The Treasuries

CLARE BUCKNELL is a Fellow of All Souls College, Oxford. She is an expert on the history of poetry and has written on literature and visual culture for the *London Review of Books*, the *New York Review of Books*, the *New Yorker*, *Harper's* and *Apollo*. She lives in London.

The Treasuries

Poetry Anthologies and the Making of British Culture

Clare Bucknell

An Apollo Book

First published in the UK in 2023 by Head of Zeus Ltd,
part of Bloomsbury Publishing Plc

9 7 5 3 1 2 4 6 8

A catalogue record for this book is available from
the British Library.

ISBN (HB): 9781800241442
ISBN (E): 9781800241466

Typeset by Ed Pickford

Printed and bound in Great Britain by
CPI Group (UK) Ltd, Croydon CR0 4YY

Head of Zeus Ltd
First Floor East
5–8 Hardwick Street
London EC1R 4RG

WWW.HEADOFZEUS.COM

The Treasuries
Poetry Anthologies
and the Making of
British Culture

Contents

Introduction   1

1 Revelation   12
   Poems on Affairs of State (1689–1707)

2 Superstition   39
   Reliques of Ancient English Poetry (1765)

3 Anxiety   76
   Beauties of the Poets (c.1780–1820)

4 Education   110
   The Golden Treasury (1861)

5 War   142
   The Battle of the Anthologies (1914–1919)

6 Politics   185
   Communism and the Anthology (1932–62)

7 Pop   225
   The Mersey Sound (1967)

8 Therapy   261
   The Anthology and Self-Help (2000–)

   Endnotes   284
   Acknowledgements   324
   Text Permissions   325
   Image Credits   326
   Index   327

INTRODUCTION

In *The British Muse* (1738), one of the earliest national anthologies of poetry, the scholar William Oldys tried to explain what the job of an anthologist was. 'We have long wanted,' he wrote in the volume's preface,

> a compiler, or reader-general for mankind, to digest whatever was most exquisite (*the flowers*) in our poets, into the most commodious method for use and application; a person, void of all prejudice, who would take no author's character upon trust [...]; one, who had not only intelligence to know what compositions of value our country had produced, but leisure, patience and attention to go through a vast diversity of reading.[1]

To be worthy of the title, Oldys argues here, any would-be anthologist ('compiler', in his terms) must be skilful, knowledgeable and patient, possessing both impeccable taste and large quantities of leisure time. 'Void of all prejudice', he or she must be strictly impartial, capable of being trusted to select, on the nation's behalf, only the most perfect '*flowers*' of its poetry and to cull the rest. Being an anthologist, this suggests, isn't so much a private job as a public one: as 'reader-general for mankind', the anthologist, like the attorney general in the legal sphere, is a public servant with an august cultural duty.[2] Britain is a serious matter; selecting and preserving its poetry, by extension, is a serious business too.

Almost two hundred years later, the poet-critics Laura Riding and Robert Graves sketched out a different version of this figure. 'The ideal anthologist,' they declared in their outspoken *Pamphlet Against Anthologies* (1928),

> is a priest of Poetry to the people, ready to give them any acceptable god. He must be free from prejudices of his own but have a steady intuition of the sort of poems that other people will like from year to year. He must, in fact, to be free from prejudice, actually dislike poetry. He must be merely a barometer of fashion.[3]

Riding and Graves, who deplored what they saw as the poisoning of early twentieth-century poetry by a wave of commercial, 'trade' anthologies, shared none of Oldys's convictions about the grandeur of the anthologist's role.* Contemporary poetry collections, they argued, were shaped by grubby financial concerns, their selections based on 'booms and depressions in poets', the likely marketability of Alfred Tennyson, A.E. Housman or Rupert Brooke.[4] All the same, in their satirical view of what the 'ideal anthologist' looked like, they alighted on one of the qualities Oldys had listed: impartiality. Like Oldys's imaginary 'reader-general' figure, devoid of preconceptions, their 'priest of Poetry' is 'free from prejudice' (so far as to be uninterested in the subject of poetry altogether): he or she is a

---

* Anthologies were certainly good business during the 1920s: few publishing houses could afford not to have at least one selection of verse on their lists. 'This is an age of Anthologies,' Collins declared in an advertisement printed in Rose Macaulay's novel *Keeping Up Appearances* (1928).

mere 'barometer of fashion', a blank space for the inscription of the public's wishes.

Impartiality and anthologising, though, don't mix. Even the supposedly objective 'reader-general', as Oldys portrays him, is interested in using poetry to project the glory of the British nation. The commercially minded priest of poetry, in Riding and Graves's caricature, may not mind what poetry he prints, but does mind his profit margins. Implicitly, both portraits acknowledge what was and is the case: that anthologies are compiled by real people, not 'ideal' figures, by editors and writers with human prejudices, interests, agendas. They exist not outside history, but in it, reflecting the ideas and priorities of their time, influencing patterns of taste, determining what's available to be read and what isn't, encouraging new and different kinds of reading publics to emerge. They seek, in some form or other, to make their mark on culture – to shape, whether briefly or enduringly, the society in which they are to be read.

Some anthologies are frank expressions of personality and taste. In *Other Men's Flowers* (1944), one of the best-loved poetry collections produced during the Second World War, Field Marshal Archibald Wavell noted that what he had compiled was 'a purely personal anthology' – a choice of verse informed by 'a part of me from which I cannot dissociate myself', and whose biases he had no desire to correct: 'my memory'.[5] Some anthologies seek to persuade their readers of the importance of particular causes or crusades. During the early days of the First World War, patriotic civilians compiled anthologies which transformed poetry into British propaganda, enlisting verse by Shakespeare, Tennyson and Kipling for the war effort. Others, have moral or religious aims, or may be party-political, calling on poetry to make a particular ideological case. The poet and scholar Michael Roberts, best-known for his *Faber Book of*

Modern Verse (1936), began his career as an editor with two Communist-leaning anthologies, *New Signatures* (1932) and *New Country* (1933), in which he brought together like-minded poets to attack the prevailing capitalist system.

Anthologies you might expect to be impartial turn out, on closer inspection, to be nothing of the kind. In the preface to his *Oxford Book of Modern Verse* (1936), an ostensibly neutral survey of the poetry of the last few decades, W.B. Yeats rattled off a string of biases. A.E. Housman was overrated, he claimed ('The *Shropshire Lad* is worthy of its fame, but a mile further and all had been marsh'); Thomas Hardy 'lacked technical accomplishment'; T.S. Eliot had made a career out of 'describ[ing] men and women that get out of bed or into it'. Wilfred Owen's poetry he ignored altogether, on the basis that 'passive suffering' wasn't a proper 'theme for poetry'.[6] His successor in the same series, Philip Larkin, claimed in *The Oxford Book of Twentieth-Century English Verse* (1973) to be disappointed that anthologists had to do any work at all, arguing that it would be preferable to leave the labour of selection up to posterity. 'At first I thought I would let the century choose the poets while I chose the poems. But outside two or three dozen names this did not really work.'[7] His hope for an *Oxford Book* 'edited by the twentieth century' had to remain fantasy: time didn't make anthologies, people did, and brought with them – as Larkin would do – preferences and biases that framed and distorted the picture they painted.[8]

Anthology reading is as much a personal business as anthology making. Hardy, one of whose ambitions, according to his wife, Florence, was 'to have some poem or poems in a good anthology like the Golden Treasury', recognized that anthologies weren't read in the same way as other books. 'There is a contingency liable to miscellanies of verse,' he noted in *Late Lyrics and Earlier* (1922): 'I mean the chance little shocks that

4

may be caused over a book of various character.'[9] Anthologies, that is, entail surprises in the reading experience, odd encounters, clashes, discoveries. They encourage unmethodical ways of reading that for other books would be inappropriate: not beginning at the beginning, dwelling on some things and skipping over others, in ways that are likely to be idiosyncratic, bound up with aspects of a reader's personality. Favourite poems or lines, discovered and then read repeatedly, may adhere in the mind to certain times of day, or to other people, or memories; they are apt to become 'associated with a habitual act', such as 'shaving, posting a letter, or eating the breakfast egg', in Riding and Graves's words – or, conversely, to get attached to extraordinary moments of stress or intensity.[10]

Readers, sensitive to this, have used anthologies in ways that make sense in the context of their own lives. When T.E. Lawrence worked for British Intelligence at the Arab Bureau in Cairo during the First World War, he travelled in the desert with a scimitar, a gun and three books in his knapsack.[11] Not many soldiers carried the Greek playwright Aristophanes' comedies or Thomas Malory's *Le Morte D'Arthur* (1469) around with them, but Lawrence was one of a large number of troops, private soldiers as well as officers, who read Arthur Quiller-Couch's *Oxford Book of English Verse* (1900) at the Front.[12] During the war and for some years after, he put together a kind of 'private anthology', as he called it, of his favourites, scribbling into a notebook poems whose tone or associations seemed to reflect things that he felt or thought in the moment.* Just under

---

* Lawrence habitually recalled poetry in extreme situations. In *Seven Pillars of Wisdom* (1926), his account of his wartime experiences in the Middle East, he recounts lying on the ground, 'passively waiting for the Turks to kill me,' having fallen from his camel, all the while humming to himself 'the verses of a half-forgotten poem' which the camel's 'prolonged stride' had brought to mind.

a third of his selections came from the *Oxford Book* – poems of joy and escape, mixed in with others, among them James Shirley's 'Death the Leveller', Samuel Taylor Coleridge's 'Youth and Age' and Arthur Hugh Clough's 'Say not the Struggle Naught availeth', darker in tone, poems about resignation, pain and loss, poems foreboding death.[13]

The instinct to collect, to stamp one's taste on culture by holding certain things up to be admired and passing over others, is an ancient one. The Greek poet Meleager of Gadara compiled what he called an *Anthologia* ('garland') in the first century BC, a collection of epigrammatic verses by forty-seven writers, each of whom was represented by a different flower. The *Palatine Anthology*, the surviving manuscript of a lost Byzantine tenth-century collection, features one book solely devoted to anthology proems, or poetic prefaces, indicating that by this early period there was already interest in how and why anthologies were to be read.[14] In the Middle Ages, European scholars compiled *florilegia*, or 'gatherings of flowers' (the Latin word was adapted from the Greek *anthologia*), collections of extracts from early Christian and pagan philosophical texts. During the sixteenth and seventeenth centuries, commonplacing – a practice, among readers, of keeping scrapbook-style collections of favourite lines, copied out under subject headings for easy reference – became a central means of learning and organising knowledge. The publisher Richard Tottel's *Songes and Sonettes* (1557), the earliest printed anthology of English poetry (which introduced readers to the sonnet in the hands of Thomas Wyatt and the Earl of Surrey), was an extension into print of a practice of manuscript collecting that had been popular for hundreds of years.[15]

By the late eighteenth century, the printed poetry anthology had become a key means by which British men, women and children encountered the culture of their nation. For reasons of price and convenience, it was a significant contributor to the period's rapid growth in the audience for imaginative literature.[16] As a kind of book which handily repackaged the 'best bits' of other books ('best' defined according to shifting categories of value, not always aesthetic), it was popular both as a teaching aid in schools and among private readers, those who lacked the means to purchase multiple individual volumes – or who felt they didn't possess the necessary taste to discern for themselves what they ought to be reading.[17]

Eighteenth-century schoolchildren learned elocution and rhetorical skills by working their way through William Enfield's *The Speaker; Or, Miscellaneous Pieces* (1774), an influential textbook anthology of verse and prose.[18] Young women were introduced to the 'safe' bits of English literature through carefully censored collections of 'beauties', mined from Shakespeare, Milton and Swift. As the adult education movement gathered pace during the nineteenth and early twentieth centuries, poetry anthologies, cheap and accessible, offered working-class students both reading material and inspiration. T.S. Eliot recommended Francis Turner Palgrave's *Golden Treasury* (1861), Quiller-Couch's *Oxford Book* and Edward Arber's *The Shakespeare Anthology* (1899) to his students when he taught University Extension classes on Elizabethan literature in London, during and shortly after the First World War.[19] In the 1960s, it was a bestselling anthology, Adrian Henri, Roger McGough and Brian Patten's *The Mersey Sound* (1967), which brought thousands of pop-loving British teenagers in touch with countercultural ideas and attitudes.

Anthologies with this level of reach and influence are public property. They represent shared touchstones, common places of resort, examples of those few books, such as the works of Shakespeare or a good dictionary, which readers from a cross-section of backgrounds might be likely to know of and draw on. As the critic Anne Ferry has suggested, they can be thought of as the literary equivalent of public museums or galleries, spaces for the display of treasures that are in some sense owned in common – bookish versions of the National Gallery or the British Museum.[20] (Ezra Pound once said that if the 'best history of painting in London' was the National Gallery, the 'best history of literature', poetry in particular, would be an anthology.[21])

Curation, though, as practised by anthologies and museums alike, isn't a transparent business. Anthologies are books that aim to say something about what they consider culturally important, what they see as worth preserving and what they don't. By selecting elements of the literary past and discarding others, they frame a version of tradition that excludes what it chooses not to remember. Some, in the guise of acting for the past, seek to shape the present and the future too. The 'Anthology Wars' in the United States, a battle for hearts and minds that went on in universities and the pages of literary reviews during the late 1950s and early 1960s, pitted an academic, traditional understanding of contemporary American and British poetry – as represented, in the ring, by *The New Poets of England and America* (1957), compiled by Donald Hall, Robert Pack and Louis Simpson – against the avant-garde 'invasion' of the Beats, as championed by Donald M. Allen in *The New American Poetry* (1960). The battle, as Louis Menand has argued, wasn't just for the right to define what the field of contemporary poetry looked like. Instead, it was about the future of cultural production, and the spaces – traditional or experimental? institutional or open to all? – in which literature could be made. Was 'poetry' a set of complex texts requiring the tools of university training to unpick? Or was it an energetic, living art of the human voice and breath?[22]

8

Anthologies make social interventions as well as literary ones. From the early modern period, many have been democratising influences on British reading culture, making poetry available to widening sections of the public. During the late seventeenth and early eighteenth centuries, the anonymous *Poems on Affairs of State* collections opened up the salacious world of court politics to outsiders, printing political satires that previously only a handful of aristocrats would have read. The *Beauties of the Poets of Great Britain* library, launched by the publisher John Roach in 1793, brought extracts from the nation's poets within reach of poorer readers with its monthly sixpenny pamphlets. Palgrave's *Golden Treasury*, which contained, its editor claimed, 'all the best original Lyrical pieces and Songs in our language', was billed as 'a storehouse of delight to Labour and to Poverty'; while *The Mersey Sound*, a slim, cheaply priced volume stamped with bubble-letter titling, was unapologetically aimed not at the usual poetry-reading elite but at the pop-cultural underground.[23]

Such books, attempts on the part of their compilers not only to redraw the map of literary culture but also to intervene in the bigger question of whom culture was for, tell us a lot about perceptions of social change. Among the social and literary elite, they were frequently sources of anxiety, prompting snobbery and disdain. 'There are poetry-lovers who can be called anthology-addicts,' Eliot commented in a lecture of 1944. 'No doubt *The Golden Treasury*, or the *Oxford Book*, has given many people their introduction to Milton, to Wordsworth, or to Shelley [...] [But] I should not say that any such person was a real poetry lover.'[24] Riding and Graves, in their *Pamphlet Against Anthologies*, refer snidely to 'the sixpence-in-purse public', and to anthologies being sold at 'railway bookstalls, leading stationers, Army canteens, Woolworth Stores, etc.'. Their chapter on 'The popular poem

9

and the popular reader', in particular, exhibits an inability not to relate the most abstract literary questions to matters of social class. 'In an anthology,' they observe, 'everything reads democratically much the same':

> Poems by Shakespeare, Donne, Shelley, Keats, become affected by the same negative poison, to a point where they are almost unrecognisable; so faces in the Underground or Overhead railways are made negative, as faces, by the spell of the cheap ticket which is the only link between them.[25]

Individual poems, this claims, lose their character by being anthologized, much as, collected in crowds or masses on the railway (united only by the 'cheap ticket' they carry), people become hard to tell apart. What part of this is statement and what metaphor isn't obvious: something that purports to be a comment on poetry, illustrated by a reference to class, starts to look, on closer inspection, like a comment about class loosely tied to a reference to poetry. Anthologies, Riding and Graves's language makes clear, aren't just books: they are also reflections of the kinds of people who read them, people seen as shadowy and indistinct, harbingers of a new, unwelcome mass culture.

The Treasuries is not a complete history of the anthology form, or a survey of the thousands of collections produced between the end of the seventeenth century and the beginning of the twenty-first. Some of the books it looks at, such as *The Golden Treasury* and Thomas Percy's influential *Reliques of Ancient English Poetry* (1765), already have a firm place in literary history. Others are much less well-known, occupying fringe positions, sometimes resembling polemics more than benign surveys of tradition. What all of them have in common, however, is the commitment they show to a particular view of culture, of readers and reading, and an investment in the possibility of using literature to stage an intervention – whether political, social, moral or psychological. Sometimes, as in the case of *The Mersey Sound*, their interventions are energetically forward-looking. Sometimes, as with the commemorative anthologies produced shortly after the 1918 Armistice, they are quiet and backward-looking, shoring up fragments against further ruin. All of them understand poetry as not just being about words on a page; all of them present poets and readers as social actors, men and women who, because they participate in culture, have the ability to shape it. The aim of the first volume of *Poems on Affairs of State* (1697), according to its compiler, was to 'charm the distracted pieces of the publick Building into one Noble and Regular Pile.'[26] He wanted nothing less than to remake the nation.

I

REVELATION

Poems on Affairs of State (1689–1707)

Around noon on 31 August 1681, a man named Stephen College was hanged and quartered in the prison yard inside Oxford Castle. Unusually, his body parts and disembowelled organs were permitted to be given to his relations for burial, instead of being displayed triumphantly in the city to discourage other would-be traitors. College was a joiner by trade, a talented artisan: he was also a political agitator, a vehement anti-Catholic and opponent of the government, who had helped construct the wooden effigies of the pope that were burned at spectacular anti-Catholic processions in the City of London in 1679 and 1680. What brought him to the scaffold in 1681, however, was his pen rather than his woodworking. In the later seventeenth century, College was one of many men and women of all political parties and backgrounds who expressed their discontent with the state of the nation in verse.[1] He was less subtle than most in the way he went about it. As a witness at his trial attested, he was often to be seen 'in the Coffee-houses, bawling against the government', reciting aloud the outspoken political satires he had composed himself.[2] Friends warned him to 'have a care of his tongue'. He 'talk'd at such a desperate rate,' it was said, 'that it was not safe for any man to keep him company.'[3] His ballads attacked Catholic noblemen at court, the allegedly Catholic-favouring Lord Chief Justice in particular, but the target of his most daring writing was the king himself: Charles II, the increasingly unpopular son of the beheaded Charles I. 'Alas!' he exclaimed in one poem, 'poor Nation, how art thou undone / By a bad Father, and now a worse, his Son!'[4]

In March 1681, the king and Parliament moved temporarily out of Westminster to sit in Oxford. College left London and followed on horseback, wearing armour and distributing ribbons bearing the slogan 'No Popery, No Slavery'. Many witnesses attested that, while in Oxford, they had seen the joiner singing a political song up and down the streets, stopping as he went to explain the meaning of some of its references to listeners. This song was more outspoken and dangerous than any of his previous productions. For one thing, it involved him pretending to speak in the voice of the king, ventriloquising him and mocking him, as if a mere subject could speak for his sovereign. Worse, at its close, it seemed to imagine and stage an act of treason: Charles being hunted down, just as his father had been, by a mob of angry parliamentarians, then captured and humiliated.

> Methinks he seems to stagger, with a hey, with a hey,
> Who but now did so swagger, with a ho;
> God's fish! he's stuck i' th' mire,
> And all the fat's i' th' fire.[5]

The government, eager to find a rebel ringleader to scapegoat, homed in on College and his song, claiming that he had devised and performed it in Oxford as part of an attempted treasonous uprising. 'This Libel lays out the very Model of the Plot,' the government's chief press censor, Roger L'Estrange, declared.[6]

Throughout his trial, College maintained that, although papers containing politically libellous material – including, allegedly, a handwritten copy of the song – had been found in his house, he had nothing to do with them. But, since what was known as 'malicious and advised speaking' – 'publishing' your words by saying them aloud for others to hear – counted as treason too, the outcome, in the hands of a jury packed with dutiful government loyalists, was a foregone conclusion. He was found guilty of high treason and executed within a fortnight of his conviction. The evidence of a poem had been enough to make him a political martyr; in a last letter he wrote from prison to his son, Stephen, he urged the boy to give up 'that folly of Riming, for [...] it will do you hurt.'[7]

College was convicted of treason largely on the basis of a poem that he sang and performed, rather than committing to print. In 1704, though, more than twenty years after his death, his 'libel' was published. Along with several other pieces attributed to him, it appeared in the latest volume of a widely read series of anthologies, *Poems on Affairs of State*, an ambitious publishing enterprise whose first instalment had appeared in 1697. The *Poems on Affairs of State* anthologies collected political poems, many of them previously unprinted, dating from the beginning of the seventeenth century to the present: they covered poetry on national politics – satires on government policy, corruption, taxation, wars – as well as poetry on public scandals, the indiscretions and misdemeanours of well-known government and court personalities of the age.

The poems they collected dating from the same period as College's song were united in their outrage at Charles's conduct and his approach to governance. They expressed dismay at the culture of hedonism and laziness that prevailed at court, the way it betrayed the mood of promise that had surrounded the young king's restoration to the throne in

1660. They vented fury about the nation's shameful naval losses during the Second Dutch War of 1665–7, and the vast taxes that had been levied to pay for them. They were anxious about a growing strain of French Catholic influence at court, and the apparent power exercised over Charles by his mistress, Louise de Kéroualle, a young former maid of honour who was known to have the ear of Louis XIV's ambassador. Increasingly, during the later 1670s and early 1680s, the mood of many of the satires darkened to one of panic and despair. The English royal line was in jeopardy: Charles, despite producing a dozen illegitimate children by seven mistresses, had no legitimate heir, and his brother, James, the next in line, was a devout Catholic. 'A colony of French possess the court,' John Ayloffe, a radical republican satirist, wrote in the mid-1670s,

> Pimps, priests, buffoons i' th' privy-chamber sport.
> Such slimy monsters ne'er approached a throne
> Since Pharaoh's reign, nor so defil'd a crown.[8]

The vigour and picturesqueness of Ayloffe's language ('Pimps', 'buffoons', 'slimy monsters', 'defil'd') is typical of the hyperbolic, pumped-up manner in which political satirists of the period went about their business. Typical, too, is the close intertwining of the personal and political, the twin spheres in which public officials moved. Owing to the informal nature of the relationships through which many political dealings took place during the seventeenth century, an 'affair of state' was just as likely to be a love affair, perhaps between a king and his well-connected mistress, as a matter of 'pure' political or ecclesiastical policy.[9] Even more than today, the business of politics could not be separated from the individuals, flawed and compromised, who conducted it.

Poems that attacked the political activities of high-profile courtiers – known as lampoons, from the French *lampons*, or 'let's drink', since they were often read aloud at boozy evenings – tended therefore to be venomously personal in nature.[10] Their idiom was both coarse and sophisticated, obscene and nihilistic. De Kéroualle, Charles's long-term favourite, was immortalized by her enemies as a 'pickled pocky Whore' and a 'stinking French bitch'; the Duchess of Cleveland, another high-profile mistress, was derided as having 'swallow'd more Pricks than the Ocean has sand'; while the unfortunate Jane Middleton, though a noted court beauty, was accused of having bad body odour (other courtiers were said to be careful to avoid 'the fair one's funky hose').* King James II's first wife, Anne Hyde, was informed that her breath smelt like cooked asparagus.[11] Charles's Lord High Treasurer, the Earl of Danby, received many delicately worded tributes ('You're such a scurvy, stinking, Errant Knight, / That when you speak a Man wou'd swear you S--te').[12] And Charles himself, though supposedly above criticism as God's representative on earth, was nonetheless fair game for the lampooners, stripped down to the weaknesses and lusts that made him human. The king was a 'fool', a 'goat' and a 'tyrant', one anonymous satirist declared:

> Silly and sauntering he goes
> From French whore to Italian;
> Unlucky in whate'er he does,
> An old ill-favoured stallion.[13]

---

* 'The fine Mrs Middleton is noted for carrying about her body a continued soure base Smell that is very offensive,' Pepys wrote in his diary in 1665, 'especially if she be a little hot.'

Few writers were willing to risk putting their names to this kind of stuff in print, and, for the most part, they would not have been able to even had they dared. In 1662, Charles's government passed a Press Licensing Act, banning any printer from operating his business without prior state approval. This meant, in theory at least, that nothing could be published without first making it past a government censor, while items that did somehow slip through the net (via underground, unlicensed presses) could still be scrutinized post-publication, then prosecuted, if their contents seemed to warrant it, for blasphemy, obscenity or seditious libel. But, as the example of College's ballad shows, there were other ways than print publication to disseminate an outspoken satire. Authors just had to be smart and inventive about how they brought their work to the readers they had in mind. Much political satire was never meant for print: instead, dangerous poems, without their authors' names attached, would be copied out by hand – sometimes by private individuals, sometimes by professional scribes – then passed around secretly between friends, or sold commercially via clandestine networks.[14] Walking home from Whitehall one evening after Christmas in 1666, Samuel Pepys encountered a colleague who passed on a new one he had heard: 'a most bitter lampoone now out against the Court and the management of State from head to foot,' as he recorded in his diary, 'mighty witty and mighty severe'.[15]

Pepys's world of circulating satires, in contrast to that of the radicals, College and Ayloffe, was relatively contained: it was made up of concentric circles of courtiers, civil servants, spies and coffee-house regulars, who were either personally involved in the goings-on at Whitehall, or interested themselves closely in state business.[16] Within such circles, most people knew or knew of one another, and could easily decipher coded references to individuals or their indiscretions. Nonetheless, though networks of poetry-sharing often didn't overlap (only a specific cohort, at least until the 1680s, would have read Andrew Marvell's anti-ministerial satires; another, separate cohort, would have read the Earl of Rochester's), they had a shared social purpose, beyond the individual disaffection they expressed, or the polemical cases they put across.* What they had in common was their ability to spread information. Anti-government libels, no matter how private or obviously vindictive their contents were, were news providers. Though they tended to be gossipy, distorted, irreverent and partial, they were a rare and necessary source of political intelligence, a key means by which men and women who maintained an interest in public affairs managed to keep themselves abreast of what was going on.[17]

During the seventeenth century, court politics was an exclusive game. Private citizens were largely kept in the dark about the workings of government, and the lives and personalities of the officials who made decisions on their behalf. Not until the Licensing Act lapsed for good in 1695 could newspapers be printed that weren't government-sponsored propaganda sheets or royal proclamations. There was no daily paper until 1702. It was a situation deliberately contrived by the Stuart monarchs, who sought to ensure that the business of government remained mysterious by means of a rigorous policy of censoring all unofficial political discourse. Subjects could not be permitted to arrogate to themselves the right to 'censure and defame the Proceedings of State', as a proclamation of 1672 declared; it was not up to them to

---

* A huge number of satires of all political stripes circulated in manuscript: many still survive, often on sheets of paper folded for easy carriage, and sometimes bearing the name and address of their intended reader on the outside.

'dispense / The laws of empire to an absolute prince.'[18] If the reality of what went on at court and in government, including the particularly egregious reality of Charles's extracurricular activities, could either be kept secret entirely, or subordinated to an official version of events, then the legitimacy of the monarch's absolute power was less likely to be called into question. But the vacuum of information, the government's 'barrier of silence', created a hunger.[19]

In 1689, not long after James II had fled to France, deposed by the new Dutch Protestant monarch, King William III, three slim volumes appeared in quick succession, all bearing the title *Poems on Affairs of State*. The timing of their publication wasn't accidental. Each contained a handful of satires by writers who had stood in opposition to James or Charles's monarchies, but whose poems, while the Stuarts were still on the throne, had remained in manuscript, as impossible to publish legally or safely. (Although slender in themselves, these volumes may have had, as the literary scholar Dustin Griffin argues, significant implications for the future development of satire in English. One likely motivation behind the former Poet Laureate (and Stuart apologist) John Dryden's *Discourse* on satire (1693), which redefined satire as a respectable literary genre with Roman pedigree, was to 'efface the memory of the "state poems"', Griffin suggests – to 'dismiss the importance' of these angry, scurrilous, partisan texts, and discredit the political case they made. Dryden had reason to feel personally attacked by the 1689 *Poems on Affairs of State* series: in an attempt to embarrass him, one of the volumes reprinted his 'Heroic Stanzas on the Death of Oliver Cromwell', an elegy for the late Lord Protector he had written many years before, whose reverent tone contrasted suspiciously with his later royalism.[20])

The 1689 volumes were followed, a few years later in 1697, by a new and much longer publication under the same *Poems on Affairs of State* title – either the work of the same anonymous compiler, or one with access to a much larger stash of manuscripts to print. The aim of this new, expanded collection, as its editor explained in a preface, was to destroy the web of secrecy that had surrounded the Stuarts' rule. For decades, successive governments had prevented the spread of political information; now, hundreds of pages of it, in the form of previously unpublished anti-ministerial satires, would be available in print. From the poems preserved in its pages, the editor wrote, readers would be able to 'collect a just and secret History of the former Times' – an impression, pieced together from the juicy tidbits of libels and songs, of what had really gone on for all those years in the corridors of Whitehall and Parliament.[21] The 'justness', or accuracy, of this new history, as the editor explained in a subsequent volume, was guaranteed by the fact that the poetry in question was the work of men on the inside. All the satires he had collected, he assured his readers, had been composed by high-ranking officials and courtiers: 'such Great Persons as were near the Helm, knew the Transactions, and were above being brib'd to flatter, or afraid to speak truth.'[22] The beans were being spilled, in other words, and by those at the very top.

In his prefaces, the editor did his best to establish the impression that he was politically neutral, acting from a place of high-minded impartiality. In publishing a large quantity of anti-Stuart satires, he argued, he had nothing but 'the Publick Good' in view: he hoped merely to 'charm', as he put it grandly, 'the distracted pieces' of England's broken body politic back into a 'Noble and Regular Pile' – an aim that must, he felt sure, 'be extreamly approv'd by all true Patriots, all lovers of the general Good of Mankind.'[23] The authors of the satires collected in his book, he assured readers, weren't prejudiced, bitter ex-courtiers, or men who had been passed over for positions and were out for revenge: they were noble and disinterested, on the side of truth, inspired 'by the injur'd Genius of their Country' to take up their pens. Like the Roman poet Catullus, who, 'in the midst of *Caesar*'s Triumphs attack'd the Vices of that great Man, and expos'd 'em to lessen that Popularity and Power he was gaining among the *Roman* People,' these writers had dared to expose the dark secrets of the Stuart state: and their work, at last, could now be shared openly in print where it belonged.[24]

All this was apt to look a little suspicious. For one thing, there was the gratuitously obscene content of many of the libels in the collection, which was hard to chalk up to disinterested patriotism (could attacking the Duchess of Cleveland's sexual appetite really be necessary for the safeguarding of the public good?). For another, all the talk about 'the general Good of Mankind' was clearly a front for political point-scoring. In 1697, releasing anti-Stuart material into the public realm was not only safe, but politically expedient too: it was likely to be welcomed by William III's ministry as a kind of declaration of allegiance, a form of more or less explicit pro-government propaganda. Whatever smeared Charles or James, celebrated William: criticism of the *ancien régime* was liable to be taken as a mark of fidelity to the new.[25]

Many of the poems in the book, accordingly, were the most outspoken and partisan of the opposition satires that had been written and circulated during the later seventeenth century, both within the court and outside it: satires by men such as the Earl of Rochester, a licentious courtier-poet who had been one of Charles's most vicious critics from inside his intimate milieu; and, from a very different world, those of the radical conspirator John Freke, who in a period of less than ten years was lucky to escape being hanged for treason three times. Openly republican satires were the only texts that didn't make it in without first being amended, prudently, by the book's editor. As the literary historian Paul Hammond has shown, the lines 'Then England rejoice, thy redemption is nigh: / Thy oppression together with kingship shall die!', which had originally formed part of an anonymous satire called 'A Dialogue between the Two Horses', mysteriously went missing in the published version, cut out because they were liable to attract the wrong kind of attention. William, although in theory a different kind of monarch, was still a monarch, and calling for 'A commonwealth! a commonwealth!' was likely to land you in hot water.[26]

The 1697 volume also commemorated, by preserving their work for posterity, the bravery of those writers who had not escaped the Stuart period alive, and who would attain, during William's reign, the status of political martyrs. College, who had died on the scaffold, featured in the collection, as did his fellow radical Ayloffe, a serial plotter who had participated in a doomed attempt to overthrow James in 1685, and met a traitor's end, after trying and failing to die by suicide by stabbing himself with a penknife.

Whose was the partisan hand behind the selection of poems? Much about the *Poems on Affairs of State* remains mysterious, but recent scholarship has suggested that one of the men at the heart of the project was a printer and bookseller named John Darby, who ran his business from Bartholomew Close in the City of London, near St Bartholomew's Hospital.[27] Darby, 'a *True Assertor of English Liberties*', as one contemporary described him, was a consistent thorn in the sides of Charles and James's censors throughout his long career, his presses regularly dismantled and confiscated by government agents as he overstepped one political line or another. In the 1670s and 1680s, he associated closely with anti-Stuart conspirators, and was responsible for printing a number of seditious works, including twenty thousand copies of the scaffold speech of one of the 'Whig martyrs' involved in a failed plot to assassinate Charles and James in 1683.[28] Having been persecuted, along with many of his friends, for his political convictions under the Stuart kings, he welcomed the Glorious Revolution of 1688, promising as it did to bring an end to both 'tyranny' (absolutist rule, of the kind practised by the Stuarts), and 'popery', the lingering threat of the return of Catholicism.

As the months and years passed, he, along with his political allies, grew dismayed: it was increasingly clear that William's kingship was not going to bring about the kind of thoroughgoing reform that had been hoped for. Though the religious threat had dissipated, William's administration was proving to be just as authoritarian in character as those of Charles and James, and a number of the public officials on whom the radicals had pinned their trust turned out to be more interested in keeping their jobs than their promises.[29] In the preface to *Poems on Affairs of State* in 1697, Darby, or an editor working for him, included a covert reference to the fact that William's rule had not inaugurated the golden age of popular liberty his early supporters had expected. There was a pointed comment about 'our present Mischiefs', evils that ought to have vanished with the Stuarts but in fact prevailed under the Dutch king.[30] But William was still around and sustained criticism was dangerous; so the reference was fleeting, and hidden away in a long piece of text apparently dedicated to attacking Charles and James.

William died unexpectedly in 1702, leaving the throne to his wife Mary's sister, Anne, another Stuart. A year after his death, a second volume of *Poems on Affairs of State* appeared. Once more, the timing seems unlikely to have been coincidental. With the king gone, the immediate danger of publishing pieces openly critical of the old administration was past. Darby and his collaborators, it seems, seized the opportunity to repeat the trick they'd pulled off with the first volume in the series, and put together a collection of poems that served as a kind of *expost facto* critique of the former regime – or a 'secret history', in the terms they would have used, of its greatest 'mischiefs'.

In its pages, evergreen poems attacking the old Stuarts were still in the mix: the volume included a vicious celebration of James's death ('all rejoice to hear the Tyrant's gone') by Darby's republican associate John Tutchin, who in 1685 had taken part in the failed Monmouth Rebellion to get Charles's illegitimate Protestant son on the throne. (Tutchin was the reputed 'Poet Laureate' of the Calves' Head Club, a shadowy group of republicans believed to meet annually on 30 January to eat, drink and sing anthems on the anniversary of Charles I's execution.) But the lead poem – heralded triumphantly at the top of the contents page – was another, more recent, satire by Tutchin, *The Foreigners* (1700), which lashed out at William's policy of handing out government positions to favoured fellow-Dutchmen. 'If Kings are made the People to enthral, / We had much better have no King at all,' the poem hinted darkly, suggesting that the right of kings to govern ought to be conditional on the assent of their people. In 1700, when Darby had first printed the satire for Tutchin, the poet was arrested by the king's messengers and indicted for libel (he was lucky to escape conviction on the grounds that he had half-disguised the proper names he used). Three years later, it was safely back in print at the head of *Poems on Affairs of State*. The volume also included poems rejoicing at William's death, the indirect result of a broken collarbone sustained in a fall from his horse, Sorrel. 'Mourn on, you foolish fashionable things, / Mourn for your own Misfortunes, not the King's,' one such satire exclaimed in bitter tones. "Twould lessen much our Woe, / Had *Sorrel* stumbled thirteen Years ago.'[31]

Those behind the second volume insisted, once more, that their production was impartial in its politics. The poems it collected, the preface explained, had been selected to exhibit 'the Spirt of the several Parties in the Nation', not just – as might be expected – the spirit of the radical group of Whigs with which Darby was affiliated.* But since William, while he was alive, was distrusted not only by men such as Darby and Tutchin, but also by Tories who longed nostalgically for the return of the Stuarts, incorporating the 'Poems of all Partys' into the volume did not mean being generous to the dead king.[32] Hatred could issue from all sides. *A Satyr upon the French King* (1697), an attack on William's peace treaty with Louis XIV by the Tory satirist Tom Brown, for which Brown, in 1697, had been arrested, was reprinted triumphantly in 1703. So too, in the third volume (1704), was a far more outspoken Tory satire: *Tarquin and Tullia* (1689), the work of a young hothead named Arthur Maynwaring.

Tarquin and Tullia had immediately attracted the attention of the authorities when it was first printed (anonymously, and through illicit means). The poem pretended to tell the story of Tarquin, a tyrannical Roman king who, along with his wife, Tullia, had orchestrated the murder of his father-in-law in order to seize power. Under this somewhat transparent historical cover – in

---

* At this period, the Whig party was split into two factions: establishment Whigs, who considered that the Glorious Revolution (that is, the deposition of James II) had achieved the measure of constitutional reform they wanted to see; and radical Whigs, or 'commonwealthmen', who argued that William's reign had not brought about sufficient change and represented a betrayal of true Whig principles. Darby was associated with the latter group.

place because it was harder for the government to pin down a libel conviction when satirists used Roman aliases for contemporary figures – Maynwaring's poem was actually a no-holds-barred assault on William and Mary. It painted them as usurpers who had wickedly dethroned Mary's father, James ('gnawed their way like vipers to a crown'), then ruined the nation they had conspired to govern.[33] 'Brutal *Tarquin*,' Maynwaring wrote,

> never did relent,
> Too hard to melt, too wicked to repent;
> Cruel in Deeds, more merciless in Will,
> And blest with natural delight in Ill;
> [...]
> Innumerable Woes opprest the Land,
> When it submitted to his curst Command.[34]

In 1689, Maynwaring was lucky and well-connected enough to escape arrest for what might have been considered 'treasonable' work. His printer, William Canning, was less fortunate, ending up in Newgate Prison two years later, following a tip-off from an informant.[35] A decade or so on, Darby and his associates were only too pleased to be able to include *Tarquin and Tullia* in *Poems on Affairs of State* without risking a similar fate – though they made sure that its tacit support for James, the fraudulently dethroned king, was undercut by the usual batch of virulent anti-Stuart satires.*

In the first three volumes of *Poems on Affairs of State*, only a handful of current political satires appeared in amongst the

---

* These included a vicious satire on James's Catholic son, who was alleged by his enemies to be illegitimate, smuggled as a baby into the queen's bedchamber in the seventeenth-century equivalent of a hot water bottle. The satire's title said it all: 'An excellent new Song, call'd, *The Prince of Darkness*: Shewing how three Kingdoms may be set on Fire by a Warming-Pan'.

older poems they printed. Though, historically, a large part of Darby's business at Bartholomew Close had consisted in finding ways to get the seditious literature of his political associates into print, in the *Poems on Affairs of State* his goal seems to have been to establish a retrospective canon of radical works: to assemble a series of examples, for the benefit of contemporaries who shared his commitments, of what principled dissent looked like.[36] (Since, too, shortly after William's accession, he had achieved official recognition in his trade by being raised to the status of liveryman of the Stationers' Company, it may be the case that he had more reason than before to keep his head down.[37]) Between 1697 and 1704, accordingly, the *Poems on Affairs of State* were comparatively silent on contemporary political matters, tending to avoid commentary on current monarchs or ministers in favour of safer attacks on dead ones. (Scholars have pointed out that this time lag would have made it difficult for many readers to 'get' political jokes, to decipher coded references to scandals that were no longer current: a bit like reading an edition of *Private Eye* five or ten years on.[38]) The second and third volumes did contain a handful of short pieces on the new monarch, Queen Anne, but almost all of them erred on the side of praise rather than criticism: if they took issue with policies advanced by her ministry, they took care to make it clear that she and her ministers weren't one and the same.

The fourth volume, the last in the series, which appeared three years after its predecessor in 1707, was a rather different beast. From its preface, which drew the reader's attention to the fact that it contained many historically 'valuable Pieces', including two previously unpublished poems by Shakespeare, the casual browser would have had little idea that what followed wasn't going to be merely a harmless compilation of old poetry, and perhaps some toothless, out-of-date satires.

The contents page, however, told the real story. In contrast to the pattern of previous volumes in the series, which were ordered chronologically so that their newest poems were clustered towards the back, here things were reversed: almost the first third of the book was taken up with new or recent commentary on Anne's reign.[39] This riskier, more contemporary approach seems likely to have been the result of a change of hands at the helm. After 1704, when Darby died, his son, John Darby Jr., probably continued to have a share in the *Poems on Affairs of State* venture, but the publisher of Volume Four was a London bookseller named James Woodward, who signed its preface and may also have been behind its selection of poems.[40]

Getting away with printing current anti-ministerial satires, while avoiding unwanted attention from government officials, meant striking a delicate balance. In places, it seems that the compiler of the new volume moderated his own selections, in order to pre-empt the censorship of material that might have been considered extreme. He handled one writer with especial care. William Shippen was a notorious propagandist and Jacobite (that is, a supporter of the old Stuart line, in favour of dethroning the queen and replacing her with James Francis Edward Stuart, the exiled son of James II), and a fierce opponent of Anne's moderate coalition government. Shippen came to prominence with a poem called *Faction Display'd* (1704), in which he inveighed against corruption within the ministry, lashing out in particular at the Duchess of Marlborough, the queen's favourite courtier and close confidante ('the Senate's Grievance, and the Court's Disgrace', as he described her).[41] As Maynwaring had done in *Tarquin and Tullia*, he used Roman aliases to disguise, thinly, the identities of the various high-profile personages he libelled, managing by this means to escape prosecution.

Shippen published a follow-up satire, *Moderation Display'd*, a few months later. This time, he had in his sights the policy of 'moderation' that Anne's ministry championed in relation to the turbulent religious disputes of the day: 'a Modern Coward Principle', he called it, 'by Knaves contriv'd, impos'd on Fools'.⁴² The poem treated the Duchess of Marlborough much as before, but wisely spared her husband, the famous military commander whose recent victory against the French at the Battle of Blenheim (1704) had made him the queen's favourite and the nation's hero. But his restraint was short-lived. Not long afterwards, he threw caution to the winds and released a second, far less politic version of the satire, whose front page promised, ominously, 'the Addition of several Characters omitted in former Editions'. This second version seemed to attack not only the government but the queen herself, insinuating that it was at least partly because of a lack of vigilance on her part that her ministers were able to be so corrupt: 'Let Justice sleep in *Anna*'s gentle Reign.' Just as controversially, it dispensed with the niceties regarding the Duke of Marlborough. Despite the general's undisputed 'Valour' and 'mighty Mind', Shippen predicted, it was inevitable that even he would fall prey to the dirty politics of the ministry, his head turned by bribes and the machinations of his nefarious wife. '*Camillo*, tho' triumphant in the Field, / Seduc'd by *Grants*, shall to this Party yield.'⁴³

Shippen defended his criticisms with reference to the same principles of openness and transparency that the first *Poems on Affairs of State* volume had preached. It was, he argued in his preface, no mere 'arrogant Presumption in private Persons, [...] to examine and censure the Actions of Publick Ministers.' Just because ordinary people existed 'in a remote Sphere, and at a distance' from the centres of power, they were still capable of judging 'what ought, and ought not to be done', and were not to be dismissed without cause as ignorant or 'rash'. All the same, as he knew, the particular accusations he was making were unlikely to be well-received: 'I am sensible a Piece of this kind will be severely censur'd.' Many readers, he knew, would 'be apt to say it is Unseasonable at least, if not False and Malicious': its attacks on Marlborough in particular weren't just politically dangerous but perverse too, wildly out of step with the jubilant mood of the nation.[44]

The compiler of the fourth *Poems on Affairs of State* volume, for his part, seems to have agreed. Although, in 1707, he opted to print both *Faction Display'd* and *Moderation Display'd*, he stuck with the (only mildly offensive) original version of the latter, stopping short of publishing the deeply 'Unseasonable', definitely 'Malicious', second edition. Shippen, no doubt, was worth taking some risks for, because he was notorious, an attention-grabbing controversialist whose satires tended to fly off the shelves. But given that a portion of the attention he generated was likely to come from government spies, the anthology's compiler must have felt that some of the positions Shippen represented, and some of the things he had alleged, were just too extreme to risk being associated with.

The ministerial henchmen came anyway. Volume Four, alone of the instalments in the *Poems on Affairs of State* series, did attract the wrong kind of attention, despite the care its compiler seems to have taken to moderate some of his selections. As the literary historian John McTague has shown, shortly after publication, and before too many copies could get out into the world, two of the satires originally chosen for the volume were swiftly cut from its pages, most likely under pressure of the threat of prosecution.[45] What distinguished them from the other offensive pieces the compiler had managed to get away with were the liberties they took with the person of the queen, as well as with noted peers of the realm, slotting into the tradition of free verbal abuse inaugurated (albeit more clandestinely) during the reign of Charles II. The most outrageous of the two satires, 'A New Ballad', didn't bother with Roman aliases and mocked Anne directly as 'Royal N---y' (probably 'Nancy' or 'Nanny', patronising diminutives of her name), dismissing her as 'more fit for a Bib than a Crown'. Like a baby, the anonymous satirist argued, she had no mind of her own, and could be pulled freely this way and that by the strong-willed Duchess of Marlborough. If only she had 'stood as much in fear of her God' as of her confidante, as the poem commented pointedly, she might have taken a more consistent approach to religious policy:

> She flatter'd the Commons with a true *English* Heart,
> And told them how nicely the Church she'd support,
> But Words are but Wind, and so is a Fart.

The duke, meanwhile, the satirist claimed, despite his military accomplishments and growing influence at court, remained a nobody: a 'little' man, controlled by his domineering wife, who would never be able to live up to the titles and honours with which he had been bestowed. It was enough, the poem sneered, to move observers 'to Spewing and Laughter' to see 'little *Jack Churchill* a Knight of the Garter.' The word 'Duke', like a magnet, adhered itself to the only possible rhyming partner: 'At his New Title they were ready to puke.'[46]

As McTague has shown, some surviving manuscript versions of the poem are even stronger in tone, daring to suggest that many people would be glad to see the Marlboroughs hanged. Before publishing the text in *Poems on Affairs of State*, the anthology's compiler, it seems, had gone through and cut out the most brazen parts of the version to which he had access, hoping by this expedient to be able to get most of the poem into print and evade official repercussions.[47] But his efforts weren't quite thoroughgoing enough. Printing a malicious libel on the queen's relationship to her most prominent courtiers, and one that also managed to impugn her integrity as a Christian, was, unsurprisingly, considered going too far, and the censors intervened. There were some things that it was not only unwise but also impossible to say. The volume was recalled, its offending pages cut out, and in their place went a more innocuous seventeenth-century song that happened to have the same title.[48]

❧

What happened to *Poems on Affairs of State* after 1707? Woodward, as his preface to the fourth volume indicates, was confident that the enterprise was just gathering pace, and that there would be at least one, if not many more, volumes in the series to come: 'The Publisher does not doubt but that he shall be encourag'd to make another Collection.'[49] In the event, though, there was no Volume Five; and the risky fourth volume, unlike its predecessors, remained out of print for a number of years after its first publication, not appearing again until 1716, by which time Anne had been dead two years and the coast was well and truly clear. It's tempting to speculate that by dancing so close to the line (and, in a couple of places, over it) the new compiler had made his project impossible to continue in the same way: he had invited attention of too invasive and smothering a kind to be able to produce another book that took such liberties with living figures. In his hands, the series had become a very different, and much riskier, political project than the one Darby had been involved in. Instead of uncovering the buried secrets of past administrations and monarchs, it had begun to write – and intervene in – the history of the present.

Poems on Affairs of State, by collecting and publishing manuscript texts that might otherwise have been lost, preserved for posterity a particular kind of satire: partisan, scurrilous, personal, fearlessly committed to smearing individuals and the institutions they represented. Because it broadened the audience for political gossip from the inner circles of the court to the reading public at large, it helped to establish a widespread appetite for such attacks, across the social classes, which persisted throughout the eighteenth century and into the nineteenth. The number of high-minded, head-shaking treatises on abusive satire produced during the first part of the eighteenth century tells us nothing if not the fact that such satire was stubbornly popular. Likewise, the many contemporary attempts to redefine satire's province – to emphasize, as Dryden had done in his 1693 *Discourse*, its classical pedigree, its noble, public-minded aims, its efficacy as a kind of extra-legal instrument of regulating morality – were swimming against the tide, trying to exclude defamatory satire from a public sphere it had already conquered.[50] 'The Satyrist and Libeller differ as much as the Magistrate and the Murderer,' insisted the essayist Richard Steele in a 1709 number of *The Tatler*, trying to force a distinction between satire (moral, corrective, quasi-legal) and libel, the name contemporaries affixed to the kind of venomous poetry found in the *Poems on Affairs of State*.[51]

If we detect a note of shrillness in Steele's claim, it's because such attempts to taxonomize, to keep different strains of satire apart, failed to describe the kind of poems people actually wrote. Alexander Pope, who tended to adopt a virtuous and public-minded literary persona, loved a libel-style smear, as the vicious portraits of loathed contemporaries that pepper his satires show. (He also owned, as a teenager, a copy of *A New Collection of Poems Relating to State Affairs* (1705), a *Poems on Affairs of State* knock-off, which he enjoyed annotating by filling in blanked-out names and guessing at the authors of anonymous poems.)[52] In response to one of his highly personal attacks, his great enemy, Lady Mary Wortley Montagu, hit back in a poem that deplored his misanthropic 'Rancour' and bullying jibes, all the while making gleeful references to his diminutive physical stature.[53]

What the *Poems on Affairs of State* series also indicated, the fourth volume in particular, was that collections of poetry could be targeted political weapons, timely interventions into live debates or scandals. In this guise, the series became a model for partisan publishers and editors later in the century. Its most high-profile successor, in the form of a newspaper, was the *Anti-Jacobin*, a weekly journal founded in 1797 by the Tory statesman George Canning, which published a mixture of new poetry and prose dedicated to attacking British and French political radicalism. Through its parodies of the poetry of Wordsworth, Coleridge and Southey (whom Canning termed, scornfully, 'Bards of Freedom'), it derided the revolutionary project perhaps more effectively than serious verses or prose treatises might have managed.[54] In 'The Friend of Humanity and the Knife Grinder', a malicious rewriting of Southey's poem 'The Widow', a caricatured republican philanthropist stops a poor knife-grinder and demands to know who's responsible for his poverty: 'Did some rich man tyrannically use you?' 'I should be glad to drink your Honour's health,' the knife-grinder replies, 'if you will give me sixpence; / But for my part, I never love to meddle / With politics, sir.' The 'Friend of Humanity' is appalled at his quietism:

> '*I* give thee sixpence! I will see thee damn'd first –
> Wretch! whom no sense of wrongs can rouse to
>   vengeance –
> Sordid, unfeeling, reprobate, degraded,

Spiritless outcast!'
[*Kicks the Knife-grinder, overturns his wheel, and exits
in a transport of Republican enthusiasm and universal
philanthropy.*][55]

Pro-government literary ventures such as the *Anti-Jacobin*,
though, were unusual. More common were anthologies
which, like the *Poems on Affairs of State*, supplied homes
for anti-ministerial critique. In 1743, an anonymous editor
(likely the disaffected politician and poet Charles Hanbury
Williams) launched *The Foundling Hospital for Wit*, an
anthology series which gathered together new satires and
songs, 'Brats of WIT and HUMOUR whose Parents chuse
to drop them'.[56] Writers who wanted inflammatory political
pieces printed, but were nervous about personal involvement,
could 'dispose of their Issue privately', as the editor put it, by
dropping off anonymous packets at a London coffee-house;
the frequency with which instalments in the series came out
would depend on the volume of new material received. If
any item – perhaps of a particularly time-sensitive nature –
required 'immediate Publication', the editor promised that
it would appear 'with the utmost Expedition'.[57] A series of
popular poems attacking the despised turncoat politician
William Pulteney, reprinted in the first two volumes of the
Foundling Hospital in 1743, did more damage to Pulteney in
a matter of months, as the writer Horace Walpole claimed,
than the outspoken opposition newspaper *The Craftsman*
had ever managed to do to his father (the former prime
minister, Sir Robert Walpole) in almost two decades. 'The
minister only lost his power,' Walpole wrote, 'but the patriot
his character.'[58] A loss of power might be temporary; losing
your character was permanent.

Two decades later, a similar anthology series, *The New*

Foundling Hospital for Wit (1768–73) dropped from the press, this time edited jointly by John Almon, a London bookseller, and his friend John Wilkes, the radical journalist and politician. Like its predecessors, this series specialized in gossip: the revelation, for targeted political purposes, of delicate information about the private lives of public figures. An innocent-looking editorial note to a poem in its third volume (1769) casually revealed that the Bishop of Gloucester's son was in fact not his son, but the illegitimate offspring of Thomas Potter, one of the most notorious rakes of the age.[59] (Potter was, to make matters worse, the son of the Archbishop of Canterbury.)*

In the same volume, Wilkes, with an eye on his career, used his editorial powers to smear two of his most prominent political enemies. Lord Le Despencer and the Earl of Sandwich had once been his friends and associates, but were now on the wrong side of the political divide as he saw it: to discredit them, and by extension the government they served, he raked up old gossip about the lewd recreational pursuits they had collectively been involved in as members of the 'Order of St. Francis', a libertine club that met at Medmenham Abbey in Buckinghamshire. Rumours about the orgiastic pursuits that went on at Medmenham had swirled in the newspapers during the preceding years (planted there by Wilkes), but the information in the anthology was new, *'never before printed'*, as its heading declared. Under the cover, once more, of an innocent editorial note, Wilkes implicated Le Despencer and Sandwich in a lurid account of the 'loves and frailties' – that is, sexual activities – of the Franciscan 'monks', who had disported themselves, Wilkes recounted, among the various erotic statues

---

* Potter was well-known for his extreme sexual predilections, which are reported to have included copulating in graveyards and sodomising cows.

and figures that Le Despencer had erected around the Abbey's grounds.[60] Wilkes himself, as his publicists (including Almon in his newspaper, *The Political Register*) declared, was in the process of fulsomely repenting for the 'sallies and indiscretions' of his youth. His fellow monks, however, the *New Foundling Hospital*'s vivid narrative suggested, had not only partaken of similar, forbidden pleasures, but had sought to hush their involvement up.[61]

In modern terms, we would call this kind of activity leaking, the anonymous disclosure, via untraceable means, of compromising political information by someone on the inside. In the later seventeenth century, poems passed around in manuscript had operated in a similar way, though more slowly, springing leaks in the impregnable machine of Stuart government by allowing gossip about courtiers and the monarch to seep out to readers. The first *Poems on Affairs of State* volumes, though they collected old libels rather than contemporary ones, likewise functioned as a kind of slow-release valve, providing scandalous tidbits and radical views that were new to many because they had always circulated privately, within and between small coteries.

In the bolder fourth volume, as in the later collections that followed its lead, the technology through which leaking happened became both riskier and more immediate: printed satires reached readers as the political information they contained was still current, and as the attacks they launched still had the power to wound. The kind of outspoken criticism it was possible for the *Poems on Affairs of State* compilers to get away with publishing in 1707 would have been unthinkable a few decades before. But books, and the layers of disguise and obfuscation they could interpolate between author and reader, or printer and reader, served as protection. Nothing could have been more immediate or radical in nature than Stephen College's song, a performance of treason that seemed to conjure out of thin air, in real time, the uprising it imagined on the streets of Oxford. But few others were like him, willing to make their own bodies, rather than paper and ink, the medium in which they resisted the state's power.

2

SUPERSTITION

Reliques of Ancient English Poetry (1765)

In March 1762, the artist William Hogarth, famous for his depictions of vice, drunkenness and delinquency on the streets of London, published a print entitled *Credulity, Superstition, and Fanaticism.* The print was an amended version of an earlier work of 1761, which he returned to at the insistence of friends who believed its message urgently needed re-communicating. The reason for their urgency was the recent appearance of a ghost.

Credulity depicts a bellowing preacher on a pulpit, his voice booming so forcefully that his wig has come unstuck from his head. From his hands dangle two puppets: a devil with horns, tail and pitchfork, and a witch wearing a conical hat, perched on a broomstick. Visual clues tell us that the preacher and his curate (pictured below him) are Methodists, part of the eighteenth-century Church of England evangelical movement which, in Tory circles, was often accused of encouraging fanaticism and helping to spread sensational beliefs about witches, devils and spirits. To the preacher's left, a thermometer propped on a book of Methodist sermons measures the mood of the congregation, its mercury rising from 'Despair' up through 'Extacy' and 'Convulsion Fits' to

'Raving'. The assembled faces below, toothless and ugly, are contorted into corresponding expressions of fear, panic and glee. In front of the pews, a young woman lies collapsed on her back in anguish, as live rabbits emerge from her skirts; she is Mary Toft, a farm labourer who, in 1726, had managed to convince a number of eminent physicians that she had been delivered of 'monstrous Births'. Next to her, a crouching man vomits a stream of old nails and bits of metal, a commonly attested symptom of possession by the Devil.

Above the thermometer measuring the congregation's mood sits a decorative panel depicting the Cock Lane Ghost, a phenomenon that had gripped London during the early months of 1762. In a grubby lodging in Cock Lane in Clerkenwell, the ghost of a young woman had begun to appear nightly, communicating invisibly via knocks and scratches on the wall, and claiming to have been poisoned by her husband. The ghost's appearances attracted large crowds, queues of coaches stretching back from the City to the fashionable West End. The eminent literary critic Samuel Johnson was part of an 'investigating committee' established to test whether or not it was real, which concluded that the landlord's daughter, twelve-year-old Elizabeth Parsons, was responsible for making sinister knocking sounds on the orders of her father, Richard.[1] In July, Richard Parsons and a handful of accomplices were convicted of conspiracy to defame the dead woman's husband.

There was more at stake in the unmasking of this ghost than the guilt or innocence of a supposed poisoner.[2] By the 1760s, belief in supernatural beings – ghosts, witches, fairies – was supposed to be the province of the uneducated common people, not of cultural elites such as Johnson and the noblemen, doctors and priests who comprised the investigatory committee. What the Cock Lane debacle revealed was that very few people were willing to declare themselves complete unbelievers until the weight of evidence on the other side started to make them look foolish. Hogarth's print showed the ghost robed in white and floating in the air according to common superstition, but clutching a large and very real-looking wooden hammer in its fist.

※

Since the sixteenth century, the question of ghost belief had divided English Protestants from Catholics. Protestant reformers argued that since Purgatory did not exist, there were, by definition, no restless souls to be found roaming the earth, haunting the living and begging for their prayers. The dead went straight to either Heaven or Hell and stayed there. By the eighteenth century, this remained the official position of the reformed Church of England. If men saw 'ghosts', orthodox preachers argued, what they were seeing were forms invented by their own guilty consciences to remind them of some past wrongdoing.[3] Prevailing ghost superstition was considered either a result of the inflammatory teachings of Methodism, or, just as harmful, a relic of the country's Catholic past, the last gasp of an age of ignorance and credulity. 'It forms a strong presumption against all supernatural and miraculous relations, that they are observed chiefly to abound among ignorant and barbarous nations,' the philosopher David Hume declared in 1748. 'In proportion as we advance nearer the enlightened ages, we soon learn, that there is nothing mysterious or supernatural in the case.'[4]

Fairies and witches fell into the same category of officially 'exploded beings'.[5] In 1736, Parliament passed a law, the Witchcraft Act, which ruled that alleged witch activities could no longer be prosecuted, because witches, in the eyes of the law, did not exist. It was now a crime for anyone to claim that a person was a witch or possessed magical powers, which in effect banned those in the legislature, judiciary or Church from formally expressing a belief in the reality of witchcraft.[6] In elite circles, such notions had long been considered old wives' tales, 'antiquated Romances, and the Traditions of Nurses and old Women', as Joseph Addison wrote in the *Spectator* in 1712. They were antediluvian, dating from an age before the rise of rationality and empirical observation. 'Our Forefathers,' Addison explained, 'looked upon Nature with more Reverence and Horrour, before the World was enlightened by Learning and Philosophy, and loved to astonish themselves with the Apprehensions of Witchcraft, Prodigies, Charms and Enchantments.'[7]

The official line about the supernatural was clear, but it didn't prevent individual doubts and fears. 'I could not have existed in the days of received witchcraft,' the essayist Charles Lamb declared in 1820. 'I could not have slept in a village where one of those reputed hags dwelt. Our ancestors were bolder or more obtuse.'[8] In his *Spectator* piece, Addison wavered enough to acknowledge that, although ghosts, fairies and witches were, undoubtedly, fabrications, there might nonetheless be 'Species of Spirits' and 'many Intellectual Beings in the World beside our selves'.[9] The obstacle that stood in the way of solid scepticism was the fact that, over the centuries, so many eminent and trustworthy witnesses in multiple countries had testified to the existence of returning spirits. 'I think a Person who is thus terrify'd with the Imagination of Ghosts and Spectres much more reasonable, than one who contrary to the Reports of all Historians sacred and prophane, ancient and modern, and to the Traditions of all Nations, thinks the Appearance of Spirits fabulous and groundless,' Addison wrote in another essay.[10] William Blackstone, barrister and Professor of Law at Oxford, was disposed to believe that 'there is, and has been such a thing as Witchcraft,' on the basis that its existence was a 'truth to which every nation in the world hath in its turn borne testimony.'[11] Johnson, likewise, thought it unwise to ignore the weight of consensus opinion. 'You have not only the general report and belief, but you have many voluntary solemn confessions,' he told his biographer, James Boswell, in answer to an enquiry about witches. The reality of ghosts, he noted, was 'a question which, after five thousand years, is yet undecided.'[12] Who was going to be sure enough to decide it now?

Ordinary people, meanwhile, continued to believe in the supernatural throughout the eighteenth century, much as they had always done. They knew from the stories they had heard since childhood, as well as what the Bible said on the subject, that spirits, witches and fairies existed, regardless of what their parish vicars tried to tell them from the pulpit.[13] Ghosts, they believed, returned to earth to bring injustices to light, haunt disloyal lovers, resolve unsettled business affairs or bear prophetic warnings. Witches – usually penurious old women, supposed to possess malevolent powers – they held responsible for local misfortunes, financial loss, illness, diseased animals, crop failure.[14] 'The common people,' wrote a doctor in 1735, 'when incapable of penetrating the reasons of their bodily sufferings, are exceeding prone to charge them on the influence and operation of superior invisible powers.'[15] Physical and mental maladies could be attributed to satanic possession: witches were thought to be able to direct evil spirits or devils to occupy the bodies of anyone whom they had a grudge against.[16] After 1736, when formal accusations of witchcraft could no longer be made, victims could still seek a cure in folk remedies, calling on Catholic priests (operating clandestinely) to exorcise them, or burying bottles filled with their urine and nail-clippings under the hearth for talismanic protection from spells.

Housewives and servants who believed in fairy-lore worked

hard to keep rooms clean and tidy, to avoid being pinched, nipped or having their milk or butter stolen; fairies, it was said, were obsessed with cleanliness and punished neglect.[17] Regular church attendance was keenly practised by those who believed that the rite of confirmation could cure rheumatism, or that churchyard soil had curative powers.[18] Those in love learned magic spells from cheap fortune-telling books, hoping to attract the object of their affection. 'Take a hollow ring of Ivory, horn or any convenient Metal,' one such book instructed, 'steep it in the Juice of Rue a night and a day, then draw thro' it the hair of a young Heifer cut between the Horns, then steep it again in Water of Fennel 24 Hours.'[19] Fortune-telling by palmistry, physiognomy and tasseography (reading coffee grounds or tea leaves) was also common. Belief in astrological signs and omens informed the decision of when to plough, when to marry or when to seek new employment.

One important source of popular superstitions was poetry. During the eighteenth century, ballads – simple songs that told a story, set to well-known tunes – were a popular form of entertainment. They were sung on street corners by vagrant ballad singers, hawked cheaply on printed sheets known as broadsides, or memorized and passed down within families and communities. The stories they told were often venerable episodes from British history or folklore, retellings of the escapades of King Arthur, St George or Robin Hood. The most attention-grabbing were embellished with wonderful characters drawn from folk superstition: giants, dragons, dwarfs, apparitions, fairies and sorcerers.

Some ballads recounted medieval tales of knights' quests and marvellous encounters. In the Arthurian ballad 'The Marriage of Sir Gawaine' (supposed to date from before the time of Chaucer), King Arthur comes up against a gigantic baron, 'twyce the size of common men', who dwells 'on magicke grounde' in a castle fenced around with spells. In return for promising the king his safety, the giant baron demands the answer to an age-old riddle, which Arthur manages to extract from an ugly, witch-like woman with a 'crookt' nose and serpentine hair. On her wedding night to Sir Gawaine (marriage to one of the king's handsome young knights being the price of her help), the 'foule' and 'grimme' woman suddenly transforms into a beautiful young lady, explaining that her former witchly appearance was the work of a wicked stepmother with magical powers:

> Shee witch'd mee, being a faire yonge maide,
>   In the greene forest to dwelle;
> And there to abide in lothlye shape,
>   Most like a fiend of helle.
>
> Midst mores and mosses; woods, and wilds;
>   To lead a lonesome life:
> Till some yong faire and courtlye knighte
>   Wolde marrye me to his wife.[20]

Other supernatural ballads popular during the period were domestic tales of woe. In 'Fair Margaret and Sweet William', a ballad believed to have been in circulation by the early seventeenth century, a young man breaks his promise to marry his lover, Margaret, who promptly dies of grief and returns to haunt him when he weds another girl:

> When day was gone, and night was come,
>   And all men fast asleep,
> Then came the spirit of fair Marg'ret,
>   And stood at Williams feet.

'I dreamt a dream, my dear ladye,' William confesses to his new bride the next morning, 'Such dreames are never good: / I dreamt my bower was full of red wine, / And my bride-bed full of blood.' Stricken by grief and guilt, he visits Margaret's house and kisses her corpse on the lips, then returns, faithfully, to her side in the grave.

Fair Margaret dyed to-day, to-day,
  Sweet William dyed the morrow:
Fair Margaret dyed for pure true love,
  Sweet William dyed for sorrow.[21]

Where aspects of the supernatural didn't appear explicitly in ballads, the fact that many of them were so old served to locate them in a hazy, romantic past, in which marvellous things were supposed to have happened as a matter of course. 'With the common people,' the poet William Shenstone wrote in 1761, 'a Song becomes a ballad as it grows in years; as they think an old serpent becomes a Dragon.'[22]

Among contemporary poets who composed fashionable, updated versions of ancient ballads, the supernatural was a favourite theme. The 'haunted lover' plot was especially popular. In 1724, 'William and Margaret', a new version of the 'Fair Margaret and Sweet William' story by the Scottish poet David Mallet, was an immediate hit in the London newspapers. 'Sweet William's Ghost', a William-and-Margaret tragedy that made Margaret, rather than William, the unfaithful villain, was the highlight of a popular Scottish anthology in 1723. In another variation on the theme, 'Lucy and Colin' (1725), Lucy dies of a broken heart the day before her faithless lover, Colin, marries someone else, a sequence of events that allows funeral and wedding to meld into one, horrifying spectacle:

To-morrow in the church to wed,
  Impatient, both prepare;
But know, fond maid, and know, false man,
  That Lucy will be there.[23]

Forty years later, around the time of the unmasking of the ghost at Cock Lane, supernatural ballads were still admired. In 1762, the critic John Newbery singled out Mallet's 'very poetical' ghost for special praise. A year later, 'Lucy and Colin' was to be found at the front of the most fashionable poetry collection of the moment, Robert Dodsley's *Collection of Poems in Six Volumes*.[24] New poets, too, were drawing on the imaginative potential of the supernatural in their work, using hedging strategies to make it clear that they weren't believers themselves.[25] In his 'Ode on the Popular Superstitions of the Highlands of Scotland' (1750), the poet William Collins presented himself as advising a fellow-writer in need of inspiration, a pretext which allowed him to describe, at length and with obvious pleasure, the supernatural beliefs of the Highlanders – their tales of 'fairy people', malevolent water-spirits and troops of bodiless, 'gliding ghosts'. One of his contemporaries, Mark Akenside, spent fifteen lines revelling in images of gothic horror ('spectres', 'guilty shades', 'everlasting woe') in his poem *The Pleasures of Imagination* (1757), having pre-emptively covered his back with a quick disclaimer to the effect that 'Superstition' was only for the 'vulgar'.[26]

The most popular strategy was for poets to write anonymously, or under pseudonyms, avoiding possible embarrassment by pretending not to have had anything to do with the supernaturally inspired work they put out. During the 1760s, several writers, Horace Walpole and the sixteen-year-old Thomas Chatterton among them, pretended to have 'discovered', rather than composed, marvellous works of superstitious invention. Populating the Highlands landscape of *Fingal* (1761), a much-admired epic poem supposed to be by an ancient Gaelic bard called Ossian (but actually the work of a contemporary Scottish writer, James Macpherson) were pale, misty ghosts, the shades of lost warriors, harbingers of doom.[27]

The broad consensus in elite circles that ghosts, witches and fairies did *not* exist was what granted poets freedom to explore. Since no one would choose to admit that they shared the superstitions of the common people, educated men and women could write about such beliefs from positions of intellectual detachment, allowing their imaginations to roam while remaining secure in their scepticism. The relative recentness of the break with credulity, of course, meant they stood on new ground, hedged around with uncertainty.[28] In the same breath as he praised Mallet in 1762 for having conjured up such a 'poetical ghost', Newbery attacked magical stories: without exception, he declared, they were 'unmeaning tales of giants, champions, inchanted knights, witches, goblins' – useless falsehoods such as 'could only proceed from the grossest ignorance, or a distempered brain.'[29] But distempered brains, it was becoming clear, produced dazzling things.

In 1765, both 'Fair Margaret and Sweet William' and 'The Marriage of Sir Gawaine' appeared in the same book: Thomas Percy's *Reliques of Ancient English Poetry*, a bulky, three-volume anthology which collected together 'Old Heroic Ballads, Songs, and other Pieces of our early Poets'. Percy, a curate and amateur scholar, was fascinated by superstitious beliefs, both as the imaginative mainstays of ballad literature and as traces of history, evidence of how ordinary men and women had conducted their lives and conceived of the world around them in unenlightened former ages. His collection of 'ancient' poems was intended for elite, educated readers, because only they, as he argued, could be trusted to know that the superstitious stories the book contained were not to be believed. It was not for credulous 'common Readers', among whom, he wrote, indulgence in marvellous tales would merely 'do hurt'. The point was not to prop up superstitions but to examine them in context, to build knowledge rather than encourage ignorance.[30]

The *Reliques* treated supernatural beliefs as just that – relics: vestiges of a lost age which could be used to piece the past together, as an archaeologist might construct history from artefacts and bones. According to the historian Joseph Ritson, writing at the end of the eighteenth century, the 1760s in Britain had marked the beginning of a period of great public interest in 'works illustrating the history, the poetry, the language, the manners, and the amusements' of the past.[31] Percy's collection, in this vein, not only displayed the poetry of former ages but also sought to bring to life aspects of a bygone society: the opinions, customs, hopes and fears of long-dead Britons. By returning belief in the supernatural back to the nation as part of its past, it was a book that made it possible to write new history, and new poetry.

✳

Thomas Percy, the son of a prosperous grocer and tobacconist, was born in 1729 in Bridgnorth, a small trading town in the middle of England. Arthur Percy, his father, despite lacking an 'academical education', encouraged his eldest boy to read widely. Alongside the usual works of Christian devotion, Thomas listed among his boyhood favourites stories about chivalry, fairies and pirates, devouring in particular the vividly embellished tales of Nathaniel Crouch, a chronicler of 'Extraordinary Adventures' and 'Wonderful Prodigies'. Through Crouch, he learned to explore the weirder byways of English history, 'the Miserable

Ends of divers Magicians, Witches, Conjurers, *&c.*': stories of 'strange Apparitions', miraculous preservations and fated deaths.[32] By the age of seventeen he had amassed and carefully catalogued a personal library of more than 250 books, which he left behind him in the care of his younger brother when he won a scholarship to Christ Church, Oxford, in 1746.

At Oxford, Percy had his sights fixed on a career in the Church. After taking his master's degree in 1751, he was appointed curate of two parishes in Shropshire near his hometown. Both were tiny, with very few parishioners, and his light duties left time for more interesting pursuits. In 1753, he paid a visit to a family friend, Humphrey Pitt, who lived a few miles away in a village called Shifnal. During his stay, he noticed that Pitt's maids were using a bundle of what looked like very old papers to light the parlour fire; curious, he asked if he could have the remains before they were incinerated. The bundle turned out be a commonplace book, or what we might think of now as a scrapbook: a handwritten collection of old poems, carefully copied out and assembled by an unknown person, in this case about a hundred years before. It was huge, five hundred pages long or more, dirty, tattered and torn in places. Later on it would become clear what an astonishing and deeply unlikely find it was, how lucky Percy had been to see it 'lying dirty on the floor,' as he recalled in 1769, just in time to save it from a fiery grave. Some of the old poems it contained were very rare, almost forgotten; some existed only in this single bundle of papers.[33] At the time, though, he had little sense of the value of what he was holding. Over the months that followed, he dipped into it when he pleased, scribbling notes in the margins, and tearing out the occasional page when he didn't fancy making the effort to copy out a poem he liked.[34]

In the autumn of 1757, however, four years later, Percy began to take his bundle of old papers more seriously. 'I am possess'd of a very curious old MS Collection of ancient Ballads many of which I believe were never printed,' he wrote to his friend, the poet William Shenstone, in November. 'It contains many old Romantic and Historical Ballads: upon King Arthur and the Knights of his round Table: Merlin &c.'[35] Samuel Johnson, whose acquaintance he had made the previous summer, had, he told Shenstone, been shown the manuscript and recommended that its contents be published, even offering to help pick out the most 'valuable pieces' and furnish the book with 'proper Notes'.[36]

Johnson's suggestions weren't the kind of thing you said no to. Percy started work on the 'ancient Ballads' in earnest in the spring of 1760, aiming, as his mentor had advised, to select the rarest gems from the manuscript and ready them for publication. Somehow, over the course of the next five years – during which he also signed publishing contracts for at least seven other literary works, conducted his duties as vicar of a new parish and had three children – the project transformed into something else entirely: a vast, ambitious collection not just of poems from the manuscript he'd rescued from the fire, but of old ballads from as many different sources as he could lay his hands on. Along with Shenstone (who liked the idea so much that he told people he'd come up with it himself), Percy read and sifted through huge quantities of manuscripts, keeping up a near-constant stream of correspondence with literary scholars and antiquarians from London, Oxford, Cambridge, Scotland and Wales.[37] With charm and deceptive humility (gifts, we might guess, acquired at the pulpit), he persuaded very busy people to devote hours of their time to helping him.[38] Richard Farmer, an eminent Shakespeare scholar, was talked into making illicit 'borrowings' of rare books from Cambridge University Library and dispatching them to him secretly in the post, only drawing the line when Percy tried to persuade him to post manuscripts too. 'I dare not own [that] I send any of y^e *printed* Books out of Town!'[39]

The collection fell into three parts. In each, Percy laid out the oldest ballads he'd found first, then led the reader forward chronologically to more modern seventeenth- and eighteenth-century pieces. Volume One contained border ballads, tales of bloody skirmishes between the armies of Scotland and Northumberland, as well as a selection of love poems and ballads that were believed to have provided the inspiration for plotlines in Shakespeare's plays. The second volume, containing a mixture of English and Scottish ballads, was meant to illustrate, as Percy explained, 'the gradual changes of the ENGLISH Language thro' a succession of FIVE HUNDRED years', moving from thirteenth-century poems to modern-day ones. The third, headed 'Ballads on King Arthur, &c.', contained famous Arthurian romances, as well as ballads retelling the legend of St George, ballads on supernatural subjects, and a collection of songs warning of the perils of infidelity and unrequited love. Many of the poems were prefaced with notes composed by Percy, explaining their history and where they had been discovered.[40] Interspersed between them were three long essays, also by Percy: an essay 'On the Origin of the English Stage', to accompany the ballads illustrating Shakespeare; an 'Essay on the Ancient Minstrels in England'; and an 'Essay on the Ancient Metrical Romances'.

The essays were where Percy hoped to make his scholarly credentials clear, to demonstrate that by publishing a collection of old scrap ballads rescued from a fireplace, he was actually making a serious contribution to the study of Britain's past. Illuminating the early history of the nation's poetry, he hoped to show, could be a means of shedding light on other, ostensibly more important things: the lives of 'ancient' people, their politics and wars, the customs and manners they adopted, the growth and change of their language. The poems he collected, he argued, were of great historical significance: according to documents he had found, the oldest ballads and medieval romances (such as the Arthurian tales) had been first composed by minstrels, greatly respected bards who were hired by kings or barons to chronicle their noble deeds in song, then perform them at court to the accompaniment of the harp. Minstrels, in this view, were like early historians, and their ballads and romances the earliest national histories.[41]

This was a necessary bit of literary upselling. During the 1760s, Percy was swimming against the tide: the majority of his contemporaries looked on romances as vulgar forms, nonsensical old tales that belonged to the past and ought to stay there.[42] According to Johnson, writing in 1765, romance-reading was something that nations grew out of as their people gradually became more learned and cultivated, in the same way that children, over the years, grew too old for make-believe.[43] Only the ignorant poor, who knew no better (largely because they had little choice in what they read or listened to), remained beguiled by romances beyond the age of ten. The 'Maturer Judgement' of adulthood, as the poet George Crabbe put it in 1781, would have little to do with them: 'My doughty Giants are all slain or fled, / And all my Knights, blue, green, and yellow, dead.'[44]

Traditional ballads were also viewed unfavourably. Despite the fact that they were rarely out of the fashionable anthologies of the day – sophisticated readers took more pleasure in them than they liked to admit – they were nonetheless associated with the common people, with rude taste, loose morals and rough, old-fashioned language.[45] They were considered entertainment for nursery children or the uneducated, absurd stories written in old-fashioned, misspelt English which had long since been superseded by the polished poetry of the modern age. Moralists disapproved of the pernicious effects they had on the minds of the innocent or ignorant. 'Children who are permitted to be familiar with footmen and other domestics hear ballads of *How the young Squire, Master's eldest Son, fell in love with the Chamber-maid*,' screeched the *London Magazine* in 1735.[46] Those who sang and hawked ballads on street-corners were considered public nuisances. Percy himself wrote dismissively to one of his learned correspondents, Lord Hailes, about 'common-ballad singers' and the 'vulgar trash' they spouted.[47] The letters he received from Shenstone, too, were littered with warnings about the danger of overvaluing ballads merely on account of their age and history. Many 'old renowned songs,' Shenstone reminded him, 'perhaps have little or no Merit; and would not have existed to this day, but for the tunes with which they are connected.'[48]

Percy wasn't the first pioneer to try to rehabilitate the ballad form. Cautious attempts had been made as early as 1707, when a poet named John Oldmixon had tried to argue that the author of a very old ballad, 'The Nut Brown Maid', must have been a gentleman, rather than a common singer. No one who wrote so movingly, Oldmixon said, could possibly have been low-born: 'By his Gallantry, we take him to be a Person that was well bred, according to his Day.'[49] In the *Spectator*, around the same time, Addison boldly compared the writers of native ballads to Homer and Virgil, on the basis that they too, though they wrote songs rather than grand political epics, had managed to combine 'Greatness' of subject matter with an arresting 'Simplicity' of style.[50] '*Homer*, the first and best of all the Poets, if we will give credit to the most antient Historians, was himself but an old blind Ballad-singer,' declared one particularly brave revisionist in 1715.[51]

The idea of linking ballads explicitly to national history also predated Percy's efforts. In 1723, Ambrose Phillips, a poet and Whig politician, put together a *Collection of Old Ballads* (unprepossessingly titled), in which each of the different songs was contextualized with a note connecting it to the real historical events which it chronicled or reimagined. 'Whatever is remarkable in History,' Phillips claimed, 'is handed down to us in Ballads.'[52] This was close to what Percy would do in the *Reliques*, but in one respect Phillips was still a long way behind him. In his *Collection*, he took an openly dismissive attitude towards ballads with supernatural elements.

It was impossible for him to exclude them altogether as a category, he was aware, because of their ubiquity. Large numbers of the most popular old ballads featured supernatural beings, or had plots that turned on supernatural happenings. What Phillips did, instead, was to tuck them away at the back of one of his volumes, making it clear that by giving space to what he considered mere foolish beliefs, he was ceding, reluctantly, to popular demand. 'Amongst the several Subjects I have hitherto enter'd upon,' he wrote,

> I have not yet touch'd upon the Miraculous, to the no little Disappointment, I am afraid, of my aged Female Readers, who [...] doubtless expect in such a Collection a Competency of Ghosts. To comply with their Taste, I have inserted the two following Songs.[53]

The idea that only 'aged Female Readers' – hardly a valued social category – liked ghost ballads was a cliché, probably a vestige of the old association between storytelling and elderly childhood nurses. Addison, in the *Spectator*, had repudiated supernatural tales as 'old Womens Fables'. 'We ought to arm our selves against them,' he wrote, and '*pull the Woman out of our Hearts*.'[54] Phillips, invoking this tradition, knew what he was doing. By declaring that he was only printing supernatural pieces in order to appease an 'aged Female' readership, he was seeking, effectively, to have his cake and eat it – to capitalize on the ballads' popularity, while making it abundantly clear that he himself was far too enlightened to enjoy them.

Percy's *Reliques* contained as many as twenty different ballads that either hinged on supernatural plotlines or contained supernatural elements. It would have been easy for him, and certainly more in keeping with the views of his contemporaries, if he had prefaced them, *à la* Phillips, with a face-saving disclaimer about popularity and the impossibility of exclusion. Instead, in his preface, where he did his best to explain to his modern-minded readers what exactly they had in front of them, he declared that all his ballads, not only the ones about real historical people or events, were eloquent fragments of the nation's past. He had selected, he wrote, 'such specimens of ancient poetry' 'as either shew the gradation of our language, exhibit the progress of popular opinions, display the peculiar manners and customs of former ages, or throw light on our earlier classical poets.'[55]

The idea that you could write the history of a people by concentrating on their 'opinions' and 'manners and customs', rather than by chronicling the regime changes, power struggles and wars that tended to be the stuff of history books, was a relatively new one. One of the many projects Percy had on the go while he compiled the *Reliques* was a translation of a work of history, the Swiss writer Paul Henri Mallet's *Introduction à L'Histoire de Dannemarc* (1755), which he was contracted for in the summer of 1763.[56] Mallet's book, which studied the religion, laws, manners and customs of the ancient Danes, argued that it was time for a new way of writing history. 'Why should history be only a recital of battles, sieges, intrigues and negotiations?' he demanded. 'And why should it contain meerly a heap of petty facts and dates?' By providing, instead, a 'picture of the opinions, customs, and even inclinations of a people,' the historian, he explained, could get to the heart of how historical men and women had thought, what they had considered important, what they'd hoped and feared.[57] And he could trace the vestiges of their rituals and beliefs in the modern European societies around him.

This had a profound influence on the way Percy treated his ballads. What he understood by 'popular opinions' and 'peculiar manners and customs' varied – like Mallet, he was interested in all kinds of manners, rituals and behaviours – but, in his work, one persistent element was superstition, the beliefs of long-dead men and women about supernatural beings, and the customs or rituals they had adopted to manage their presence.

In his editorial notes, accordingly, whenever the subject matter of a ballad gave him the opportunity, he dived eagerly into the history of superstitious belief. As he explained in his introduction to 'The Witches' Song', a ballad in Volume Three in which a *Macbeth*-style gaggle of witches crow about their gruesome activities (stealing a skull from a charnel house; collecting hair clippings from a hanged murderer), he was interested primarily in what he called superstitions of 'genuine English growth', the opinions 'of *our own vulgar*': beliefs that would shed light on specific aspects of native popular history.[58] When he introduced the song 'Robin Good-Fellow', a seventeenth-century ballad about the 'merry jests' of the Puck figure who also features in *A Midsummer Night's Dream*, he marvelled at the extent and sophistication of the old English superstitions around fairies and sprites, comparing them, as a system of beliefs, to the complex mythology of ancient Greece and Rome.[59]

Popular fairy belief was one of his favourite subjects. Generally, the information in his notes was keyed to particular words or ideas in a ballad that might need contextualizing.

When it came to fairy superstition, however, his commentary went far beyond what was strictly necessary. 'After these *Songs* on the *Fairies*, the reader may be curious to see the manner in which they were formerly invoked and bound to human service,' he noted after a ballad called 'The Fairies Farewell'. 'It will afford entertainment to a contemplative mind to trace these whimsical opinions up to their origin.'[60] While hunting through the collections of the Ashmolean Library in Oxford for old ballads, it transpired, he had become sidetracked by 'the papers of some alchymist', which contained, among other curiosities, 'a variety of Incantations and Forms of Conjuring both *Fairies, Witches*, and *Demons*.' He was so fascinated by the alchemist's instructions for binding a fairy into servitude that he included them in full:

> *An excellent way* to gett a *Fayrie*. First, gett a broad square christall or Venice glasse, in length and breadth 3 inches. Then lay that glasse or christall in the bloud of a white henne, 3 Wednesdayes, or 3 Fridayes. Then take it out, and wash it with holy aq. [water] and fumigate it. Then take 3 hazle sticks, or wands of an yeare groth: pill [strip] them fayre and white; and make them soe longe, as you write the *Spiritts* name, or *Fayries* name, which you call, 3 times on every sticke being made flatt on one side. Then bury them under some hill, whereas you suppose *Fayries* haunt, the Wednesday before you call her.[61]

In late 1761, Percy wrote to the Welsh scholar Evan Evans, one of his long-suffering helpers, to ask if Evans could supply him with further information about the history of popular fairy lore. Like Mallet, he was convinced that fairy beliefs had arrived in Britain from 'the northern nations' (that is, they had been carried over from Scandinavia by early medieval Danish invaders), and he wondered if any of the ancient Welsh writers Evans read ever mentioned or described such creatures. 'Does the opinion entertained in Wales of those fanciful beings suppose them as diminutive in size, as our English Notion does?' he enquired.

> You know that the English vulgar notion of *Fairies* hath always been that they are a very diminutive race of beings of a middle nature between men and spirits: resembling the former in their actions &c, and the latter in their power of being invisible &c that they exchange their offspring with those of the human race; that they are fond of dancing and make those green circles sometimes seen in the grass &c. &c. &c.[62]

Evans proved, unexpectedly, to be a mine of information about 'the vulgar notion of Fairies in Wales' – still upheld, he said, by credulous 'old women' – and corroborated Percy's guess that the English and Welsh superstitions were connected. Just as in England, fairies in Wales were 'supposed to haunt desarts, groves and meads, and to be dressed in green,' he wrote. 'Their chief diversions are music and dancing, and those green circles you mention are occasioned by them.'[63] A summary of this, credited to 'a learned friend in Wales', was reproduced faithfully in the *Reliques*' note to 'Robin Good-Fellow'.[64]

Underpinning all these investigations into the minutiae of superstitious beliefs was Percy's conviction that ghosts, witches and fairies counted as historical information. It was perfectly possible, as he saw it, to dismiss the supernatural as *not true* while at the same time considering it *true to history*. When supernatural beings cropped up in old ballads, they could be noted as interesting representations of ancient beliefs without threatening to encroach on anyone's rationality or religious faith.[65] The 'most credulous' old poets, those with 'the greatest passion for the marvelous', as he wrote in his translation of Mallet's book, might 'falsify' the history of their age by filling it with tales of giants and fairies, but, in doing so, 'without perceiving it', they revealed its 'manners of life and modes of thinking', the strange superstitions that structured its reality.[66] Incredible, supernatural ballad stories, in other words, might not supply the most true-to-life picture of the events of the past, but nonetheless supplied an honest one: because they were full of marvels, they spoke to what people had once believed in and revered. Romances, though they seemed allergic to facts, were invaluable resources for the social historian, chronicling the past in spite of themselves.[67] 'This is doubtless the best, if not the only use, we can make of those old reliques of poetry, which have escaped the shipwreck of time,' Percy concluded. 'All our poetry is historical,' Evans agreed in a letter of 1764. 'The Bards [are] not only valuable as poets, but historians.'[68]

In one way at least, the Enlightenment brought eighteenth-century men and women closer to superstition, not further away from it. In 1777, John Brand, an antiquarian, produced an updated edition of a work of 1725, Henry Bourne's *Antiquitates Vulgares*. In his book, Bourne had catalogued a number of the superstitions 'held by the Common People', but, because he was a curate with orthodox religious views, he had also sought to regulate or quash those that he felt were 'sinful and wicked'. In a chapter on the belief that ghosts who walked the earth tended to vanish at dawn, Bourne claimed that what observers had really seen flying around at night weren't purgatorial souls but 'good and evil Angels attending upon Men', orthodox theological beings which had no power to hurt them under God's protection.[69]

When he came to update and revise the book, fifty years later, Brand made it clear that his job wasn't to reassure anyone: he was a historian, not a priest. 'The good Man,' he wrote mockingly of Bourne, 'has played the Conjurer so far as to *raise* us *Spirits*, but does not seem to have had so much of the *Scholar* in him as to have been able to *lay* them.' What interested him, instead, was the ancientness of such 'flimsy' ideas, what they might reveal about the primitive people who had invented them, and whether it might be possible to trace them back through the centuries to 'the distant Countries from whence they were first perceived to flow'. 'Wisdom', he believed, could be 'extracted from the Follies and Superstitions of our Forefathers.'[70] Returning spirits were no longer a theological threat; they were just historical data.

All of this meant asking readers to compartmentalize, to separate what they knew to be real in the later eighteenth century from what an ordinary person might have believed three or four hundred years before. As the historian Richard Hurd pointed out in 1762, no one in modern times refused to read Homer and Virgil on the grounds that their poems contained pagan gods and superstitions. The exploits of Athena and Poseidon weren't taken as an affront to rationality or the Christian religion. If that cognitive dissonance was possible, why couldn't it be applied to old ballads and romances, which also contained 'magic and enchantments', but were – just like the *Iliad* and *Aeneid* – clearly the products of a bygone age?[71] And why, for that matter, could it not be applied to old English and Celtic supernatural beliefs in general, which, if they lingered at all in the modern age, did so among the common people and seemed to pose no threat to the superior rationality of the enlightened?

Providing everyone was clear that superstition was dead, the historical approach afforded educated men and women the freedom to think analytically about a subject that had always resisted objective study. Hurd went a step further and argued that it wasn't even necessary to assume that people in the past had really believed in supernatural beings in order to treat their superstitions as historical evidence. By the word *giant*, he claimed, English writers had never truly meant 'an imaginary being of superhuman size given to terrorizing the locals'. Instead, right from the start, giants had been metaphors, images of dominance called up by inventive poets to represent feudal barons and the outsize power they exercised over their people.[72] Percy took the same line in his notes to the ballad 'The Dragon of Wantley' in the third volume of the *Reliques*. The dragon in the poem's story, he explained, had never been an actual fire-breathing monster: it was a fictional embellishment of the poet's, representing a real-life Yorkshire landowner who had been caught stealing tithes and estates.[73] None of this, of course, was to say that supernatural beliefs were a lie, or that they possessed no reality for the people who had encountered or used them; simply that, in some scenarios, they had grown up from specific social or political situations, and had been a kind of language, a means for men and women to make sense of the hostile forces structuring their reality.

☙

The first completed pages of the *Reliques* were sent to be printed in February 1762. Almost three years later, the presses were still rolling, as individual sheets shuttled back and forth from the printer to Percy and his scholarly correspondents, constantly being tweaked or rewritten. A series of rapid changes had to be made in 1764, when the Countess of Northumberland, a well-known society figure, agreed to be the book's dedicatee. At the last minute, Percy reversed the order of his volumes so that the border ballads, retelling the noble history of the Countess's ancestors, came first. Then, since a lady's name was going to be affixed to the project, he combed the entire thing for smut or profanity. The ballad 'Cock Lorrel's Treat' had to go; thankfully, a line about a lady being 'bare / alle about the buttockes' had already been wiped from the poem 'The Boy and the Mantle'.[74] 'I am only affraid lest she should expect the contents to be of a higher nature than she will find them to be,' he wrote nervously to Hailes, his Scottish antiquarian friend. Time ran out in the autumn, when the Countess requested to see Percy's finished handiwork. 'By almost harassing myself to death and every one else concerned in this work,' he reported to Hailes, 'I got the book finished and a set finely bound by the *given time*. I presented it and had the happiness to have it very honourably received.'[75] It was ready for the public on Valentine's Day, 1765, more than a decade after Percy had first rescued the torn, smudged manuscript from the fire.

The *Reliques* was a hit. A month after publication, close to half of the first 1,500 copies had already sold, a result 'far better than I could have expected,' as Percy told Hailes.[76] During his trips down to London that spring, he was a regular guest at high society tables, popping into Northumberland House – the West End home of the Countess – for breakfast or dinner, and calling on Horace Walpole, to whom he'd sent a copy of the anthology.[77] 'I can acquaint you with a delightful publication of this winter, a collection of old ballads and poetry in three volumes,' Walpole wrote to a friend. Percy's dragon tales were perfectly timed, he pointed out; just at that moment, the French were in uproar about a terrifying, howling, man-eating beast supposed to be prowling the Gévaudan region (modern-day Lozère). 'Pray set this against our ghost in Cock Lane,' Walpole exclaimed, 'and tell me how much this age is enlightened!

How little Sir Isaac Newton thought that in little more than thirty years he should be less talked of than a second Dragon of Wantley!'[78] Three years later, in 1768, by which time the French dragon had been slain, metaphorically speaking, and the *Reliques* had gone through a successful second edition, Percy was elected to Johnson's starry London dining society, the Club, where his fellow dinner companions included Edmund Burke and Adam Smith. In 1770, he was made a Doctor of Divinity, the highest degree the University of Cambridge had to offer. By 1782, he was a bishop.[79]

Percy, ever an assiduous social climber, was pleased to be talked about and delighted by the impression his anthology was making in fashionable circles. The historian in him, though, was just as pleased by the reception of the book among scholars and antiquarians. Several were sufficiently impressed by his research to draw on his conclusions in their own work. Thomas Warton, the future Poet Laureate, quoted from the *Reliques* at length in his heavyweight *History of English Poetry* (1774–81), slightly modifying his own ideas about the origins of supernatural poetry in the light of Percy's discussion of ancient Scandinavian beliefs about giants, dwarfs and fairies.[80] Brand, compiling his history of popular superstitions, found the *Reliques* a goldmine of information about ancient fairy beliefs, on which Percy – thanks to his friend Evans and a nameless seventeenth-century alchemist – had become something of an authority.[81] Vicesimus Knox, a popular essayist who liked to disparage antiquarianism as 'raking in a dunghill', confessed to enjoying the feeling of time-travel as he leafed through the *Reliques*, describing the pleasure of having been able to project himself into the past 'by an effort of imagination'.[82]

Reviewers, too, appreciated the book as a piece of history-writing as well as a literary collection. According to William

Kenrick in the *Monthly Review*, it offered readers 'the certain gratification of taking a retrospect of past ages', 'tracing back our distant claims to the honours, or virtues, of our progenitors.'[83] Dipping into it was like encountering men and women who were very different, but in some ways very similar, to oneself. The *Critical Review* commented that readers would find in Percy's book 'an ethic history of our ancestors', meaning that in its poems and notes the ethos – the character, values and opinions – of long-dead people would shine through. As Percy had hoped, the reviewers were intrigued by, rather than dismissive about, the old-fashioned superstitions that appeared in his ballads. 'Some of the witches' songs give us lively ideas of antient credulity,' observed the *Critical Review* approvingly.[84] Kenrick, in the *Monthly*, had no problem with the supernatural content of Percy's ballads. He did pick up on one offence against logic in 'Margaret's Ghost', in fact, but it wasn't to do with the ghost: the culprit was the line 'When night and morning meet', which, he argued, was nonsense because – as Newton would have pointed out – 'no two objects can meet unless they move contrary ways, and are both present.'[85] Superstition was fine; a faulty understanding of physics wasn't.

One of the most important things Percy's anthology suggested was that the progress of enlightenment involved tangible losses as well as gains. 'Ignorance and superstition,' Warton declared in his *History of English Poetry*, 'so opposite to the real interests of human society, are the parents of imagination.' Ghost, witch and fairy beliefs, though thoroughly debunked in the eyes of the educated, could nonetheless be a marvellous resource: they constituted 'fictions [...] more valuable than reality', as Warton put it, fantastic lies that were worth hanging onto as, inexorably, society moved forward towards truth and light.[86]

The imagination, as growing numbers of critics and philosophers argued, seemed to be stimulated most by what it was unable rationally to understand. 'It is our ignorance of things that causes all our admiration, and chiefly excites our passions,' Edmund Burke observed. 'Knowledge and acquaintance make the most striking causes affect but little.' The most sublime and dazzling ideas, those that lent themselves readily to art, were also those that couldn't be subjected to the power of reason, whose causes remained strange and obscure.[87] According to the critic William Duff, writing in 1767, the 'boundless region' of the supernatural provided more scope than any other for poetic flights of fancy. In the representation of 'Witches, Ghosts, Fairies, and such other unknown visionary beings,' Duff suggested, poetic genius could 'indulge its adventurous flight without restraint', unhampered by the usual obligations to believability and verisimilitude. To imagine and depict the invisible, he argued, required a rare imaginative brilliance: it was the 'most pregnant proof of truly ORIGINAL GENIUS'.[88]

The return to the supernatural imagination brought with it a new openness to popular beliefs. By tracing the lineage of the nation's superstitions, rooting them in the history of its people, Percy's book helped to imbue the 'vulgar' traditions of common folk with meaning and dignity. Long-held native superstitions, the Shakespeare scholar Elizabeth Montagu argued in 1769, possessed a quasi-religious significance: they were 'hallowed traditions', 'consecrated' by centuries of faithful belief into a kind of 'holy ground' of the imagination.[89] The best supernatural fictions, it was now believed, Shakespeare's marvellous ghosts and witches among them, succeeded in capturing the imagination because they were rooted in tradition, in the ancient superstitions that ordinary people had grown up with. Neither Homer nor

Virgil, as the critic Hugh Blair observed in 1763, had gone to the trouble of inventing the vast mythology of gods and marvellous creatures that structured their poems: it already existed in the 'traditionary stories' and 'popular legends' they knew from childhood. (Homer, one critic remarked, had been at a disadvantage in this regard: if he had lived in England during the medieval period, the 'superior' nature of the superstitions then current would have allowed him to write even better epic poems.[90])

In a dramatic reversal of the old, snobbish attitude towards popular 'credulity', it was now argued that the only way to guarantee you were writing a good supernatural story was to keep your characters and plots in line with traditional beliefs. 'A poet is by no means at liberty to invent what system of the marvellous he pleases,' declared Blair.[91] Boswell, Johnson's biographer, who loved magical romances and hoped one day to 'write a little story-book' of his own, described the ingredients he would need: 'It will require much nature and simplicity and a great acquaintance with the humours and traditions of the English common people.'[92] According to Montagu, anyone trying to depict a supernatural personage had to take care to 'fix it in such scenes, and display it in such actions, as are agreeable to the popular opinion.' Witches were to be pictured 'holding their sabbath', and ghosts 'whispering a bloody secret [...] at the midnight hour', because that was what was expected of them. As usual, Shakespeare was held up as an exemplary model. Since it was commonly believed that spirits who roamed the earth vanished away at cockcrow, he had directed Old Hamlet's ghost to disappear likewise, holding fast to tradition in order to conjure a supernatural presence that felt, in some sense, solid and real.[93]

During the mid-1790s, when the first generation of British Romantic poets was beginning to write and publish, traditional tales of the supernatural were at the peak of their fashion.[94] The many ballad anthologies that appeared during the second half of the century, inspired by the *Reliques*, had become increasingly unapologetic about the popular, 'unsophisticated' poetry they contained. 'Vulgar' poetry no longer needed special pleading; the simpler a poem was, it was argued, the more faithfully it would be able to depict the real shapes of 'life and nature', and the unreal ones too. Poets were especially eager to promote the ballad revival, feeling that it offered models for their work which, because they belonged to the distant past, would still leave room for them to experiment freely. Percy could 'never be mentioned with too much respect,' the poet Robert Southey declared, for succeeding in 'awakening the public to the merits of our old writers.'[95] In his *Lectures on the History of Literature* (1818), the German critic Friedrich von Schlegel observed that, after Percy, ballad fever had 'engrossed the whole of the English literature'. 'The universal passion was for the ancient national ballads,' Schlegel recalled, for the 'melancholy echoes of the lost poetry of a more heroic time.'[96]

In March 1796, the fashionable *Monthly Magazine* printed a new English translation of 'Lenore', a powerful ghost ballad of 1773 composed by the German poet Gottfried Bürger. At university in Göttingen in the 1760s, Bürger had come across Percy's *Reliques* and become fascinated by the traditional ballad form, the possibilities of the supernatural ballad in particular. His poem 'Lenore', or 'Ellenore' in the English version, told the story of a slain soldier, William, who returns from the dead on horseback to carry off Lenore, his faithful lover, so that they can be buried together.

To British readers who knew the old ghost tales in the *Reliques*, the story would have had a familiar ring to it. In the Scottish ballad 'Sweet William's Ghost', printed in Percy's third volume, Margaret grieves for her dead lover so desperately that she no longer wishes to live, and pleads with his ghost to be allowed to join him in his coffin:

> 'Is there any room at your head, Willie?
>   Or any room at your feet?
> Or any room at your side, Willie,
>   Wherein that I may creep?'

William insists there is no place for her:

> 'There's nae room at my head, Margret,
>   There's nae room at my feet,
> There's no room at my side, Margret,
>   My coffin is made so meet.'[97]

The plot of Bürger's ballad unfolds somewhat differently. Unlike Margaret, who begs Willie to be allowed to die with him, Lenore, galloping on horseback behind a lover she believes to be alive, has no idea that their destination is a graveyard rather than their bridal home. But, in a nod to Percy's text, Bürger has her ask William the same sinister question:

> 'And where is then thy house, and home,
>   And bridal bed so meet?'
> ''Tis narrow, silent, chilly, low,
>   Six planks, one shrouding sheet.'
>
> 'And is there any room for me,
>   Wherein that I may creepe?'[98]

The conclusion of Bürger's story is horrifying. In a dramatic rendition of the 'vanish at cockcrow' trope, Lenore watches

William shrivel and transform into a dry skeleton as dawn comes: 'His head became a naked scull; / Nor hair nor eyne had he.' William, it turns out, is not really William at all, but the embodiment of Death himself, arrived with 'scythe and hour-glass' to drag her to the tomb where her lover's bones are. Lenore receives, against her will, what Willie stubbornly refuses to give Margaret: 'endless union' in the grave, the promise of a coffin big enough for two.[99]

The appearance of the translated 'Lenore' in 1796 had an 'electrifying' effect on the British literary scene, as the critic Mary Jacobus has shown.[100] The *Monthly Review* diagnosed 'an increased relish among us for the modern German school of literature – a school of [...] the marvellous, the horrid, and the extravagant.'[101] Walter Scott, who had heard the ballad's translator, William Taylor, read an early draft aloud in Edinburgh in 1794, was so inspired that he composed his own version of the story, 'William and Helen'. Rival English translations appeared in quick succession in 1796, capitalising on Bürger's sudden celebrity. Charles Lamb, who, by his own confession, had been 'dreadfully alive to nervous terrors' since childhood, dashed off an incoherent letter to his old schoolfriend Samuel Taylor Coleridge in July: 'Have you read the Ballad called 'Leonora'... If you have !!!!!!!!!!!!!!!'[102] Wordsworth, with whom Coleridge corresponded about the poem at length, bought copies of both Bürger's ballads and Percy's *Reliques* from a bookshop in Hamburg while travelling with his sister, Dorothy.[103] Southey wrote his own Bürger-inspired ballad, 'Donica' (1797), which told the story of a young princess who becomes ghostly pale and seems to die in the arms of her lover, reviving only to be snatched, finally, by Death at the altar.

Both 'Lenore' and 'Donica' reappeared, a few years later, in the most famous supernatural poetry collection of the Romantic age. *Tales of Wonder* (1801) was a two-volume anthology of macabre ballads compiled by Matthew Lewis, the author of the sensational Gothic novel *The Monk* (1796), a rollercoaster tale of witchcraft, devil worship, murder and lust. His anthology, which the young Percy Shelley owned and inscribed with little marginal drawings of ghosts and monsters, combined new supernatural compositions – thirteen original ghost ballads of Lewis's own; eight by Southey; four by Walter Scott – with traditional English and Scottish ballads, and translations or imitations of German and Danish ones.[104] 'The Plan, which I propose to myself,' Lewis wrote to Scott in 1798, calling on him to join the project, 'is to collect all the *marvellous* Ballads that I can lay my hands upon. [...] [A] ghost or a witch is a sin-qua-non ingredient in all the dishes, of which I mean to compose my hobgoblin repast.'[105]

Beyond the obvious spooky pleasures of the 'hobgoblin repast' Lewis proposed, he, Scott and Southey were interested in what the supernatural ballad might do for modern British poetry more widely: they believed that drawing on a fresh, full-blooded European form might help to 'renew [its] spirit'.[106] Accordingly, Taylor's celebrated 'Lenore' translation featured prominently at the close of the second volume of the book, while, in Volume One, Scott provided a translation of another supernatural Bürger ballad, 'Der Wilde Jäger' ('The Wild Huntsman'). Several pieces from Percy's *Reliques* appeared too, among them 'The Marriage of Sir Gawaine', with its depiction of witchly powers of transformation; the tragic tale of 'Fair Margaret and Sweet William'; and 'Sweet William's Ghost', the likely inspiration for 'Lenore'. Among the new ballads was a story of a ghostly maiden stuck in purgatorial limbo, who appears each night and then vanishes, per superstitious tradition, at cockcrow; and the tale of a witchy old woman on her deathbed, who recounts, trembling, how she once enjoyed 'suck[ing] the breath of sleeping babes', anointing herself with 'infants' fat', and feasting on 'rifled graves'.[107]

When it came to such sensational texts, Lewis had a difficult line to tread. By the beginning of the new century, as he was aware, the supernatural ballad revival had begun to be looked on with disfavour: not only by the critical establishment, which had long been hostile to the 'corrupting', amoral influence that Gothic literature threatened to exert, but by many writers and readers too. The intensity, during the mid-1790s, of the fashion for German or German-inspired tales of horror could not sustain itself, and left in its wake an emerging moral disgust, bound up with a disinclination, on the part of more sophisticated audiences in particular, to fall for sensational tricks.[108] Wordsworth, who believed that both British and German poetry had been 'absolutely redeemed' by Percy's *Reliques*, and whose *Lyrical Ballads* (1798) sustained the revival of the ballad form, nonetheless had mixed feelings about its supernatural aspects.[109] In his poem 'The Idiot Boy', collected in *Lyrical Ballads*, young Johnny saddles up his pony to fetch the doctor for a sick neighbour in the middle of the night, embarking on a moonlit gallop that recalls the terrifying, spectral night-ride of 'Lenore'. When he is gone too long, his mother fears for his whereabouts in the typical language of supernatural balladry: 'Perhaps, with head and heels on fire, / And like the very soul of evil, / He's galloping away, away, / And so will gallop on for aye, / The bane of all that dread the devil!' But Johnny, it turns out, is just slow and lost, not Lucifer incarnate, or a 'horseman-ghost', as his mother imagines; what powers the narrative, as in other Wordsworth ballads, are emotions and the states of mind they create, not forces beyond human control. 'Why stand you thus, good Betty Foy?' the narrator enquires at the end of the poem. 'It is no goblin, 'tis no ghost, / 'Tis he whom you so long have lost, / He whom you love, your Idiot Boy.'[110]

Wordsworth's humorous about-turn wrongfoots the reader by setting up expectations of supernatural agency it proceeds to disappoint. Compiling *Tales of Wonder*, Lewis sought to disarm his critics by doing something similar, swerving disconcertingly from the Gothic melodrama of his ballads to dry humour. His editorial notes, unlike Percy's careful, scholarly annotations, frequently take a comic, shoulder-shrugging tone. 'I have taken great liberties with this Ballad.' 'I forget where I met the original of this Ballad.' 'I once read in some Grecian author, whose name I have forgotten, the story which suggested to me the outline of the foregoing ballad.'[111] He made deadpan summaries of the plots of his texts, which intimated that he found it hard to take them seriously. 'A young man arriving at the house of a friend, to whose daughter he was betrothed, was informed, that some weeks had passed since death had deprived him of his intended bride. Never having seen her, he soon reconciled himself to her loss.'[112]

More radically, he included, alongside the many 'straight' ballads of terror he collected, several parodies and burlesques: jokey, spoof pieces, which played off the fact that most readers knew the supernatural playbook by heart and some could recite it backwards. Among his own contributions in this vein was a spoof of the unfaithful lover ballad, a comic tale in which cheating Sally is punished for her bad behaviour, not by having a terrible dream and voluntarily consigning herself to the grave, but by being forced to eat a fatal quantity of rhubarb.[113] Then there was 'The Sailor's Tale', a ballad in which the lugubrious ghost of a seaman returns from his watery grave to tell a friend the story of his demise:

'Dear Tom,' quoth he, 'I hither come a doleful tale to
    tell ye!
A monstrous fish has safely stowed your comrade in
    his belly;
Groggy last night, my luck was such, that overboard
    I slid,
When a shark snapped and chewed me, just as now
    you chew that quid.'[114]

Here, the comic rhyming ('tell ye' / 'belly') does as much work
as the narrative to prompt our laughter. Ghosts aren't supposed
to be chatty or colloquial, or to compare shocking events (a
shark chomping on its prey) to mundane activities (chewing
tobacco). The supernatural, 'The Sailor's Tale' makes clear,
becomes funny at its peril: humour, by drawing attention to
itself, has a tendency to stop storytelling in its tracks, hobble
the suspension of disbelief.

Ghost stories like these are as much divorced from history
as they are from belief. By the beginning of the nineteenth
century, five years after the appearance of the translated
'Lenore', supernatural tales were everywhere in both elite
and popular culture, the ancient and the new promiscuously
mixed up together. Running through Lewis's anthology, the
pre-eminent macabre collection of the period, was a 'guiding
parodic intelligence', as one critic has put it – a slippery,
sophisticated refusal to take such stories seriously, either
from the perspective of a believer or an antiquarian.[115] From
the vantage point of the 1760s, as the educated world stood
nervously on the cusp between scepticism and a new openness,
Tales of Wonder, with its strange conflation of 'straight' terror
and weary, urbane humour, would have been an impossibility.
But Percy's rehabilitation of the supernatural had made it into
a cultural resource that could be used more than one way:

sufficiently defanged, what once was marvellous and strange was apt to look familiar, predictable, capable of prompting enlightened laughter in place of fear.

3

ANXIETY

Beauties of the Poets (c.1780–1820)

In October 1818, John Keats wrote to his brother and sister-in-law from London, having cut short a visit to Scotland because of a bad sore throat 'which came of bog trotting in the Island of Mull'. He wrote merrily about seasickness and how it had its uses in silencing the over-talkative; about bad jokes (his own); about the beautiful pattern of light and shade he had seen in a gateway in Whitehall; and about everything else that happened to be 'uppermost in Mind'. Eventually he came, as if in passing, to the matter of his own work. Earlier in the year, his first long poem, *Endymion*, had been savaged by two of the nation's most influential literary reviews. 'This is a mere matter of the moment,' he told George, his brother, and George's wife Georgiana, with practised confidence. 'I think I shall be among the English Poets after my death.'[1] By the phrase 'among the English Poets', he didn't just mean that he expected his work to be sympathetically re-evaluated by posterity, or that he hoped future readers and critics would speak of him in the same breath as the great English poets he admired. What he had in mind was something more specific.

One of Keats's most beloved possessions was a copy of *The Poetical Works of Edmund Spenser*, a cheap edition of

Spenser's poetry in eight volumes that belonged to a bigger series. *The Poets of Great Britain Complete from Chaucer to Churchill* (1777–83) was a vast edition of the works of fifty British poets in 109 volumes, masterminded by a Scottish publisher, John Bell. Keats could not afford the large numbers of books his contemporaries, Byron and Shelley, possessed; but, had he been wealthy enough, he could have filled his house in Hampstead with collections like Bell's. From his earliest childhood, the bookshops and street-stalls in London were packed with poetry. In 1795, the year he was born, a *Complete Edition of the Poets of Great Britain* appeared in thirteen volumes, produced by another Scotsman, Robert Anderson. During his schooldays, Samuel Bagster launched *The Poets of Great Britain* (1807) in a record-breaking 124 volumes. Three years later, Alexander Chalmers brought out a new *Works of the English Poets* in twenty-one volumes. In 1818, the year Keats wrote to George and Georgiana about Scotland, Thomas Campbell was busy putting the finishing touches to a seven-volume *Specimens of the British Poets*, to be published a few months later. Throughout Keats's short life, and for twenty years before he was born, the literary market was dominated by voluminous standard editions of the most celebrated 'English Poets'. Behind that curious capitalized phrase in the letter to his brother and sister-in-law lay the thought of being included in such books, to be eagerly bought up by a growing audience of poetry readers alongside Chaucer, Spenser, Shakespeare and the other writers he had revered since childhood.[2]

Ambitious *Works* such as Bell's didn't come out of nowhere. Since 1710, it had been legal for any publisher to reprint the works of older British poets and playwrights, once their exclusive copyright periods (twenty-one years, in the case of works published prior to 1710) were up. In practice, however, the handful of London booksellers who owned these venerable literary properties fiercely protected what they insisted were rights in perpetuity. Scottish publishers, determined to break the monopoly, reprinted out-of-copyright titles wherever they could. In 1765, Robert and Andrew Foulis, two brothers who ran a press in Glasgow, were the first to come up with the idea of releasing standardized pocket editions of the British poets as part of a series. But they were unable to sell their titles south of the border, where they would have been accused of piracy by London booksellers who still insisted that they held legally enforceable rights to the material. It took a landmark court case in 1774 – when a London bookseller tried to sue the Scottish publisher Alexander Donaldson and was ruled against by the House of Lords – to break the deadlock and enshrine the idea of limited copyright in law.[3]

Suddenly, the poems and plays of great writers were available for anyone to reprint and sell, once the protected twenty-one-year period had elapsed. It was a decisive moment, as the historian William St Clair has argued, not only for 'the progress of reading', but for 'the subsequent course of the national culture widely defined.'[4] 'The Works of *Shakespeare*, of *Pope*, *Swift*, *Gay*, and many other excellent Authors of the present Country, are, by this Reversal, declared to be the Property of any Person,' one journalist wrote excitedly. A huge corpus of older literary works which had languished in private ownership had been 'returned to unrestricted common public use': the 'gates of the great private estates' were 'thrown open'.[5] Bell, who had dashed off an eleven-volume edition of Shakespeare's works as soon as the ink was dry on the House of Lords decision, set up shop in London and began manufacturing and selling his *Poets of Great Britain* under the English booksellers' noses, vastly undercutting their offerings with his elegant, well-printed volumes priced at a shilling and sixpence each.[6] The only way forward was to compete. Ventures and volumes multiplied. By the mid-1790s, the London publisher Charles Cooke was offering individual titles in his *Pocket Edition of Select British Poets* series for sixpence apiece.[7]

Today, standard editions of poets and playwrights, such as the Oxford World's Classics or Penguin Classics series, are fixtures of bookshelves and classrooms, so it's difficult to imagine a world without them. But to late eighteenth-century readers, particularly readers with modest incomes who had previously been unable to afford their own expensive copies of Shakespeare or Milton, they were revolutionary.[8] Taken together with Samuel Johnson's *Works of the English Poets* series (1779–81), Bell and Anderson's editions achieved sales of over half a million volumes, an extraordinary figure for the time. The Foulis, Cooke, Bagster and Chalmers titles also sold in unprecedented numbers.[9] Each copy, moreover, would be likely to pass through several hands. In a short period, a vast amount of printed material that had been jealously guarded for the wealthy was available at cut-price rates, within reach of those whose reading previously would have been limited to cheap ballads, tracts and ragged secondhand volumes.[10]

The appearance of the standard editions was part of the wider 'reading explosion' of the late eighteenth century, as St Clair has called the period of rapid democratization and growth after the 1774 copyright decision.[11] Both the size of the book industry and the audience for imaginative literature shot up. 'I suppose that more than four times the number of books are sold now than were sold twenty years since,' one bookseller, James Lackington, noted in 1791, an estimation modern data analysis has broadly confirmed.[12] Social groups who had read widely before 1774 probably took advantage of the lower prices to read more; but, equally, as St Clair has argued, groups who had previously read very little were eager to acquaint themselves with new authors and texts. Lackington wrote:

> The poorer sort of farmers, and even the poor country people in general who before that period spent their winter evenings in relating stories of witches, ghosts, hobgoblins, &c now shorten the winter nights by hearing their sons and daughters read tales, romances &c and on entering their house you may see *Tom Jones*, *Roderick Random*, and other entertaining books stuck up on their bacon racks.[13]

Not everyone welcomed the change unreservedly. The sheer volume of words now in the public domain could feel overwhelming.* Vicesimus Knox, the essayist, despaired in 1778 that trying to fix on a course of reading had become like wading through a sea of books without a map. Previously, Knox said, the general 'scarcity of Books' had been 'the principal obstacle to the advancement of learning'. Now, 'the multitude of them is become, in the present age, scarcely less injurious to its interests.' To read even just the works of the most well-known authors would be 'an employment sufficient to fill up every hour of laborious application', and most people didn't have many hours free in the first place.[15] The size of the apparent task was daunting and the multitude of options distracting. Given the 'vast quantity of poetry or verse of all kinds' readers now had to grapple with, Knox argued, not to mention the multiplication

---

* In his utopian novel *L'An 2440* (1770), the French writer Louis-Sébastien Mercier pictured a dream Paris of the future with almost no books in it. The city's royal library, in his vision, is cleansed of its hefty tomes; its former book-lined 'galleries of immense length' are swapped for 'one small cabinet'.[14]

of 'crowded and bulky tomes' on science, moral philosophy, the antiquities, philology, theology and travel literature, it would be impossible for anyone 'either to collect or to read all that is excellent, much more all that has been published.' There was a constant 'danger of confusion and distraction, of a vain labour, and of that poverty which arises from superfluity.'[16]

A few years later, however, Knox found a way to make the 'too many books' problem work to his advantage. In 1784, he published an immensely successful anthology of extracts from well-known English prose writers, *Elegant Extracts, or Useful and Entertaining Passages in Prose*. In the next five years, he worked to put together similar selections of poetry and correspondence (each with the word 'elegant' in the title). As far as he was concerned, collected editions such as Bell's or Anderson's had performed a valuable service in making more literature available to more people; but their hundreds of volumes were clogging up library shelves, piling up on desks and putting off the very readers whom they would benefit most. Handy compilations of extracts could step in to save inexperienced readers the time and effort of having to read everything. As Laura Riding and Robert Graves, with more than a touch of snobbery, told the story in their *Pamphlet Against Anthologies*,

> The general public looked with pride not unmixed with dismay on this new acquisition. It was an impressive shelf-full, but was one really expected to read it all through? If so, did one have to start at the beginning, go on till one came to the end and then stop? The print too, they pleaded, was rather small. So some charitable gentlemen, friends of the booksellers, came to their help.[17]

These 'charitable gentlemen', with an eye on the commercial opportunities the new superfluity of books created, set about convincing the public that anthologies were the way forward. Being well-read nowadays, they argued, meant not reading everything: to read intelligently, as Knox claimed, was to read 'in the classical sense of the word, LEGERE, that is, to *pick out*, to select the most valuable and worthiest objects.'[18] Better still was to cede judgement to books that handpicked such 'worthiest objects' for you.[19]

The availability, during the late eighteenth century, of convenient collections that shrunk down other books contributed significantly to the period's 'reading explosion' – just as, ironically, the groaning multi-volume editions they capitalised on had done.[20] By excerpting the most celebrated passages from multiple texts, and preventing readers not only from having to read more than one book, but having to buy more than one too, anthologies of extracts made the newly reprinted 'classic' literature yet more accessible to men and women of ordinary means. One very popular anthology format began to dominate the literary market in the early 1780s, targeted in particular at female readers, families and schoolchildren.* In 1781, George Kearsley, an entrepreneurial London bookseller, had brought out a popular selection from Samuel Johnson's works, which he titled *The Beauties of Johnson*.[21] Capitalizing on its success, he advertised heavily and formed a small army of compilers – hack writers who needed the money – tasked with churning out 'beauties', selections from all the fashionable

---

* Among schoolchildren, anthologised extracts were known as 'spouting' pieces, texts to be learned by heart and declaimed in class. 'I confess myself utterly unable to appreciate that celebrated soliloquy in *Hamlet*, beginning "To be or not to be," or to tell whether it be good, bad, or indifferent, it has been so handled and pawed about by declamatory boys,' commented Lamb in his essay 'On the Tragedies of Shakespeare' (1812). Lamb would have been exposed to volumes of 'spouting' extracts at school at Christ's Hospital during the 1780s.

out-of-copyright authors it was possible to transform into revenue sources.

Within months (in some cases weeks), the *Beauties* of the works of Shakespeare, Milton, Pope, Swift, Laurence Sterne, Oliver Goldsmith, David Hume and Henry Fielding all appeared in Kearsley's shop, and were swiftly imitated by competing presses eager to get a share of the new market.[22] 'Virtually every English author of great contemporary repute was ransacked for passages,' the historian Richard Altick has observed.[23] The vogue was so great that the popular *Lady's Magazine* renamed its 'Specimens of British Literature' column 'A Supplement to the Beauties of Johnson' in 1782, judging – probably correctly – that it would get more traction that way.[24] Kearsley's collections sold for half a crown, or two shillings and sixpence, directed at book-buyers with modest incomes, and representing a vast saving on the alternative of buying all the works of a given author (owning all of Shakespeare or all of Milton, say, would be out of reach for most). But even this could be undercut. In 1793, the bookseller John Roach brought 'beauties' within the reach of poorer readers with *Roach's Beauties of the Poets of Great Britain*, a series of twenty-four pamphlets issued monthly for just sixpence, each containing a poem or two.

'Beauties' volumes promised the best: the finest insights, the most impeccable morality, the loveliest descriptions, the 'vetted and the venerable'.[25] They were patchworks of highlights, collages formed by breaking up wholes and slotting together the pieces. 'Literary cooks have, of late, served up to the Public divers ragouts and olios under the stile and title of the BEAUTIES of Johnson, the BEAUTIES of Sterne, &c.,' observed a reviewer in 1782.[26] Like stews ('ragouts and olios'), made up of a variety of ingredients and seasonings carefully mixed together, they combined ingenious selections of finely chopped morsels, especially designed for palates that weren't exactly sure what they wanted.

Kearsley, as 'literary cook'-in-chief, adopted a method of rearrangement that countless 'beauties' editors imitated. His books excerpted brief passages – which might, in prose, be as little as a resonant sentence, and in poetry, just a line – and then gave each passage a sententious title: 'Charity'; 'Faults'; 'Hypocrisy'; 'Women's Frailty', and so on. These titles (not, that is, the real titles of the works the passages came from) would then be sorted in alphabetical order in a table of contents, encouraging readers to skip forward to the themes or ideas they were interested in. A reader looking through the contents of Kearsley's *Beauties of Shakespeare* (1783), for instance, might piously turn to the page marked 'Good Deeds', or have her eye caught by the entry 'Drunkenness'; in either case, she would have no idea which lines she was getting, or which play they belonged to, until she read them. Some compilers went a step further and sorted their extracts into generic categories, which helped readers work out how they were meant to react to what they read. 'Pathetic' told you that you were getting sentimental passages to tug on your heartstrings; 'Moral', 'Sacred' or 'Didactic' meant that you could be sure you were reading things in line with good Christian principles; 'Descriptive' would supply you with glowing portraits of churchyards, mountains and country villages; 'Narrative' pieces were likely to be stirring and patriotic. A pious reader of Henry Headley's *Select Beauties of Ancient English Poetry* (1787), for instance, might skip to 'Didactic and Moral Pieces' and pick out, say, 'Faith', 'Church Monuments' or 'Reflections on Death', secure in the knowledge that wherever these extracts turned out to be from, they wouldn't be shockingly immoral.

Entering the 'beauties' market (becoming a 'beauty-monger', in the snide phrase of the writer Hannah More) was a smart move for booksellers.[27] Roach, for instance, earned much more by selling a few extracts at a time in individual pamphlets, and spinning his series out over twenty-four months, than he would have done by selling full works. But while they capitalized financially, 'beauties' publishers were careful to stress that their chief motivation in compiling collections was the desire to aid their readers. Only a handful of people, the editor of Kearsley's *Beauties of Johnson* noted in his preface, possessed or had access to all of Johnson's works: for the 'generality of the public', who weren't blessed with libraries, selections provided a shortcut to surveying the whole landscape.[28] 'Beauties' volumes were compact and inexpensive, presenting as less intimidating to the casual reader than 'books of a larger size and of a more erudite appearance', as Johnson observed of Kearsley's *The Beauties of Isaac Watts* (1782).[29] And, since they were small enough to be carried on the person, they allowed reading and learning to happen anywhere: the 'pocket volume', Knox wrote, 'accompanies the reader in his walks,' 'in the coffee-house', and even to work.[30]

The underlying point being communicated in these assurances of affordability and convenience was that 'beauties' weren't for the cultural elite. 'To those who have made the poetry of this country a subject of serious and deliberate investigation, the following Extracts will afford neither entertainment nor instruction,' declared Headley in the introduction to his *Select Beauties of Ancient English Poetry*. The learned were being told frankly not to bother.[31] According to the poet Oliver Goldsmith, in his preface to *The Beauties of English Poesy* (1767), 'compilations' of verse were 'chiefly designed for such as either want leisure, skill, or fortune to choose for themselves.'[32] For George Croly, the compiler of an 1828 *Beauties of the British Poets*, the point was simple: 'The writings of the great poets of England cannot be put into the popular hand too often, in too pleasing a form, or under too accessible circumstances.'[33]

'Popular', of course, didn't mean everyone. 'A large and a respectable body of the public' was how Headley described his envisaged audience, using 'respectable' to limit what he meant by 'large'. According to Knox, volumes of extracts were designed for a 'numerous' and 'very respectable' portion of the population – that is, numerous, but not that numerous.[34] The kinds of people they and the other beauty-collectors had in mind weren't working-class readers, who might perhaps have been able to afford Roach's sixpenny pamphlets out of their wages on an occasional basis, but would have had little time – or, after a gruelling twelve- or fourteen-hour day, little energy or inclination – to read them. Instead, they were those whom the nation's growing wealth during the eighteenth century had provided with opportunities for leisure.[35] As early as 1731, the schoolmaster John Clarke noted that those with 'a pretty good deal of empty Time upon their Hands', 'Persons of Genteel Professions or Trades', might dedicate their free hours to improving their minds, and could profitably spend them on poetry.[36] Knox suggested that 'elegant miscellan[ies]' were well-suited to merchants, lawyers and other men from the professional classes, those whose 'life of business' called for something they could 'read, comprehend in a short time, and relinquish', and which would serve as a pleasant distraction from profit and loss.[37] But such 'occasional readers', as he and Clarke agreed, weren't only male. 'In the present age,' Knox wrote, 'it is not uncommon to see wisdom and taste united with a fine assemblage of features in a delicate female face.' 'Ladies', in his emphatic italics, were swiftly becoming one of the most 'numerous' and 'important' groups of readers in the nation, and they deserved to have their 'literary wants' met.[38]

Here, the 'beauties' collections really came into their own. The problem with reprinting great poems and plays in full was that not all writers, especially those who had written several centuries ago, could be trusted to live up to the high moral standards of late Georgian Britain. It was clear that 'many books of earlier times could not be read in their complete form without peril to the soul.'[39] They used indecent or obscene expressions; they were full of un-Christian profanities; and the habits and manners they portrayed weren't exactly compatible with what went on in polite modern drawing rooms. To be suitable for an audience of 'impressionable' young females, classic authors had to be presented selectively. By combing through the works of Shakespeare (a noted purveyor of 'barefaced obscenities' and 'nauseous vice'), Swift or Sterne – as well as modern writers known for their bad behaviour, such as Byron – anthologists could serve as human shields, protecting delicate readers from having to see or imagine anything untoward.[40]

The idea, according to the most well-known Shakespeare beautifier of the period, Thomas Bowdler (whose name lives on in our words 'bowdlerize' and 'bowdlerism'), was that anthologies should do what would otherwise have to be done by cautious male guardians: they could pre-censor poems and plays so that husbands and fathers reading aloud to their families wouldn't have to omit words silently as they went along. The express aim of his *Family Shakespeare* (1807), Bowdler explained, was to cut from the Bard's works everything that was 'unfit to be read aloud by a gentleman to a company of ladies.'* With his selection in hand, even the 'most religious' and 'chaste' of

---

* Not everyone agreed that he'd succeeded. 'Mr. Bowdler has [...] left many things in the text which, to a delicate taste, must still appear coarse and reprehensible; and only effaced those gross indelicacies which every one must have felt a blemish,' commented the *Edinburgh Review* in 1821.

listeners could enjoy the plays without fearing an encounter with 'words and expressions […] of such a nature as to raise a blush on the cheek of modesty.'[41] Friedrich Engels, remarking on the popularity of such 'family editions' among the middle classes as late as the 1840s, described them as 'castrated': 'cut down in accordance with the hypocritical morality of to-day.'[42]

No 'beauties' volume of the period was complete without a set of throat-clearing prefatory remarks about the primary importance of Christian virtue. Readers of William Dodd's *Beauties of Shakespear* (1752) – an early experiment in the format – were promised 'much excellent and refin'd morality' and 'much good divinity'. Kearsley's *Beauties of Shakespeare* vowed to be 'very serviceable, in impressing on the memory of Youth some of the sublimest and most important lessons of Morality and Religion.'[43] Knox, in the preface to his prose *Elegant Extracts*, declared that the book would allow readers to 'imbibe' the 'purest principles of Virtue and Religion'; in his verse *Extracts*, he swore blind that the poetry in the collection was a straight road 'to learning and to virtue'.[44] John Bullar, the editor of an 1822 *Selections from the British Poets*, explained the process through which he had ensured that nothing immoral crept into his book:

> The principle of selection has been very rigid. While it has led the Compiler to seek for beauties, it has compelled him to ascertain that no poison lurks among the flowers. On the other hand, it has induced him occasionally to admit pieces of rather questionable poetic merit, on account of the strict accordance of the sentiments which they contain, with those of that sacred book; from which, the further we depart, the more dangerous is our error.[45]

'Occasionally', in other words, Bullar had opted to include average or bad poems ('pieces of rather questionable poetic merit'), on the basis that they contained very good morality, and chosen them over poems commonly acknowledged to be exceptional works of literature, whose morality was dubious.[46] In the hunt for 'beauties', aesthetic criteria were outweighed by the cardinal importance of being sure that 'poison' didn't 'lurk' where it shouldn't.

In the case of authors positively known for their indecency – Swift, Sterne and Byron, for instance – poison lurked everywhere and constant vigilance was required. The editor of Kearsley's *Beauties of Sterne* (1782) saw himself as doing the world a service by making the controversial author of *Tristram Shandy* accessible for the first time to the innocent and virtuous. '*Chaste*' readers were usually forbidden to 'penetrate beyond the title-page of *Tristram Shandy*', for fear they might encounter a few too many hints about penetration of a different kind.[47] Now, they were equipped with a tasteful collection of passages 'selected for the Heart of Sensibility', all delicately extracted and given pleasing moral titles ('Conjugal Happiness'; 'Consolation'; 'Forgiveness'). 'Every loose Expression is carefully avoided,' Kearsley assured potential buyers in his advertisement for the book.[48] Swift was similarly treated, subjected wherever necessary to the 'literary pruning knife' so that all 'offensive flowers' were lopped from the 'bouquet' of his works.[49] In Byron's case, it was his epic poem *Don Juan* (1819–24), with its endless mockery of conventional morality, that posed an especial problem for publishers seeking to capitalize on his popularity. In the poem's famous shipwreck scene, in Canto II, there are, among other things, jokes about Catholics, Jews, cannibals and the sanctity of human life.[50] By the time J.W. Lake, the compiler of *The Beauties of Byron* (1829), had finished with it, the scene was thirty verses shorter and included none of these things.

By cutting as they did, the beauty-mongers were playing to the views of contemporary moralists and educationalists about the evils that would result from exposing impressionable minds to poetry in unregulated doses. According to the authors of conduct manuals, a taste for books in young people, young women in particular, needed careful supervising if it were not to run into dangerous channels. Reading, it was believed, strongly influenced mental patterns and behaviours, either reinforcing virtuous inclinations or encouraging corrupt ones. Those whose inclinations were still malleable enough to be shaped were urged to choose their books in accordance with orthodox Christian principles, to moderate the volume of titles they consumed, and submit to the guidance of wise elders who knew what was good for them.[51] 'I sincerely wish you may read nothing but what you may retain for improvement,' the pedagogical writer Ann Murry instructed an audience of young ladies in 1785. 'Be cautious what books you peruse.'[52]

Poetry didn't have to be actively immoral to wreak havoc: the mere fact that it was imaginative in nature was enough. Tall tales and extravagant descriptions might seem harmless, but because they appealed to readers' senses and imaginations rather than to their reason, they were felt to weaken capacities for rational self-discipline. 'A passion for poetry is dangerous to a woman,' declared a 1789 treatise on female education. 'It heightens her natural sensibility to an extravagant degree, and frequently inspires such a romantick turn of mind, as is utterly inconsistent with all the solid duties and proprieties of life.'[53] Like novels, which were blamed for making girls act as foolishly as their favourite heroines, poetry, if indiscriminately embraced, was believed to transform its female readers into flighty, hyper-delicate creatures, their heads turned by the marvellous and improbable, their virtue half-seduced away from them by descriptions of love and passion.[54] 'The inexperienced,' wrote Knox sadly, 'long to be actors in the scenes which they admire.'[55] As far as the evangelical preacher John Angell James was concerned, poetry was basically dark magic. 'Poetry is a bewitching, and if not of a strictly moral character, a dangerous species of writing,' he proclaimed in 1828. If indulged in without restraint, it was liable to 'debase' the intellect, to 'unfit the mind' entirely for 'useful pursuits'.[56]

Some poets, it was believed, were unsuitable to be read at all, let alone unrestrainedly. 'We hear passages [...] quite unequivocal in point of impiety, repeated with enthusiasm by young ladies from the works of a noble, but profligate and infidel poet,' Hannah More wrote darkly, referring to Byron.[57] Those poets who could safely be recommended – Milton, for instance, or the eighteenth-century religious poets Edward Young and William Cowper – were to be read occasionally and cautiously. 'Only a *limited* perusal of poetry,' as one preacher put it sternly, 'as a recreation, and a recreation only.'[58]

In 1804, the critic and biographer John Aikin sought to lay out what the acceptable parameters were. His *Letters to a Young Lady on a Course of English Poetry* was an advice manual aimed at female readers in possession of 'a set of the English Poets' (perhaps Bell's or Anderson's), who required a guiding hand to steer them through volumes and volumes of uncensored material. Even young ladies 'well-grounded in the principles of morality', as he argued, couldn't always be trusted to work out for themselves what was 'valuable' and what was 'dubious matter'; guidance was necessary both to screen them from the dubious in the first place (to 'suppress in merited oblivion', as he put it, 'all such pieces as appear entirely unfit for your perusal'), and to teach them how to do the screening for themselves.[59] Reading safely, Aikin explained, was like crossing treacherous ground without stumbling, learning to 'pass lightly and unhurt' over words and passages that might otherwise trip you up. Swift's poetry, for instance, might be 'grossly tainted with indelicacies', but if young women learned to recognise and avoid the bad bits as they went along, they could 'pick [their way] very nicely' through its moral minefields.[60]

On this view, the 'beauties' volumes provided a valuable service, because they did the way-picking and the mine-clearing themselves. Female readers who owned all of Swift's works in a complete 'English Poets', though they might equip themselves with Aikin's guide, had little choice but to steer themselves through the treacherous waters that awaited them. Readers armed with a copy of Kearsley's *Beauties of Swift*, on the other hand, needed no further aid, and could take any path they liked the look of with full confidence. 'If you could read poetry with a judicious friend, who would lead your judgment to a true discernment of its beauties and defects,' the conduct-book writer Hester Chapone suggested, 'it would inexpressibly heighten both your pleasure and improvement.'[61] As far as the beauty-mongers were concerned, what they offered was exactly that sort of 'judicious' friendship – a guiding hand on the arm, an improving voice in the ear, a careful management of the landscape so that all the dark ways were gone and only bright straight paths remained.

Conservative anxieties about young women's reading weren't necessarily to do with the content of the books female readers enjoyed. Often, they were bound up with larger fears about the place women occupied in the world, and the possible effects of too much leisure and too much intellectual independence on their willingness to stay put. By the late eighteenth century, there was a venerable tradition of equating intelligence and bookishness in girls with unmarriageability. Young ladies who lost themselves in poetry, it was argued – either their own or other people's – tended not to bother paying attention to their appearance and put off men accordingly. Female 'wits', as the satirist Jane Collier put it in 1753, were usually taken to be 'slatterns'.[62] In 1778, Knox described the stereotypical figure:

> Her attention to the muses has excluded the graces from any share of her notice. If you call upon her in the morning, you find her with slipshod shoes, with no apron, with matted hair, a dirty face, a cap awry, and fingers begrimed with ink.[63]

Knox's slipshod poetess, we notice, isn't incidentally dirty and unkempt; she is dirty and unkempt because she has been up all night writing, with ink-stained fingers, hair 'matted' from falling asleep at the desk, and no apron on yet. Her literariness and her unfeminine aspect are impossible to separate.

Bookish girls who didn't put men off with their disregard for their personal 'graces', it was believed, would frighten them away with their cerebral powers. 'Oh! ye lords of ladies intellectual, / Inform us truly, have they not hen-pecked you all?' enquires Byron in *Don Juan*. 'Literary ladies will, I am afraid, be losers in love,' explains a male character in the novelist Maria Edgeworth's *Letters for Literary Ladies* (1795). 'Cupid is a timid, playful child, and is frightened at the helmet of Minerva.'[64] Those helmeted harridans who did manage to ensnare a husband were considered likely to lose him again through careless management of the home. Most men, as Collier noted, would 'rather have a woman who could make a pudden, than one who could make a poem.'[65] (The idea of a wife who could make both puddings and poems was inconceivable.) Ladies who 'aspired to the sublime delights of philosophy and poetry,' according to Edgeworth's character, would no doubt 'despise the duties of domestic life.' Nobody wanted a wife who would be away 'weeping over some unvarnished tale' at just the moment 'she should be ordering dinner, or paying the butcher's bill.'[66]

Bookish women, moralists claimed, were arrogant, pedantic (a word that was often used of female learning to make it seem excessive and wrongheaded) and self-centred, wasting time reading and writing when they could be attending to duties that better suited their capabilities. If they were absorbed in a book, they weren't doing – or were doing half-heartedly – some more important task in the home. In an essay of 1819, Hannah More attacked what she called 'the increased and increasing prevalence of idle reading' among leisured women. Burying one's head in novels and frivolous poetry was 'scarcely less mischevious', she claimed, than squandering time in the 'ever multiplying haunts of public dissipation': inveterate readers, in other words, were as immoral in their choice of pursuit as frequenters of pleasure gardens, theatres or brothels. Whether a woman's time was 'consumed in unprofitable reading at home, or in frivolous diversions abroad,' the 'effect on the state of the mind' was 'not very dissimilar'. Both led, eventually, More warned darkly, in the same direction: to the divorce courts.[67]

What observers professed to worry about most was the possibility that bad reading would have consequences for the constitution of women's brains. The female mind was conceived of as a *tabula rasa*, a 'passive, soft, unresisting medium for external impressions', able to be moulded freely for good or ill.[68] Frivolous novels and poems, on this basis, were medical problems: because they could be absorbed at speed with little need to pause for thought, they let the 'muscles' that performed difficult mental work slide into disuse, as John Angell James claimed. They 'prostrate[d] the understanding' and 'enervate[d] the will'.[69] Educators, More suggested, ought to 'imitate the physician'. 'If the latter prescribes bracing medicines for a body of which delicacy is the disease, the former would do well to prohibit relaxing reading for a mind which is already of too soft a texture.'[70] The female brain was pictured as delicate in nature, vulnerable to the impress of any new idea; it needed to harden its defences, not relax them further.

Toughening up the female mind, of course, did not mean transforming it into a masculine calculating machine. The 'mental atrophy' that frivolous reading supposedly produced was a problem because it might weaken a girl's resistance to romantic temptation, not because it would threaten her ability to learn Greek. There was value in strengthening and exercising girls' rational faculties, but not to the extent that they would consider the management of the home beneath them, or might ponder learning astronomy rather than home economics.[71] Happily, as Knox argued, there was no reason to suppose that 'intellectual acquisitions' would make a wife 'incapable or unwilling to superintend the table'. A 'woman of improved understanding and real sense', it was suggested, was in fact likelier to accept her station in life contentedly than an uneducated one.[72] The aim, in other words, was progress within conventional limits: the formation of a class of young women who weren't frivolous, read suitable books and thought carefully about them, but could still dress their hair nicely and make a pudding.

How to go about fashioning these women? For More, in the first full-length book she published on the subject of female education in 1799, the answer lay in a prescribed diet of reading. Feeble, untrained minds, she argued, needed to be treated like feeble or delicate bodies, given a course of stiff medicine to bolster and invigorate them. 'Study,' she wrote, 'is to be considered as the means of strengthening the mind, and of fitting it for higher duties, just as exercise is to be considered as an instrument for strengthening the body.' A course of serious and pious books would 'act upon the constitution of the mind as a kind of alterative' (that is, a tonic), 'bracing the intellectual stamina' of women who had thus far been exposed to frippery and trifles.[73] In the 1770s, John Aikin and his sister Anna had argued a similar case around Gothic novels, whose terror-giving properties, they believed, served to 'ventilate' the mind, waking it up and keeping its imaginative muscles 'on the stretch'.[74] More didn't have novels in mind; she was in favour of girls attempting to digest what she called 'strong meat', serious philosophical or historical texts. But the underlying idea was the same. Some reading was unhealthy, relaxing the mind, impairing its 'powers of resistance' and breeding habits of laziness and indolence. Other reading, meanwhile, of a 'dry tough' kind, in More's unappealing phrase, was like wholesome physical exercise, building up the muscles and sinews of the intellect.[75]

At the top of More's list of books to be avoided, along with romantic novels and impious poetry, was a surprising category: anthologies of 'beauties'. Beauties volumes, we might think, given their careful excavation of only those literary tidbits that could be considered morally unexceptionable, would have served her programme well. In fact, in her view, '*Abridgments, Beauties*, and *Compendiums*' formed 'too considerable a part of a young lady's library': they were, as she argued repeatedly, 'an infallible receipt for making a superficial mind'.

By obviating the need for self-directed study, More suggested, 'beauties' inhibited the development of intellectual independence. Because they were formed of small scraps and excerpts rather than sustained arguments, they encouraged laziness, desultoriness, undisciplined habits of skim-reading and dipping in and out. Real learning, instead, was the fruit of 'unwearied assiduity' and in-depth investigation: to be properly digested, More said, knowledge needed to be drawn from the 'true spring, the original works of the author', not consumed 'severed' and handed over on a plate by a *beauty-monger*. What she referred to, dismissively, as 'a few fine passages from the poets [...] huddled together by some extract-maker' could not possibly 'fill the mind or form the taste', and would supply readers with the superficial appearance of learnedness without actually strengthening their intellectual capacities. Like all frothy, insubstantial print forms – magazines; collections of occasional poems; books of trivia or jokes – anthologies were well-suited to the bookshelves of fashionable fools.* 'Nothing that is valuable can be obtained without sacrifices,' she concluded. 'If we would purchase knowledge we must pay for it the fair and lawful price of time and industry.'[76]

Knowledge and learning were connected to manners. The question of private reading, what went on inside women's heads when they lost themselves in a book, wasn't separable, several writers claimed, from their public behaviour, the way they conducted themselves out in the world. The kind of thin, meretricious knowledge typically supplied by anthologies of extracts, More and others argued, tended to encourage unmerited pride and conceit in the young females who devoured it. 'A little learning,' wrote Collier and her co-author Sarah Fielding in their novel *The Cry* (1754), 'is well observed to be a dangerous thing.'[77] Erudition bred humility, an awareness of the vast extent of human knowledge and all that remained

---

* Not just female fashionable fools. In More's satirical poem *Florio: A Tale, for Fine Gentlemen and Fine Ladies* (1786), the foppish male title character is described as doing his reading 'while he dress'd: for true 'tis, / He read Compendiums, Extracts, Beauties'.

to be read and understood; readers who relied on 'beauties' selections, by contrast, were given to believe that they already knew everything worth knowing about Shakespeare's plays or Hume's philosophy. Such books opened 'an inlet to arrogance', in Collier and Fielding's words; they encouraged 'impertinence' and even 'insolence' – in a word, showing off.[78]

Anthologies were eminently quotable. Their composition, as treasure troves of glinting fragments, encouraged young women to pick out passages they especially admired, learn them and store them up to impress rivals and suitors at social occasions – a practice that could be readily seen through, because just about everyone present would have read the same selection. 'It is not difficult to trace back to their shallow sources the hackney'd quotations of certain *accomplished* young ladies,' More wrote snidely. A diet of bits and pieces from the usual sources, Knox's *Elegant Extracts* or Kearsley's *Beauties*, made 'readier talkers', as she put it, but 'shallower thinkers'.[79] Too often, as Edgeworth argued, girls gathered knowledge with the sole aim of 'displaying' it, and could easily be 'betrayed into a miserable ostentation of their learning' by the prospect of 'public applause'.[80] Knox himself acknowledged – though not in the context of his own anthologies – that there were connections between 'superficial and ill-directed reading' and female 'vanity'. Girls who dropped bits of Latin into conversation or casually quoted lines from *Paradise Lost* were likely, he said, to be bitterly disappointed with the reception they met with. 'Affectation of learning' tended merely to 'draw upon itself the contempt and hatred of both sexes' – the contempt, that is, of both male targets and female rivals.[81]

Novelists of the period made ready connections between ostentatious quoting and poor moral character. In Collier and Fielding's *The Cry*, the villain of the piece is an amorphous crowd of shrieking gossips, known collectively as 'the Cry', who serve as a stand-in for everything fashionable and superficial about contemporary society. Their 'learning', as we might expect, consists of memorized quotations from 'many different books', which they deploy aggressively to score points or humiliate an enemy. 'This sort of knowledge the *Cry* think necessary towards shining in conversation,' the narrator explains. 'It is of the utmost consequence to [...] their ever-busy bustling lives.'[82] At the other end of the moral spectrum, the heroine of Samuel Richardson's *Clarissa* (1747) is a model of intellectual comportment, 'well read in the English, French, and Italian poets', but nonetheless able to keep her learning to herself. 'Seldom,' Richardson notes approvingly, 'did she quote or repeat from them, either in her letters or conversation [...]; principally through modesty, and to avoid the imputation of [...] *affectation*.'[83]

Jane Austen considered beauty-mongers cynical profiteers, petty thieves who made a living from patching together 'some dozen lines of Milton, Pope, and Prior', as she put it in *Northanger Abbey* (1817).[84] Her novels give us several examples of characters looking silly spouting bits and pieces from anthologies. Catherine Morland, *Northanger Abbey*'s dreamy, credulous protagonist, devotes her teenage years to packing her memory with the sort of literary tidbits which, she considers, all romantic heroines-in-training ought to know ('those quotations which are so serviceable and so soothing in the vicissitudes of their eventful lives'), ending up with a jumble of clichéd lines that couldn't possibly be of service to anyone.[85] The least likeable Bennet sister in *Pride and Prejudice* (1813), Mary, besides playing the piano too much at parties, is known to 'read great books and make extracts'.[86] In *Emma* (1815), foolish, impressionable Harriet Smith puts together an anthology of 'all the riddles of every sort that she could meet with', a pursuit Austen duly skewers.[87] In the same novel, Mr Woodhouse, Emma's well-disposed but rather silly father, tries his best to help Harriet out by recalling one of the 'many clever riddles' circulating during his boyhood, but can never get past the first line: 'Kitty, a fair but frozen maid...'[88] Sharp-eyed readers during the 1810s might have recognized the line as from a poem by David Garrick, which had done the rounds in *The New Foundling Hospital for Wit* (1771). If they had, they would also have known that the unfortunate Mr Woodhouse has on the tip of his tongue a particularly filthy bit of innuendo.*

Then there is Mrs Elton, the unpleasant, self-absorbed wife of the Woodhouse family's curate, who peppers her conversation with evidence of her reading, from the showy Italian '*caro sposo*' she directs towards her husband, to her attempts to one-up her interlocutors by quoting lines of poetry. Nothing quite works as she hopes. At the end of the novel, she falls into the same trap as Mr Woodhouse by forgetting most of the (very inappropriate) fable she wants to quote; and, in conversation with Emma, whose disdain habitually brings out the worst in her, she tries to show off with some 'charming lines' from Thomas Gray's 'Elegy Written in a Country Churchyard' (a favourite of the beauty-mongers), which, of course, she misquotes.[89] Quotation, in the novel, invariably misses the mark, falls flat or backfires. In Mrs Elton, though, what's most egregious is how nakedly ostentatious it is.

More would have known exactly what to make of Mrs Elton's showy quotation habit. 'Some ladies,' she wrote in 1799, 'are eager to exhibit proofs of their reading, though at the expence of their judgment, and will introduce in conversation quotations quite irrelevant to the matter in hand.' The way they

---

* The answer to the riddle is supposed to be 'the chimney-sweeper', but its references to 'the hood-wink'd boy', or 'little urchin', who quenches a 'flame' 'kindled' by two serving maids, leaves open an alternative possibility.

talked, she explained, could be put down to their education, or lack of it:

> Their acquirements have not been woven into their minds by early instruction; what knowledge they have gotten stands out as it were above the very surface of their minds, like the *appliquée* of the embroiderer, instead of having been interwoven with the growth of the piece, so as to have become a part of the stuff.[90]

The embroidery metaphor More uses here vividly illustrates her point. The kind of 'learning' young ladies acquired from flicking idly through anthologies could be thought of as superficial in a literal sense: it floated on the 'very surface of their minds', like ornamental needlework on top of a piece of fabric, rather than being stitched properly into the 'stuff'. The words 'piece' and 'stuff' here, though, are ambiguous. They seem to refer both to what women know (the extent of their learning, the materials they've consumed), and to the total structure of their minds, the materials they have to think with in the first place. The two are connected: what you read governs how you think, or how you're unable to think.

Embroidery, of course, was a gendered choice of metaphor on More's part. During the eighteenth and nineteenth centuries, it was a characteristically female activity, both performed by women and associated with them because of its delicate, decorative qualities. Her comparison here – likening kinds of female learning respectively to well-woven fabric (in which threads of knowledge, built up over time, become part of the deep texture of the mind), and to superficial appliqué work – assumes that there is something about women's brains that makes them distinctively feminine, different to male ones. No male brain during the period would have been compared to a piece of sewing, embroidered or otherwise. What her metaphor also makes clear, though, is that in her view women's minds aren't all alike: within certain parameters, and governed by the kind of education they receive, they may grow to be more or less superficial, more or less decorative, in their makeup. Any woman, in other words, may opt to double down on her mental 'femininity' or push back against its limiting aspects.

At the turn of the nineteenth century, More was writing in accordance with a longstanding intellectual tradition of associating the decorative and ornamental with femininity. As the literary theorist Naomi Schor has shown, in early modern writing on art and literature there was a common tendency to gender small details (the fine, the decorative, the peripheral, the incidental) as female, while essentials (the substantive, the significant, the general) were treated as masculine.[91] In her *Reading in Detail* (1987), Schor cites the example of the French anthropologist Julien-Joseph Virey, who attempted, in a treatise of 1810, to ground this cluster of ideas about femininity and detail in a theory of women's congenital makeup. Women's 'soft and all-impressible imaginations', Virey argued, allowed them to 'perceive detail better than the masses [of men]'; but this fineness of perception barred them, correspondingly, from perceiving and comprehending wholes. While men tended to 'consider the species and general things', women would naturally 'fasten on the individual and settle on particular objects'. 'All that is strong, vast, sublime,' Virey concluded, 'is better perceived by the one, all that is delicate, gracious, and fine is better felt by the other.'[92]

More argued a version of this in her treatise on female education. Women, she declared, were 'acute observers' and 'excel[led] in details', but did 'not so much generalize their ideas as men'; 'their minds' could not 'seize a great subject with so large a grasp.'

A woman sees the world, as it were, from a little elevation in her own garden, whence she takes an exact survey of home scenes, but takes not in that wider range of distant prospects, which he who stands on a loftier eminence commands. [93]

Because they thought in particulars, in other words, women struggled to make things add up: they lacked 'that power of arrangement which knows how to link a thousand connected ideas in one dependent train.' They could not, as the clergyman John Bennett put it in 1787, 'arrange, combine, abstract, pursue and diversify a long strain of ideas,' lacking a capacity for '*deep* meditation'.[94] Where male thinking was synthesized, female thinking was miscellaneous, contradictory and fragmented; men saw the bigger picture, and women only the pieces.

Young ladies who confined their reading to anthologies only ever had pieces to go on. As the critic Leah Price has observed, More was conscious that the 'disconnected' nature of anthologies could be said to 'echo' the fragmentary workings of the female mind.[95] Reading only the 'crippled mutilations' of longer works, she believed, exacerbated intellectual limitations that women already possessed by virtue of their sex. Rather than being taught 'how to think, to compare, to combine, to methodize', their education was made up of scraps, the 'beauties' of different poems or plays that a nameless editor had happened to select and arrange, and which by their nature couldn't be read in the same way as an argument or a complex plot.

It does not make a full mind; [...] neither does it accustom the mind to any trains of reflection: for the subjects, besides being each succinctly, and, on account of this brevity, superficially treated, are distinct and disconnected; they form no concatenation of ideas, nor any dependent series of deduction.[96]

The Mrs Eltons of this world, in other words, talk as they do because they lack training in 'reflection', 'deduction' and 'concatenation': nothing they have read has taught them how to fashion 'disconnected' details into something larger and more consequential, to weave – in the terms of More's metaphor – fine embroidered details into the texture of a piece of fabric, rather than merely sticking them on the surface. A mind fed on a diet of fragments resembled, as the clergyman Joseph Robertson put it in his *Essay on the Education of Young Ladies* (1798), 'a magazine of trifles and follies': a throwaway jumble of odds and ends.[97]

✿

Right from the start, the question of what 'beauties' volumes were for was hard to separate from the question of *whom* they were for. Invariably, they were marketed as for someone and not for someone else. The *Elegant Extracts*, as Knox explained, were for schoolboys and girls, and for men of business and ladies of the house who wanted something to flick through in spare moments; they were not for serious scholars. Headley's *Select Beauties of Ancient English Poetry*, as he was careful to note, was for a 'respectable' public, which meant that it wasn't for those whose income dipped below a certain point. Not everyone was in agreement with these classifications. Bowdler's *Family Shakespeare* was meant for genteel parents who didn't want to be embarrassed by obscenities and profanities; but, in the opinion of at least one reviewer, it still wasn't really suitable for 'delicate' readers. Kearsley's volumes of *Beauties* were, according to the bookseller himself, for '*chaste* lovers of literature'; but, according to More, Austen and others, they were exactly what respectable young women should not be wasting their time on.

The question of whom 'beauties' were for mattered because so many people read them. If they had been less fashionable, or sold fewer copies, there would have been little debate. As it was, possessors of 'a shelf or two of Beauties, Elegant Extracts and Anas' seemed to form 'nine-tenths of [...] the reading public',* as Coleridge commented darkly in 1817.[98] A vast 23,000 copies, at a conservative estimate, of Knox's poetic *Elegant Extracts* sold in various editions between 1796 and 1824, years after it had first been published.[99]

High sales figures, of course, meant a greater diversity in the economic backgrounds of those who were buying and reading. Since the period of the 1774 copyright decision, the reprinting of older literary texts had been associated with changes in the makeup of the reading public. Those who were opposed to the new legal situation argued that the loss of perpetual copyright would mark the end of a golden age of hierarchy and exclusivity. If readers from the middle classes or below could get their hands on a competitively priced reprint of Shakespeare or Milton, critics warned, works of great genius were effectively being classed – in price terms at least – with 'the Ephemera of Literature who are born and die in a day'.[100] It was like 'letting the mob in to vote', as the poet Thomas Moore put it, opening up the market to the preferences of the lowest common denominator.[101]

Several Romantic-period writers, John Clare, Leigh Hunt and William Hazlitt among them, disagreed, recalling having

---

* An 'ana' was a collection of the observations, anecdotes or table-talk of some well-known person, usually a gossipy, ephemeral publication capitalizing on fame.

'doated on' cheap editions of the poets, Cooke's sixpenny books in particular, as schoolboys and young men with little money to spare. 'I bought them over and over again,' Hunt wrote, 'and used to get up select sets, which disappeared like buttered crumpets; for I could resist neither giving them away, nor possessing them.' He comforted himself during long days of lessons at Christ's Hospital by 'thinking of the sixpence in my pocket', imagining scurrying to Paternoster Row to 'buy another number of an English poet'.[102] For other writers, including Moore, Coleridge, Wordsworth and Shelley, the growth of the trade in affordable reprints meant the emergence of a new reading public they didn't trust and found it hard to communicate with. More cheap books bred more readers, a 'foolish crowd', as Shelley put it, of men and women lacking taste and discrimination, whose commercially driven choices would shape literary production for the worse.[103] 'Our readers have, in good truth, multiplied exceedingly, and have waxed proud,' wrote Coleridge archly in 1816, implying that not only was the book-buying and periodical-reading public now considerably bigger than before – which was bad enough – but also that it dared to have ideas and preferences of its own.[104]

If, per his exaggerated estimate, it was true that books were now 'in every hovel', anthologies seemed particularly to blame.[105] Since they collected passages from multiple books in affordable single volumes, they lowered the minimum price of access to poetry, plays and essays, placing them within reach of new readers lower down the social scale.[106] In practice, of course, not all those who could read had enough to spare from their wage packet to buy even the cheapest of the 'beauties', individual sixpenny volumes from Roach's series; but, in the eyes of cultural conservatives, 'not everyone' was still too many. The cheapness of the books, and the perceived unsavouriness of those reading them, served to cheapen their contents. 'Elegant extracts, Anthologies, are sickly things,' Francis Palgrave – father of Francis Turner Palgrave, future creator of *The Golden Treasury*, the most famous anthology of all time – declared. 'The splendid bouquet decays into unsavoury trash, and as trash is thrown away.'[107]

As early as 1782, the year Kearsley's collections began to dominate the market, reviewers in the established literary periodicals made it clear that they considered the popularity of the 'beauties' a deplorable social trend. 'Extracts from celebrated writers, called their *Beauties*, are become so hacknied as to be disgustful,' sneered the *Monthly Review* in December 1782. 'The common price for the possession of each of these *Beauties* is half a crown.'[108] Here, the connection between cheapness, ubiquity ('hacknied', 'common') and undesirability ('disgustful') is relatively subtle. A month earlier, however, a review in the *London Magazine* of Cooke's *The Flowers of Literature* had lain its cards on the table. Cooke's book, the reviewer snarled, was a 'crude and ill-sorted selection', a 'vile catch-penny' designed to cash in on the trend Kearsley had started; Cooke himself was 'predatory', 'impudent' and piratical, one of a 'swarm of servile imitators' bent on thieving original work from writers and starving them out of the market.[109]

'Crude', 'vile', 'catch-penny', 'impudent', 'servile': this is language that pretends to describe the book trade and one of its more enterprising salesmen, but seems more about the sort of people the reviewer feared would be able to afford Cooke's book. Catchpennies – cheap and inferior books or pamphlets, designed to make quick sales – enabled the creation of a class of cheap and inferior readers, a 'swarm' of men and women who were 'crude', 'impudent' and 'vile' just like Cooke himself. Swarms (of insects, say, or bacteria) were never good news: they happened in vast numbers and brought with them infection and plague. People swarmed, but not people from the upper echelons of society. Swarms meant crowds, masses, mobs, the poorer or criminal classes assembling in alarming and unknowable numbers. (Things that 'swarmed' during the early 1780s, according to a search of one of the most read newspapers of the period, included aggressive 'Bees', 'Sons of WHORES', 'Reptile Vagabonds' and 'French Privateers'.[110]) With the book trade in mind, we might recall More's attack on beauty-mongers for producing 'swarms of *Abridgments*, *Beauties*, and *Compendiums*'; or the novelist Clara Reeve's disgust in 1785 at the state of the publishing industry, brimming over with bad cheap print:

> They [novels] did but now begin to increase upon us, but ten years more multiplied them tenfold. Every work of merit produced a swarm of imitators, till they became a public evil, and the institution of Circulating libraries, conveyed them in the cheapest manner to every bodies hand.[111]

What the 'swarm' metaphor makes clear here is that numbers are the problem. Catchpenny novels, Reeve says, have 'increased' and then 'multiplied [...] tenfold' in quantity, each commercial hit spawning a 'swarm' of eager imitators. The spread of libraries has then allowed these books to penetrate to the very bottom of the social scale, making them available 'in the cheapest manner' to 'every bodies hand'.

Some 'bodies', as Reeve suggests but doesn't say, weren't supposed to have the spare time or money to read for pleasure. During the late eighteenth and early nineteenth centuries, opposition to cheap books on the basis that they were 'hacknied', 'crude' or immoral served as a convenient disguise for an uglier truth: that many people simply didn't want them to be in 'every bodies hand', and feared what might happen if they were.[112] The popularity of anthologies brought with it a pervasive sense of loss of control, offering an index of the chaotic rate at which the affordability and reproducibility of printed books seemed to be growing. It was 'the emergence of the reading public as a social problem', in Altick's words.[113] The sour response of the literary establishment to the thought of new readers, with their modest shelves of 'beauties' and 'extracts', signalled the existence of larger underlying fears – about what else these people read, what they spent their time doing (or not doing), and what they might come to want.

4

EDUCATION

*The Golden Treasury of the Best Songs and Lyrical Poems
in the English Language* (1861)

In 1916, the young American poet Ezra Pound approached
a London publishing agent with an idea for a new kind of
anthology. He wanted to put together a massive twelve-volume
collection of the 'best' poetry from across the world, bringing
together in one place all the poems he thought had changed
the course of literary history. The agent was impressed by
Pound's ambition and took his proposal straight to Macmillan,
the publishing house that had made its name in the previous
century by cornering the popular poetry market. The response
was swift. 'In two days,' Pound wrote, 'came a hasty summons'
from the agent once more: 'would I see him in person?'

> I found him awed, as if one had killed a cat in the sacristy.
> Did I know what I had said in my letter? I did. Yes, but
> about Palgrave? I did. I had said: 'It is time we had
> something to replace that doddard Palgrave.' 'But don't
> you know,' came the awestruck tones, 'that the whole
> fortune of X & Co. is founded on Palgrave's *Golden
> Treasury?*'[1]

Pound had done something worse than killing a cat in church. He had impugned the editor of the best-loved collection of poetry in the English language, 'that doddard' Francis Turner Palgrave: Palgrave, otherwise known as the great 'benefactor', the genius who had brought the British public its 'national anthology' and injected new life into its literary culture.[2] And he had done it to the publishing house whose reputation Palgrave had made almost singlehandedly. Macmillan, of course, turned Pound down.

Pound didn't forget his early run-in with the British literary establishment. In 1929, he recorded the story for posterity in a long *New York Herald Tribune* article, and in the mid-1930s he was still to be found complaining about 'that stinking sugar teat Palgrave' and his book.[3] But the reading public, British, American and Commonwealth, went on buying *The Golden Treasury*. The anthology sold 10,000 copies in the first six months after it appeared in July 1861, although Macmillan had only issued 2,000 in the first print run. There were 61,000 copies in circulation by 1884 – a vast number for a poetry book at that or any time – and 140,000 by the time of Palgrave's death in 1897, each of which was likely to have passed through the hands of several readers. More than 650,000 had been printed by the Second World War.[4] As an accessible, intellectually serious attempt to gather together all the 'best' English poetry in one volume, it became a model for the heavyweight collections that came after it, household fixtures such as the *Oxford Book of English Verse* (1900) and the *Faber Book of Modern Verse* (1936).

As the years passed and the popularity of Palgrave's book continued unabated, it attained the status of a kind of national symbol. It was as British as the poetic landscapes between its covers, Shakespeare's 'greenwood tree', Thomas Gray's country churchyard, the hills, pathways and stones of Wordsworth's

Lake District, the wild lands of the Scottish border ballads. Robert Frost, who first came across it in 1892 and admired it all his life, held it responsible, perhaps only half-jokingly, for his decision to uproot his family from New England and move across the Atlantic in 1912. 'I said I had come to the land of *The Golden Treasury*. That's what I went for.'[5]

❧

Francis Turner Palgrave was born in 1824 in Great Yarmouth, on the Norfolk coast. His father, Francis Cohen, a lawyer and medieval historian, was the son of a once-wealthy Jewish stockbroker who had lost all the family's money. In the year of his son's birth, Cohen married a Norfolk woman, Elizabeth Turner, converted to Anglicanism and swapped his Jewish name for an English one, Palgrave, his mother's maiden name. His conversion was made in the hope of greater professional recognition: he was, according to a contemporary, 'much the greatest of all the historians of early England', but his own 'un-English' beginnings, and his un-English name, stood in the way of success.[6] It took another ten years of hard work before he was offered an official academic position as Deputy Keeper at the newly created Public Records Office. Francis, his son, was fourteen before his father could afford formal schooling for him at Charterhouse.

The home education the Palgrave children received in the meantime was exacting and rigorous. Francis studied Latin from the age of four, could recite long English poems at six, and was put to work at Greek when he turned seven.[7] 'He takes pleasure in learning a few Latin words,' his mother wrote approvingly in her journal when he was four and a half. In 1834, when Francis was nine, his parents wrote to his grandfather to say that he and his little brother Gifford had enjoyed 'three weeks' holiday', during which they had 'learnt perfectly all the first book of the *Aeneid* by heart.'[8] At Charterhouse, he secured all the form prizes, became Head of School in his final year, and, in 1843, won a scholarship to Balliol College, Oxford.

Balliol in the 1840s had a particular atmosphere: it was a place where clever ex-public school boys were transformed into political firebrands. Along with many of his contemporaries, Palgrave came under the influence of his charismatic Classics tutor, Benjamin Jowett, a religious reformer, modernizer and convinced republican who campaigned, years ahead of his time, for working men and women to be admitted to the universities. Jowett invited Palgrave into the Decade Club, an exclusive Balliol debating society where he socialized with the young poets Matthew Arnold and Arthur Hugh Clough. No subjects were off the table at the 'pugnacious' meetings of this society (nicknamed 'The Decayed' for its risqué reputation), but it was especially concerned with questions of radical politics.[9] In this, it reflected the mood of the times. The 1840s was a period of intense working-class agitation, as the Chartists, a mass movement pushing for working men's suffrage, submitted petitions to Parliament, demonstrated at large public meetings, wrote tracts and launched strikes across Britain. Palgrave and Clough, under Jowett's guidance, committed themselves to political and social reform, and to the cause of republicanism. 'Palgrave too,' Clough wrote to Arnold's brother, Tom, in July 1848, 'has become, [...] partly by revolutionary sympathy, a very suspect person at Oxford and next to myself is I suppose accounted the wildest and most *écervelé* [hare-brained] republican going.'[10]

By 'revolutionary sympathy', Clough was referring to Palgrave's keen interest in what had recently been taking place in France. In the early spring of 1848, an uprising on the streets of Paris had resulted in the abdication of the king and the establishment of a Second Republic. Palgrave made the journey across the Channel to observe the situation for himself in April, accompanied by Jowett and two Oxford colleagues, Robert Morier and Arthur Stanley. In the grounds of the Tuileries Palace, below a fluttering Tricolor flag, he watched ordinary people gather in large numbers, thronging with a 'quiet, resolute air', as he observed in his diary, through what had just recently been 'royal precincts'. 'Everything looked bright and propitious as the Dawning.' With Stanley, he managed to gain admission to two Republican Club meetings at the Sorbonne, where crowds of citizens met to debate the future of their new democracy. 'Although the assembly was almost entirely composed of the working classes,' he wrote, its 'democratic sentiments' were peaceful: 'there was not [...] a word of "levelling violence" or "lawless fury".' A week later, he, Jowett and Stanley found themselves standing with the Provisional Government to watch a review of the new Republican troops, 'a long stream of bayonets that poured for 12 hours incessantly, from the distant Tuileries to the Place de la Concorde.' 'We saw them,' Palgrave added, 'for S.J. and I joined the Regiment, and marched round close before them, with bare heads, to the sound of drums and shouts of *Vive la République!*'[11] It was a unique political education.

After graduating, Jowett's best students tended to end up in one place, where he maintained a tight network of connections: the Education Office of the Civil Service. Matthew Arnold worked there as an inspector of schools, as did his former Balliol tutor, Ralph Lingen, and Clough joined the department a few years later. On his return from France, Palgrave abandoned a fledgling academic career to follow the same path, accepting a teaching post as part of an experimental new venture in adult education.

Kneller Hall was a training college in Twickenham for working-class young men, who were educated at the state's expense and then sent off to gruelling teaching positions in workhouses and prison schools. As the new Vice-Principal of the Hall, serving under one of his Balliol mentors, Frederick Temple, Palgrave was paid to instruct the young men in English literature, history and composition, as well as to teach them how to be teachers themselves.[12] He used his distinguished contacts to turn the school into something resembling an Oxford college, inviting Clough, Arnold and his new friend Alfred Tennyson (who lived close by in Twickenham) to give poetry readings and socialize with the students.[13] The idea was that the exposure to refined conversation and progressive ideas would elevate the students' ambitions, turning them into cultivated teachers capable, in their turn, of improving their pupils.

But the experiment was a failure. The two years the young men spent at Kneller Hall were just enough to equip them with aspirations and high ideals, which the reality of the education system soon put paid to. The profession they entered turned out to be considerably less dignified than they had been brought to believe. Money was short, so, instead of beginning their careers at district schools at a distance from the workhouses, Palgrave's ex-students were compelled to sleep, eat and teach inside the worst institutions of the Victorian social system, becoming prisoners of the places their work in education was supposed to be making obsolete. They were expected to oversee the workhouse boys' daily routine and cleanliness as well as their studies – 'to see them washed and combed, to attend to them at meals, to see them go to bed and get up,' as one exhausted teacher wrote. When the boys refused or were unable to keep their rooms clean, the young men had to 'take mop and broom' and do it for them.[14] Soon, word got out among potential Kneller Hall students about the working and living conditions they were likely to be signing up for. In 1854, under the pressure of rapidly declining enrolment rates, the college closed and Palgrave and Temple returned to central London.

Kneller Hall was Palgrave's first exposure to a social problem that would occupy him for much of his career. In the mid-nineteenth century, the education of the adult working classes was a question that had begun to interest many who shared his middle-class, professional background. The kinds of ideas and solutions they experimented with tended to depend on their political views and economic position. Industrialists and factory owners, who weren't interested in educating their workers for education's sake, but instead wanted them to understand better the science behind the mechanical work they were doing, sponsored the founding of mechanics' institutes, establishments with libraries where workers could attend lectures on technical subjects and borrow books. Their motives for putting up the money were moral as well as economic: by offering vocational tuition, the mechanics' institutes were supposed to increase workers' efficiency at their jobs, but also – by keeping them busy, and instilling in them what were thought of as middle-class virtues of industry and discipline – to draw them away from recreational drinking and other frowned-upon activities.

'Adult education,' as one historian has put it, 'had for most middle-class liberals an added value as a social policeman.'[15] Workers who had been inculcated with sound middle-class principles and given access to middle-class kinds of knowledge, it was believed, would be far less likely to protest against their labour conditions or enter into a violent confrontation with their employers. They were being educated to help them 'get on', to rise socially and financially, as they were told; it was a system that looked, at least from the outside, as if it were something from which everyone benefited.[16]

As time went on, the humanities, literary studies in particular, began to feature with increasing regularity on the lists of lectures offered at the institutes. By 1848, of the more than 150 lectures delivered across the Yorkshire institutes, 109 were on literary subjects, with a further twelve on music and the fine arts; in 1851, an analysis of a thousand lectures delivered at institutes across the country showed that more than half were literary or historical in nature.[17] Charles Dickens, the Shakespearean actors Charles and Fanny Kemble, and Keats's friend Charles Cowden Clarke were regular guest lecturers.[18] The Brontë sisters' father, the Reverend Patrick Brontë, spoke at the Keighley Institute in Yorkshire. Oscar Wilde, on tour lecturing about 'The Value of Art in Modern Life' in a frantic bid to earn money, stopped off at an exhausting number of mechanics' institutes all over the United Kingdom.[19] Of the literary lectures, those 'on Poetry and the Drama' were 'most of all attractive', as one Birmingham report noted in 1836. George Dawson, an institute lecturer who was called to give evidence to the Parliamentary Committee on Public Libraries in 1849, told MPs that poetry was both 'a great deal read' by working people – in Chartist periodicals, where it was excerpted, or in old volumes bought cheaply from secondhand bookstalls – and also written by them. 'Anybody connected with a newspaper knows what an enormous flood of poetry the working classes send in the course of a year.'[20]

The move towards literary lectures, away from vocational, technical learning, can be explained partly on the basis that it was what the institutes' students wanted. One disapproving commentator affected not to understand their preference for 'light literature, criticism, music, and the drama' above 'plain and easily understood discourses on the elements of the sciences, and their application to the useful arts', but to us it's likely to seem reasonable enough.[21] Uninterested in attending scientific lectures, they were nonetheless keen to acquire 'a little of the cultural elegance', the lightness, polish and ease which they believed their social superiors possessed, and to which they saw tuition in literature and the arts as a kind of shortcut.[22]

As their employers saw it, there were few drawbacks to the change. If industrial workers were to be weaned off the 'degrading pursuits' they seemed to take such pleasure in (intoxication, 'sexual excess' beyond what was strictly necessary within the marriage bond), poetry seemed more likely to refine and civilize their tastes than a stiff course of mechanical engineering.[23] Anything that tended to make them look and behave more like the middle classes, without stimulating them to think that they could *be* middle class themselves, was all to the good. The kind of literature the institute lecturers taught wasn't political or otherwise subversive in character, and poetry in particular had the advantage of encouraging 'higher thoughts': it would inspire its readers, instructors hoped, to look inwards rather than dwelling on their material circumstances. Poetry, F.W. Robertson, one of the founders of the Brighton Mechanics' Institute, told his members, enabled 'the man of labour to rise sometimes out of his dull, dry, hard toil and dreary routine of daily life', into a brief 'forgetfulness of his state': it was a kind of temporary balm for the spirit. David Lester Richardson, a college principal in colonial India, praised it for its ability to 'effectually beguile men from the circle of mean and selfish thoughts', to distract them, conveniently, from the real difficulties of their lives. 'Even in penury and solitude,' Richardson suggested, 'a mind of true refinement can echo the noble sentiment of [the poet James] Thomson: "I care not Fortune what you me deny..."'[24]

The institutes weren't the only organisations to turn towards literary tuition. During the years Palgrave spent at

Kneller Hall, the first Working Men's College was founded in
Camden, north London, by a group of Christian Socialists.
The group's hope was that the collegiate environment they
intended to foster for working-class students would provide
a kind of counterweight to the age's spirit of materialism, a
space to combat its ethos of 'competition, selfishness, and
greed'.[25] In the eyes of their leader, F.D. Maurice, a progressive
theologian whose politics had recently got him sacked from
King's College, London, education wasn't a utilitarian
proposition, something you could justify on the grounds that
it was likely to improve a man's usefulness or his wage-earning
potential. The benefits the working classes would derive
from education were, Maurice argued, of an intangible kind:
learning promised intellectual enrichment, spiritual freedom,
independence of mind, the development of a selfhood capable
of bearing with dignity the monotonous nature of machine
labour. What it did not and could not promise, in Maurice's
view, despite his progressive politics and those of the college's
other founders, was the elimination of class distinctions. As
Dickens put it, giving a speech at the opening of Manchester
Library in 1852, the point of providing a working man with
books was to supply him with a resource to 'cheer him through
many of the struggles and toils of his life', to encourage his
'self-respect' – not to give him the means of swapping those
toils for an easier life.[26]

To this end, the subjects the college offered when it
opened its doors in 1854 weren't the technical, vocational
ones initially favoured by the mechanics' institutes, but
the humanities. On signing up, the machinists, carpenters,
decorators, goldsmiths, warehousemen, clock-makers, tailors
and boot-makers of north London were offered programmes
in English literature, history, politics and law, which their new
teachers pressed on them as intrinsically superior in nature to

mathematics or the sciences. John Ruskin, already famous as a painter and art critic, offered a well-attended drawing class, bringing in the Pre-Raphaelite artists Dante Gabriel Rossetti, Ford Madox Brown and Edward Burne-Jones to teach alongside him. Classes in French, English grammar, Latin and singing were consistently popular.[27] In the first year after the college opened, Maurice offered a course on 'Political Terms illustrated by English Literature', an attempt to get his students to understand political theory via the characters and scenarios of literature.[28] The college's instructors defended ardently the idea that the English literary tradition belonged to everyone, as the birthright of the many rather than the few. 'Poetry [...] is addressed to all men,' Vernon Lushington, a volunteer teacher, wrote in the *Working Men's College Magazine* in 1861.[29]

Emphasis was placed on literature's spiritual benefits, its ability to provide a therapeutic antidote to the social and moral poisons of industrial progress. Henry Morley, an academic and critic who taught evening classes for working men at King's College in the 1850s, claimed that great literature offered 'a natural corrective' to materialism, a means of 'sustain[ing] the spiritual side of life' in unspiritual places.[30] Those whose livelihoods revolved around the operation of machines, it was believed, had lost touch with traditional art and culture, becoming detached from their heritage in a way that only fresh acquaintance with literature could mend. The greatest English poets (Shakespeare, Milton and Wordsworth, according to Maurice) spoke to their readers like ordinary men, as if in conversation; but their voices were such as could make 'the deepest minds of a grand age of English history intelligible to our age.'[31]

Such claims, though lavish, weren't out of step with the kinds of arguments regularly made by the cultural establishment for the power of literature during the mid-nineteenth century. A.J. Scott, one of the first professors of English Language and Literature at University College, London, wrote in 1849 that the 'living contact of spirit with spirit' that readers sensed when they engaged with imaginative literature constituted a unique kind of moral education. Poems and novels, because they stimulated internal reflection on questions of human behaviour, provided a finer and deeper understanding of right and wrong than young men or women could glean from being preached at from the pulpit.[32] According to Arnold, who fought during his time in the Education Office to get English Literature recognized as a compulsory school subject alongside Latin and Greek, it was nothing less than therapy on a national scale. 'In poetry,' he predicted, 'the spirit of our race will find, as time goes on and as other helps fail, its consolation and stay.' Poetry would keep people going, he argued, when the resources of religion, philosophy and even science were exhausted. 'More and more mankind will discover that we have to turn to poetry to interpret life for us, to console us, to sustain us.'[33]

In theory, of course, such therapeutic qualities could be sought and found in classical literature, in the revered ancient texts on which school and university curricula had long been founded. But not everyone was equipped with the necessary tools to turn to the Classics for consolation: there were obvious barriers to entry. By Palgrave's time, there was a growing belief among educationalists that the necessary 'helps' could also be located, with considerably less effort and without recourse to a dictionary, in England's native literature – a long line of authors and works which was increasingly valorized for what it seemed to say about English history and the values of the English people. While classical poetry continued to be highly prized, English literature became, during the second half of the century, 'one of the central symbolic expressions of the "imagined community" of the English people', as the literary historian Stefan Collini has argued: a cherished source of pride, patriotism and national identity.[34]

No less than its military triumphs, its advances in science or the spectacle of its great cities, England's literature, its poetry in particular, was considered one of the characteristic achievements that had made the country what it was, a storehouse of cultural riches that those inheriting could be proud of. In its glory, it held a mirror up to the people who had made it: it was an expression, educators and critics claimed, of the rugged spirit of the English people, evidence of their exceptional native qualities and of the steady continuity of those qualities through times of difficulty and upheaval. 'Literature is the autobiography of a nation,' declared the novelist and Working Men's College teacher Charles Kingsley in 1848.* 'There comes a time in every national history when the people seem to waken up to some knowledge of themselves,' argued the *Spectator* in 1861. 'The poet who expresses this first phase of self-knowledge – like Shakespeare for England, and Burns and Scott for different phases of Scotch life – are borne on the crest of a national wave.'[35]

In the present, literature could serve as inspiration: an exhortation to the living to meet the high moral standards of the past. Young subjects of the British administration in India were fed a substantial diet of English literature at school and university (it was a compulsory element of all arts and social science degrees), as a means of instilling in them an elaborate

---

* Kingsley, incidentally, was no fan of 'beauties' volumes or *Elegant Extracts*. 'The young,' he observed in a lecture of 1848, 'have been taught to admire the laurels of Parnassus, but only after they have been clipped and pollarded like a Dutch shrubbery [...] cut up into the very driest hay.'

respect for the values and achievements of their colonizers.[36] 'The English language and its magnificent literature have done more to expand the Indian mind during the last 50 or 60 years than any one thing else,' gushed a contributor to the Sadler Commission enquiry into the state of colonial education at the turn of the century. 'All the present advance of India is due to the study of English literature and of the ideals it embodies by Indians.'[37] As the destined creators and enforcers of this culture, young Englishmen applying to be colonial administrators were required to brush up on their literary history as well as their grasp of political economy. In 1855, Jowett joined a commission tasked with crafting a suitable examination for entry into the East India Company's civil service, in which a thorough knowledge of literature ('our poets, wits and philosophers') was required for the highest marks.[38] Austin Dobson, a poet and civil servant on the Board of Trade, put together a specialist *A Handbook of English Literature* (1874) for exam candidates, full of such germane information as where Milton had gone to school and how much Burns earned per annum on his farm.[39]

In this climate, established living poets were public figures, voices to be listened to on questions of culture and politics alike. In 1864, no one considered it especially surprising that Giuseppe Garibaldi, the dashing military commander at the head of the campaign for Italian unification, made a point of calling on Tennyson at his house on the Isle of Wight during a visit to Britain: he was interested in talking about Italian and English poetry, but also wanted to get the poet's views on the state of play in Europe.[40] A journalist for the *Daily News*, having tracked down Garibaldi, infiltrated the grounds of Tennyson's house to get a glimpse of the famous bard. 'I had just left a hero, and was within a stone's throw of a poet,' he reported shrilly (presumably from behind a hedge).[41] As early as 1831, a review of Tennyson's poems claimed that poets were men who could 'act with a force, the extent of which it is difficult to estimate, upon national feelings and character': they could 'influence [...] unnumbered minds', 'command the sympathies of unnumbered hearts'.[42]

Palgrave, one of Tennyson's most vocal admirers, was a committed believer in both the centrality of poetry to public life and the greatness of English poetry in particular. France's literature he dismissed outright as inherently less 'poetical' than England's; Germany, he considered, despite its promising beginnings, had 'never yet reached the place to which a nation so highly gifted for poetry appeared naturally entitled.' English poetry, by contrast, had flourished over the centuries by picturing and absorbing the finest qualities of the English people, reflecting them back to themselves as if through a splendid mirror. In Spenser and Milton's works, 'we see England,' Palgrave wrote, 'from Elizabeth to Cromwell, interpreted to herself.' Its ability to present the nation with its own image was unique. Goethe and Schiller's works were magnificent, Palgrave acknowledged, but couldn't be said to 'stand in that intimate relation to the mind of Germany at large which our great poets occupy towards Englishmen.' According to the chauvinist perspective he shared with his class and generation, English poetry at its best was, and always had been, 'a spontaneous expression of the national spirit'. It followed that it was the natural and proper inheritance of all who considered themselves Englishmen, all who had a vested interest in the progress of the nation.[43]

❦

At Oxford, Palgrave had wanted to become an architect. Since childhood, he had been fascinated by fine art and beautiful buildings, filling up teenage diaries with records of trips to ancient Roman sights in Italy. His journal entries during his trip to France in 1848 mingled enthusiastic commentary on the new power of the *citoyens* with descriptions of cathedrals and arches. Pressure from his father, however, who considered architecture an unsuitable profession, pushed him towards the civil service, where the reformist notions he had come into contact with at Oxford and in Paris began to take shape in the context of education.

His ideas were shifting and changing. Like many other idealists of his generation, young men who had watched, dismayed, as the European revolutionary movements of the late 1840s collapsed or disavowed their principles, his political commitments gradually became less radical in nature.[44] He repudiated his former republicanism, turned away from questions of suffrage extension and began to focus instead on the possibilities of social reform through education, on the civilizing and humanizing role of the arts in particular. His experience of teaching at Kneller Hall, though the experiment itself had been abortive, had left him with a core belief similar to that of Maurice and the founders of the Working Men's College: a conviction that literature, and poetry in particular, ought to have a central place rather than a peripheral one in the growth of popular education. From the early 1850s, in his spare hours away from the desk at the Education Office, he wrote a stream of articles and lectures on literary subjects, many targeted at audiences who didn't share his background and whose level of prior education he couldn't presume on. In these he returned, again and again, to the problem of how great literature could be made to broaden its reach.[45]

The issue wasn't, as he saw it, that working-class people weren't reading enough; it was more that they were reading the wrong things, wasting their time and attention on throwaway newspaper articles and cheap sensational novels. 'Journalizing prolixity,' he wrote in an 1853 article for the Education Office's house journal, *The Educational Expositor*, 'is the natural predilection of uneducated readers.' 'We read and read,' a contributor to the *Working Men's College Magazine* agreed in 1861, 'but what? Newspapers, magazines, railway novels, as miscellaneous and as rapidly succeeding one another as the dishes at a Lord Mayor's dinner.'[46] Readers read, too, for what Palgrave considered the wrong reasons, going to books 'for something almost similar to what they find in social conversation' – gossip, wit, chit-chat. Those with little time on their hands, he argued, ought not to approach books as if what they contained were merely a continuation of everyday life, supplying the same ideas and feelings they could get by opening a penny newspaper. What they needed was the opposite: a few books of a special kind, to be treasured, 'kept and studied and known by heart', whose rewards would be lasting and transformative.[47]

Chief among those books, as he instructed an audience of adult students at the South London Working Men's College in Southwark, ought to be great works of poetry, which held out the prospect of lifelong pleasure and joy to those who read them.* Since, as he pointed out, pleasure and joy weren't evenly distributed commodities in society, those who stood to gain the most from reading poetry were the kinds of men

---

* The South London Working Men's College was founded on Blackfriars Road in 1868 by William Rossiter, a former apprentice trunk-maker who had retrained as a teacher after attending classes at the Working Men's College in Camden. Ruskin donated money to help establish the new college's library; the evolutionary biologist T.H. Huxley was its first principal.

ranged out on the benches in front of him. For them, he warned, indifference to poetry represented

> indifference to a source of high, enduring, and spiritual pleasure – nay, to one of the few, the very few, sources of such delight which life affords us, and of which, the more dusty, dry, and commonplace life tends to become, the more we have need.[48]

'It seems to satisfy a want that we have long been conscious of,' Clough had written in a review of the working-class poet Alexander Smith's book, *City Poems* (1857), 'when we see the black streams that welter out of factories, the dreary lengths of urban and suburban dustiness [...] irradiated with a gleam of divine purity.'[49] As the industrial economy made the forms and routines of work uglier and drearier, poetry's ability to 'irradiate' working experience, to transform and brighten the days of those who could read it, became proportionately more important. The drier and dustier 'commonplace life' was, the more critical its role became. 'Every great poem,' Palgrave argued, represented 'an addition to the value of life – a pleasure which money cannot give, nor poverty take from us.'[50]

Such poetry was for everyone, he told his audience, because it was something a reader was bound to feel or sense before he had time to think about what it said: its mark was that it would 'infallibly reach the heart, and through it the intellect of every Englishman who [sought] to understand it.'[51] There was, in his view, a 'natural and happily common bias' towards poetry, in children as well as adults, and the ability to know which poems were worth reading – that is, possessing taste – was also something innate, a capacity that didn't have to be bred or acquired at school. Almost everyone appreciated beauty and was drawn to it, even if they couldn't say why. 'Taste, in any sense worth having,' Palgrave explained to his listeners, just meant 'a natural turn or instinct towards any subject (which almost every one has something of),' a propensity which, if they desired, could then be 'trained and exercised by information and experience.'[52]

Training one's taste, when it came to poetry, wasn't easy. It meant, according to Palgrave, studying, for each new poem you came across, its style and technical properties (shape, rhyme scheme, metre), the history of the age during which it had been written, the other great poems it could be compared with, the life of its author, and so on. But such rigorous private study, as he argued at the South London Working Men's College, was particularly suited to those who were industrious and self-motivated, tailor-made for the kinds of men who had voluntarily enrolled in adult education. Those who considered that they'd acquired all the education they needed at public school and Oxford, thank you very much, were far less likely to attempt it. The typical 'man of wealthy leisure', he explained, being 'under less external stimulus to improve himself', often exhibited little desire to do so, tending to remain, instead, in a kind of pleasant 'intellectual babyhood'.[53]

'It is astonishing how much may be accomplished in self-culture by the energetic and persevering,' the writer and campaigner Samuel Smiles had argued in *Self-Help* (1859), his bestselling manual of advice for self-improvement, praising men and women who were 'careful to avail themselves of opportunities', and used 'the fragments of spare time which the idle permit to run to waste.'[54] Palgrave shared his age's faith in the value of working-class self-culture, but considered that nothing – and certainly not the practical courses of study Smiles recommended, in mathematics, mechanics or economics – was more worthwhile than spending one's time buried in a poetry book. Even second-rate poetry, as he argued in his preface to *The Golden Treasury*, was 'better worth reading than much of what fills the scanty hours that most men spare for self-improvement.'[55] First-rate poetry, of course, was best of all.

In the summer of 1860, he went on a walking tour of Cornwall with Tennyson and the Pre-Raphaelites William Holman Hunt, Thomas Woolner and Valentine Prinsep, all of whom had taught at the Working Men's College in Camden. They brought their London manners and odd clothes to the West Country, confounding the locals and their fellow hotel guests, talking emphatically and flamboyantly about painting, sculpture and (especially) 'the character of English poetry of all periods'.[56] Palgrave recalled that he had proposed the idea of compiling an anthology of poetry to Tennyson 'during a walk near the Land's End'. Their lengthy conversations about the book, Holman Hunt recalled, went on 'at times on the heights of a cliff or on the shore below':

> We could watch Tennyson in his slouch hat, his rusty black suit, and his clinging coat, wandering away among rocks, assiduously attended by our literary friend, and if by chance the poet escaped his eyes for a minute, the voice of Palgrave was heard above the sea and the wind calling 'Tennyson, Tennyson!'[57]

A plan was hatched. With Tennyson consenting to act as judge and censor over the final selection for the anthology, Palgrave began combing through old multi-volume collections of English poetry to create a shortlist. He gathered the poems he liked by copying them out longhand, or cutting them straight out of books with scissors, then brought his piles of papers in stages during the autumn of 1860 to two friends he trusted, Woolner and a colleague from the Education Office, George Miller.* (In the fair copy of the anthology he produced, Palgrave noted that the selection process with Woolner and Miller went on 'in courts of poetry held here & elsewhere': 'here' may refer to the Office itself.[58]) They commented on each piece in a shorthand Palgrave devised: 'P' meant print; 'O' omit; 'P (?)' maybe print; 'X' must print; and 'P XXX' great enthusiasm.[59] He took the draft manuscript with him to Farringford, Tennyson's house on the Isle of Wight, when he went to stay with the family for Christmas. Though a different gift would probably have been preferable, Tennyson dutifully went through the entire selection in ten days, approving most of the choices and rejecting a handful of others. Palgrave deferred to his taste with an almost religious reverence.

The chief selection criterion was simple: excellence. 'This little Collection,' Palgrave wrote in the book's preface, 'differs from others in the attempt made to include in it all the best original Lyrical pieces and Songs in our language [...] – and none beside the best.'[60] Its aim, in other words, was not to miss a single excellent short poem in the British literary tradition, and not to include a single one that wasn't excellent. The title, in this context, was significant. Early and mid-Victorian readers were used to buying poetry anthologies with titles such as *The Book of Gems*, *The Amulet*, and so on, variations on the precious stone theme, many of which were made up of new poems produced to order. ('I have been so beGemmed and beAmuletted [...] that I have given all these things up,' Tennyson wrote crossly in 1831, after he was asked one too

---

* 'I am glad to think,' Miller's grandson wrote in a letter to *The Times* several decades later, 'that [...] he employed his great learning and talents on a work which has brought "sweetness and light" to many more homes than the Education Acts, which he spent the most part of his life administering.'

many times to contribute to a fashionable poetry annual.)[61] No jewels, though, shone brighter or were more valuable than gold: it stood for the finest and best, the standard against which other valuable things were measured. Putting 'golden' in front of 'Treasury', moreover, evoked a vision of glittering riches, a metaphorical version of the real Treasury in London where the nation's wealth was safeguarded.[62]

In 1861, as Palgrave noted a few years later to his publisher, Alexander Macmillan, the idea of compiling an anthology on the basis of poetic quality alone was something of 'a new idea'. Early and mid-Victorian collections, especially those targeted at specific populations (families, children, the poor), tended to make their selections on the grounds of 'suitableness', or moral appropriateness, rather than, simply, 'goodness as Poetry'.[63] The pocket volume *Affection's Gift* (1848), for instance, collected the only morally acceptable part of Byron's oeuvre, his *Hebrew Melodies*, alongside sacred poetry by Thomas Moore and Felicia Hemans; while Charles Mackay's massive tome, *The Home Affections, Pourtrayed By the Poets* (1858), celebrated familial love, rigidly excluding 'every composition which might give offence to the pure-minded'.[64] To Palgrave, prioritizing aesthetic excellence seemed a more promising way to reach a broad readership. Men and women who lacked the spare time to read widely would benefit from being supplied with only the very best, poems whose beneficial human and spiritual effects flowed directly from their literary superiority. 'There can be no more useful help for discovering what poetry belongs to the class of the truly excellent, and can therefore do us most good, than to have always in one's mind lines and expressions of the great masters,' Arnold argued.[65] *The Golden Treasury* compensated for its readers' unfamiliarity with the tradition by providing all the finest 'lines and expressions' in one place: its 'vigilant conscientious selection', in the words of a teacher in the *Working Men's College Magazine*, ensured that only 'sterling literature', 'the great works of great men', made it through.[66]

Not all 'great works', however, were suitable for the readership Palgrave envisaged. The *Treasury* was made up of 'lyrical pieces' – short poems, often focussing on a single idea or situation, in rhyming verses – for two reasons: because the lyric was the poetic form that both he and Tennyson favoured, but also because it lent itself to autodidact reading. Short poems (more than half the pieces in the *Treasury* had twenty lines or fewer) could be read quickly in snatched moments of leisure or during shift-breaks; they could be learned by heart without great difficulty, to be recited to oneself or aloud to fellows, a common autodidact practice recommended by the Working Men's College to its students.[67] Lengthy epic poems, on this score, were out. 'Imagine a clerk on his much-bothered walks from banks and wharves to the counting-house and back, chanting Milton's "Paradise"!' exclaimed one East Londoner in the college's *Magazine*.[68] So, for similar reasons, were poems written in highly wrought or complexly allegorical language, which seemed to resist being taken to heart.[69]

'First-rate lyrics,' Palgrave declared to a lecture audience in Oxford, were for everyone: they represented 'the voice of humanity', 'our own experience given back to us in song.'[70] Though they might communicate the idiosyncratic thoughts and feelings passing through 'a single mind', they appealed nonetheless to 'the common human heart', establishing touchstones of feeling.* Wordsworth, who had written in the

---

* Palgrave was a keen poet himself. When it came to choosing a selection of his own pieces for publication, he rejected several on the grounds that they were 'too personal' in nature – not, in other words, sufficiently universal or meaningful to other people.

Preface to his *Lyrical Ballads* (1805) that a poet was simply 'a man speaking to men', was Palgrave's model for this kind of writing. He admired Wordsworth's desideratum that lyrical poetry ought to be written in a version of the 'language really used' by ordinary men and women, and should picture 'incidents and situations from common life', readily intelligible to all. 'Many are the poets,' he wrote, quoting Wordsworth.[71]

The *Treasury*'s selection committee was united in its admiration for popular songs and ballads. Palgrave, Woolner and Miller included Thomas Hood's poem 'The Bridge of Sighs' (1844) – described as 'slovenly and cockneyfied' by the reviewers – as well as street songs their readers might recognize, such as the old ballad 'Sally in our Alley', the tale of a shoemaker's apprentice, which all four selectors, including Tennyson, argued should be printed. (Tennyson, in fact, was the driving force behind the selection of several songs and ballads, by Robert Burns in particular, which the others were less sure about.[72]) They rejected, correspondingly, any poetry whose language needed a lot of glossing, or which couldn't be understood without knowledge of its author's life and times. Palgrave was of the opinion that too much editorial intervention gave the impression that poetry was fundamentally difficult when it didn't have to be. Like Maurice, who, as both a scholar and a teacher, had no time for in-depth commentary or philological pedantry, he was 'impatient of anything that came between the reader and the author'.[73]

The only notes he included were tucked away at the back of the book, designed for more inquisitive readers.[74] Here he explained classical allusions for the benefit of those who had never studied Latin or Greek ('*That busy archer*: Cupid'; '*Cynthia*: the Moon'), glossed difficult language ('*feateously*: elegantly'), and filled in possible gaps in readers' historical knowledge.[75] From a note he scribbled on his fair-copy manuscript in June 1861, it seems that Alexander Macmillan was even keener than he was to keep potentially off-putting classical references to a minimum. Each of the four sections of the anthology, in his original plan, was to have a Latin tag from Virgil as its motto, and the contents page a fragment from Euripides. But Macmillan decided otherwise, anxious about the erudite impression such additions, left untranslated, might make. 'Macmillan wd. have these struck out, lest they shd. give the book a learned look.'[76]

Throughout the anthology, the emphasis was on the pleasure of free intellectual discovery: on roaming at will, rather than being told where to go. Within its pages, the *Treasury*'s poems weren't arranged in strict chronological order. Instead, they were loosely grouped around topics or ideas, 'in gradations of feeling or subject', as Palgrave explained, so that they followed on, one from the other, like harmonious variations on a theme. What he wanted was for his readers to come across little chimes and connections between the various pieces naturally, in the process of leafing through the pages, and to begin fitting these connections together to build up a literary picture for themselves. This was, as before, an arrangement suited to self-taught readers. The fact that, as autodidacts of the period reported, they tended to read 'without any order or method' – that is, without knowing, or having ever been taught, how to read efficiently – forced them to develop their own mental categories and procedures, a kind of discipline borne of 'improvisational reading'.[77] The *Treasury* let them read as they wished: it was envisaged as 'a storehouse of delight to Labour and to Poverty', as Palgrave described it in his dedication to Tennyson, a place where readers who were accustomed to doing so could work out for themselves what they found most nourishing, or, if they wished, could devour greedily everything they came across.[78]

Macmillan, whose publishing business was less than twenty years old when he agreed to take on Palgrave's project, was cautious about the book's prospects. In 1860, his house list chiefly comprised school textbooks aimed at the colonial market, in traditional, safe-bet subjects such as mathematics and theology. He had published Smith's *City Poems* in 1857 (the working-class collection noticed by Clough), but made few other inroads into the trickier world of poetry publishing. When his conservative first print run of 2,000 copies of the *Treasury* began to sell out rapidly in the autumn of 1861, two months after publication, he agreed to produce a second impression – and then, before the year was out, a third and a fourth. 10,000 copies vanished off the shelves in six months.[79]

The book's snowballing popularity seemed to have more to do with word-of-mouth reputation than with the good graces of the London literary world.* In its first months, just a few of the established literary periodicals picked it up for review.[80] The *Westminster Review* observed, in its backhanded way, that the book was 'a model of what such works should be', in comparison with the 'heap of good, bad, and abominable poems' readers were usually presented with.[81] Some critics noted that Palgrave appeared to have a broader-than-usual readership in mind - to have taken into account the wants and interests of the average 'plain man', as the *Spectator* put it patronizingly, as well as those of the cultural establishment.[82] J.A. Froude, editor of *Fraser's Magazine* and one of Palgrave's political allies at Balliol, commented that the book contained

---

* Partly because it had been published in July, out of the major reviewing 'season', and partly because it was perceived as just another poetry anthology in a crowded market, only a handful of critical notices appeared in the months after publication. (Palgrave's strenuous attempts, through various avenues and contacts, to get it reviewed in *The Times* came to nothing.)

a number of very 'popular and favourite pieces' that its compiler must have been tempted to omit, 'almost certain' as they were to be found 'in every house where there are any books at all'. But since the anthology was destined not only for the usual book-lined middle-class homes, but also for homes where there were very few or no books, its inclusion of the most well-known things made sense. The collection would not 'be what it is meant to be,' Froude concluded, '"a storehouse of delight to labour and to poverty",' 'if its greatest valuables had been omitted.'[83]

The *Treasury* met with its most enthusiastic reception in the *Working Men's College Magazine*, owing in part to Palgrave's close friendships with several of the college's instructors. Arthur Munby, a civil servant who taught part-time, introduced his students to it as 'the best anthology of and in our language'. To review the book adequately, he said, was a hard task – the reader was left with a kind of 'vague but glowing sense of the benefit received' – but its excellence, as he saw it, lay in its comprehensiveness, and the fact that Palgrave had provided inexperienced readers with notes to guide them. To 'pillars' of the literary community, Munby acknowledged, these notes were likely to seem 'pedantic, dogmatic, superfluous', either so obvious as not to need saying, or inappropriately opinionated. (Matthew Arnold, commenting on the book in 1864, claimed that several of them were written in a provocative, alienating style, which could be ascribed to Palgrave's awareness of the audience he was writing for. The 'promiscuous multitude', he observed – he also called it a 'mob' – no doubt preferred 'big words' and 'outrageous' opinions to the kind of calm, reasoned criticism favoured by their betters.[84])

Munby, though, seeing things from a different perspective, argued that the notes, in view of the 'loving appreciation' of poetry they represented, and the 'insight' they provided 'into the very heart of the matter', would be an object lesson in how to read with attention and sympathy for readers not yet equipped with a trained critical sense. 'Even when you have made up your mind about the beauty of a poem, it is interesting to know why others, and especially keen and competent observers, admire it,' he wrote. Among men and women who had had 'little opportunity of comparing the poets of different nations and different times', who had 'not *studied* Poetry, but only *felt* it', reading what Palgrave had written would 'open their eyes'.[85]

❀

Whether eyes were opened, and how far, is a difficult question. Tracing working-class reading habits tends to be harder than studying the reading culture of the elite, because the documentary evidence available is comparatively thin on the ground: by and large, working-class readers tend to leave fewer records or recollections behind them. The accounts we do possess, moreover, of working-class self-education tend to be exceptional, histories of struggle, luck and the will to succeed which, by definition, only exist because of the extraordinary qualities of their subjects.[86] The daily routine of Thomas Cooper, shoemaker, autodidact, Chartist and founder of the Shakespearean Chartist Association – who rose at 3 a.m. every morning to read, reciting poetry while he worked at his cobbler's stall in the hope of memorising *Paradise Lost* and all 'the best plays of Shakespeare' – teaches us a lot about a man so driven that he had a physical breakdown at the age of twenty-one, but provides scant ground for drawing wider conclusions.[87]

What seems clear, though, is that many working-class readers of *The Golden Treasury*, as it continued to be reprinted in the years and decades following its first appearance, thought of it (with varying degrees of self-consciousness) as a tool to help them get on in the world. They did not, as their accounts of how they approached their reading show, consider poetry exclusively in the light in which Palgrave, and Maurice too, viewed it – as an uplifting, spiritualising force, a source of pure pleasure and joy. Where, for Palgrave, poetry's benefits were immaterial (he called it a delight 'which money cannot give, nor poverty take from us'), many of his readers found it difficult to separate the interests and ambitions it generated from the question of their own social mobility. 'Pre-packaged collections of classics', after all, as the historian Jonathan Rose has pointed out, were an obvious recourse for adult readers 'racing to make up educational deficits' in a bid to improve their social prospects, in view of the curated convenience and cheapness they promised. 'Any number of [readers],' according to Rose, 'testified to the inspiration of Palgrave's *Golden Treasury*,' its capacity to spark the imagination and lead them to other authors, books and ideas they might not otherwise have found.[88]

One such reader at the beginning of the twentieth century was Harold Brown, a miner from the age of fourteen who retrained to become a teacher and writer. In his autobiography, Brown recalled being supported by the charitable Workers' Educational Association through 'years of study', all of which 'had to be done after my day's work – evening classes, reference rooms in public libraries.' The books he remembered as his 'constant companions' were 'the majestic works of Shakespeare [and] Palgrave's *Golden Treasury*': 'I turned over the pages and never lost sight of my good fortune at having access to such riches.'[89] His contemporary, the future Labour MP Philip Inman, born in 1892 in a two-up, two-down cottage in Yorkshire to a mother who cleaned gravestones in the local churchyard, paid to enrol on a postal tuition course in English, French and Latin when he left school to become a salesman. He recorded the progress of his reading and commented on favourite authors in an exercise book. 'I found Palgrave's *Golden Treasury* what its title implied, a valuable treasure house,' he recalled. 'It was one of my permanent bedside books.'[90] Reading and rereading its poetry, for both men, wasn't a spiritual escape from worldly aspiration: it was itself a source of aspiration, part of a systematic process of self-culture.*

The *Treasury* was a set text at Working Men's Colleges and in courses taught via the University Extension movement, a late-Victorian initiative which sent lecturers from the universities of Cambridge, Oxford and London to teach adult learners across the country – as far as the remote mining communities of Northumberland, in some cases, where the miners, 'after a day's hard work in the pit', walked 'four or five miles through cold and darkness and rough roads' to hear them.[91] During the First World War, the young T.S. Eliot worked as an extension lecturer for the universities of London and Oxford, regularly travelling up to teach in Ilkley, Yorkshire, a three-hour journey from London by rail. He put the *Treasury* on his reading lists, recommending it in 1918 to his Elizabethan Literature class in Southall, west London, which was attended by a small number of committed students who stuck at their reading despite the disruptions of wartime, family bereavement and the flu epidemic. 'Read: A few translations of Italian Sonnets in Rossetti's *Early Italian Poets*, and sonnets in the *Golden*

---

* For Inman, Austen's novels had a similar ability to open up new worlds. 'Some day, I thought,' he wrote, 'perhaps I would get to know a world in which voices were always soft and modulated and in which lively and witty conversation was more important than "brass".'

Treasury,' he instructed them when they took on 'The Lyric and the Sonnet'.* The *Treasury*, along with Arthur Quiller-Couch's *Oxford Book of English Verse* (1900) and the Everyman's Library, which he pointed his students towards for editions of Christopher Marlowe and Ben Jonson, was cheap, well-known, and the sort of thing that working men and women (often women, of course, during the war years and immediately afterwards) could be expected to borrow from a library or find on a shelf at home.[92]

At the Front, working-class readers found other uses in Palgrave's book. V.W. Garratt, a factory worker and keen autodidact who 'studied the Everyman's Library *Sartor Resartus* when he was being paid to solder gas-meter fittings,' was sent to France shortly after the beginning of the Somme offensive, in the summer of 1916.[93] His job was to carry the wounded on stretchers from the advanced dressing station, just behind the line, through the winding trench network back to the collecting post, from where they would be taken to hospital. It was 'a most difficult and exhausting job', as he recalled, 'for in parts the patient had to be carried shoulder-high and with as little jolting as possible during the three hours' journey.' In the lulls between deliveries of casualties, while his friends hunted rats in their dugout, Garratt read and wrote:

> My own favourite practice was to lie in the sombre light of a candle reading the *Golden Treasury*, or else scribbling out verses of my own composition. To extol

---

* Later Eliot would be more dismissive of the *Treasury*, considering it a hangover of Victorian literary culture. In 1933, he referred snidely to the nineteenth century as 'the epoch of Ward's *English Poets*, and of *The Golden Treasury*, birthday albums and calendars with a poetical quotation for each day.'

the visions of the mind in poetic praises was temporarily
to forget the surrounding dirt and destruction.[94]

By the end of Garratt's war, his copy of the *Treasury* looked
'like a battered warrior' itself, its binding 'limp' and 'creased'
after being caught in a storm in Palestine. On the passage home
via southern Italy, he had it stashed safely in his kitbag along
with the diaries he had kept over the years, a 'close companion'
to be 'preserved at all costs'.[95] In 1939, when he came to write
his autobiography after a career as a journalist on Fleet Street,
having been sponsored through university by the government,
it was still in his possession, and retained a kind of totemic
power. For the generation of working-class readers he belonged
to, as for the two generations before his, it had been a symbol of
achievement and ambition – a storehouse not only of civilizing
cultural riches, but of glimpses of another sort of life.

5

WAR

The Battle of the Anthologies (1914–1919)

'**O**ut of the storm of battle,' proclaimed the novelist Hall Caine in the autumn of 1914, 'a great new spirit of brotherhood has been born into the world':

> In love of justice and in hatred of oppression, speaking in many voices and many tongues but from only one soul, which enkindles the earth as with a holy fire, men and women of all civilised countries have drawn closer and clasped hands.

At first glance, this reads as another uplifting comment on amity between the Allied and neutral nations of the type that countless journalists had been scribbling in the months following the outbreak of the First World War. But Caine had something very specific in mind when he referred to a 'new spirit of brotherhood' and 'clasped hands': he was talking about the miraculous coming together of hearts and minds represented by a single book. His claims were part of the preface to an anthology, *King Albert's Book: A Tribute to the Belgian King and People from Representative Men and Women Throughout the* World (1914), which he had compiled and dedicated to King Albert I in the wake of Germany's violation of Belgian neutrality. His ambitions for the project were considerable, as its preface made clear. No bigger claims, it's reasonable to say, had ever been made for an anthology in the history of British literature.

King Albert's Book was no hastily curated Christmas stocking-filler. It brought together almost 250 lavish tributes to Belgium's plight and her courageous resistance, supplied by willing 'princes, statesmen, churchmen, authors, artists, and composers of all civilised countries, except the countries of our enemies.'[1] In its pages, Winston Churchill rubbed shoulders with Aga Khan, Claude Debussy, Claude Monet and the former American president William Howard Taft. Guglielmo Marconi, fresh from inventing the long-distance radio transmission, sat alongside Emmeline Pankhurst, Edith Wharton, Thomas Hardy and Andrew Carnegie. These celebrities' offerings in poetry, prose, painting and music constituted, according to Caine, 'the spiritual message of the civilised world to the suffering millions' – or, in the words of an advertisement in the *Glasgow Herald*, one of three British newspapers which clubbed together to sponsor the book's publication, nothing short of 'the world's voice on the war'.[2] Caine himself, a well-connected writer and energetic patriot, worked hard to solicit contributions from very important people in a short space of time, with the professed aim of raising money for the Belgian Fund, an organization run by the *Daily Telegraph* dedicated to helping the country's refugees.

Alongside the shilling that each sale contributed to the fund, however, *King Albert's Book* had another, less openly avowed, purpose. On 16 December, a 'Special Cable' from London appeared in the *New York Times*. It announced the imminent appearance of the anthology for sale in the United States ('Over

250,000 Copies' were already 'in Booksellers' Hands'), and the many contributions from distinguished Americans it contained. The advertisement quoted some ringing lines Caine had elicited from Joseph Choate, the former US ambassador to London, to the effect that Germany was without doubt the war's guilty party and that American citizens, despite their nation's neutrality, should feel free to take sides privately ('our hearts go whither they list').[3] Such messaging, targeted at engaging the sympathies of the nation whose eventual role in the conflict was considered of paramount importance by both sides, was Caine's way of doing what he could, as a prominent literary figure with powerful connections, for the war effort.

It may seem strange that men who usually wrote novels should have been involved in large-scale propagandistic missions, whether privately undertaken or steered by the government. In Britain in 1914, though, the written word, rather than the newer technologies of radio and film, was still considered the most effective way of making a political case, and distinguished members of the literary establishment – novelists, poets, playwrights, journalists – the best public communicators.[4] During earlier wars, those who could read had represented a minority proportion of the population overall. In 1914, though, more than a generation after elementary education (to age thirteen) had been made compulsory for all children in England and Wales, rates of illiteracy were at a historic low, and the prestige of literature at a corresponding high. The war occurred, as the literary historian Paul Fussell has shown, 'at a special historical moment when two "liberal" forces were powerfully coinciding in England.' On one side, the traditional 'belief in the educative powers of classical and English literature was still extremely strong'; on the other, 'the appeal of popular education and "self-improvement" was at its peak,' and this education was still a largely 'humanistic' business, focusing on literary subjects as it had done under Victorian figures such as Palgrave and Maurice.[5] Shortly before and during the conflict, there was 'proportionately more popular interest in authors and the world of authors than at any time before or since,' as the historian John Gross has argued, and readers possessing these interests were taught by newspaper critics to revere English literature as the greatest of all European literatures, and its modern exponents as men and women of national importance.[6]

Such readers, alongside their counterparts abroad, formed a body of potential patriots whose sympathies and energies could be won for the Allied cause through literature, Herbert Asquith's government seems to have been aware from the beginning. In early September 1914, thirteen of the writers involved in Caine's *King Albert's Book*, including Caine himself, were called to attend a meeting of 'eminent authors' at Wellington House in London, the headquarters of the newly established War Propaganda Bureau. Its head, Charles Masterman, a member of Cabinet and a writer himself, hoped to recruit prominent poets, novelists and critics to produce pamphlets and books for the cause, imagining that thoughtful, well-argued work by distinguished literary names would carry more weight than propaganda authored by civil servants.[7]

Some well-known writers needed no encouragement and had to be reined in – literally, in one case. The British Ambassador in Italy threatened to resign unless 'a certain eminent novelist' were restrained from 'riding into Rome on a donkey with all the circumstances reminiscent of Palm Sunday.'[8] Others contributed more productively. Caine, we can be sure, was inspired or encouraged to compile his anthology of heavyweights after the September meeting, and to prepare it for the American market. Another, warier, conscript was Thomas Hardy, who recalled, characteristically, the 'tragic cast' of the September sunshine that shone in upon the group of literary men at the meeting, all of them eager to help, but as yet 'unforeseeing' the extent of the awful events that were to come.[9] Hardy wrote a short patriotic lyric, 'Song of the Soldiers' (later retitled 'Men Who March Away'), as soon as he returned to Dorset, which was published in *The Times* on 9 September and – significantly for Masterman's envisaged American audiences – in the *New York Times* the next day. For Caine's anthology, he produced a 'Sonnet on the Belgian Expatriation', lamenting the flow of refugees from the 'ravaged street, and smouldering gable-end' of Bruges, Antwerp and Ostend.[10] He was not, as he told the novelist John Galsworthy – another Masterman conscript and Caine contributor – a natural writer of poems for causes, given to 'seeing the other side too much'. But he produced several new pieces for the British and American papers and agreed to countless requests from anthologists to reprint them free of charge, giving up 'every scrap' he wrote, as he told the publisher Charles Watts in 1915, 'to aid some charitable object that this brutal European massacre has rendered necessary.'[11]

Of the major literary forms, poetry, it was believed, had a special role to play in wartime. 'War and poetry owe much to each other,' declared the critic John Bailey in the *Times Literary Supplement* in October 1914.[12] From the first days of the conflict, traditional poetry, whether explicitly on the subject of war or not, was mined as a source of comfort, diversion, inspiration and national feeling. Civilians and soldiers alike lionized the British poetic inheritance as part of what made their nation superior to its foes. Sir Arthur Quiller-Couch, holder of the prestigious King Edward VII Chair of English Literature at Cambridge, gave his students an easy laugh in a lecture of November 1914 by mocking the German accent: 'The Germans are congenitally unfitted to read our poetry; the very structure of their vocal organs forbids it.'[13]

In a similar vein, the Oxford Professor of Poetry, Sir Herbert Warren, explained in March 1915 that the British were 'pre-eminently a poetical nation': no other modern country 'had a finer or richer poetical literature – not France, or Italy, certainly not Germany.' If the war were to be fought on poetry alone, Warren claimed, Germany wouldn't stand a chance:

> Put in naval language, they had one super-Dreadnought, the Goethe, a powerful ship, but hardly equal in guns or speed to the Shakespeare. They had two or three Dreadnoughts, the Lessing, the Schiller, [...] and a flotilla of minor vessels, but nothing like the number or variety of the English armament.[14]

Members of the Establishment, in 1914, were full of such pronouncements about the value of the native literature and its contribution to Britain's special destiny in the world.[15] Many of the soldiers who fought their war for them also believed, in as fervent a manner, in the significance of poetry as a means of national self-expression. Encamped in the trenches or behind the lines for long stretches, they read and wrote prolifically, ordering a steady stream of books to the Front. Individual volumes of Keats, Wordsworth, Blake, Browning and Housman made their way across the Channel, but anthologies too were hugely popular companions – especially Quiller-Couch's own *Oxford Book of English Verse* (1900), a chunky, thousand-page selection from across the history of English poetry, which, in Fussell's view, all but 'preside[d] over the Great War', shaping the way participants imagined and responded to it.[16] With its thin India paper leaves, the *Oxford Book* was just portable enough to be carried abroad in knapsacks or posted to the trenches, and because it contained the equivalent of many books in one, it was practical.

'You really couldn't very well carry more than one book at a time in your pack,' explains Private John Ball, the protagonist of *In Parenthesis* (1937), an epic poem about the war by the poet and former soldier David Jones. Many men, as Ball does in the poem, chose the *Oxford Book* as their 'one book'. Its pages, in Jones's telling, become stiff and dirty, 'abominably adhered, especially for split finger-tips'. In his trench bay, Ball opens it and begins reading the medieval Scottish poet William Dunbar's 'Lament for the Makers', an elegy for lost companions snatched by Death ('He has tane Rowll of Aberdene, / And gentill Rowll of Corstophine; / Two better fallowis did no man see'). Each stanza of the elegy ends with Dunbar's admission that he fears his own end: '*Timor Mortis conturbat me.*' 'There is no new thing under the sun,' thinks Ball, and closes the book.[17]

Soldiers' letters home, particularly officers' letters, show them drawing on poetry in order to process and communicate, in a language their non-combatant relatives would understand, what they were seeing around them.* Key literary passages, such as one from Milton's *Paradise Lost* on light and darkness, as Fussell has argued, became frameworks for the way many conceptualized their war.[18] Shakespeare, for obvious reasons, was an especially popular recourse. 'Death has no terrors for me in itself,' wrote Lieutenant Ernest Polack shortly before the Somme offensive in late June 1916, quoting Hamlet to make his point: 'If 'tis not now, 'twill be to come.' (It came three weeks after his letter.) Lieutenant Robert Wallace McConnell, sailing to Gallipoli in 1915, wrote to his father that the beauty of the night and the full moon had reminded him 'very much

---

* Simon Featherstone cautions that though poetry was 'seen as an appropriate response to war by all classes', the culture of pervasive, unapologetic literariness some historians have sketched wasn't always shared by private soldiers.

of the 5th Act in the *Merchant of Venice*,' and that this in turn had prompted thoughts of home. 'It's strange that beauty and loveliness seem to wake up in darkness and sadness.'[19]

Shakespeare and Milton were available to be quoted – ad infinitum – but they weren't around to write verse on the subject of this modern conflict. In their stead, living poets were urged to shoulder the burden of their inheritance, to produce work equal to the great historic occasion the war presented. Repeatedly, they were reminded of their symbolic importance and duty. 'A great work by an Englishman is like a great battle won by England,' Gerard Manley Hopkins told the future Poet Laureate Robert Bridges in 1886 (Bridges would respond to the call years later by publishing a wartime anthology).[20] The pronouncements of poets on the war were felt to carry as much weight – or more – than those of politicians and journalists, because while the latter concentrated on unpacking the significance of current events, poets were like visionary eagles, soaring ahead and looking to the future.[21] 'It is of the future that the world most anxiously desires to hear from its poets, from the seers whose privilege it is to look above and beyond the battlefield,' gushed the *TLS* in January 1915. 'Happy the nation,' agreed the *Times*, 'that in its fateful hour has a voice to "nerve its heart", to remind it what it has been, and what it is, to tell it to endure.'[22] This conviction persisted well into the war.* In 1917, the critic Edmund Gosse

---

* And into the next one. In his anthology *Other Men's Flowers* (1944), Field Marshal Wavell attacked modern poetry for its lack of 'vision': 'We – the rank and file – want leadership and encouragement from those gifted with power over words, not defeatism and depression. A poet is a man to whom vision is given beyond his fellows. Of what use is that vision if he expresses it in words unintelligible to all but a small circle, and doubtfully to them? The world soon begins to suspect that he has no vision, and is therefore no poet. And without vision, as the prophet said, the people perish. We might well have perished in this war without Mr. Churchill.'

chastised Siegfried Sassoon for the bitter tone of his new book, *The Old Huntsman*, anxious that its satires would adversely affect morale and 'relax the effort of the struggle'.[23] Poetry was a powerful weapon, and it had to be directed for the war, not against it. 'It is not for invective that we look to our poets in these days,' warned the *TLS*.[24]

In 1914, poets took up their responsibility in huge numbers. During the first three months of the war, just about every newspaper and journal in the country was swamped with enthusiastic sonnets and quatrains by established poets and first-time versifiers from the civilian population.[25] Very few submissions were rejected. The *St Helens Reporter* took in a poem entitled 'A Voice from Hell, Supposed to be from a German in the Infernal Regions' by one Bertha Brownsword, which began: 'After long years of lechery and sin / I died, and lo, to Hades came my soul…'[26] Uniformly patriotic and written in a high moral key, such verse made stirring reference to the past Christian and classical heroes in order to rouse the courage of Britain's present-day sons, urged them to go forth bravely just as they would on the football field, and vouchsafed that although the war would bring the nation great pain, suffering would cleanse and renew its spirit (a process presided over by God, who had, of course, already picked sides).[27]

Women poets – often wives or mothers of volunteers – contributed prolifically; working-class poets submitted to their local paper; Old Boys and university graduates published in school or college records; and the group of Establishment poets that Masterman had brought together (Hardy, Rudyard Kipling, G.K. Chesterton, Henry Newbolt and William Watson, among others) found a home in *The Times*.[28] *The Times*, indeed, seems to have borne the brunt of the 'virtual stampede into print', publishing its first war poem, Newbolt's 'The Vigil', on the morning of 5 August, mere hours after the declaration of war, and recording a year later in August 1915 that, ever since, 'a steady stream of verse has poured into this office every day.'* 'Last August we used to receive as many as 100 metrical essays in a single day, and, although the number declined as the war became a test of endurance, the stream has never run dry,' its editorial boasted wearily.[29] The *TLS* commented in October 1915 that the war had not yet produced the number of poems the Trojan War had done, 'but it is making them up quickly.'[30]

The general impression, as the critic Marion Scott noted in 1917, was of 'an enormous increase in poetical output', a 'voluminous *quantity*' that must surely contain, hidden within it, some 'first-rate *quality*'.[31] Other observers were less sanguine. The *Daily Mail*, which was responsible for publishing many of them, declared 'A Serious Outbreak of Poets' ('it is at least a possibility that Germany and England may have to call "stop the war" in order to stop the poets'); Hardy's wife, Florence, complained that on top of having to deal with the awful news, 'she did not reckon on the additional infliction of the newspaper poets & prophets.'[32] 'Mr. Dooley', a fictional Irish bartender who had a column in the Chicago press in which he made acerbic comments about international affairs, argued that the bombardment of innocent civilians by 'concealed batteries iv [of] poets' had made the war an even more frightful experience for the British public than it needed to be, and that several of the explosive fragments raining down on people's heads must surely be in violation of the Geneva Convention.[33]

In short order, the deluge of poems in the newspapers became a deluge of volumes of poetry, a trend encouraged

---

* The critic Harold Monro laid out the timeline: '*The Times* for August 5th gave prominence to verses by Henry Newbolt; on the 6th to a sonnet by William Watson; on the 7th R.E. Vernède occupied a large space, and on the 8th an expected but unfortunate poem by the Laureate took up its position.'

by publishers anxious to exploit the demand for war-related material and aware of the importance of looking patriotic.[34] Fears that book sales would decline during wartime proved unfounded. 'People were reading poetry as they had not done for many years,' Robert Graves wrote, recalling the climate that had enabled him to sell out two editions of his volume *Fairies and Fusiliers*.[35] Never before, 'in the world's history', as Gosse claimed in 1917, had there been 'an epoch which has tolerated and even welcomed such a flood of verse as has been poured forth over Great Britain during the last three years' – 'more than five hundred volumes of new and original poetry', according to his own records.[36] The real number was far higher. An authoritative bibliography lists some 2,225 men and women who published verse during the war, of which the great majority – four-fifths – were civilians.[37] There were similar trends in the United States, even before it joined the war in 1917, as poetry in the newspapers became increasingly war-focused and collections of war poetry sold in high volumes.[38]

The war anthology swiftly became the publishing enterprise of the moment. Caine's *King Albert's Book* was part of a wave: three anthologies responding to the conflict were rushed out in September 1914 alone, and twelve in 1915.[39] In January 1915, the *Athenaeum* reviewed nine recent collections, of which five were war anthologies. 'No one who [has] read these through can have any excuse for ignorance of the war poetry of England,' the reviewer observed tartly.[40] In August, *The Times* tried to get a grip on the situation by advertising an 'anthology of the anthologies' as a special supplement, reprinting sixteen of what it considered to be the best new war poems that had been published in its pages and subsequently snatched by greedy compilers.[41]

The fact that more poetry collections 'were rained down upon the heads of the British public than bombs from the Kaiser's zeppelins,' in one critic's words, isn't necessarily surprising. On the supply side, there were suddenly a lot of new poems about war that could be rehoused for profit, not to mention old ones by Shakespeare, Milton, Tennyson *et al.*, which were always available for reuse. And there was a demand to match: contemporary readers seemed to possess a voracious appetite for patriotic war verse.[42] But it also made sense in the context of the literary market in 1914. Heavyweight anthologies of traditional favourites, such as the *Golden Treasury* and the *Oxford Book*, remained hugely popular; but a vogue had also sprung up for slim anthologies of contemporary poetry, generated by the success of a publication of 1912, *Georgian Poetry*. In this collection, younger poets of the post-Victorian generation – Rupert Brooke, D.H. Lawrence, John Masefield and others – had joined forces to revolt against what they considered the archaic, sentimental values and styles they'd inherited from their elders.[43] Brooke's friend Edward Marsh, Winston Churchill's private secretary and a wealthy patron of the arts, shepherded the poets together and financed the volume, sending out a hundred advance copies to important people in the literary world. *Georgian Poetry* 'went up like a rocket'. Seven months after publication, it had reached its sixth edition; by the summer of 1914, its tenth.[44]

As individuals, the poets Marsh promoted might not have made much of a splash. Together, though, published in the same volume, they seemed to herald a new corporate strength in the poetry world. 'The literary health of an age is not to be judged by the occurrence of transcendent genius, but by the number and variety of its writers of excellence,' the *Westminster Gazette* observed in 1914. The collective counted for more than the individual: at no other time since the Elizabethan age, the *Gazette* argued (when not only Shakespeare but also Christopher Marlowe, Philip Sidney and Edmund Spenser had flourished as poets), would a book with the cohesiveness and strength of *Georgian Poetry* have been possible.[45]

Corporate publication of verse swiftly became the vogue, ushering in what has subsequently been called 'a great age of anthologies'.[46] Why risk publishing individually when you could publish together with likeminded fellows? The Georgians' success was the envy of other groups, as the poet Harold Monro recalled.[47] Ezra Pound's anthology *Des Imagistes* (1914), a key text of early Modernism, can be understood partially as a response to *Georgian Poetry*, envisaged, according to Marsh, as a kind of 'post-Georgian' project by poets 'who don't like being out of G.P.'. Pound subsequently produced three other anthologies, each seeking to carve out space for Modernist innovation.[48] Volumes and ventures multiplied. Within months of *Georgian Poetry*'s appearance, Marsh's poets were writing to tell him that they had been approached by other anthologists with plans for similar collections. 'There seems to be a number of anthologies in preparation just now,' James Stephens, one of the Georgians, observed to him in the summer of 1913. 'Whether your magical 6th edition is responsible for them or not I don't know, but I am contributing to three and have refused to contribute to ten.'[49] Everyone who was anyone was either anthologizing or being anthologized.

⚶

War benefitted the anthology and the anthology benefitted war. In 1914, both were good business. Patriotic publishers seized their moment: anthologies became the literary equivalent of poster campaigns, put to work recruiting volunteers, shaming shirkers and raising money for charitable funds. Like other forms of propaganda, they were almost exclusively civilian productions: compiled by civilians, marketed to civilians, and made up of work by civilians.* 'This is the book to take in the train just now,' the *TLS* wrote approvingly of *Remember Louvain!*, a 1914 anthology edited by the *Punch* journalist E.V. Lucas. 'Let us read the news from the front, and then let us turn to this book to give it higher value.'[50] Newspapers over the breakfast table, a book of poems for the train on the way to work: this was a vision of life with the guns heard, if at all, in the very far distance.

Patriotic citizens who purchased an anthology for their commute were entitled to feel that they were doing their bit for the cause. Publishers, uncertain about what the war would mean for business, saw that they could boost sales and cultivate a magnanimous public image by donating anthology profits to war funds – an arrangement enabled by the fact that many poets were willing, for similar reasons, to gift pieces and waive copyright. 'Give gladly, you rich,' ordered the poet William Watson on the opening page of a 1914 anthology, *Poems of the Great War*:

> – 'tis no more than you owe –
> For the weal of your Country, your wealth's overflow!
> Even I that am poor am performing my part;
> I am giving my brain, I am giving my heart.[51]

The idea, as the publisher John Lane explained in his collection *Songs and Sonnets for England in War Time* (1914), was that enthusiastic poets like Watson who wanted to 'give their brains' should donate each of their poems to one anthology

---

* In 1914, the idea of the soldier poet, or trench poet, now such an evocative symbol of the war experience, was yet to emerge. During earlier conflicts, poetry about war had been written by men and women at home, not by active troops, and it seemed reasonable to assume that this division been writing and fighting would hold.

only, to prevent 'any possible overlapping' and ensure that the public didn't encounter the same tired specimens over and over again.[52] Of course, there were only so many poems by famous names to go round, so duplication happened almost immediately. Newbolt's 'The Vigil' cropped up in both *Poems of the Great War* and *Songs and Sonnets*, as did Chesterton's 'France', and it was a rare anthology that was missing any of Kipling's 'Hymn Before Action', Hardy's 'Men Who March Away' or Binyon's 'For the Fallen' ('They shall not grow old…'). As the war went on and the stacks of anthologies multiplied, possessing a distinguishing characteristic became important: there were collections 'By Poets of the Empire' and 'By Women Poets of the Empire'; collections of elegies for the fallen; collections of poems on the war in the air and at sea.[53]

All were propaganda opportunities. In 1914, with recruitment top of the agenda, what mattered was pleading the war's cause and differentiating Britain's noble ambitions from Germany's vicious ones. Unlike Germany, poets argued, Britain wasn't interested in a war of aggression: she wanted merely to secure Belgium's freedom from the oppressor, defend her own people against the threat of invasion, and stamp out the strain of barbaric militarism in Prussian society.[54] Germany, it was claimed, had shown her true colours. 'Through Luxembourg and Belgium they are marching in their might, / They trample on the weak, / Our overthrow to seek; / They tear up every treaty, and they laugh at every right,' screeched the imperialist writer Ian Colvin in 'The Answer', printed in *Songs and Sonnets*. Another *Songs and Sonnets* contributor was clearer still as to whose fault the war was: 'If Europe must be crucified, / Not ours the guilt! Let it be known.'[55] Robert Bridges, the Poet Laureate, prefaced *The Spirit of Man* (1915), his high-minded anthology of English and French poetry and philosophy, with an incongruous rant about what he called 'Prussia's scheme for the destruction of her neighbours' and the unscrupulousness of the German people.[56]

Anti-Teutonic sentiments were evergreen, but they made for better propaganda if they could be backed up with particular examples of German aggression.[57] 'Shall thy fate, fair Lusitania, / Mark the climax of a mania?' exclaimed one poet in the aftermath of the torpedoing of the ocean liner in 1915.[58] Lucas's *Remember Louvain!* was rushed out in September 1914 to capitalize on the international press frenzy surrounding the looting and burning of the Belgian town of Louvain by German troops in late August. 'This little collection of poetry bearing upon the fineness and sacredness of the struggle which England is making,' Lucas declared, 'has been hastily brought together in the hope that it may have some quickening and stimulating influence in these times of national trial.' It was divided into sections with stirring titles ('Liberty'; 'The Call to Arms'; 'Great Hearts'; 'Great Deeds'), and opened with a letter by 'a little gentle lady, the wife of a clergyman', who declared piously that she was 'so glad to have a son to go', and only wished that she had ten sons, or could go herself. Captains Shakespeare and Milton were conscripted into the ranks of Lucas's poets: Shakespeare with 'King Henry's Rally' (otherwise known as the 'Once more unto the breach' speech in *Henry V*), and Milton with a sonnet that Lucas presumptuously retitled 'To the Germans at Louvain'.[59]

The republication of stirring sixteenth- and seventeenth-century poetry in a book about a twentieth-century war was not untypical. The fighting in Flanders, of course, had very little in common with Henry V's siege at Harfleur: gone were the gleaming swords, the banners and the decisive cavalry charges; in their place came machine guns, gas and the stasis of trench warfare. But the 'Agincourt ideal' – a popular understanding of what battle was like based on the distant past – provided a powerful dream of war that collections of poetry kept alive. Partly, this was a question of precedent. Traditional poetry about war, though sometimes violent and bloodthirsty, wasn't realistic in nature; it had always preferred to idealize, to invoke heroic battles and individuals from history or legend, rather than describing the situation on the ground. (Henry's speech at Harfleur is a good example, dwelling as it does on the legends of St George and Alexander.) This was as it should be, contemporary critics felt. 'Poetry has always preferred to see the heroisms of war and, as far as possible, not to see its brutalities,' J.C. Bailey wrote in the *TLS*. 'It is the very essence of [its] business to be magnifying mirrors of that fraction of our life which is great and significant.'[60] Civilian editors and poets in 1914 duly looked to history, finding the glories of the past far more inspiring than what they understood of the present.[61]

The effect, from the beginning, was to obscure the mechanized nature of the new war. Looking back on 1914 from the vantage point of 1940, the poet Edgell Rickword recalled the 'virgin ignorance' of highly educated portions of the civilian population, 'inured to colonial wars, pacifications of backward peoples,' but with no real sense of the destructiveness of modern European warfare.[62] Those who read the poetry of the patriotic anthologies could have been forgiven for imagining that the struggle against Germany was essentially a late-medieval crusade, or that rather than wading through muddy trenches, soldiers would be doing battle in galleons in the manner of Sir Francis Drake.

The most popular collections were like poeticized history textbooks, re-runs of the version of Britain's past that was taught in schools – a glorious unfolding story of chivalric derring-do, naval victories and civilizing missions to benighted foreign lands.[63] *Lyra Heroica* (1891), a much-reprinted collection of verse for boys, set the tone, bolstering notions of 'the glory of battle and adventure', 'the sacred quality of patriotism' and 'the beauty and the blessedness of death', via stirring poems by Shakespeare, Scott, Byron and Kipling.[64] Why imagine defeating an enemy when you could 'vanquish' him, or think of dying when you could 'fall' or 'perish' instead? Why think of the Front as a complex network stretching for miles, when it could be simply 'the field', recalling ages past when battles were fought by small armies on a single patch of ground?[65] Why look to the recent past and the humiliating defeats of the Boer War, when you could remember victorious Drake and Nelson?

Poems of the Great War, the anthology opened by Watson's stirring call, contained a typical selection of historical myths. There was a piece by the poet R.E. Vernède (who would go on to fight and die of his wounds in 1917), asking God to 'grant to us the old Armada weather'; a contribution by the popular writer Alfred Noyes, in which Britain is pictured embracing her destiny 'as her fleets cast off the North Sea foam'; and a poem by the playwright J.B. Fagan, in which Fagan reports excitedly that 'Old Drake is beating his drum'.[66] In *Songs and Sonnets*, the novelist Henry de Vere Stacpoole warned anyone foolish enough to 'dream that Drake is dead' to think again; while the *Punch* editor Sir Owen Seaman (one of Masterman's group of writers) urged young men 'Forth, then, to front that peril of the deep,' and referred shamelessly to the need to 'keep / The storied scutcheon bright' – as if anyone in 1914 would be fighting with a shield. (In the same volume, Francis Coutts went a step further and encouraged soldiers to 'draw thine own armour on' in order to 'ward the foeman's darts'; arrows had not been used in battle since the seventeenth century.) In 'The Call', another typical piece, Vernède transformed the whole nightmare into a chivalric fairytale, presenting the Germans as a bunch of 'ogres' jealously guarding the 'fair Princess' of civilization.[67]

Women Poets of the Empire (1916), meanwhile, edited by the poet Charles Forshaw, showed women writers – who would not have been exposed to *Lyra Heroica*, or to the typical public school education – still reading the same history books and dreaming the same dreams. Edith Mary Cruttwell's 'Gallipoli, May, 1915' reimagined one of the most disastrous campaigns in military history as a latterday Christian crusade against the Turks: 'Have patience yet awhile: / The Holy Wisdom's gates shall open wide / And the Cross blazon on the central dome.' In 'Forward, England!', Jane E. Pemberton returned dauntlessly to the seafaring theme: 'Think of Nelson, Howe, and Drake! / Britain's Empire is at stake.'[68]

Poems of To-Day, an anthology of 1915 that went through thirteen reprints before the end of the war, devoted a third of its pages to 'History' poems. In this section, Drake and Nelson were both present and correct, Drake several times. A pre-war piece by Noyes, 'The Moon is Up', captured the storybook mood of romance in which the war was fought in the public imagination:

> The moon is up: the stars are bright:
>   The wind is fresh and free!
> We're out to seek for gold to-night
>   Across the silver sea!
> The world was growing grey and old:
>   Break out the sails again!
> We're out to seek a Realm of Gold
>   Beyond the Spanish Main.[69]

Going into battle was an adventure: it was like voyaging (in spirit at least) back to the Elizabethan age, when the world was new and ripe for discovery and an unconquered 'Realm of Gold' still existed beyond the seas.* As such, it represented an opportunity for the display of courage and daring that had long been awaited. Noyes was not alone in believing that Britain had grown 'grey and old' during the later Edwardian years: there was a widespread feeling, among Tory commentators in particular, that the empire on which the sun never set was becoming sickly, decadent, in the manner of the Roman Empire shortly before its fall. It teetered on the brink of losing its standing in the world, threatening to collapse through military weakness and the slow moral and physical 'degeneration' of its people.[70]

War, on this view, was a welcome proving ground, a chance for Britons to test their strength and redeem themselves. 'I had hopes that England'll get on her legs again, achieve youth and merriment, and slough the things I loathe,' Brooke wrote from a military camp in Dorset.[71] Modern life left so little room for bravery, for youthful heroism or glory; this was a chance to reclaim forms of acting and being in the world that had seemed consigned to the history books. 'The language of romance and melodrama has now become true,' enthused the Oxford Greek professor Gilbert Murray in 1915. 'We have entered ourselves upon a heroic age.'[72] War promised a second chance – a breath of fresh air, a body of clean water, a fire to purge and renew. For too long, as Binyon declared in a contribution to *Poems of To-Day*, Britons had been corrupted by 'fatted sloth and fevered greed'; war would force them to rally and 'cast aside [their] slumbers', to face their 'hour of peril' and emerge 'purified'.[73] 'Our national follies and sins have deserved punishment,'

---

* Elizabethan fever persisted into the next war. In 1943, the poet Robert Nichols suggested that 'the courage of the Somme had a peculiar quality, a "bravery" in the Elizabethan sense, which was never recovered.'

Bridges wrote gravely in *The Spirit of Man*. Only in 'the brave endurance of sufferings' was there hope, and a chance to reform. 'We can even be grateful for the discipline.'[74]

From the beginning, it was assumed that civilians, not soldiers, would write the poetry of the war. Civilian poets had the freedom to look at events without being distracted by the exigencies of the battlefield; their distance from the conflict, contemporaries suggested, was what equipped them to view it as part of the larger story of the British nation.[75] 'The finest poem which the war has so far produced,' declared the *TLS* in October 1914,

> is the Poet Laureate's 'Thou Careless, Awake!' with which *Poems of the Great War* rightly opens. For Mr. Bridges, like Wordsworth, has in him the unfailing tranquillity of those who see passing events *sub specie aeterni*.[76]

Bridges, in other words, by virtue of being at a considerable remove from the action, had achieved the 'tranquillity' which, according to Wordsworth, was necessary for the expression of poetic emotion. Rather than seeing events up close, and living them as they happened, he saw them '*sub specie aeterni*', or from a high and universal perspective, like an eagle on a lofty perch. Precisely because he wasn't there, he could communicate the grandeur and significance of the historical moment.

Not everyone agreed with this view of things. From the earliest months of the war, there were those who disliked the lofty attitudes that the civilian anthologies represented. The dissenting voices were few, but strident. In September 1914, the poet Richard Aldington declared that no good verse could possibly come out of the war, because civilian patriotism encouraged forms of behaving and thinking that were fatal to artistic expression. 'This kind of social feeling does not produce art,' he declared in Pound's literary magazine, *The Egoist*.[77] His contemporary John Gould Fletcher, writing in the same magazine, found the contents of the anthologies 'hopelessly banal'. Rather than putting the reader 'face to face with the imaged reality', or seeking to convey an emotional truth about the war, they dealt in 'indefinite abstractions', apparently interested only in 'giving the Allies laurels and the Germans a black eye'.[78]

Harold Monro, Marsh's collaborator on *Georgian Poetry*, observed that the problem was a lack of specificity. 'We get an impression of verse-writers excitedly gathering to *do something* for their flag,' he wrote; but

> As soon as they begin to rack their brains how that something may be done in verse, a hundred old phrases for patriotic moments float in their minds. [...] We feel as if we would gladly hold the heads of some of our poets down to their verses, and force them to answer us: 'Did you feel this? If so, have you written it as you felt it? Are these phrases your own? Are they the result of your experience?'[79]

J.C. Squire, another Georgian, agreed that abstraction was to blame. The phrases that filled the 'shabby patriotic verse' of the anthologies, he argued in 1914, weren't the poets' own; once upon a time, they might have been vivid and particular, able to gesture to some living reality in the world, but now they were mere formulae, interchangeable like building-blocks. 'Put England down as "knightly", refer to "Trafalgar" (which has always done good service as a rhyme to "war"), summon the spirits of Drake and Grenville from the deep, introduce a "thou" or two, and conclude with the assertion that God will defend the Right – and there's the formula for a poem.'[80]

Two things, in short, were wrong with the poems in the civilian anthologies. In the first place, the scenes they described and the emotions they tried to express were general, abstract, which made them vague and unconvincing. In the second place, they relied too much on history, on Trafalgar, Drake, the crusading knights and all the other ghosts that stood in the way of a credible reckoning with the present. From a modern perspective, the solution – that civilian poets should step back and allow the fighting men to try writing the poetry of the war – seems obvious enough. But it was not obvious in 1914, and only slowly began to be raised in literary discussion. When the critic John Middleton Murry reviewed a new anthology of French war verse, *Les Poètes de la Guerre*, in May 1915, he tentatively suggested that it was superior to similar English productions because much of the poetry it contained 'was composed in the fighting line'.[81] A few months later, Arthur Clutton-Brock made the case in the *TLS* that civilian poets would never be able to write effectively about things they'd never seen, and that those who tried to do so were merely pretending, 'assuming the character' of the kind of writer they felt they ought to be. 'Art, unfortunately,' he wrote, 'will not come when duty calls.' Powerful verse about war could only be the fruit of experience. 'It is out of himself, out of his own real states of mind, that a poet can make his poetry.'[82]

❧

The creation of the soldier poet as a species was Rupert Brooke's posthumous work.[83] When the news of Brooke's death on the romantic Greek island of Skyros (he was en route to Gallipoli) reached England in April 1915, there was an outpouring of public mourning. Churchill, encouraged by Marsh, set the tone, writing a lavish obituary for the *Times* in which he stressed Brooke's patriotism, selflessness and serenity in the face of death. Newspapers which had, as Graves wrote, 'slated [Brooke] as an impudent undergraduate versifier when his first poems were published a few months before,' now 'paid him heroic honours.'[84] Shortly after his funeral, the war sonnets he had composed in 1914 (including 'The Soldier', with its opening 'If I should die, think only this of me') appeared in print, the text supervised by Marsh and accompanied by a dashing sketch of the author.

The unprecedented popularity of the volume in the months and years that followed came from the fact that it reflected, straightforwardly and beautifully, the ideas about war that the civilian poets had made orthodox.[85] Using the conventional high language of honour and sacrifice, Brooke claimed that fighting and dying would be the making of Britain's young men, cleansing them of the grubby, decadent habits into which they had fallen in peacetime. Their country would be made both richer and purer by the gift of their young lives laid down freely. If the message of Christian sacrifice needed to be made any plainer, it was hammered home on Easter Sunday 1915, when the Dean of St Paul's Cathedral used 'The Soldier' as the text for his sermon on Christ's death and resurrection.*

---

* 'Some Dean quoted Brooke's soldier-sonnets [...] from the pulpit of Westminster Abbey,' Monro reported airily, perhaps deliberately getting the venue wrong. The poet Charles Hamilton Sorley commented in April 1915 that 'The Soldier' had been 'over-praised'. '[Brooke] is far too obsessed with his own sacrifice, regarding the going to war of himself (and others) as a highly remarkable sacrificial exploit, whereas it is merely the conduct demanded of him (and others) by the turn of circumstances where non-compliance with this attitude would have made life intolerable.'

Brooke's *1914, and Other Poems* was reprinted twenty-five times before the end of the war. Its impact on soldiers from all social classes was powerful. A few serving men, as Brooke's own example shows, had written, or tried to write, poetry on the war as early as 1914; but now many began attaching lyrics and sonnets to their letters home, writing in a recognisable, Brookeian idiom.[86] Publishers, as before, were not slow to pick up on the commercial possibilities of the trend. With increasing regularity, slim volumes of verse by aspiring poets in uniform began to appear on the market, adorned, if the soldier in question happened to die before he was published, with an epitaph and a wistful author photograph in khaki. Posthumous volumes could expect a particularly large readership. 'The spectacle of "whom the gods love" dying young has always fascinated mankind,' Squire observed darkly in the *New Statesman* in 1916. To die young, in battle, was to be touched with a heroic glow that the living could not share. In the eyes of readers at home, nothing could be more beautiful and pathetic than verse written by men who knew that their death might be just around the corner, and whose poems, consecrated by the fact of their mortality, stood as eternal 'memorials of promise unfulfilled'.[87]

The 'unofficial publisher in general to the poets of the British Army' was William Galloway Kyle, a journalist and editor who ran a publishing firm under the trade name of Erskine Macdonald. Kyle, responsible for multiple volumes of soldier poetry, was well aware that death in action equalled marketability.[88] He wrote the preface to his first major anthology, *Soldier Poets: Songs of the Fighting Men*, in September 1916, as battle continued to rage on the Somme, and in the final paragraphs he took the opportunity to cast a mournful shadow over the names of several of the poets he published:

[Here are] poems by Lieutenant Geoffrey Howard and the late Lieutenant W.N. Hodgson, M.C., who left Oxford to join the Army and found a grave in France in July last. [...] And as this volume is going through the press we hear that Sergeant Streets, who was a miner before he enlisted in August, 1914, and Corporal Robertson have been 'missing' since July 1. This is their priceless legacy. No further introduction or commentary is needed.[89]

Kyle recognized that allowing the tragic facts of these deaths to speak for themselves had more emotive power than any 'commentary' of his own he might add. But there was another reason why he opted to stand back and let the soldiers speak. The idea behind his anthology was the one that critics had begun tentatively to articulate in 1915: that serving soldiers, because of, rather than despite, their proximity to the action, might give a better and more honest account of battle than civilians could. Kyle was a civilian himself, but in the interests of promoting the work of his poets, he let rip at a caricatured version of the typical civilian versifier:

The soldier poets leave the maudlin and the mock-heroic, the gruesome and fearful handling of Death and his allies to the neurotic civilian who stayed behind to gloat on imagined horrors and inconveniences and anticipate the uncomfortable demise of friends.[90]

Civilians, Kyle claims here, are those who 'stay behind' (implicitly, by choice), while their braver relatives and friends march away and fight for them. They 'gloat' at the thought of dangers they can only 'imagine'; they get a kind of 'maudlin' pleasure from dwelling on the idea of death (the merely 'uncomfortable' 'demise of friends'); and they embody, in their fears and neuroticism, the fatal spirit of 'decadence' which, according to their own poetry, has weakened Britain and her empire.

This is an early version of an argument that would exert a huge influence over the way subsequent readers thought about war poetry, and about who was best fitted to write it.[91] No longer was the question merely an aesthetic one – a debate about whether distance from war or proximity to it made for a better perspective, or whether traditional words or new ones were more suited to the subject matter. Now, the question was also a moral one. Civilians, Kyle's preface suggested, did not deserve to write the poetry of the war because they were hypocrites: cowardly stay-at-homes who took secret delight in imagining the gruesome scenes at the Front, while maintaining piously that the Germans had to be crushed and that the young men they sent to their deaths were accomplishing a high and noble purpose.

As the journalist E.B. Osborn observed in his anthology *The Muse in Arms* (1917), the largest collection of soldier poetry produced during the war, there were myriad differences between the ways serving men thought about Britain's war versus how non-combatants tended to think about it. In these differences, the moral superiority of soldiers as men and patriots was plain to see. Soldiers, unlike civilians, didn't hate the enemy: as good Christians, they looked on the Germans 'in sorrow rather than anger'. In contrast to many at home, they weren't jingoistic flag-wavers, given to bragging about how much they loved their country. They 'never put to their lips the brazen trumpet of self-advertising patriotism.' Instead, they fought and gave their lives selflessly for the sake of the next generation; and the officers among them, in particular, as Osborn wrote, were distinguished for their supreme spirit of 'comradeship', the 'all-engrossing love' they displayed for their men.[92]

From this list of approved qualities – the dislike of jingoism, the inclination to pity, the affection for one's fellow men – we might be forgiven for expecting something like the poetry of Wilfred Owen in the soldier anthologies Osborn and Kyle published.[*] But there was nothing of the kind. Owen came to public notice too late to have been included, but Sassoon, Graves and Isaac Rosenberg, each of whom we might expect to have been given several pages in the 1917 volumes at least, were either absent or briefly featured. (Sassoon was represented – in Osborn – by just two poems, one of which, 'Absolution', was in an early, Brookeian manner, which the experience of the trenches soon stamped out of him.) Overwhelmingly, and despite the fact that the poets they included had actually been to war and seen action, the volumes contained verse that had a lot more in common with the contents of the civilian collections and the ideals of Brooke's sonnets.[93]

Soldier Poets, Kyle declared, showed above all the 'exultant sincerity' and 'unconquerable idealism' of the fighting men. 'The spirit that has turned our soldiers into poets,' he wrote, 'is the spirit of the V.C. – brave and debonair.'[94] Osborn went a step further, arguing that the poetry in his collection illustrated the 'sunny joyousness' that had, according to a misty-eyed observer, been seen on the faces of British troops before the Battle of Arras in 1917. 'They were not merely unafraid; they all gloried in the thought of the great ordeal to come. [...] They went up in sunshine and with singing to win undying fame and deathless gratitude.' Soldier poetry was remarkable, Osborn said, for its

---

* Kyle published two high-profile collections: his second, *More Songs by the Fighting Men*, appeared in December 1917.

'blithe, unconquerable courage', exhibiting the astonishing capacity of the 'British warrior' to 'remember the splendour and forget the squalor' of war. It was an 'enduring expression' of willing sacrifice: an assertion, qualm-free, of the righteousness of the war and of Britain's moral place in it.[95]

The majority of the soldiers Kyle and Osborn published belonged to the officer class, and came from public school and university backgrounds. Others had received more perfunctory educations, but were enthusiastically self-taught. Both groups produced poetry that was as much steeped in romantic history and myth as that of their civilian elders, drawing on the same evocative reference points. The enemy was once more the 'foeman'; trenches were 'the field'; the weapon of choice (in imagination at least) remained the 'sword'. There was much talk of fighting for 'Honour and the Cross'.[96] Osborn's preface brought up both Agincourt ('Agincourt, Agincourt! / Know ye not Agincourt? / Oh, it was a noble sport!') and the adventurous Elizabethans, comparing his soldier poets to 'modern Sidneys and Raleighs'. Drake's exhausted shade was yet again dragged up to serve as an example.[97] In Kyle's anthology, Lieutenant Joseph Courtney, an army surgeon, imagined dead soldiers resurrected with their 'lances raised', as if fresh from a medieval joust. The prime minister's son, Herbert Asquith, wrote an elegy commemorating 'a clerk, who half his life had spent / Toiling at ledgers in a city grey', who realises his romantic dreams by dying in battle: 'His lance is broken; but he lies content / With that high hour, in which he lived and died.'* He goes, of course, 'to join the men of Agincourt.'[98]

---

* Edmund Gosse was not taken by this poem. 'I read him [Asquith] forward and I read him backward, and I see nothing. If he were a Herbert Snooks [...] no one would ever have looked at his verses. And people say that the "age of privilege" is passed!'

The soldier anthologies, to a greater degree than their civilian counterparts, were also steeped in Greek and Roman myth. At late-Victorian and Edwardian schools, boys encountered war as culture before they encountered it in the flesh: war meant Achilles, Patroclus and Hector on the plains of Troy, a set of visions, words and ideals, a page in a book of poetry. Homer's *Iliad* was where they learned what it meant to go into battle, and in the epitaphs of Simonides they learned about death and glory. In public schools in particular, the teaching of the Classics was central to the curriculum: most headmasters were classicists by training and encouraged the devotion of a disproportionate number of classroom hours to the subject. As the historian Peter Parker has shown, the most attractive of the ideals it enshrined – courage, manliness, comradeship, patriotism, nobility in death – were embraced by masters and pupils as models for living, and, once war broke out, as models for dying too.[99] After 1914, when reality had taken the place of books, literary experiences continued to entangle stubbornly with real ones. 'We've been gliding through a sapphire sea, swept by the ghosts of triremes and quinqueremes,' Brooke wrote delightedly from a ship bound for the Aegean in 1915.[100]

The textbook for this way of viewing the world was J.W. Mackail's *Greek Anthology* (1890; revised in 1906), a selection of Greek verse which, in the years before the war, was ubiquitous in school classrooms. (Cyril Connolly called it 'one of the sacred books of the inner culture' at Eton, 'the very soil of the Eton lilies.'[101]) Its evocative introduction offered a vision of ancient Greek culture, Greek attitudes to mortality in particular, which stuck in the imagination. In death, Mackail wrote, 'the Greek genius [had] its fullest scope and most decisive triumph': its poetry made beauty out of something terrifying, transforming the deathbed moment into a calm and painless leave-taking.

'There is none of the horror of darkness, none of the ugliness of dying; with calm faces and undisordered raiment they rise from their seats and take the last farewell.' To die in battle, according to this vision – especially, to die young, in perfect health and unspotted by the corruptions of life – was to live forever, and win lasting fame. 'Being dead they have not died,' ran one of Mackail's translated epigrams, 'since from on high their excellence raises them gloriously out of the house of Hades.'[102]

Whom the gods love die young. The fact that Death had a habit of sweeping away 'the finest and most beautiful things the soonest', as Mackail put it, became a point of honour in elegiac war writing.[103] 'This life has closed at the moment when it seemed to have reached its springtime,' Churchill observed in his obituary of Brooke, lamenting the loss, but, with an echo of Mackail, also suggesting that there was consolation in the thought of losing something before it had faded and withered.[104] Fighting men seemed to 'consecrate' themselves to death 'out of a feeling of the fullness of living', as the poet Robert Nichols wrote: the act of dying was perceived as 'a sort of flowering'.[105] It made England flower too. 'Happy is England in the brave that die,' declared John Freeman in a poem for Marsh's wartime *Georgian Poetry* volume (1917): 'Happy in all her dark woods, green fields, towns, / Her hills and rivers and her chafing sea.'[106] The springtime of sacrifice was the eternal springtime of the land.

Versions of this idea came up repeatedly in the soldier anthologies, where they formed part of the larger notion of war as a theatre of courageous sacrifice. In *Soldier Poets*, Kyle anthologized Dyneley Hussey's 'Youth', a poem whose imagery seems to come straight out of Mackail's fated Greek universe ('Short is the time, / O flower, and full of storms; / The summer sky is dark with warlike forms'); and Sydney Oswald's 'The Dead Soldier', in which the 'goodly harvest' and 'golden grain' of a lost soldier's life are 'garnered in' before time (autumn in spring). On a similar theme, Kyle chose Oswald's 'Dulce et Decorum est pro Patria Mori', an elegy which – unlike Owen's famous, bitter poem of the same title – adopts with complete sincerity Horace's sentiment about the sweetness and rightness of dying for one's country: 'Full soon they died, yet made / A name of lasting glory.' Among his selections, too, were classically-inspired poems by soldiers who had not come from public school backgrounds, but shared the same Greek ideals. 'Danger and Death were as wine,' Private H. Spurrier exults in his contribution to *Soldier Poets*; 'glory is ours, we have won her.' In 'Youth's Consecration', Sergeant J.W. Streets, a miner before the outbreak of war, declares that he will 'go to death calmly, triumphantly': 'We are Olympian gods in consciousness.'[107]

The idea of going to one's death calmly – Mackail's vision of a gentle, 'undisordered' departure – stands behind the many representations in the anthologies of dying as falling into a slumber, like 'lights out' in the boarding school dormitory. This was, perhaps, a necessary transfiguration of the hyper-violent reality; but, as Nichols observed, it managed to transfigure reality a little too successfully. 'They [civilians] couldn't understand anything,' he remembered a fellow-officer telling him incredulously, recounting the story of how he had been away from the Front in a civilian hospital and tried to convey some of his experiences to his companions. 'My pals hadn't been blown to bits by trench-mortars. They had "fallen in France" and one gathered that the falling was soft or, if it wasn't, well, that just meant an extra halo.'[108]

Fictions like these had a profound appeal. The soldier anthologies were popular both with civilians who found in them confirmation of everything they wanted to believe about the war, and with serving men, for whom they offered both inspiration and a kind of escape. It was likely no coincidence that several of them appeared in the aftermath of the Somme, when what they had to say was most powerfully desired and needed.[109] *Soldier Poets* was twice reprinted before the end of 1916; by 1919, Osborn's *Muse in Arms* had gone through five impressions.[110] Owing to the wartime paper shortage, which tended to discourage ambitious ventures unless they were likely to be huge successes, all the collections were major publishing events and heavily advertised. Kyle's two volumes were triumphs of marketing: they were published bound in cloth for the civilian market, and, separately, in a specially designed 'trench edition' for the troops. Owen was among those who had a copy of *More Songs by the Fighting Men* delivered to him at the Front.[111]

Kyle's preface to *More Songs* provides a sense of the excitement with which his first anthology was greeted. The selections in *Soldier Poets*, he wrote, had inspired

> many articles, sermons, and speeches, including an address by the President of the Board of Education. [...] No literary work of our day has possessed so much genetic force or been of greater influence. It was well said that 'Soldier Poets' was of greater service to the Allied cause in America than many Blue Books and specially prepared statements.[112]

The claim that *Soldier Poets* had done more to get the US into the war than any official British propaganda document is difficult to verify. But the anthology certainly made an impression at home. Readers remarked on the 'fresh spring of life' that fighting men, under Kyle's aegis, had breathed into English poetry.[113] Marion Scott spoke for many when she explained that what she admired most about the collection was its fidelity to the past as well as the present. The best of its poems demonstrated, she wrote, an old-fashioned 'nobility of thought': 'the clear-eyed faith and complete self-surrender which make so many men in our Army comrades of the Paladins of old.'[114]

In literary circles, Edgell Rickword recalled, the arrival of *Soldier Poets* 'caused a certain flutter': 'there were bold speculations on a renaissance of English poetry to be attributed to the moral stimulus of the war.' *The Telegraph*, in a thrilled review, called the phenomenon of soldier poetry a *'miracle'*, declared outright that verse-writing had been *'reborn in the throes of war'*, and praised Kyle's chosen poems for 'their fecundity and their power'. The anthology had the right kind of ethos, the reviewer felt: like the war itself, a modern 'great Crusade', it was an inspiring appeal to 'chivalry and hardihood and moral fervour'.[115] Gosse, writing in the *Edinburgh Review* in 1917, took a similar view, effusing about the 'beautiful gallantry' of soldier poetry and the poignancy of youthful mortality in language that wouldn't have been out of place in Mackail's Greek anthology. 'On many of these poets a death of the highest nobility has set the seal of eternal life,' he observed. 'They were simple and passionate, radiant and calm, they fought for their country, and they have entered into glory.' The most extraordinary among them, he suggested, could not possibly have done anything but die young: they were men of 'our old, heroic type', soaring beyond a time and place they were too great for. Death merely 'quenched' them.[116]

The idealizing representations of the anthologies had done their work.

In November 1914, in the midst of the initial war anthology boom, John Gould Fletcher, the Imagist poet, wrote a pair of articles for *The Egoist* in which he suggested that anthologies were likely to be a pernicious influence on attitudes to the war. Beyond the sheer badness of the poetry they contained (which he spent a lot of time on), he claimed that they encouraged – and modelled – a kind of groupthink, bringing together poems that shared a common attitude. 'Curiously enough, the next "poem" in this peerless assembly, by Henry Newbolt, expresses precisely the same sentiments,' he observed of the contents of *Poems of the Great War*. 'Have the poets taken to spying on each other?'[117] By virtue of their selection principles, anthologies encouraged the writing of poetry that had nothing to do with modern warfare, and were complicit in preserving the ignorance of volunteers as to what they were really signing up to. The patriotism they exuded was of a cosy, self-reinforcing kind ('Oh, scented soap, chocolate boxes, the village smithy under the spreading chestnut tree, and all the rest!'), and constructed by the usual misleading, arcane diction – 'storied scutcheons', and so on.[118] Anthologies, Fletcher suggested, were at bottom profiteering ventures, even when they were framed as being for charity. *Songs and Sonnets* was 'a book of Britannia wares' designed to line Establishment pockets.[119]

Both the charge of groupthink and the suggestion of a profiteering motive would recur in subsequent years. In 1917, even Gosse, who had so much admiration for soldier poetry, had to admit that, beyond a few starry exceptions, the publishing climate had encouraged 'a mass of standardised poetry made to pattern', 'uniformly meditative, and entirely without individual character'. Among the civilian poets, the situation was especially bad: he noted 'a family likeness which makes it impossible to distinguish one writer from another', a common 'horrible confidence in England's power of "muddling through"'.[120] Middleton Murry, reviewing the fourth volume of *Georgian Poetry* in 1919, argued that one of the reasons it was such an inadequate response to the war was the uniformity of its contents. 'The corporate flavour,' he wrote, 'is one that we find intensely disagreeable.'[121]

Safety in numbers, it was recognized, allowed both bad poetry and greed to flourish. 'Many young authors acquired spurious reputations under the cloak of Patriotism,' Monro wrote in 1920: 'these might, in fact, be called War Profiteers.'[122] Riding and Graves sneered at wartime collections in their 1928 *Pamphlet Against Anthologies*, categorizing them as a species of 'trade anthology' (that is, a collection treating poetry 'as a commodity destined for instructional, narcotic, patriotic, religious, humorous and other household uses'). War anthologies dealt, Riding and Graves said, in the 'marketable sentiment' roused by moments of national crisis, using the power of this sentiment to mask fabrications and omissions in the version of events they put forward. 'That the War was technically won by weight of numbers and munitions after a gross display of atrocities on both sides – all this is history. But the anthologist and his poet have no more respect for history than for poetry.' The anthologies were cynical 'barometers of fashion', they concluded, exploiters and creators of popular ignorance.[123]

Writers at the Front who despised the sentimental view of the war weren't slow to blame it on poetry and the anthology boom. 'God! How I hate you, you young cheerful men,' exclaimed Lieutenant Arthur Graeme West in a poem of 1916,

> Whose pious poetry blossoms on your graves
> As soon as you are in them, nurtured up
> By the salt of your corruption, and the tears
> Of mothers, local vicars, college deans,
> And flanked by prefaces and photographs
> From all your minor poet friends –[124]

This is an attack on a specific literary event: the elegiac soldier-poet collection, characterized by its 'cheerful', 'pious' poetry of self-sacrifice (think of Osborn's description of the 'sunny joyousness' of the verse he'd collected); its fetishization of poets who die in action (poetry 'blossoms' on their 'graves' the minute they are 'in them'); its sentimental paratexts ('prefaces and photographs'); its roots in a hypocritical civilian culture of weeping 'mothers, local vicars, college deans'. In December 1917, Owen wrote about the same fashionable lies in his poem 'A Terre':

> This bandage feels like pennies on my eyes.
> I have my medals? – Discs to make eyes close.
> My glorious ribbons? – Ripped from my own back
> In scarlet shreds. (That's for your poetry book.)[125]

Here, just as in the soldier-poet anthologies, there are morbid classical allusions: the feeling of the bandage across the speaker's face, 'like pennies on my eyes', recalls the mythic Greek custom of placing coins on the eyes of the dead to pay the ferryman on the river Styx. But the soldier in question is not dead, and not on his way to Elysium; he's just 'blind, and three parts shell'. Likeness, here ('This bandage feels *like* pennies on my eyes') reminds us of difference, of the gulf separating real experience from myth: the fact that something is like something else is another way of saying it isn't the same. Greek mythology, Owen suggests, is less an illuminating analogue for the war than a means of transforming or obscuring it; and literary allusions are part of the problem, part of the mass of seductive images and ideals ('medals'; 'glorious ribbons') that anthology poetry sells. 'That's for your poetry book.'

Owen's wartime reading supplied him with abundant material for these kinds of ironic attacks. In *Poems of To-Day*

(1916), a copy of which he owned, a note from the editor instructed readers to listen out for 'the passing-bell of Death', ringing delicately in the poetry of Brooke, Binyon and Newbolt. Owen repurposed the phrase in the bitter opening lines of his 'Anthem for Doomed Youth' (1917), observing that few in Flanders heard any bells when they died: 'What passing-bells for these who die as cattle? / – Only the monstrous anger of the guns.'[126] His 'Dulce et Decorum Est', from the same period, fed off both Sydney Oswald's pious 'Dulce et Decorum est pro Patria Mori' in *Soldier Poets*, and Corporal H.J. Jarvis's poem of the same title in *More Songs*. The connections suggest that he reserved much of his anger for a particular target: not the hypocrisy of the civilian population (though he attacked that too), but the hypocrisy of his fellow soldiers, who ought, as he saw it, to have known better. What he had in his sights wasn't patriotic myth-making *per se*, but myth-making in this war by serving poets who weren't interested in telling the truth about their experience, and by anthologists who encouraged their magical thinking.[127]

For some enemies of the patriotic war anthologies, the most effective way to hit back was to beat the anthologists at their own game. Towards the end of the conflict, collections began to appear which stood in opposition to the standard soldier-poet volumes, critiquing them by showing in practice what an adequate artistic response to the war might look like. *Wheels* (1916–21), edited by the poet and critic Edith Sitwell, was a rebellious, anti-Establishment anthology series for new verse, whose first number appeared shortly after the bloodbath of the Somme. Sitwell and her brother Osbert, who had seen action and been wounded in 1915, were pacifists and loathed both the enterprise of the war and its conduct.[128] The 1916 and 1917 volumes in their series were saturated with the war, with images of it and moods drawn from it, but not in a way that most literary reviewers either expected or liked.

The young poets *Wheels* showcased, the *TLS* commented disapprovingly, were 'on the whole, dour and morose'; they seemed to see 'nothing bright in the present, and no bright hopes in the future.' Unaccountably, they appeared to have refused 'to do any of the brave things associated in popular literature with the title of poet – to lead, to uplift, to amaze.'[129] They disliked 'mothers, generals, heroes, the Church', the middle-aged and elderly in general. They dealt in awful images of 'iron and blood', 'clinging mud', decay and decomposition, bodies hanging from trees like 'blackened rag[s]', worms waiting underground – a world of horrors propped up, they argued, by the 'monstrous myths' of the patriotic anthologies and their poetry.[130] As one of their number, Helen Rootham, observed, war had been able to kill so many because its nature had been disguised: boys had joined up expecting a 'Great Adventure', but found something else entirely.[131]

Two years on, Bertram Lloyd, a conscientious objector and political campaigner, published *Poems Written during the Great War* (1918). Lloyd's anthology brought together writers from several countries, united in their hatred of conventional patriotism: some were civilians and some serving soldiers, as he explained in his preface, but all loathed the 'cant and idealization and false glamour' that had 'overlaid' the reality of the conflict. War, being profoundly unpleasant, Lloyd argued, needed people to invest in pretending it wasn't, to romanticize it and dress it up: it was, of necessity, 'the most showy fact in human history'.[132] The poems he collected were bent on stripping back the spectacle and the glamour, and did so through their diction – spare, plain, ugly – as well as the scenes they depicted. 'This bloody steel / Has killed a man. / I heard him squeal / As on I ran,' wrote Wilfrid Gibson baldly in 'The

Bayonet'. Words could not be trusted: it was better to keep them to a minimum.

In 'They', Sassoon – to whom Lloyd devoted several pages – put the comfortable myths of the anthologies into the mouth of a pontificating old bishop. 'When the boys come back / They will not be the same,' the bishop remarks sagely to his congregation, 'for they'll have fought / In a just cause.' When 'the boys' do come back, their version of events is somewhat different:

'We're none of us the same!' the boys reply,
'For George lost both his legs; and Bill's stone-blind;
Poor Jim's shot through the lungs and like to die;
And Bert's gone syphilitic...'[133]

As the choice of the bishop character suggests, Lloyd and his poets blamed the war and its prolongation on the 'grand old men' of the political and ecclesiastical establishments, the 'radiant, pink, well-nourished Anglican[s]', the 'genial' and 'cruel' armchair patriots, who liked to make 'noble toothless' speeches while dispatching their grandsons to France.[134] The last four years, terrible though they had been, had at least shown up the 'moral bankruptcy' of this statesman class for what it was. Young men had been betrayed by their elders into giving themselves to a false cause, then lost their youth to 'utter disillusionment and cynicism', in Lloyd's words. His anthology expressed, above all, the alienation of the young from the old, or the young-who-were-no-longer-young from their former selves. 'We would be young, be young, once more,' one of his poets, the German Heinrich Hutter, lamented.[135]

This, of course, is the version of the war – the sense of waste, the revulsion against conventional patriotism, the ironic awareness that the best had been sacrificed by the worst – that we recognize now. By 1930, a little over a decade after the appearance of Lloyd's anthology, it had become orthodox, consolidated by the publication of outspoken war memoirs by Graves and Sassoon, growing admiration for Owen's poetry, and the influence of Frederick Brereton's *Anthology of War Poems* (1930), a collection which, even more than Lloyd's, foregrounded critical, disaffected trench poetry above the songs of the old 'melodious patriots'.[136] Calling civilian poets 'silver-haired swashbucklers' and 'poetical armchair-warriors', as Lloyd had done rebelliously in 1919, was, by the end of the 1920s, positively conventional, at least in younger circles.[137]

What's perhaps surprising is how long it took to get there. In 1918 and 1919, Lloyd didn't expect to be widely read or understood. 'The fact that this collection of poems,' he wrote in his second anthology, *The Paths of Glory* (1919), 'contains so little in any way tending to glorify the idea of War in general, will perhaps seem strange to some readers.' Few people wanted stark realism: in the years immediately following the war, the general need was for reassurance that the hundreds of thousands of deaths had been worth it, that sons and brothers had died for ideals and traditions that were still live, and which would have more meaning for their loss.[138] In this climate, Brooke remained the most popular soldier-poet (perhaps, the most popular poet) by some distance.* While Sassoon's *Counter-Attack* was given mixed reviews in July 1918, Brooke's *Collected Poems*, published the same

---

* Julian Grenfell, famous for 'Into Battle' (1915), his poem celebrating the visceral 'joy' of combat, came a close second. The *Saturday Review* commented in July 1921: 'Can his [Sassoon's] warmest admirers pretend that posterity is likely to rank anything of his with that wonderful song of Julian Grenfell's, like the passionate trilling of the larks in the air above "No Man's Land"? No, they cannot.'

month, was heralded and then reprinted sixteen times in the course of the next decade.[139]

Anthologists, now arrogating to themselves the great task of memorializing the war, felt no pressure to change their methods. They brought out new collections that looked very much like the old ones: in 1919, George Herbert Clarke published a massive two-part *Treasury of War Poetry*, in which he held up for admiration 'patriotism, courage, self-sacrifice, enterprise, and endurance', and reserved special praise for Binyon, Newbolt, Watson and Brooke; a year later, there was Jacqueline Trotter's *Valour and Vision: Poems of the War*, in which Trotter reprinted the old favourite sea-pieces and battle-pieces, took very selectively from Sassoon and Graves, and professed to show 'the honour of our Nation's purpose in the Great War'.[140] More than twenty years later, in the midst of another war, when Field Marshal Wavell – who had fought and lost his left eye at the Battle of Ypres in 1915 – made a collection of his favourite poems, *Other Men's Flowers* (1944), the names were the same: Julian Grenfell, W.E. Henley, Kipling, Newbolt, Brooke; Herbert Asquith with his lance-toting volunteer.[141] Such books 'saw their task as an urgent saving up of England's heritage,' as the critic Alexandra Harris has put it, an effort, in time of war, to pack up and keep close what might otherwise be lost.[142]

In 1912, with the arrival of *Georgian Poetry*, anthologies had represented the future. During the war years, they seemed future-looking still, leading the turn away from civilian verse and towards a new kind of poetry written from the battlefield. But their focus remained resolutely on the past. They suffused popular literary culture with Christian and classical values of self-sacrifice, which expedited the creation of a volunteer army, and allowed the trench experience to be reimagined as a part of an unbroken historical continuity. The majority of serving soldiers who published verse stuck to these values. The vast majority of readers, unmoored by bereavement, held fast to them too.[143] 'Old habits of thought and feeling die hard,' Rickword wrote in 1940, 'especially when they are reinforced by all the influence of the social forces which resent change.'[144]

In 1919, Osborn, building on the popularity of his *Muse in Arms* anthology, published *The New Elizabethans*, a set of short biographies of well-known poets who had 'fallen' in the war. As the title suggests, he presented his subjects not as modern soldiers but Renaissance men, bold, exuberant Drakes, Raleighs and Sidneys. In the languorous Edwardian years, he explained, such men 'had a fear that the age of adventurous living was over for ever.' But 'then came the war, and personality was matched with opportunity.'[145] It was what everybody wanted to believe. In Osborn's jubilant vision, the war hadn't been a tragedy, though it had taken many youthful lives; it had been what those lives were made for.

6

POLITICS

Communism and the Anthology (1932–62)

*N*ew Verse no. 1 (1933), the first number of the most influential poetry magazine of the decade, opened with a section simply entitled 'WHY'. In it, the editor, Geoffrey Grigson, set out his reasons for founding a new poetry periodical in what he called 'such an ulcerous period as our own'. His aims, he said, were literary and highbrow: to provide a home for 'respectable poems' which wouldn't otherwise appear in print, and to try to halt somewhat the process of 'vulgarising' which he perceived to be underway in the arts. What Grigson wasn't interested in, he insisted, was politics. *New Verse* would belong 'to no [...] politico-literary cabal'; if it encouraged bomb-dropping, its bombs would be of a strictly metaphorical kind, aimed at 'masqueraders' and 'big shot reviewers'. There would be no political rhetoric, no speechifying, no platform. 'The object of *New Verse*,' he wrote, 'needs expansion in no complex or tiring manifesto.'[1]

It might seem strange that Grigson felt the need to declare that he was not writing a manifesto, and that his literary magazine wasn't a political organ in disguise. But the readership he envisaged in 1933 would have seen nothing odd in the connection between poetry and politics, and in the assumption that, ordinarily, new undertakings in the literary world would be accompanied by a quasi-political declaration. Since the appearance of the Italian poet Filippo Tommaso Marinetti's *Manifesto of Futurism* in 1909, in which Marinetti had announced the birth of a new art movement, avant-garde projects in art and literature had launched themselves by forceful manifestos, setting out how they intended to transform – if necessary, by destroying – their present cultural moment.[2] 'The essential elements of our poetry shall be courage, daring, and rebellion,' Marinetti had written. 'There is no beauty except in strife. No masterpiece without aggressiveness. Poetry must be a violent onslaught upon the unknown forces.'[3] Marinetti followed his first manifesto with a string of others, prompting the emergence of rival artistic movements all launched with angry declarations. *Des Imagistes* (1914) was a 'group manifesto', its creator, Ezra Pound, declared. *Blast* (1914), a manifesto for the Vorticist movement, contained lists in violent block capitals of things and people the Vorticists – Pound, Wyndham Lewis, Henri Gaudier Brzeska – didn't like: the Victorians, the Futurists, the weather. 'We are Primitive Mercenaries in the Modern World,' Lewis declared cryptically.[4] In 1922, with some reason, John Middleton Murry observed that 'most of the famous statements on style [...] are protests.'[5]

Early twentieth-century literary and artistic manifestos aped stylistic features of the political manifesto: its short, direct sentences; its bold lists of declarations; its cultural diagnoses and suggested remedies. In their politics, though, they often broke with the socialist history of the manifesto form, which had come into being as a distinctive genre of political text with Marx and Engels' *Communist Manifesto* (1848).[6] Lewis, for instance, made a point of declaring that 'We are against the glorification of "the People",' and that

Blast was interested in 'THE INDIVIDUAL' rather than any one social class.[7] In 1933, however, when Grigson set about putting together the first numbers of *New Verse* and writing his pointed anti-manifesto, new literary ventures tended to be either tacitly or outspokenly left-wing in their politics. By ejecting politics from his magazine, Grigson was well aware that what he was really doing was ejecting socialist politics. The word 'new' in *New Verse*, he argued in the magazine's second number, didn't imply a 'deterministic', Marxist view of history: it meant 'only fresh, contemporaneous, new written'. Newness didn't have to be political, and neither did the magazine's contents. 'If there must be attitudes,' he added grudgingly, 'a reasoned attitude of toryism is welcomed no less than a communist attitude.'[8]

Grigson might have wanted to publish both sides, or to publish no sides, but when it came down to it he couldn't: the writers whose work he admired and wanted to see in print were, almost to a man or woman, political and left-wing. To a degree unprecedented in British literary history, a large majority of the poets and novelists of his time had laid their partisan cards on the table, and many combined growing political consciousness with activism. 'Verse will be worn longer this season and rather red,' quipped the journalist Hugh Gordon Porteus in 1933.[9] The Thirties literary generation shared a set of attitudes which had developed, often acutely, out of 'the great social, political and moral changes going on around them.' They were marked as writers by the experience of growing up in the bitter years of the First World War and its aftermath, and by the social and political extremes of the era in which they reached adulthood. In the early 1930s, 'a series of events took place that cracked the world of the 'twenties beyond repair,' as one of their number, John Lehmann, put it.[10] The situation at home and in Europe seemed to be approaching crisis. At the lowest point of the Depression, in the summer of 1932, there were three and a half million unemployed in Britain; the Labour Party, on which the hopes of many were pinned, had collapsed; and, inspired by Mussolini's programme in Italy and Hitler's rise to power in Germany, Oswald Mosley's bands of Fascist blackshirts were beginning to be seen on the streets.

In such circumstances, as contemporaries noted, the 'forcible intrusion of social issues' into the individual consciousness seemed to make adopting a position and being public about it not so much a choice as a necessity. 'The mere statement of social realities today,' wrote the poet Stephen Spender in *New Verse* in 1937, 'involves one in taking sides.'[11] The question was considered to be an especially urgent one for writers and other artists. As Cecil Day Lewis, a poet and devout Communist Party member, explained in 1937, capitalism in its later stages was a hostile environment for culture and those who made culture: under its 'reactionary' and 'repressive' structures, freedom of expression would 'die by inches'.[12] You simply couldn't be 'an intellectual and admire Fascism', the writer Cyril Connolly argued, since to approve of Fascism was to approve of 'the intellect's destruction'.[13] One reason so many British writers lined up to express their support for the Republican cause during the Spanish Civil War (1936–9) was that they feared a victory for Franco's Fascists would mean the end of artistic freedom. The struggle, as Spender and Lehmann argued in their anthology, *Poems for Spain* (1939), was a cultural as well as a political one, a fight to save 'the conditions without which the writing and reading of poetry [would be] almost impossible in modern society.'[14]

Writers could respond to the imperative to take sides by becoming politically active: by writing pieces for free, signing petitions and giving to funds; joining the Communist Party, travelling around the country giving talks at local meetings and speaking to workers; even, from 1936, joining one of the International Brigades in Spain.* But for poets and novelists, taking sides was also a question of literary style. On the page, if nowhere else, writers encouraged themselves and others to commit: to be clear, take a position, say something and mean it. 'The equivocal attitude, the Ivory Tower, the paradoxical, the ironic detachment, will no longer do,' declared 'Authors Take Sides on the Spanish War', a questionnaire designed by *Left Review* to test the strength of the *literati*'s political commitment.[15] After all, as the poet Louis MacNeice pointed out, a writer's 'first business' was '*mentioning* things': what a poem said about the world, and what kinds of life it touched on, was of paramount importance. Both he and Spender issued pleas for what they called 'impure poetry', poetry that was steeped in contemporary reality, holding itself accountable to moral and political, rather than merely literary, concerns.[16]

Here, beyond the importance of not averting one's gaze, there was a second, compelling, consideration: that political literature might not just be able to reflect the world it described, but change it too. If a certain kind of writing, clearly expressed and read by a large enough number of people, could make a difference in the anti-Fascist cause, surely it was a poet's responsibility to commit to producing it.

❈

* However, professions of activity and unity could sometimes be misleading. The membership of the British Communist Party peaked at just over 18,000 in 1939; many major literary figures of the decade, including Auden, MacNeice, Isherwood and Orwell, never joined. As for Spain, though prominent writers did volunteer and fight, it has been estimated that over 80 per cent of the Britons in the International Brigades were members of the working class, not artists.

John Lehmann confessed to feeling 'bewitched' by the idea that 'writers and artists had a large role to play' in the political life of the decade.[17] His first book of poetry, *A Garden Revisited*, appeared in 1931, shortly after he'd left Cambridge and gone to work for Virginia and Leonard Woolf at their publishing house, the Hogarth Press. It caught the attention of Michael Roberts, a tall, bespectacled young poet and scholar who reminded Lehmann 'at once of a giraffe', and came to him with the idea of putting together an anthology. Roberts had in mind, he said, a collection that would be like a map of the generation he and Lehmann belonged to: it would present the emerging young poets of the decade 'as a *front*', as if they formed a coherent new movement.[18] Day Lewis, Spender, W.H. Auden, William Empson, Julian Bell, Lehmann himself: all were under thirty-five, part of a generation 'deeply marked' by the legacy of the First World War, though they had been too young to fight in it; and all came, as Lehmann acknowledged, from 'much the same layers of English middle-class life', public school, Oxbridge. *New Signatures* (1932), by bringing them together and making 'high and confident claims' for what they had in common, was the first attempt in English literature to define a particular Thirties identity and diagnose the forces that had shaped it.[19] It took its title from a poem by Day Lewis, addressed to his friend Auden: 'I, who saw the sapling, prophesied / A growth superlative and branches writing / On heaven a new signature.'[20]

Newness was important to Roberts for two reasons: first, because it signalled a breach, a clear departure from what had gone before; and, second, because it made the young poets he had gathered together seem contemporary, hyper-modern, synonymous with their moment. In Auden and Day Lewis's ability to incorporate images from modern industrial life

– collieries, pylons, factories – into their poetry, Roberts saw a determination to grapple with the special difficulties of living in the twentieth century.* New, intractable social problems called urgently for fresh solutions; the times had changed, so poetry had to do the same, or relinquish its usefulness as a way of interpreting and explaining the world. 'We may appreciate the elegance of poetry written by men whose whole experience was different from ours, but we cannot accept it as a resolution of our own problems,' he argued in *New Signatures*. 'New knowledge and new circumstances have compelled us to think and feel in a way not expressible in the old language at all.'[21]

Not everyone liked this attempt to mark a generational shift. Grigson, in *New Verse*, called Roberts 'too conscious of "novelty", too aware that he is "modern",' apparently bent on dragging writers who didn't have a lot in common into a collective attempt to define, proleptically, what the Thirties was going to be about.[22] But Roberts and Lehmann believed that their contemporaries could be grouped together under the same flag: they seemed to share a definite, positive attitude to the social crises of their time, an investment in the redemptive possibilities of action and change. 'These new poems,' Lehmann wrote in a blurb for the book,

> are a challenge to the pessimism and intellectual aloofness which has marked the best poetry of recent years. These young poets rebel only against those things

---

* Later, Roberts would be less sure that employing such images counted as defining the modern age. In his *Faber Book of Modern Verse* (1936), he quoted the American poet Hart Crane: 'To fool oneself that definitions are being reached by merely referring frequently to skyscrapers, radio antennae, steam whistles, or other surface phenomena of our time is merely to paint a photograph.'

which they believe can and must be changed in the postwar world.[23]

The comment about pessimistic, intellectually aloof poetry would have been read by contemporaries as primarily a reference to T.S. Eliot's work, *The Waste Land* (1922) in particular – a poetry that had appealed to the immediate post-war generation in its detached, desolate way of seeing the world.[24] In his later, more comprehensive anthology, the pioneering *Faber Book of Modern Verse* (1936), Roberts reprinted extensive amounts of Eliot's poetry, including the whole of *The Waste Land*, for its influential 'development of poetic technique'.[25] But *New Signatures*, in 1932, demanded something different. Lehmann, in his autobiography, explained that the making of the book had coincided in his life with a period of intense political awakening: he had watched, horrified, as the Labour government fell in the General Election of 1931, and, influenced by Spender's reports of communism in action in Berlin, he had gradually moved 'further to the left', from socialism and anti-imperialism towards Marxism.[26] His hopes for *New Signatures* were related to his hopes for politics: he wanted to publish young, rebellious poets who weren't crippled by pessimism, and who seemed to believe in a connection between writing and action. 'The way out of the Waste Land was that which led into the Socialist International,' a later critic remarked.[27]

Roberts, in his preface, communicated a more cautious version of the same faith. He attacked poets of 'recent years' (Eliot again) whose persistent sense of futility left them at a 'hopeless disadvantage': younger men, he acknowledged, might 'sympathise' with their feeling of post-war disillusionment, but would not 'succumb to it'.[28] He insisted that there was such a thing as simple morality, and that 'efforts to root out

ugliness and evil' were 'necessary and valuable'; he argued that
though modernity had done away with absolutes, individuals
should still be 'prepared to defend and to suffer for their own
standards'; and he asserted that it was possible to have hope
for the future, in the full knowledge of what usually happened
to such hopes.[29]

Reviewers admired the new stance, which was taken as
uniting the young poets together as one. The 'purpose' of those
in *New Signatures*, the *TLS* commented approvingly in 1932,
was not to wallow in the depressing, negating feelings which
their 1920s predecessors had courted, but to fashion a new style
from their despair. 'A style involves a faith. It is a new kind of
faith as it is a new kind of style.'[30] We might compare here the
attitude of the art collector Samuel Courtauld, who composed
a 'private anthology' of his favourite poems in 1939, rejecting,
as unsuitable for the age, all verse he found 'self-centred' and
'introspective'. 'All the familiar futilities – pessimism, disillusion,
despair, exhibitionism, jealousy and cowardice – are especially
hateful in a time like the present.'[31]

Roberts' vision for socially engaged poetry in *New Signatures*,
unlike Lehmann's, was only tentatively Left in its politics.[*] He
called his contributors 'revolutionary', but didn't pin down
what their 'revolutionary attitude' was revolutionary towards,
and referred just once to communism, which he portrayed, not
very politically, as 'good citizenship', or a kind of Christian
solicitude for the welfare of others.[32] As events in Europe
gathered pace, though, his attitude hardened. *New Country*

---

[*] Samuel Hynes has observed, in the context of Auden's long poem
The Orators (1932), that apparently partisan works of the early 1930s
were often ideologically ambiguous, able to point either Left or Right. In
Roberts' preface, words such as 'evil', 'standards' and 'faith' don't have
to lean just one way.

(1933), his second anthology, appeared during the period of heightened anxiety and partisanship that followed Hitler's rise to power and the beginning of the suppression of leftist opposition in Germany. 'In reading it,' Lehmann wrote, 'one [could not] help being struck by the very rapid increase in the pace of the swing towards the Left.' Not only was its tone different, but it had dropped the less political contributors in *New Signatures* (William Empson, for one, was gone), in favour of recruiting a handful of 'bluntly revolutionary' new voices, including the Marxists Edward Upward and Charles Madge.[33] In its outspokenness, it seemed to have crossed the border that divided literature from propaganda, as some reviewers noted: it was a statement of literary intent, but also a political declaration.[34] Where the Futurists and Vorticists had co-opted the form of the political manifesto to make an intervention into the worlds of art and literature, in *New Country* Roberts brought the literary manifesto back in touch with politics – and with communist politics in particular.

However unsuitable a poetry anthology might seem to us as a vehicle for doing politics, in the Thirties it made sense. Beyond the fact that literature in general was believed to be a political matter, there was the fact that the anthology was a collective form: as a collaboration between writers, it offered a platform for marshalling like-minded individuals together under the same flag. Roberts opened *New Country* with a lengthy preface – his manifesto – in which he pre-emptively announced the end of capitalism. 'I think, and the writers in this book obviously agree,' he declared, 'that there is only one way of life for us: to renounce that system now and to live by fighting against it.' The old social order, he argued, was dying, and it was becoming clearer daily where the future lay. 'If our sympathies turn towards revolutionary change, it is not because of our pity for the unemployed and the underpaid but because we see at last that our interests are theirs.' To the smug middle classes ('you, the readers of the *Observer*, *The Times*'), he had advice, and a warning. 'We know that you have a stake in the present scheme of things, but you know as well as we do, that the smash will come soon, before you have time to retire on your savings. [...] How long will you go on talking as though your 1910 were coming back?'[35]

Halfway through his preface, Roberts seemed to remember that he was supposed to be talking about literature rather than political theory. 'How,' he enquired suddenly, 'is all this to affect our writing?' Drawing on a passage from the *Communist Manifesto*, in which Marx and Engels describe the moment when an enlightened portion of the bourgeoisie, seeing that the proletariat 'holds the future in its hands', breaks off to make common cause with the workers, he argued that it was up to middle-class writers to evolve a literary style able to cut across the social divide.[36] Here, the fact that he was producing an anthology, not a political essay, worked in his favour. By publishing poetry and fiction which, in various ways, embodied his ideas, he could illustrate what the new classless style might look like. His injunction to writers to remain 'intelligible', for example, made sense when read alongside a poem such as Rex Warner's 'Hymn', with its bold, clear refrain:

> Come then, companions. This is the spring of blood,
> heart's hey-day, movement of masses, beginning of good.[37]

Likewise, his call to novelists to 'turn for [their] subject-matter to the working class' was answered by a short story by T.O. Beachcroft, 'A Week at the Union', in which Beachcroft narrated, realistically and plainly, the death of a poor old woman in a provincial workhouse infirmary.[38] It was possible for *New Country*'s readers to take such fiction merely as fiction (though its politics wouldn't have escaped them), but in the light of Roberts' manifesto about style, it became something else: a glimpse of a new socialist art.

New Country, with its provocative statement of a collective programme, set the template for other literary-political anthologies. In 1936, Lehmann launched *New Writing*, a periodical for contemporary British and European fiction and poetry, opening with a paragraph headed 'MANIFESTO'. '*New Writing*,' this ran, 'is first and foremost interested in literature, and though it does not intend to open its pages to writers of reactionary or Fascist sentiments, it is independent of any political party.'[39] As reviewers weren't slow to remark, almost without exception *New Writing*'s submissions were 'written from a single point of view': that of sympathy with 'the workers'.[40] Its first number contained a story of Berlin working-class life by Christopher Isherwood; pieces by the communists Tom Wintringham, Ralph Fox, Edward Upward and Alec Brown; and one by the German-Jewish writer Anna Seghers, who had been arrested by the Gestapo and forced to flee to Paris.

In Letters of Red (1938), an unmistakeably communist anthology compiled by the writer Eric Allen Osborne, had splashed across its endpapers a vivid cartoon depicting Fascist censorship in Japan, Germany and Italy. Over the page was an epigraph from the prominent zoologist Sir Peter Chalmers Mitchell, who had recently escaped a Nationalist prison in Málaga. 'Fascism is a pathological condition, a disease of Society,' Mitchell wrote. 'Unfortunately, it is contagious. [...] I fear that a very slight change in economic conditions would produce the virulent phase even in England.' Each of Osborne's contributors, in what he described as a 'crusade against

Fascism', hammered home the same message. Communism was the only way out of the economic trap; Fascism, if not actively combatted, would spread. 'It Will Happen Here – unless...'[41]

In manifestos, words like 'unless' carry real weight: they gesture towards possibility, the hope of things being otherwise, attempting to will a future into being by envisioning it.[42] *New Country*, the reviewers noted, seemed to express a 'wish actively to influence others, [...] to point the way – apparently the Communistic way – to better things.'[43] Roberts' preface was full of future-facing rhetoric, prose that fell halfway between prophecy – confident, far-sighted – and something more like wish-fulfilment. Lehmann described its characteristic note as one of 'strain and impatience, almost of hysteria at times, about the urgency of the revolutionary situation.' In time, Roberts tells us, middle-class writers will see 'more and more clearly' that their interests are bound up with those of the workers; in time, their writing will become 'more and more' popularly intelligible; the demarcation between the old order and the new will become 'more and more' obvious.[44] 'More and more' might add up to something, but it's not clear what: a gap seems to obtrude between the situation that is envisaged and where the middle-class writer finds himself now.

Roberts, though, tasks writing itself, poetry in particular, with bridging the divide. Poets who believe in change, he claims in *New Country*, don't just 'hint at the attitudes of the future': their work actively 'helps to make' those attitudes by means of creative innovation. Writing, in the end, he argues, is what will 'make the revolutionary movement articulate', giving shape and voice to things that would otherwise be impossible to imagine. (In his *Faber Book* introduction, he admired Gerard Manley Hopkins, though no political revolutionary, for his ability to see and articulate questions other people couldn't yet perceive. 'The problem which is his today is the world's tomorrow.'[45])

Day Lewis believed that poetry was a kind of 'incantation', a magical process of naming and creating new states of mind.[46] In the language of the old, tired world, with its 'outworn forms and sentiments', the revolution was unimaginable, and therefore impossible: it was only by creating afresh – by fashioning new images, new forms, and re-investing language with energy – that committed writers would be able to articulate it and hasten its course.[47] 'Already now the old forms can no longer adequately reflect the fundamental forces of the modern world,' Edward Upward declared. 'The writer's job is to create new forms now.'[48]

Communist novelists and poets, Spender wrote in 1935, were distinguished by their ability to 'foretell' future possibilities, to explain what the world would or could be as well as what it currently was. Upward claimed that it wasn't possible to tell the truth as a writer unless you mixed faithfulness to the reality of the present with a latent awareness of what was to come. The 'greatest books', he argued, were those that managed to 'sense the forces of the future beneath the surface of the past or present reality.'[49] The poet and activist Nancy Cunard, whose writing was suffused with it, called this awareness 'an inner sense of probability'. 'No light word – Probability,' she noted in 1931. 'It links conviction with instinct, is almost instinct itself, is the feeling of coming things.'[50]

Cunard's great Thirties work, *Negro: An Anthology* (1934), was a glimpse into the future. A hyper-ambitious, sprawling collection of essays, poetry, music and photography by 150 different contributors, it explored the rich cultural history and political destiny of Black peoples around the world. In its nine hundred pages, photographs of African sculpture sat alongside documentary histories of slavery; discussion of the treatment of African nations by colonial powers framed Harlem Renaissance poetry and jazz scores; anthropological studies of language and religion were juxtaposed with excoriating commentary on ongoing race controversies, such as the trials of the Scottsboro Boys in Alabama.*

The '150 voices' in her book, Cunard noted in its foreword, included a number of Black writers.[51] The request for submissions she had dispatched in 1931 declared that she wanted, pre-eminently, 'outspoken criticism, comment and comparison' from Black scholars of politics, law, anthropology and the arts, whom she invited to document, factually and dispassionately, subjects that in the hands of white writers had tended to shade into exoticized 'romance or fiction'. Potential publishers were informed that 'no book like this has ever appeared before in the world, because of its character and representativeness.'[52] Among other prominent names, James W. Ford, the Communist Party USA's Vice-Presidential nominee in 1932 and the first African American on a presidential ticket, contributed an essay on 'Communism and the Negro'; the Harlem Renaissance poet Langston Hughes opened the collection with his poem 'I, Too'; the boxer Bob Scanlon wrote an essay on his career and the history of Black boxing. The sheer number of contributors, Black and white,

---

* In 1931, nine African American teenagers were accused of raping two white women in Alabama. All but one of them were initially sentenced to death, but this verdict was challenged in a series of high-profile appeals and re-trials over the ensuing years. The case unfolded as Cunard was working to compile her anthology. She became Honorary Treasurer of the British Scottsboro Defence Committee in 1931, raising funds for the cause. Her protest petition, the 'Scottsboro Appeal', demanded 'unconditional liberation for the innocent boys, and an end to lynchings and frame-ups'.

was part of the point. Struggle and protest, Cunard argued, were collective acts, and could be most effectively articulated in a book which was itself the work of many. What rang through the anthology, as she wrote in her foreword, wasn't a single note but a 'chord': 'the chord of oppression, struggle and protest', which might be either 'trumpet-like or muffled', but remained 'insistent throughout'.[53]

Cunard, a humanitarian and idealist, had no overarching party-political agenda. But her hopes for the eradication of race discrimination harmonized, in the 1930s, with the anti-discrimination programme of the US Communist Party. 'Progressive members of the race are aware that they must fight every way they can to advance,' she wrote in her foreword. '[They] have realised that it is Communism alone which throws down the barriers of race as finally as it wipes out class distinctions.' Several of the contributors to her section on US politics were card-carrying Communists, who denigrated what they called the 'murderous humanitarianism' of capitalist-colonial rule, and held up, as its opposite, a future 'Communist world-order' committed to race and class equality.[54] 'Oppressed and degraded' Black Americans, Ford, the Communist Party politician, argued in his essay, would see their economic conditions and political prospects transformed by the 'progressive and ennobling' power of revolution, and could model their activities on the example of Soviet Russia, where, he claimed, 'all races, colors and nations' had come together in a 'voluntary union' of proletarian solidarity. Cunard agreed that the Soviet Union had, as she put it, 'once and for all solved the "problem" of races,' managing to turn 'instilled conflicts into cooperation, wiping out the false concept of "inferiority".'[55] What the Soviets had achieved (or were believed to have achieved) under Stalin could be managed, her book argued, in the West, accomplished by the kind of pioneering alliance of voices and arguments represented in its pages.

When she tried to find a publisher for *Negro* in the early 1930s, Cunard struggled. For most traditional firms, her radical politics and attention to sensitive race questions made her manuscript impossible to take on. Eventually, the small, left-leaning London firm Wishart & Company agreed to publish her, but only on the condition that she paid the costs of production herself. When *Negro* appeared in 1934, it went almost unnoticed by the American press, where she had most hoped for positive notices; the single print-run of 1,000 copies failed to sell out.[56]

Cunard's difficulties point us towards one of the major anxieties that dogged leftist writers during the Thirties. As far as she was able, she pushed for copies to be sent to public libraries, so that the cost of the book would not be a barrier to low-income readers.[57] But, in practice, the kinds of people most likely to read her work were middle-class, progressive men and women like her: readers who spoke like her, thought like her, had come through public school and Oxbridge, and – since they had chosen to pick up her book – needed little convincing of the importance of the political issues at stake.

What was the point, middle-class writers worried, of trying to write for a working-class readership, if working-class readers never saw their work? A 'highbrow' poet, it was estimated in 1938, would be lucky to sell 800 copies of a book in a year, and his readers would come predominantly from within the ranks of the middle-class intelligentsia. Rather than speaking to an 'ideal working-class audience of [the] imagination', he would in fact reach enlightened members of exactly the suburban middle class whose values his poetry set out to attack.[58] Thirties poets put the blame for the situation on everyone but themselves. To a large extent, they claimed, it was the fault of the reviewers and critics, who were supposed to interpret literary works so as to make them more intelligible, but instead seemed to want to do the opposite, wilfully 'translat[ing]' poetry into a complex, theoretical language.[59] Then there was the fact that much of the poetry of the early twentieth century seemed to have driven away potential readers by dint of its sheer difficulty. Literature had become 'sectarian'; writers had grown comfortable addressing increasingly tiny cliques. In 1938, MacNeice quoted pointedly from Eliot's famous statement about the need for complexity in modern poetry. 'The poet must become more and more comprehensive, more allusive, more indirect,' Eliot had written. It was his job not to write to be understood, but to write against common understanding – 'to force, to dislocate if necessary, language into his meaning.'[60]

Style wasn't just style, it was politics. As Thirties writers saw it, the Modernists and the critics hadn't just driven a wedge between poetry and ordinary readers, they had also made it much harder for poets to have socialist principles and act on them. If left-wing literature, they argued, was to mean anything to the kinds of people – the unemployed, the exploited, the proto-revolutionary – whom it described and addressed, it had, somehow, to learn to communicate itself to them – to 'the widest possible circles of ordinary people engaged in the daily struggle for existence,' as Lehmann put it.[61] In an ideal world, Day Lewis argued, poetry, like fiction, would be 'popular', not 'exclusive' or 'esoteric'; it would be seen as 'everyone's business'. 'Words and poems survive if they are relevant to the experiences of many people in many places at many times,' declared the communist poet Charles Madge.[62] For Auden, too, one measure of poetry's success as an art form was the range of human experiences it could speak to. The ready association between poetry and rarefied genius was an unhelpful one, he maintained; literature was made, after all, of 'language – the medium of ordinary social intercourse', a basic fact it seemed to have forgotten.[63]

Where they could, poets and editors tried to show their readers that things were changing. The literary journalist Janet Adam Smith, in her anthology *Poems of Tomorrow* (1935), praised the political straightforwardness of Day Lewis and Spender, the way their poetry steered clear of 'obscurity' and didn't prevaricate about taking a side.[64] Roberts, similarly, devoted a large chunk of his *New Signatures* preface to assuring readers that his book would give no space to 'ambiguity', 'recondite allusions', show-off erudition or any of the other trappings of 'esoteric poetry'.* To be effective, he believed, even poetry at the cultural vanguard had to be comprehensible: 'A leader, though he may sometimes be compelled to go ahead to reconnoitre, must not be out of sight of his followers.'[65] He had chosen the writers assembled in his book, he said, because they worked in verse rhythms 'not alien to the normal movement of English speech', and used symbols and metaphors that would make sense to readers beyond their coterie.

The alternative to massaging the work of middle-class poets in a bid to prove that poetry had changed its spots was to publish new working-class voices. Lehmann's original title for *New Writing*, his literary periodical, was *The Bridge*, in view of its aspiration to close the gap between sections of culture – British and European, elite and working-class – that were usually worlds apart. His editorial approach, as he explained in his autobiography, had been to combine the writing of two

---

* In several cases, this involved massaging the truth. It was fair to say that William Empson, who had launched his career as a critic with a book called *Seven Types of Ambiguity* (1930), liked both ambiguity and erudition.

distinct 'teams' of contributors: those who, like him, came from a solidly middle-class, metropolitan background, and

> those, like George Garrett, B.L. Coombes, Leslie Halward and Willy Goldman, who started without any of these advantages, and when they wrote of mines, seamen, factory workers or East End tailors, were writing from the inside, out of their own experiences.* These I was particularly interested to encourage; it was, in my view, one of the main reasons for the existence of *New Writing* to break down the barrier between these and the other team, to provide a place of cross-fertilization of their talents.⁶⁶

In *New Writing* no. 2, there were contributions from 'leather-workers, plasterers, dock-labourers, seamen, wood-cutters, and tailors' apprentices'; in no. 3, there were stories, some informed by personal experience, of miners in the pits, men struggling on the dole, workers fighting in Spain, hunger marches against unemployment.⁶⁷

It was a seductive notion in the Thirties, the idea that a book, by calling attention to working-class voices and giving them as much space as elite ones, could imagine a future in which class distinctions were no longer meaningful. Osborne's *In Letters of Red* anthology brought work by Auden, Grigson and Upward into contact with a short play by a London taxi-driver, Herbert Hodge, and poetry by a former errand boy, Peter

---

* Garrett, Coombes, Halward and Goldman were particularly successful working-class writers encouraged into print during the Thirties. Garrett was a merchant seaman and labour organiser; Coombes was a coal miner; Halward was a toolmaker, plasterer and labourer; Goldman, whom Lehmann brought onto the *New Writing* editorial team, was a tailor and docker.

Lagger. *Poems of Freedom* (1938), an anthology compiled by the New Zealand journalist John Mulgan, printed little-known poems by historical working-class writers – Chartists, radical Irish poets, political balladeers – alongside Shakespeare, Milton and Blake, and recent work by Auden, Day Lewis, Rex Warner and Spender. The theme was political protest: the book was to be a 'record', as Auden wrote in its introduction, of 'what people in many different social positions, from a peer like Lord Byron to a poor priest like Langland, [...] have noticed and felt about oppression.'[68] By showing how similarly men from different social backgrounds had responded to injustice, it connected them together in a long tradition of victimhood and rebellion, showed their common cause.[69]

As the book's contents page indicated, the poetry of Langland or the Chartists could be co-opted to make a political point as readily as new working-class writing. In the two anthologies Auden compiled himself during the Thirties – *The Poet's Tongue* (1935), co-edited with John Garrett, and *The Oxford Book of Light Verse* (1938) – he sought to connect with ordinary readers by rehabilitating the popular poetry of the past. 'In spite of the spread of education and the accessibility of printed matter, there is a gap between what is commonly called "highbrow" and "lowbrow" taste, wider perhaps than it has ever been,' he noted in *The Poet's Tongue*. Closing it meant reminding readers that literature hadn't always been made by the cultural elite. Verse, he suggested, could be thought of at bottom merely as 'memorable speech', as jokes, proverbs or slang were memorable speech: and, as such, it could encompass any content, from the traditional, 'highbrow' themes ('the eternal verities'), to the completely ordinary stuff of everyday life, provided that it was in some fashion memorable. Poetry, like people, Auden said (with a typical touch of provocation), was capable of being 'profound and shallow, sophisticated and naïve, dull and witty, bawdy and chaste in turn'; it wasn't always concerned with life's Great Questions.[70]

Auden's contents pages mingled poems by supposedly 'highbrow', classic authors with folksongs, ballads, nonsense poems, riddles, sea shanties, Christmas carols, nursery rhymes and saucy ditties. In the *Oxford Book of Light Verse* – a very different kind of book, as its startled publishers soon came to realize, to the authoritative selections compiled by senior academics that had previously appeared under the 'Oxford Book' imprimatur – lyrics taken from Shakespeare's plays mixed with anonymous Shetland ballads; Pope's *The Rape of the Lock* consorted with the nursery rhyme 'Jack and Gill'; political songs rubbed shoulders with Edward Lear's 'The Jumblies' and 'The Owl and the Pussy-Cat'.[71] In *The Poet's Tongue*, selections were organised alphabetically according to the first letter of their opening word ('A carrion crow sat on an oak'; 'A farmer's dog leapt over the stile'), rather than by author or period, encouraging readers to think of them as part of the same jumbled, democratic community. Seamus Heaney described this approach as having about it 'a slight whiff of the counter-cultural'.*

Neither of Auden's books made explicitly socialist arguments or recommendations. His assertion, in *The Oxford Book of Light Verse*, that democratic societies would survive only if all citizens, not just the wealthy few, were 'fully conscious

---

* Heaney and Ted Hughes adopted the same method of arrangement in their anthology *The Rattle Bag* (1982). 'At the back of our editors' minds there was always the example of W.H. Auden and John Garrett's 1930s anthology *The Poet's Tongue*,' Heaney wrote in the *Guardian* (25 October 2003). 'Auden and Garrett had shown the way to combine street rhymes and Shakespeare songs and had generally democratised the heritage without in the least dumbing it down; and it was also from them that we got the idea of printing the poems according to the alphabetical order of their titles.'

and capable of making a rational choice', wasn't necessarily radical in its implications.[72] Left- and right-wing critics alike, nonetheless, found evidence of a clear political programme. Robert Graves sneered at the 'hypothetical proletarian reader' to whom *The Poet's Tongue* seemed to be addressed, suggesting that Auden, by being so 'dogmatic' in his politics, had dishonestly 'vulgariz[ed]' the poetry he'd collected.[73] Left-wing reviewers, by contrast, hailed the book as proof that Britain's poetic tradition had always included working-class voices. 'It is an anthology that claims that real English poetry has been shaped by the people in every generation,' observed Montagu Slater, the communist editor of *Left Review*. According to the American poet Louise Bogan, Auden and Garrett had succeeded in showing that poetry

> rises from the throat of whatever class, in whatever century. They have brought our attention back to the voice speaking in a landscape where trees bear laurel at the same time that fields grow bread.[74]

The 'landscape' of poetry, in other words, might be striated by class ('laurel' trees, symbolic of the high-cultural literary tradition, versus wheatfields, the province of the workers); but Auden and Garrett's book had proved that it was one landscape nonetheless. Their anthology supplied a bridge across the divide, a view of the scene comprehensive enough to take in the laurels and the fields at once.

❦

To the surprise, no doubt, of his editors at the University Press, Auden used his introduction to *The Oxford Book of Light Verse* as an opportunity to give readers a lesson in Marxist literary history. Marxists believed, he explained, that the kind of literature writers could produce was determined by the structure of the society they lived in. In pre-industrial England, when society had been, relatively speaking, simple, more homogenous and less stratified, poets and other artists had occupied a settled place in the life of their community: they had been sufficiently 'rooted' within it, as he put it, to be able to share its interests and shape its common culture. Many of the greatest achievements in poetry, he explained – Shakespeare's plays, for instance – had come out of such 'small, compact, homogenous communities'.[75]

From the beginning of the nineteenth century, however, as the economic structure of society grew more complex and small communities dispersed in favour of aggregating in great, sprawling cities, the relationship between the poet and his community had become less straightforward. 'Isolated in an amorphous society with no real communal ties, bewildered by its complexity,' Auden wrote, 'artists were driven to the examination of their own feelings and to the company of other artists. They became introspective, obscure, and highbrow.' They worked, typically, in isolation, mining their private feelings and experiences for material, and opted, increasingly, for introspective, egotistical forms in which to express themselves – the lyric poem, the self-exploratory novel, the autobiography. (All modern poems, Madge complained in 1936, seemed to 'begin with "I"'; all novels were really autobiographies in disguise.[76]) The process, Auden said, culminated at the end of the nineteenth century and the beginning of the twentieth in literary movements that divorced themselves, intentionally, further and further from the common language and interests of the social group. The result? 'Writing gets shut up in a circle of clever people writing about themselves for themselves. Talent does not die out, but it can't make itself understood.'[77]

Nonetheless, Auden argued, writing happened because people wanted – paradoxically – to be read and heard, to feel that they were in conversation with an audience who listened to them and understood them. 'They feel alone, cut off from each other in an indifferent world where they do not live for very long. How can they get in touch again?'[78] In his early poems and those of his contemporaries, there are images shaped by this paradoxical feeling of connection-in-loneliness, of watching on from the outside with complex feelings. In 'The Secret Agent' (1928), an unrhymed, disconcerting sonnet, Auden positions a 'trained spy', a solitary, estranged figure, in a web of broken connections: 'They ignored his wires: / The bridges were unbuilt and trouble coming.' Lehmann, in a poem called 'A Little Distance Off' (1935), imagines standing at a remove from a large mass of people, far enough away to observe how individual faces in the crowd blur into a single, perfect whole: 'You stand / A little distance off and cannot change / Your isolation for their many.'[79]

Such lines get their energy from reaching for what they cannot have. 'We shall not begin to understand post-war poetry,' Day Lewis wrote in 1934, 'until we realize that the poet is appealing above all for the creation of a society in which the real and living contact between man and man may again become possible.'[80]

That was the diagnosis, and the remedy that followed from it was that modern writers, if they wanted to reach a wider audience, needed somehow to reintegrate themselves and their work into the life of the community – to join the crowd, become part of things once more. Writing in a way that didn't involve being crippled by feelings of self-division meant subordinating oneself, wholeheartedly, to a larger collective, finding a way to 'sink the ego', in the contemporary phrase.[81] Marxist critics argued that this came about through politics: real commitment to the cause of the workers, learning how to accept the obligations and inconveniences of collective action, how to 'feel, think, and say "we", instead of "I",' as the writer Alick West put it. Not just, in other words, supporting the workers' cause from a position of detached bourgeois sympathy, signing petitions on its behalf or writing articles about it, but really joining it – 'abandon[ing] individualism for a consciously social life.'[82] 'The whole point of artists adopting a revolutionary position,' Spender explained, 'is that their interests may become social, and not anti-social.'[83] Writers suffered from an 'unnatural apartness', the novelist Storm Jameson argued, from 'the life of farmers, labourers, miners, and the other men on whom the life of the nation depends'; they had to learn how to reintegrate, to make their writing part of the general output of labour and energy.[84]

In practice, making common cause with the workers was difficult. With the exception of once-in-a-generation events, such as the First World War and the Spanish Civil War, which threw middle- and upper-class volunteers together with soldiers from all backgrounds, actually encountering and forming relationships with working-class communities was something bourgeois writers liked to talk about, but rarely did.[85] (Part of the appeal of both war and revolution in this respect was the fact that they were communal experiences: they represented the chance to be a cog in a very large and undeniably important machine.) Spender recalled meetings of the Writers' Association for Intellectual Liberty, at which members engaged in absurd games of one-upmanship as to who was 'most closely in contact with the working classes'.[86]

What writers could do, however, and without having to abandon the way of life to which they were accustomed, was to rethink the way they wrote in light of the new emphasis on the collective. What if the problem wasn't the way they lived their lives, but the literary forms they chose to express and order their ideas? Some kinds of prose or poetry, it was argued, were better suited than others to getting to grips with social, rather than individual, experience.[87] The communist novelist Arthur Calder-Marshall recommended that writers should try what he called 'composite' novels, or novel cycles, sprawling, epic narratives about the fortunes of a society rather than the life and times of a solitary protagonist.[*] The novelist Naomi Mitchison, in an abortive experiment, tried writing a book with the help of an advisory group of workers who did some of the same jobs as her characters, consulting them about the proper layout of a foundry and which swear-words she ought to use. (In 1936, the magazine *New Masses* printed her enthusiastic piece about the project under the title 'We're Writing a Book'.)[88] Jameson, following Orwell's approach in *The Road to Wigan Pier* (1937), declared that writers ought to be producing factual, documentary-style records of working life, which they should research by living and collaborating with the workers in question. 'It is not necessary – in a great many instances it would be impossible or undesirable – for a writer to work alone,' she observed. 'A writer living in a Nottinghamshire mining village could not possibly do his job properly without the help of confidential reports from the workers.'[89]

Poetry offered similar collaborative possibilities. MacNeice praised Auden's poem 'Night Mail', produced to narrate a documentary film about the overnight London–Glasgow postal train, because it was a good example of 'collaboration with other craftsmen'.[90] Then there was the 'Oxford Collective Poem', a project orchestrated by Madge in 1937, in which twelve current

---

[*] Such as the French novelist Jules Romains' *Men of Good Will* (1932–46), a vast, 27-volume novel cycle with a huge cast of characters, depicting French life and society over a period of twenty years: not the most straightforward example to follow.

Oxford undergraduates were tasked with writing a line each about life in their city. In a protracted series of stages, they integrated the lines they'd written into unified poems, passed around and edited the results as a group, then voted on what became the final product. Madge was proud of the repeatable, scientific quality of his 'experiment', as he called it. Poetry written to order by collectives, he suggested, differed usefully from regular, single-author poems, since the latter could 'only be written once, under an exceptional stimulus (love, alcohol, political passion etc.), by an exceptional person.'[91] The alchemy, in other words, that most people would have considered at the heart of imaginative writing – the effect of a particular, intense stimulus on a particular person, at a particular moment – was merely a handicap; what you needed was poetry that could be 'turned out continuously', by anyone and at any scale, as if on a factory production line.*

Roberts much preferred thinking in terms of 'we' and 'us', rather than 'I' and 'me', in his anthologies. 'New knowledge and new circumstances have compelled us to think and feel in ways not expressible in the old language at all,' he declared at the beginning of *New Signatures*. The epigraph he chose for the volume came from a poem by Day Lewis, full of the appropriate plural pronouns:

> Now our research is done, measured the shadow,
> The plains mapped out, the hills a natural bound'ry.
> Such and such is our country.[92]

'I' all but vanishes in *New Country*. 'Roberts in a long preface "usses" and "ours" as though he were G.O.C. a new Salvation

---

* Critics disapproving of the project were quick to insist that there was a difference between writing a poem and delivering a product. 'All true poems are *created*, not manufactured,' the poet D.S. Savage objected.

Army,' Grigson snarled in a review, comparing Roberts' habit of speaking plurally to the manner of an officer addressing his troops.[93] The statements the preface makes are characteristically collective. 'We must make clear our politics.' 'We're all in the same boat.' 'We're asking you to help us abolish the whole class system.' 'How is all this to affect our writing?'* Uses of 'I' slip quickly back into safety in numbers. 'I think, and the writers in this book obviously agree, that there is only one way of life for us.'[94]

Tacitly, all the 'we's and 'us's – a grammar of togetherness – are there to suggest what *New Country* and *New Signatures* argue explicitly: that the individual viewpoint is less significant than the viewpoint shared and believed in by the group. The 'essence of the communist attitude', Roberts claimed in *New Signatures*, lay in a simple 'recognition of the importance of others', and of one's own comparative unimportance in the larger scheme of things – one's place merely as a little 'cog' in a 'golden and singing hive', as Spender put it in an early poem.[95] Similar to the experience of fighting in the First World War, belonging to a political movement, in Roberts' eyes, offered something 'rare in our competing, individualist world': the opportunity to feel part of something larger than oneself, however uncertain in its circumstances and implications. Having missed the war himself, he cited as a formative experience a group expedition he had once undertaken as a student in the Jura mountains, when solicitude for the welfare of the group had overtaken whatever private discomforts he might have felt. 'Impatience and fatigue and personal delight and suffering disappeared, and I remember only, at the end of

---

* This was a common trope in Thirties political writing. The questionnaire Cunard put together for *Left Review* in 1937, 'Authors Take Sides on the Spanish War', was full of reassuring-sounding 'ours' and 'us's', designed to project the illusion of easy consensus. 'It is clear to many of us'; 'we are determined'; 'we wish the world to know'; etc.

each day's work, standing at nightfall on the last spur of the ridge, counting the tiny figures moving down the slope in sight of food and warmth again.'[96]

Bonding over a walking tour in Switzerland, of course, much like getting together with eleven fellow-undergraduates to write a poem, wasn't exactly the same thing as making common cause with the workers. The idea of the collective, in the hands of middle-class writers, had a tendency to become nebulous and symbolic, to shift fluidly into safer or more congenial realms of experience – team-feeling, public school-style comradeship, Christian self-sacrifice, a determination to leave no man behind.[97] Roberts may have commented grandly in *New Country* that his book served to show 'how some of us are finding a way out of the individualist predicament,' but few would have been convinced that collecting the work of various male middle-class writers in the pages of a book was the same thing as sinking the ego in a mass movement.[98] The subtitle he and Lehmann chose for *New Signatures*, 'Poems By Several Hands', is revealing in this context. 'By Several Hands', in the 1930s, would have struck an odd, old-fashioned note: it had been a popular title-phrase choice for anthologies and miscellanies during the eighteenth century. But since 'hand' could refer to a factory worker or manual labourer as well as to the hand that held the pen, it's likely that Roberts and Lehmann hoped to bring a particular set of associations to bear – to suggest, idealistically but disingenuously, that poets working together on the same book were like a crew of men on a job; that producing an anthology was a similar kind of labour to building a ship, or digging out coal; that everyone was part of one supreme, exhilarating, mass effort.

New Writing and *Left Review*, because they made a point of seeking out and printing the work of working-class writers, were perhaps the only literary enterprises that really got close to a version of collective action. *New Writing*'s first number, the *TLS* commented in 1936, though it contained stories and poems from many different perspectives, seemed to have a kind of unity to it: throughout, the idea of 'an effective brotherhood born between victims of oppression' was a theme. 'The oppression takes various forms – sometimes it is war, sometimes fascism, sometimes the social system,' the reviewer wrote, 'but always it is this sense of broader comradeships breaking through the hard shells of confining, destroying individualisms.'[99] Lehmann described *New Writing* as his contribution to 'the common effort we felt we were all engaged in' politically during the decade, capable of doing more, as an enterprise, than 'any poem – any poem that I could write – in the short time still left to us.'[100] His hope for it, which the *TLS* seemed to articulate, was that it wouldn't just portray 'comradeship', but, in an important sense, realize it too, by displaying the shared political convictions and humanity of writers across the classes. One of the 'confining, destroying individualisms' in its sights, that is, was the individualism of writing, and the isolation of individual writers – who, now, in its pages, could be transformed into members of a collective, political actors working together towards a common end.

What the finished copies of *New Writing* obscured, of course, were the difficulties Lehmann encountered in recruiting his working-class contributors: the advances he paid out to the serially unemployed to keep them in paper and ink; the reports he received from others of trying, unsuccessfully, to concentrate on their prose after long working days, surrounded by the squeals of children, the clatter of dishes, and 'all the other noises and smells that cannot be escaped in crowded tenement flats'; the loss of those men who, having found work, could no longer prioritize their writing; the ghosts of stories that did make it into his office, but had no time or opportunity to be edited and had to be cut.[101]

Only a few published pieces had life-changing consequences for their authors. Few were read or remembered in the years that followed. In the end, as Lehmann recognized, what really broke down social barriers wasn't well-meaning anti-Fascist literature, but war: the conflagration that enveloped Europe in 1939, like the one of twenty years before, had little respect for class.

❧

'By 1940,' the journalist Anthony Hartley wrote in 1963, looking back on the period, 'the thirties were no longer relevant.'[102] The decade's political ideals turned out to have short sell-by dates. In 1939, the Republican cause in Spain, invested with the hopes of a generation of left-wing intellectuals, was defeated, and news filtered through of the brutal actions of Soviet NKVD agents behind the lines. In the same year, the Nazi-Soviet pact, the grubby rapprochement of Stalin's Soviet Union with Hitler's Germany, prompted droves of British Communists to leave the Party. Simultaneously, what a later generation would consider as the 'rather melodramatic approach to politics' taken by Thirties writers was beginning to show the cracks: what had all the poetry, the essays and the novels actually achieved, beyond fervently expressing commitment and urging others to commit as well?[103]

Roberts, as early as 1936, had begun to back away from the vanguard, declaring that it was the prerogative of writers merely to see problems clearly, not to 'attempt the politicians' statement or formulation and vote on it.' 'Primarily poetry is an exploration of the possibilities of language,' he wrote in his *Faber Book* introduction. 'It might be argued that a too self-conscious concern with "contemporary" problems deflects the poet's effort from his true objective.'[104] Auden, in his introduction to *Poems of Freedom* in 1938, went off-message

1. Engraved portrait of Stephen College after an unknown artist (1795), picturing the artisan and Whig radical as a political martyr.

By Irish Oaths, & wrested Law I fell,
A prey to Rome, a Sacrifice to Hell.
My bleeding Innocence, for Iustice cryes
Heare, Heare, O Heaven for man my suit denyes.

POEMS

ON

Affairs of State,

FROM

The Reign of K. *James* the First,

To this Present Year 1703.

Written by the Greatest Wits of the Age,

VIZ.

The Duke of *Bucking-ham.*	Mr. *John Dryden.*
The Earl of *Rochester.*	Dr. *G——th.*
The Earl of *D——t.*	Mr. *Toland.*
Lord *J——s.*	Mr. *Hughes.*
Mr. *Milton.*	Mr. *F——e.*
Mr. *Marvel.*	Mr. *Finch.*
Mr. *St. J——n.*	Mr. *Harcourt.*
	Mr. *T——n,* &c.

Many of which never before Publish'd.

Vol. II.

Printed in the Year 1703.

2. Title page of the second volume of *Poems on Affairs of State* (1703).

3. Engraving by William Hogarth, *Credulity, Superstition and Fanaticism. A Medley* (1762), purporting to show the inflammatory effects of Methodist preaching.

4. Engraving of Thomas Percy, after a portrait by Sir Joshua Reynolds, showing him holding his 'MSS.', or manuscript of old ballads.

RELIQUES

OF

ANCIENT ENGLISH POETRY:

CONSISTING OF

Old Heroic BALLADS, SONGS, and other PIECES of our earlier POETS,

(Chiefly of the LYRIC kind.)

Together with some few of later Date.

VOLUME THE FIRST.

DURAT OPUS VATUM

LONDON:

Printed for J. DODSLEY in Pall-Mall.

M DCC LXV.

5. Title page of Thomas Percy's *Reliques of Ancient English Poetry* (1765). The Latin tag below the image of a harp amidst Gothic ruins reads: 'The work of bards endures'.

6. Mezzotint after a portrait by Archer James Oliver (1809), showing Vicesimus Knox, creator of the popular *Elegant Extracts* anthologies.

7. Hannah More, writer and moralist, painted at her desk by Frances Reynolds (*c.* 1780).

8. Chalk and pencil drawing of Francis Turner Palgrave by Samuel Laurence (1872).

9. Photograph of the Working Men's College in London, in the Great Ormond Street (Camden) location it moved to in 1857.

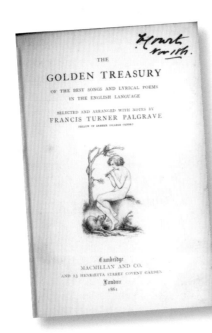

10. Title page of the first edition of *The Golden Treasury* (1861). The vignette, after a sketch by Thomas Woolner, shows the Greek god Pan at his pipes.

11. Photograph of Sir Arthur Quiller-Couch, editor of *The Oxford Book of English Verse* (1900), at home in Cornwall (1943).

12. A soldier balances rifle, pack and book as he reads in the trenches.

13. Front cover of *More Songs by the Fighting Men* (1917), edited by Galloway Kyle, the second of Kyle's popular anthologies of poetry by serving soldiers.

14. Photograph of Michael Roberts, editor of *New Signatures* (1932) and *New Country* (1933), reading a French poetry anthology.

15. Photograph of Nancy Cunard (1932), taken during her stay in Harlem, New York, as she gathered material for her forthcoming *Negro: An Anthology* (1934).

16. John Lehmann pictured alongside volumes of *New Writing*, the experimental, border-crossing anthology periodical he edited for Penguin from 1936.

17. Portrait of Adrian Henri by Edward Lucie-Smith (1970). Lucie-Smith edited *The Liverpool Scene* (1967), in which Henri appeared alongside Roger McGough and Brian Patten.

18. Roger McGough (left) photographed as part of his comedy/music trio The Scaffold (1968). The other two members were John Gorman and Mike McGear (Paul McCartney's brother).

19. Portrait of Brian Patten by Edward Lucie-Smith (*c.* 1970).

20. Allen Ginsberg reads his work to a crowd of 7,500 at the International Poetry Incarnation, Royal Albert Hall, London (11 June 1965).

21. The 'alive and rowdy and pop' front cover of the first edition of *The Mersey Sound*, published in the Penguin Modern Poets series (1967).

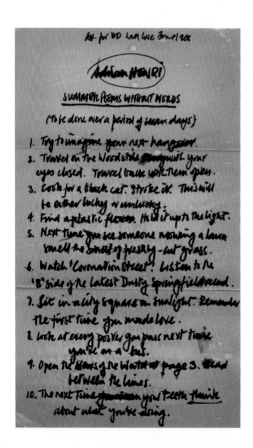

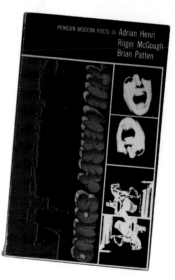

22. Adrian Henri's 'Summer Poems Without Words', one of his 'action-pieces', or sets of instructions issued to audiences at live readings. '1. Try to imagine your next hangover.'

to declare that all grandiose claims about 'poets as a social force' were 'bosh'. 'Those who go to poetry expecting to find a complete guide to religion, or morals, or political action, will very soon be disillusioned,' he wrote. 'Reading this anthology will teach no one how to run a state or raise a revolution.'[105] Hartley's assessment of the Thirties literary achievement was cynical, but hardly unfair. 'All their exhortations and manifestos brought no other consequence upon themselves than that of an increasing literary success.'[106]

Swiftly, an image of the decade and its literary culture crystallized. In the late 1940s and early 1950s, when readers discussed poetry, the poets they tended to think of were Thirties figures such as Auden and Spender, and the picture they formed in their minds of what 'a poet' looked like was a quintessentially Thirties one: 'a left-winger just back from the Weimar republic or Spain, aggressively introducing pylons or power-stations into his verse.'[107] For the generation of young writers who embarked on their careers in the immediate post-war period, dissecting this mythical figure, pointing out the flaws or hypocrisies in its stance, became a key means of differentiation, a way of insisting that their work was less naïve than what had passed before for socially engaged poetry.[108]

For some, the problem lay in the gulf between the social world of Auden, Day Lewis, Spender, *et al.*, and that of the workers who formed, mostly without knowing it, their subject matter. From their particular class position – often lower-middle class, as the products of grammar schools, the scholarship system and other instruments of post-war social mobility – the new generation of poets, known collectively as the 'Movement', queried what their public school-educated, well-connected predecessors could possibly have known about real life. 'The poetry of the 1930s may have been left-wing, but it was profoundly upper-class,' the poet John Holloway declared. Far from managing to swap 'I' for 'we', the individual view for the collective, it had merely reinforced the old barrier between the elite and everyone else, the faceless masses 'out there' whom it addressed. 'It reads "you",' Holloway said, 'not "we".'[109] His contemporary D.J. Enright saw in Auden's poem *The Orators* a disdainful portrait of what Auden had called, characteristically, 'our proletariat'. 'What, we are inclined to ask, is this "proletariat"?' Enright asked. 'What kind of animal is it, with so many heads, speaking so many different languages? Does Auden know the whole truth about each one of its heads?'[110]

Others felt that what was wrong was the Thirties poets' political commitment *per se*, their belief that big ideas about changing the world could actually work in practice and not go sour.* 'Politics were considerably more fashionable in those days than they are now,' Enright said drily. The poet John Wain dismissed the entire decade as a kind of drawn-out, childish game of dressing-up, 'the last age [...] in which people had the feeling that if only they took the trouble to *join* something, get a party card, wear a special shirt, organise meetings and bellow slogans, they could influence the course of events.'[111] Donald Davie's poem 'Remembering the Thirties' (1955), which Spender compared to 'rotten eggs' being flung at his generation, spun the convictions and antics of the Thirties into the plot of a boy's adventure story, a romantic 'saga' with a hint of the ridiculous about it:

---

* The Thirties poets took to censoring their former selves in this respect. In a review of Day Lewis and Lehmann's *The Chatto Book of Modern Poetry* (1956), John Press noted that the editors had 'smuggled out of sight' all evidence of their own 'boisterous past'. 'I should have welcomed one or two of Mr. Auden's early poems,' Press wrote, '[or] Mr. Day Lewis's savage outbursts at the complacency of the governing classes in the days of the National Government.'

POLITICS

It dawns upon the veterans after all
That what for them were agonies, to us
Are high-brow thrillers, though historical;
And all their feats quite strictly fabulous.[112]

Fabulous, but historical. The problem with big ideas, as
Davie recognized, was that they made catastrophes happen:
'the Anschluss, Guernica'. By the 1950s in Britain, not only
fascism but communism too was associated with repression,
persecution and brutality. Being a communist could be excused
only, if at all, as a youthful phase, to be abandoned as part of a
general, necessary disillusionment. 'My generation came up to
university in the time of the Molotov-Ribbentrop pact,' Davie
wrote. 'There was no excuse for us if we were starry-eyed about
the Stalinist Left.'[113]

Auden's generation missed both world wars, but poets
of Davie's age often served in the Second, beginning their
working lives as writers and lecturers in the shadow of the
concentration camp and the atom bomb. In their eyes, the true
enemy, which linked fascism with communism, was ideology:
any kind of inflexible, self-contained worldview which, if
applied forcefully to life, meant violence and the suppression
of freedoms.

'I would call any system of ideas which is self-consciously
complete and final, and which is regarded as suitable for
imposition on the whole human race, as in emotional effect
totalitarian,' the poet Robert Conquest wrote in 1957.[114]
Conquest had been a member of the British Communist Party
at university in the late 1930s, but had broken with it at the
start of the war, and had first-hand experience of the realities of
communist organization from serving as a liaison officer with
Bulgarian forces in 1944. As an expert on Eastern Europe, he
was employed by the Foreign Office to help run an anti-Soviet

propaganda unit.[115] The anthology he produced of the poetry of his contemporaries, *New Lines* (1956), was a literary event, the volume that helped to establish the careers of Philip Larkin and Kingsley Amis, but it was a political statement too. *New Lines*, as Conquest conceived it, was to be a calculated response to the manifesto-style anthology of the Thirties, whether *New Signatures*, *New Country* or *New Writing*: it was an attempt to take a stand against the tyranny of ideals, to resist the lure of all systems, ideologies and 'isms'.[116]

The poets collected in its pages, Conquest wrote in his preface, were united by a suspicion of '*a priori* dogmas' and 'great systems of theoretical constructs'. Their writing was 'empirical in its attitude', interested in 'the real person or event', or in the world as it actually was rather than as it looked through Left or Right ideological lenses.[117] Politics, whether in the sense of theoretical world-building or commentary on real events, was conspicuously absent from the book, as was rhetorical grandstanding, which some poems dismissed explicitly as fruitless, or belated. 'I might have been as pitiless as Pope,' Davie wrote in a poem called 'Too Late for Satire', referring to the eighteenth-century political satirist,

> But to no purpose; in a tragic age
> We share the hatred but we lack the hope
> By pinning follies to reform the age.

The closest Conquest came to admitting anything remotely political into his collection was his choice of Davie's 'Rejoinder to a Critic', a poem in which Davie claimed that extremities of feeling, intense love and intense hatred, had been responsible for the war's violent excesses. Love, these days, like hate, Davie said, had a 'radio-active fall-out'; among those injured by its touch could be counted 'Half Japan'. After Hiroshima, as the poem concluded, 'How dare we now be anything but numb?' Not engaging, not committing, it implied, was the only justifiable mode of artistic response.[118]

This, as Enright argued, was the poetry of 'chastened common-sense' – unexciting, undramatic, maybe, but a necessary pushback against two decades of polarization and hysteria in art and life.[119] Where writers of the Thirties had been keen to take a side, to claim that they were part of something all-encompassing and greater than themselves, the younger generation preferred to disdain collective enterprises. 'We hardly cared or even knew about each other's views,' Conquest said bluntly.[120] It was difficult, as he explained in *New Lines*, to say what connected the group of poets he had brought together (beyond their negative feelings about ideology), because the whole point was that they were not 'a group of doctrine-saddled writers forming a definite school complete with programme and rules.' Literary collectives, in other words, had nothing to do, even metaphorically, with political ones. Enright's own anthology, a similar volume entitled *Poets of the 1950's* (1955), didn't represent a 'movement', as he insisted in its introduction; it was merely an 'interim report', a 'presentation of selected poems by individual writers', some of whom happened to share common attitudes. 'It is in a sense a tribute to the state of the country that there should be so little political excitement in Britain today,' he added.[121]

※

Conquest cheerfully printed the *Observer*'s comment about *New Lines* on the jacket of *New Lines II* (1963): 'No book in recent times has been met with such a huge volume of abuse.'[122] Critics noticed and reacted to its calculated lack of politics, and to the Movement's apparent rejection of political consciousness more generally. Davie's line in 'Rejoinder to a Critic', 'How dare we now be anything but numb?', wasn't an expression of principle, the poet Charles Tomlinson sneered in 1957, but 'a total failure of nerve': it constituted a retreat from side-taking where side-taking would seem to be most warranted.[123] 'A reader of our post-war poetry would find it hard to discover there many of the basic facts about the world in which we live,' the critic John Press observed in 1963, commenting on the direction British poetry had taken in the last decade. The overwhelming political facts that had driven Lehmann, Spender and their contemporaries to write – the rise of fascism abroad and at home; mass unemployment; hunger marches on the streets – might be all in the past, he argued, but there was enough misery and deprivation in postwar Britain to provoke a poet's political 'indignation' – as well as, further afield, enough to despair about in the spread of communism, the brutal suppression of revolution in Hungary, the flood of refugees. 'Why have our younger poets withdrawn from the public world?'[124] The typical approach among Conquest's group, according to the poet and critic Al Alvarez, seemed to be to pretend that all was well with the world even when it wasn't – to go on behaving, out of 'embarrassment, shyness, humiliation, misplaced good manners', as though 'nothing unusual were happening'.[125]

In 1960, Penguin commissioned Alvarez, then the *Observer*'s poetry critic and an influential champion of new voices, to compile an anthology of contemporary poetry.[126] The result, a collection Alvarez titled *The New Poetry*, appeared in 1962, featuring several familiar Movement names – Larkin, Amis, Davie, Enright – but also younger poets, Thom Gunn, Ted Hughes and Geoffrey Hill, and a handful of American writers, John Berryman, Robert Lowell, Sylvia Plath and Anne Sexton. Its title, as well as the choice of some of its contributors, seemed to reference Donald M. Allen's avant-garde *The New American Poetry* (1960), published two years previously in the United States. In a long preface, whose forceful, manifesto-like argument recalled the politicized introductions of *New Signatures* and *New Country*, Alvarez attacked what he called the principle of 'gentility' in British life, as represented by the moderate attitudes of the *New Lines* poets.

'Gentility,' he wrote, 'is a belief that life is always more or less orderly, people always more or less polite, their emotions and habits more or less decent and more or less controllable; that God, in short, is more or less good.' It was a stance, he said, which was 'becoming increasingly precarious to maintain.' Over the last half-century, the emergence of violent forces of disintegration – in the shape of two world wars, the concentration camps, the threat of nuclear destruction – had required of those who held tight to it almost impossible levels of repression, self-deception, or both. 'Once upon a time,' Alvarez explained, 'the English could safely believe that Evil was something that happened on the Continent, or farther off, in the Empire where soldiers were paid to take care of it.' Now, however, evil was impossible to compartmentalize and tidy away, not least because psychoanalysis had revealed that frightful, internal versions of its external shapes operated in the most ordinary-seeming consciousnesses.[127]

The point was not, he continued, that British writers needed to start producing poetry that dealt directly with psychoanalysis or hydrogen bombs or Auschwitz. What they did have to do, however, was drop the old gentility pretence, 'the disease so often found in English culture.' Poetry required, Alvarez argued, 'a new seriousness', an openness to 'the full range' of human feeling, in all its rawness and ugliness – as he saw in Lowell and Berryman's work, with its ability to 'cope

[...] with the quick of their experience', even to 'disintegration and breakdown'; and in Plath's poetry of the early 1960s, which he championed in the *Observer*, a body of work that occupied, perilously, a 'narrow, violent area' between the sayable and unsayable.[128]

No one now was calling on poets to change the world, as Lehmann and Roberts had once sought to do. Poetry that confined itself to making political cases must 'cease to be poetry and become propaganda,' as Alvarez wrote. But the way it responded to or interpreted the world mattered, if for no other reason than it was, inexorably, *part* of things, under the same shadow of public menace and private breakdown as everything else. Not subscribing to an ideology or a party, refusing to engage one way or another, wasn't a magic solution, for poets or for anyone else; the 'mass evil' of the century made no exceptions, would not look away for those who refused to look at it. 'All our lives, even those of the most genteel and enislanded, are influenced profoundly by forces which have nothing to do with gentility, decency, or politeness,' Alvarez argued.[129] Poetry, since it was shaped too, sometimes despite itself, by those forces, was obliged somehow to grapple with them head-on. 'By blood we live, the hot, the cold,' Geoffrey Hill wrote in 'Genesis', one of the pieces collected in *The New Poetry*. 'There is no bloodless myth will hold.'[130]

7

POP

The Mersey Sound (1967)

In 1961, the scholar and translator John Willett made what would have seemed to most readers of the *TLS* a bizarre and unwelcome prediction. Poetry, Willett said, appeared to be escaping from the pages of books: live readings by poets in front of an audience, often accompanied by jazz musicians, were in vogue, and you could attend poetry concerts, listen to poetry on the gramophone and watch poetry performances on television. 'As a reviewer who has sat alone in a theatre on a first night with the author of the play, one would accept that anything over four for poetry is a bit of a sweaty press,' observed a *Guardian* journalist at a Liverpool reading in 1966. At this reading, instead, remarkably, 'one hundred and fifty were squashed into the tiny auditorium,' with another hundred listening via loudspeaker from an overspill room. The channels through which poetry operated and reached people were changing. In the course of the decade, Willett suggested, they might well change beyond recognition. 'We are not all that far from the day when a truly first-class poem will find its way into the Top Ten.'[1]

To a post-war readership, taught to think of poetry as something written by dead people who by definition were unable

to perform it live, the idea of a poem making it into the charts
like a pop song would have been unfathomable. But Willett
was right to observe that a new relationship between poetry
and popular entertainment was beginning to form. From the
late 1950s, avant-garde poets had started to experiment with
the possibility of combining spoken poetry with live jazz, blues,
dance and cinema, touring the country and putting on shows
for enthusiastic paying audiences. Regular poetry nights were
organized at unlikely venues: fashionable coffee bars, dimly lit
club basements, rowdy Edinburgh Fringe theatres. They were
attended by the kinds of people who habitually came to such
places anyway, teenagers, students, drinkers, music-lovers. 'In
the past five, six, seven years,' declared the poet Adrian Mitchell
in 1966, 'British poets have been stomping the island giving
adrenaline transfusions in cellars, town halls, clubs, pubs,
theatres, anywhere.'[2]

Once upon a time, Mitchell and his collaborators argued, all
poets, whether you called them bards, minstrels or troubadours,
had earned their living by stomping up and down the island
reciting their work. Poetry, in its early forms, had been an oral art
rather than a literary one: it relied on living voices to deliver it and
pass it on, and through it poets had felt close to their audiences,
sharing with them the live experience of speech, rhythm and
music. But their connection had been fatally disrupted. The
invention of the book, and with it the emergence of an idea
of 'literature' as something fixed and written down, had come
between them. 'Books – however beautiful – are more and more
distant branches, and not the roots of cultural communication,'
wrote the poet and performer Michael Horovitz. Live bards had
become dead authors; collective audiences had fragmented into
individual, lonely readers.[3]

Pop music, in this context, seemed like a model of everything
poetry had once been. Where poetry was dead, pop was

alive. Where poetry was, or at least seemed, elitist, pop was democratic. Where pop realized its purpose in performance, in a live moment shared and collaborated in by performers and audiences, poetry meant solitariness, introspection, solo writing or solo reading.[4] What held modern poets back, avant-garde writers argued, wasn't their craft but their medium. To many commentators in the 1960s, it was obvious that pop and poetry worked in similar ways as art forms. Lyricists such as Bob Dylan and Leonard Cohen, it was pointed out, wrote songs whose formal qualities, romantic imagery and metaphors wouldn't look out of place in anthologies; the Beatles experimented with collages of styles, stream-of-consciousness lyrics and accidental effects.[5] The difference lay in whom pop musicians spoke to, and how they communicated. To survive and flourish, counter-cultural critics argued, poets had to 'jump the book', abandon the written word and 'follow the Beatles into the clubs and dancehalls' where the real audiences were.[6]

Willett was more right than he knew. In 1965, the poetry world had its first 'pop concert', the International Poetry Incarnation, when an international group of writers booked out the Albert Hall and read their work to a chanting, gyrating, pot-smoking crowd of 7,500. In 1967, three poets from Liverpool – Adrian Henri, Roger McGough and Brian Patten – achieved mainstream success in bestselling anthologies, *The Liverpool Scene* and *The Mersey Sound*, volumes that more closely resembled pop LPs than poetry books. The same year, Corgi Books released a collection called *Love, Love, Love* (a lyric from the Beatles' new hit 'All You Need is Love'), which excitedly compared its poets to 'today's better pop lyricists'.[7] One year on, even Willett's 'Top Ten' prediction came true. In November 1968, McGough hit the number one spot with his group, The Scaffold, and their music hall-style ballad 'Lily the Pink'. 'Pop goes the poetry,' observed *Critical Quarterly* sourly in December. The following year, when Mick Jagger read Shelley aloud at a Rolling Stones concert in Hyde Park, accompanied by the release of a cloud of butterflies, the cycle of influence seemed complete.[8]

☧

McGough began reading to live audiences in 1961. He was in his early twenties, holding down a teaching job at St Kevin's Comprehensive School outside Liverpool, and escaping two evenings a week into town on the bus with his 'poetry survival kit': tight jeans, a Sartre-style black roll-neck sweater, a packet of Gauloises, a notebook. His destination was a regular poetry night organized at Streate's Coffee Bar in Liverpool, a 'candle-lit, whitewashed basement with a distinct Left Bank flavour.'[9] The Streate's night had been set up a year earlier by two young jazz-and-poetry enthusiasts, an Irish writer, Johnny Byrne, and eighteen-year-old John Frederick 'Spike' Hawkins, who before he moved to Liverpool had cultivated a reputation for eccentricity by making his home in a hedge in rural Buckinghamshire. There were two regulars in particular whom McGough hit it off with. Adrian Henri was a bearded, bespectacled painter, part-time lecturer and blues enthusiast, who had been persuaded by the poet Pete Brown (aka 'Pete the Beat') to try reading his poetry to audiences. Brian Patten, who first performed his work in November 1961, was fifteen years old and just out of school, working as a reporter on the local paper and spending all his free time reading and writing poetry.[10]

By 1963, the three were performing regularly in theatres, bars and clubs, offering programmes of poetry mixed in with other kinds of popular entertainment: taped or live rock music by local 'Merseybeat' groups (part of the thriving scene from which the Beatles had recently emerged); dramatic sketches;

comic and satiric segments; surreal dialogues. By presenting their poetry as part of an evening that also included music, comedy, drink and drugs, they made it something other than 'Poetry with a capital "P"', as McGough explained – it was just an element in the total experience of a night out.[11] 'To-night the bar is pretty busy,' reported a journalist from the Everyman Theatre in 1967. 'There's been a poetry reading and that makes everybody thirsty.' Those who showed up to listen and watch, 'in their uniforms of corduroy, denim and PVC', weren't what anyone at the time thought of as a typical poetry audience; they were a pop audience, composed of the same teenagers and twenty-somethings who made up the beat music scene.[12] 'What is exciting about [Sampson &] Barlow's,' Henri wrote of the folk club Patten had hired for Monday evening readings, 'is not so much the poets as the audience. The girls on the front row there are mostly the ones on the front row when the Clayton Squares play the Cavern.'* At O'Connor's Tavern, a windowless, smoky hole lit by a 'torrid orange light', where there was live music downstairs and poetry upstairs, you could encounter just about anyone in the audience – including, on one occasion, a convicted murderer and his crew, a bunch of 'serious Liverpool heavies' whom Henri gamely entertained with his set.[13] 'I'm accepted – by the hard cases, the bruisers – as just a bloke who writes poetry,' McGough explained to a journalist.[14]

The marriage of pop and poetry wouldn't have worked everywhere, but it succeeded in the corner of Liverpool in which Henri, McGough and Patten lived because of its particular

---

* The Clayton Squares were a well-known local beat group; the Cavern Club stood at the heart of the Liverpool rock scene and was the site of the Beatles' appearances in the early 1960s. The idea of getting close to 'the girls on the front row', for Henri, McGough and Patten, was a powerful motivation for live performance. 'We give readings, do gigs (one night stands) at universities, clubs and events,' as McGough put it in 1966.

demographic makeup. 'No other city in Britain has an area with such a high density of artistic and intellectual talent,' enthused the *Liverpool Daily Post* over what it called 'Liverpool's Left Bank', the area of rundown, bombed-out Georgian streets criss-crossing between the two cathedrals:

> Into this small compact area [...] the intelligentsia, beatnik, literati, arty, tarty-arty, bohemian and dilettanti have come together to form their own inward-looking society, with their own norms, uniforms, heroes, ambitions and vices. The annual turnover of students to the Art College and the University ensures a continued introduction of new ideas, new faces and new hangers-on.[15]

The architecture of the area, as the newspaper noted, lent itself to the needs of a 'shifting, floating population' of the working class, itinerant or would-be bohemian, its large townhouses ripe for conversion into cheap flats and attic bedsits. Henri, the *Weekend Telegraph* reported in a long piece on the area in 1967, lived on Canning Street 'at the top of a house teeming with artists, beat groups, poets and birds.'* 'The painters, musicians and dancers are all mixed up together, living on top of each other in a small area.' Everyone knew each other; everyone collaborated or competed with one another; everyone spent their evenings in the same small handful of disreputable pubs and bars.[16] It all felt, a reporter for the *Guardian* observed in 1966, 'rather like a West Coast Greenwich Village before self-consciousness arrives.'[17]

---

* Henri in fact lived on the first floor, not 'at the top', and 'teeming with artists...' was an exaggeration.

For some, following the example of the middle-class student hippies who had colonized the cheap flats of Notting Hill earlier in the decade, the area and its gritty, unpredictable scene represented a fantasy of bohemia, a way of experiencing forty years on what it might have been like to have lived in Paris during the 1920s, or, in the *Guardian*'s more recent analogy, parts of San Francisco in the 1950s. 'When I went home at Christmas I kept thinking [about] all the people in those back streets who would have to stay there,' Maggie Brown, a fashion student at the Art College, told the *Liverpool Daily Post* soulfully.[18] For residents from local working-class backgrounds, on the other hand, Henri, McGough and Patten among them, the cheapness of the area and its ready supply of collaborators represented a rare – perhaps unique – chance to experience an alternative life to the one they would have lived. Patten wrote, as he told his publisher, 'under a broken skylight my machine going rusty with rain and actually in my overcoat till the holes are blocked up.'[19]

What united both groups, the student bohemians and the working-class artists alike, was an emphasis on living for the moment: on being young, on experiencing and creating without fear, on avoiding, as far as was possible, the trammels of duty, responsibility and consequence that ordinary people found themselves enmeshed in. 'I'm not trying to earn myself a place in history with poetry,' McGough commented to a journalist. 'My work is about now.'[20] The idea of being sixty-four, as the Beatles had it, was a mixture of shocking and laughable. 'Everyone in this community seems to be living for themselves,' Maggie Brown observed in her interview. 'All values are subjected to the current desire.'[21] If adult life was a combination of nostalgia and future-facing prudence – savings, pensions, mortgages, playing by the rules and deferring gratification in the hope of being rewarded later – the alternative was a kind of perpetual adolescence, characterized by its lack of investment in anything but the present.

This comes across sharply in Henri's poetry, which builds up a world designed to exclude anyone even remotely close to middle age, a 'country of Now' in which adults are alien, suspect presences, or unpleasant reminders that there's such a thing as growing old.* ('Don't worry,' his speaker tells a teenage girlfriend in one poem, perhaps only half in jest: 'Everything's going to be all right / There'll be voluntary euthanasia for everyone over 30.') In his poems, images of youth culture – 'Top of the Pops', 'girls in bikinis', a 'chocolate Easter Egg', 'a red bra with I LOVE YOU written inside one of the cups', 'Magic colouring books', packets of crisps, Paul McCartney – aren't merely symbols, stand-ins for more 'important' feelings or realities, but feature just as themselves, the salvageable, compelling flotsam and jetsam of the moment.[22] He carried a notebook around with him and scribbled down ordinary words, images and objects that struck him as he encountered them, establishing a practice of creating art out of 'whatever was to hand'.[23] His lists recorded what modernity looked like as it happened and on its own terms, rather than holding it up to be seen through, or measured against an idealized past.

In its obsession with youth, the Liverpool scene reflected the priorities of pop culture at large. As the jazz musician and critic George Melly put it, pop in all its forms – including both the mainstream trends in music and fashion that young people subscribed to en masse, and the 'underground', alternative culture of the avant-garde – 'suffer[ed] from a severe Peter Pan complex.' The pop community was 'prepossessed', Horovitz

---

* 'The communal voice of their poetry speaks,' the critic Jonathan Raban wrote of the three Liverpool poets, 'of the dreary disaster of having to grow beyond the age of fourteen.'

wrote, 'not with the past, or the future – but with NOW.'[24] For the first time, it seemed to those observing, the people who made culture – poets, pop bands, fashion designers – were as young as their teen and twenty-something fans, and shared with them a particular set of attitudes.[25] 'Young people,' Patten's publishers wrote deferentially in an advert for his first solo collection in 1967, were remarkable for having grown up in 'an infinitely more confusing, fast moving world than their elders,' which they alone were equipped to communicate and explain.[26] Now that the adolescent gap between childhood and adulthood had been renamed as 'teenage', and given its own set of rebellious behavioural characteristics, being young began to seem like a state of mind, an inherently fascinating and different way of being in the world. 'Who, these days, isn't young, a Beatles fan, and fond of the sound of his own voice?' the *TLS* commented drily in 1967.[27]

Youth was taken as a guarantor of authenticity, of freshness of perspective, of being at a distance from (and uncorrupted by) the moral extremities of the war years, as well as the staidness of the decade that had followed. The American Beat poet Allen Ginsberg, enlisted to hype up Patten's first solo collection, considered it sufficient accolade to point out on the cover that the teenage poet was 'younger than the atom bomb' – part of the 'Post Atomic generation', as his publishers added for good measure. 'Patten's generation – younger than the new Hiroshima – plays – is – poetic Adam,' Horovitz wrote excitedly in 1968; the young seemed to have no past, no future, to be somehow 'reborn each day with the entire universe'.[28]

The 'Post Atomic' generation, defined by the avant-garde poet and artist Jeff Nuttall as those who had not reached puberty at the time the bombs dropped on Hiroshima and Nagasaki, occupied a particular historical position. Their youth, as

Nuttall argued in *Bomb Culture* (1968), meant that in 1945 they hadn't yet entered into the future-building obligations (family life, a steady job, a mortgage) that encouraged their elders, even after the bombs had fallen and the age of nuclear threat had begun, to 'pretend as cheerfully as ever' that things were the same as they'd always been. Younger people might sustain the same pretence, but did so reluctantly or hostilely, unable to 'conceive of life *with* a future' in a world where, suddenly, it was impossible to trust the moral compasses of authorities and institutions, and in which humanity's end-date might turn out to be unpleasantly close at hand.[29] Western society, advanced, rational, civilized, had nonetheless built the weapon that promised its own destruction: it had shown itself to be 'suicidal', 'hostile to life', as the philosopher Norman O. Brown put it, exhibiting its own, terrifyingly large-scale, Freudian 'death instinct'.

The way out of the crisis that loomed, according to the avant-garde, was to knock down and rebuild: to get rid of the old order and replace it with a culture centred on living, not dying, one in which human fulfilment was considered a matter of desire, pleasure and self-expression. 'Unlike the Lost Generation, which was occupied with the loss of faith,' the journalist John Holmes explained to the readers of the *New York Times Magazine* in 1952, 'the Beat Generation is becoming more and more occupied with the need for it.' 'The wish to live must be rekindled in the species,' Nuttall wrote, 'the drift to suicide redirected.'[30]

On the individual level, at least, this could be translated into a handy slogan: make love, not war. 'Square' society, suicidal society, was sexually repressed; in the alternative culture partially being realized in bohemian circles, desires were there to be acted upon, not sublimated. Joe Orton, in his diary, called the idea 'complete sexual licence'. 'It's the only way to smash

up the wretched civilization. [...] Much more fucking.'[31] Adrian
Mitchell, known for his rousing anti-Vietnam War readings,
argued in 'Peace is Milk' (collected in the 1967 *Love, Love,
Love* anthology) that the solution to the societal impulse to
'Choose death' lay in choosing pleasure, or what the book's
editor termed 'Universal Love':

> Make love well, generously, deeply.
> There's nothing simpler in the savage world,
> Making good love, making good good love.[32]

As poets, McGough, Henri and Patten were less comfortable
with grand, universal subjects, preferring particulars. 'I think
generally when people write about the Bomb and things it's too
big, you know, too vast, to think about,' McGough told Edward
Lucie-Smith, critic and editor of the *Liverpool Scene* anthology.
They also retained a healthy scepticism about the power of the
male libido to stop the world ending. ('While the mushroom
cloud is growing outside on the horizon we're laying the birds
in the back yard.'[33]) In the poems they wrote and performed
during the 1960s, though, the subject of the bomb, along with
a more general anxiety about running out of time, habitually
overlapped with the idea of 'sexual licence' – sex featuring as
either a defiant antidote to 'bomb culture', or as the best and
only way to fill the perhaps very short window left to everyone
on earth. Patten's prose-poem 'Before it happened' features a
scene in which 'crowds commit mass love in city streets', an
inverted, carnival version of the mass suicide implicitly about
to be committed by society at large. Sex in the last four minutes,
the final romp, takes place anywhere it can: 'Pale and lyrical
couples wandered into stables, bedrooms, empty cinemas and
other places of refuge for a final Good Time.'[34]
In McGough's 'At Lunchtime   A Story of Love', the poet's

speaker persuades the young woman sitting opposite him on the bus to take off 'her / greenhat, put her bus ticket into her pocket' and 'makelove', on the basis that, 'this being a nuclearage', time is running out:

> The buspeople, and therewere many of
> them, were shockedandsurprised and amused-
> andannoyed, but when word got around
> that the world was coming to an end at lunch
> time, they put their pride in their pockets
> with their bustickets and madelove one with
> the other.

McGough's customary trick of running words together ('makelove', 'nuclearage', 'shockedandsurprised') has a special appropriateness here, as the little verbal connections and collisions come to represent, in miniature, those unexpected bus couplings – the sudden coming together of musty 'white mothballbodies', now free and 'doing naughty things'. By the end of the poem, it's the next day, no bomb has dropped and the world hasn't ended after all, but everyone has discovered that they quite like pretending it's about to: 'In everybus / In everystreet / In everytown / In everycountry / people pretended that the world was coming / to an end at lunchtime.'[35] A world, in a sense, as McGough points out, has come to an end – the world of sitting politely on buses and letting the usual inhibitors (fear, embarrassment) get in the way of the free expression of desire.

Those who liked the world just as it was, thank you very much, reacted with horror to the poem's 'supposed call to permissiveness'. 'Concerned housewives,' McGough recalled in his autobiography, contacted headteachers when 'At Lunchtime' was used as a text in schools; newspapers and MPs were written to; questions were raised in the House of Commons. Thousands of miles away in the US, a copy of the collection the poem appeared in was denounced in California. In Virginia, irate parents had it publicly burned.[36]

'At Lunchtime', like Patten's 'Before it happened', sketches an imaginary before-the-bomb scenario, using the threat of imminent doom to picture the kind of 'what if you could' behaviour sanctioned by societal awareness of the end. What both their poems steered away from capturing, conversely, was the moment of the bomb itself, or what its immediate aftermath might look like. This kind of representation was challenging because of the severe, full-stop finality it involved: the fact that, once the bomb came, nothing else could or would ever follow it. How could you seek to convey what that meant in a literary form which, by its nature, could be read by multiple readers, live more than one textual life? Poems could be reprinted, reproduced, performed live by their author on different occasions; if they pictured the end of the world, they had to go on doing so, impossibly, every time they were read, like miniature dramas of resurrection.

In 1964, Henri found a solution in an artform he'd been experimenting with since reading an article about 'happenings', avant-garde spectacles organized by the artist Allan Kaprow in New York. Happenings, or 'events', as Henri called his own activities, were like 'three-dimensional paintings': they were productions that unfolded live and involved a mixture of dramatic performance, poetry reading, painting, music, film and improvisatory audience participation, all in a carefully staged physical environment.[37] Often they were designed to shock. A happening in London in 1964 involved various girls being 'painted [and] slapped about with wet fish and strings of sausages,' and the serendipitous arrival of an irate caretaker on the scene; in 1966, at an event staged by the Austrian artist Hermann Nitsch, a lamb's carcase was 'ritually paraded' in front of the audience, its entrails inserted into one of the performers' trousers and threaded out through his fly buttons.[38] Henri's events, by contrast, were more about immersive fun than high-concept terror. 'City' (1962) involved poetry, dance, a backdrop that Henri painted live as the event unfolded, and a background of jazz; 'Nightblues' (1963), staged in a cinema, featured McGough reading his work to the accompaniment of a local rock group, 'a girl dancer from Oldham', and the spectacle of Patten, 'now and again disclosed by the curtain', sitting at a typewriter and pretending to type a 'great epic poem' that he never completed or read aloud.[39]

'Bomb Event' took place in December 1964 at the Cavern Club, the regular home of the Beatles when they performed in Liverpool. At the appointed time, the low-ceilinged brick chamber was plunged into darkness; '350 teenagers', 'jammed between the arches and pillars', fell into a hushed silence. As the Clayton Squares saxophonist Mike Evans recalled in *Mersey Beat* magazine, things started with a bang: 'There was a huge explosion, girls screamed while the lights flickered and we broke into our first number, "Danger Zone".'[40] From there, the event rattled through a mixed programme of bomb-related entertainment. There was music from the Squares (a version of Charles Mingus' jazz song 'Oh Lord Don't Let Them Drop That Atomic Bomb on Me'); a parodic lecture from Henri on household protection against nuclear attack, formed of extracts from the *Civil Defence Handbook* mixed up and read in the wrong order; Patten acting the part of a zombie, wrapped in bandages; Henri reading his poem 'Tonight at Noon' ('In forgotten graveyards everywhere the dead will quietly / bury the living') to the accompaniment of 'very soft weird music'; Henri being silenced on stage by a figure the *Mersey Beat* described as 'a monster, very effectively clad, [who] came onto the stage and strangled him.' During the worst bits, the cloakroom girls screamed and hid under the counter.[41]

Finally, after a pop group, the Excelles, had performed an appropriate rendition of 'Don't Say Goodnight and Mean Goodbye',

> they went straight into 'Silent Night'. For four minutes they sang the standard Christmas carol. All the time they were singing, the countdown of a four-minute warning was given over the PA. 'When the countdown reached 10, the group sang louder until, at zero, they stopped. The lights went out and there was a tremendous explosion. Girls were screaming again as a false ceiling, made of paper and powder, representing fallout, collapsed.'[42]

The faked bomb – the countdown, the darkness, the explosion, the fallout – was cathartic, even a good night out, because it wasn't real. But in one sense it had a kind of truth to it. Henri's events, like Kaprow's happenings, were never repeated: though they were scripted and rehearsed rather than improvised from scratch, they were conceived as one-offs. A hundred small circumstantial factors – the size and behaviour of the audience; the lighting of the room; whether the equipment worked; the mood of the performers; the weather outside – added up to make them unique immersive experiences, living environments that you couldn't remake authentically on another day.[43] In the case of 'Bomb Event', this quality of unrepeatability was key to the meaning of the spectacle, getting at the heart of what the bomb signified in a way that words on the page or a regular performance set couldn't. Viewed from a particular angle, the bomb was like the ultimate happening: immersive, all-encompassing, unrepeatable in a new, hyper-significant way.

The *Mersey Beat*'s reporter did his best to convey for the paper's readers what had happened at the Cavern 'the night the bomb dropped', but recreating its bizarre twists and turns was hard to do in retrospect. No single account, or combination of accounts, could register the experience in its totality: to get it, you had to have been there. The live moment could be captured in a recording or transcribed for the page, but as a slice of time it was marked off at either end by the dimming and brightening of the lights, framed and separated off from the ordinary course of things.

Henri, McGough and Patten, the latter two in particular, rarely wrote poems with the sole objective of performing them, and all of them agreed that the printed page, not the live poetry reading, was the place where poetry achieved whatever 'permanent value' it held.[44] But their work gained something, or became something else, in the process of being presented to an audience and incorporated into a live set. Henri liked to improvise on the text of his poems like a jazz musician, adding extra lines to pieces, such as the list-poem 'I Want to Paint', which could grow or change on the night without losing their shape. ('I want to paint / Pictures that children can play hopscotch on / Pictures that can be used as evidence at Murder trials / Pictures that can be used to advertise cornflakes...') What audiences were likely to know or not know, or what they were likely to find funny or moving, could be taken into account in performance, and details of people and places altered accordingly. A poem set in Liverpool, such as Henri's 'The New "Our Times"', could, for a reading at the Fringe, suddenly change its locus to Edinburgh, with the police constable character renamed 'Angus MacKay'; a poem imagining McGough, to everyone's surprise, being installed as 'Chair of Poetry at Oxford' might switch to imagine the even more unlikely scenario of Beat novelist and professional heroin addict William Burroughs being installed instead.[45]

Other poems transformed more dramatically in performance. Henri's reading of 'The Entry of Christ into Liverpool', a collage of sights and sounds, was accompanied at O'Connor's by live drums, trumpets and a tin whistle, the instruments picking up on lines in the text as if they were stage directions ('THE SOUND OF TRUMPETS'); performed, the poem was able to capture a three-dimensional urban environment, a cacophony of simultaneous noise.[46] Then there were the avant-garde experiments with audience participation. At Sampson & Barlow's readings, Henri might pass around scraps of paper, ask everyone present to scribble down a word or phrase, then assemble them to form complete 'poems' which would be different every time. On other nights, he might solemnly hold up a series of empty picture frames for inspection, an act entitled 'Silent Poems'.[47] His 'action-pieces', or 'poems without words', involved issuing audience members with lists of simple tasks to complete in the following seven days, on the grounds that a 'poem' could be any act or way of being in the world that involved attentiveness to one's surroundings and a willingness to look at things in a new way. 'Travel on the Woodside ferry with your eyes closed. Travel back with them open,' one prompt read. 'Look at every poster you pass next time you're on a bus.' 'The next time you clean your teeth think about what you're doing.'[48]

The wordless poems were meant to be taken with a pinch of salt, but there was a serious thought behind them. Henri's insistence that just about anything could be a poem – teeth, *Coronation Street*, the *News of the World*, a hangover – expressed a larger feeling of disenchantment among avant-garde writers with what they called 'Poetry with a capital P': a determination to re-evaluate, on their own terms, what counted as creativity, and not to respect writers or books simply because their reputations had survived the test of time. The more extreme advocates of the position declared that there was a difference between 'poems' (written down, in books, stuck in the past, useless to the present) and 'poetry', which they defined, *à la* Henri, as any kind of creative, energetic act, any attempt to bring 'new realities' into being. 'True poetry cares nothing for poems,' declared the social theorist Raoul Vaneigem in *The Revolution of Everyday Life* (1967). 'What better way could there be of abolishing the poem than realising it?'[49]

True poetry, in other words, existed out in the world, in the realized, creative acts of revolutionary individuals; it was rarely found locked inside books – which, in most cases, were 'betrayals' of the values poetry represented, as vestiges of the old, hierarchical world that poets were now tasked with blowing to bits. Attacking the movement in *Encounter*, the poet Douglas Dunn remarked grimly that it seemed as if words themselves had been declared superfluous. 'The medium is a handicap, an artefact of education and the literary past; soul is everything.'[50]

This was unfair – words were still very much necessary – but in some of the more extreme antics of the literary avant-garde, observers could have been forgiven for detecting a desire to throw off the chains of verbal communication. At the International Poetry Incarnation at the Albert Hall in June 1965, an event to which an audience of 7,500 turned up to see Allen Ginsberg (recently deported from Czechoslovakia), Lawrence Ferlinghetti, Gregory Corso and other 'celebrity' Beats temporarily in London, the spectacle, rather than the poetry, was what most people remembered. 'Relatively few read their poems,' Horovitz admitted. According to Paul McCartney's friend Barry Miles, one of the event's organizers, a lot of what was read was 'awful bullshit'. Henri, McGough and Patten watched from the wings with mixed feelings. Ginsberg himself got too drunk to read well when his turn came; the poet Harry Fainlight had a debilitating acid trip at the rostrum and was 'virtually howled' from the stage.[*] The highlight of the night, from a performance perspective at any rate, was a rendition by six poets of the German artist Kurt Schwitters' 'Sneezing Poem', which involved, as might be guessed, no words, but was made to last ten minutes and 'brought the house down'. ('It's the only international poem in the world,' the poet Christopher Logue joked.[51])

Those in the audience, 'sitting and standing and chanting, dancing and smoking pot,' decked out in flowers, weren't necessarily there for the poetry; they were there for what poetry, on this strange night in June, seemed to represent – a party atmosphere, a spirit of permissiveness, a feeling of ritualistic, quasi-sacred togetherness, all presided over by Ginsberg, bearded like a 'too-long exiled biblical prophet', chanting, clashing his finger-cymbals and leading the crowd in Tibetan mantras. 'The occasion had become religious, / With drums and bells,' the poet Robert Gittings wrote rapturously afterwards. Poetry, like pop, was suddenly 'communal, tribal, a shared experience,' as Melly put it, not an art for lonely individuals; whatever else it was, it was definitely alive. 'The whole great grounded ship of poetry burst into leaf and grape, / And dolphins curved and leapt.'[52]

Poetry's ship had run aground in the first place, the avant-garde argued, for one important reason: print. On the page,

---

[*] 'None of us who had even the remotest connection with that event have ever been able to hire the Albert Hall again,' Sue Miles said. 'Ever, ever, ever, ever, ever. They check.'

even the most spirited contemporary poetry was 'only half alive', as Horovitz wrote in 1967, a 'preview of life' rather than life itself. Poems in books were like 'unlaid eggs', desperate to be birthed, 'demanding voice; demanding meaning; demanding movement.'[53] The pieces collected in *Torch*, Hull University's literary magazine, in McGough's view, weren't even half-alive: 'perhaps "Taxidermy",' he thought, 'would have been a more accurate name for a magazine full of objects which at first glance appeared to breathe, but which on further examination were stuffed and lifeless.'[54] Literary culture as it went on in the pages of the established reviews and journals was dismissed as dull and stifling. When Patten, as a teenager, started his own poetry magazine, *Underdog*, he avoided commissioning reviews or articles, hoping to allow the poems to speak for themselves. Poetry, he wrote in 'Prosepoem Towards a Definition of Itself', 'should be seen in the company of thieves and lovers rather than that of journalists and publishers.'[55] All three poets disliked the idea, ventured by their editor at Penguin, of prefacing their work in *The Mersey Sound* with a critical introduction.[56]

Academic criticism, in the eyes of disaffected ex-students such as Horovitz, was the worst culprit of all, with its 'isolated armchair mentality', its determination to split poetry off from life, its cold-blooded manner of analyzing, like a scientist at the dissecting table, the dismembered minutiae of printed texts.[57] All the self-important peering at the page, the 'meticulous verbal analysis', Lucie-Smith wrote in his introduction to *The Liverpool Scene*, was considered 'laughable' in the performance world, where how a poem was constructed or which influences it drew on didn't matter half as much as what it was able to do. Rather than existing as an 'artefact', a static object in space, to performers poetry was like a 'service', or an 'agent', a means of eliciting an emotional response or establishing an intimate relationship. Pop music was a vehicle for heightening (sometimes manufacturing) its listeners' desires, a way of making them feel and want more deeply. Pop poetry, whether intoned into microphones at Sampson & Barlow's or screamed through megaphones at CND marches, offered a similar focal point for emotion, channelling laughter, anger or pheromones.[58]

The most significant thing about poetry, in this context, as Henri pointed out, was that it was a 'perfect communications system'. 'The difference between painting and poetry to me is that painting's like a public address system – the message goes out but you're not aware of it being received,' he told Lucie-Smith. 'In poetry you are aware of somebody at the other end of the telephone.'[59] Paintings languished in galleries or private collections, where artists rarely got to see how viewers reacted to their work; live poetry audiences let you know immediately how they felt. The performance setting worked like a 'telescope', as Nuttall put it, collapsing the gap between artist and audience. As Henri and Patten tried to explain to a hostile group of fellow-poets at the 1964 Edinburgh Festival Poetry Conference, the 'basic issue' facing poetry now was one of '*communication*'.[60] If established poets turned their noses up at the idea of forming instant, emotive connections with the people who consumed their work, how could they compete with other entertainment forms – pop concerts, cinema, television – which communicated instantaneously, and thrived by knowing how to give audiences exactly what they wanted?

Most people in the literary world disliked the idea of poetry competing at all. The critical reviews reserved their worst insults for the Liverpool poets because of their performance methods, which seemed bent on transforming poetry into entertainment of the most easily digestible variety. As a group, according to David Harsent in the *Guardian*, they were 'a fetchingly bittersweet cabaret turn'; to Douglas Dunn, they were 'small-town, demotic Mantovanis'; the poet Roy Fuller compared them to 'ham tragedians'; elsewhere they featured as 'a three-headed pantomime horse'.[61] Sections of the avant-garde joined the attack, feeling that the line ought to be drawn somewhere. Jeremy Robson, who had pioneered the poetry-and-jazz movement in the UK, expressed horror at the idea of '"pop" poetry', and commented meaningfully on the 'grossly inflated' reputations of 'certain showmen'. Horovitz claimed that there was a difference between 'sparking direct contact' with a live audience and getting 'tied to the *Business* of entertainment': becoming part of 'the industry', going fully 'pop', selling out.[62]

The Liverpool poets had 'gone pop', their detractors argued, because they seemed more preoccupied with audience satisfaction than with the integrity of their work. By attempting to communicate directly, in the manner of music and television, with a mass youth public (a group Robson referred to as 'the lowest [...] common denominator'), they were felt to be in danger of ceding creative control to the fans they wrote for. Mass audiences, 'in poetry as in television or music or the cinema', the poet Grevel Lindop suggested, were in the position of 'consumers', able to impose through money and numbers their 'own criteria upon the artist'. What audiences wanted, in other words, audiences got: at Liverpool readings, the 'extent to which the audience determines what it is going to hear,' Lindop wrote, 'should not be underestimated.' He gave the example of McGough's poem 'Why Patriots are a Bit Nuts in the Head', reliably enjoyed by the poet's young, left-wing, pacifist listeners for the simple reason that it 'flattered' their 'unthinking assumptions', told them what they wanted to hear.[63] Lucie-Smith noted the same tendency at work during the Albert Hall event, observing spectators 'applauding the echo of their own sentiments' as they listened to Mitchell perform his 'slightly smug poem about Viet Nam'. Such readings were 'preachings to the converted', the poet Peter Porter argued: audiences came along 'to have their tyres pumped up', to hear what they expected to hear in the manner of pop fans at an album tour.[64]

And it wasn't just a question of politics. Live audiences, Porter suggested, eagerly lapped up not only poets' views on the world but also the smallest details of how they expressed them, their 'throwaway cracks' and verbal tics.[65] Some kinds of writing, evidently, were more successful than others at grabbing an audience's attention, flattering their intelligence and setting up patterns for them to anticipate. The fact that this was so, Lindop argued, explained a lot about Henri, McGough and Patten's poetic styles: their habitual punning, their striking metaphors, their way of repeating lines so that they came around like pop choruses ('I want to paint...'). Their ways of writing seemed to pander to the anticipated desires of fans at the most basic, structural level – more proof, as the critics saw it, that the poetry they wrote wasn't truly their own, its meaning and shape conditioned by a thousand tiny adjustments made with a pop audience in mind. It was no coincidence, as Lindop observed, that the most characteristic elements of their styles were also those that looked a lot like the 'techniques of advertising'. As with newspaper ads, television jingles and commercial slogans, the aim seemed to be to set up a hook as rapidly and economically as possible. 'Where there is a mass-audience to be held and entertained,' he concluded, 'it is inevitable that the poet will welcome the techniques of mass-persuasion.'[66]

Henri, McGough and Patten weren't unduly perturbed by the idea that they were giving audiences what they'd paid for; the whole point, as they saw it, of reading at bars and clubs was to attract people the same age as them who cared about the things they cared about, and with whom they could communicate directly and intimately.[67] To Henri, at least, too, there was nothing especially insulting about the comparison between his work and advertising copy. In 'Notes on Painting and Poetry', the essay he wrote to accompany his first solo collection, *Tonight at Noon* (1967), he suggested that writing poetry in the mid-twentieth century was fundamentally a matter of reuse, rather than invention. The sheer volume of specialist ad-language in the public sphere at all times – messaging, jingles, slogans – was an extraordinary, unprecedented literary resource, and it was up to poets to exploit it – to take their cue from pop art's fascination with the 'humble and despised' objects of consumer society.

'I think my concern should be with the whole area of language as it impinges on me, now,' he wrote:

> Certain specialist uses of language seem particularly relevant: that of advertising (hoardings, slogans, tv ads) or newspaper headlines, where the aim is to transmit a message (or feeling) as quickly as perception allows... Far from drawing away his coat-tails in disgust at the taint of 'commercialism' I can't help feeling that this new and different and economical use of language should be investigated by the poet.[68]

Henri investigated the 'taint of "commercialism"' in his poetry by putting ad-language into uncomfortable contact with other kinds of texts, and into uncomfortably surreal situations. His poem 'On the Late Late Massachers Stillbirths and Deformed Children a Smoother Lovelier Skin Job', in *The Mersey Sound*, combines, not quite at random, lines from John Milton's Sonnet XXXVIII ('On the Late Massacre in Piedmont') with slices of type from the *TV Times* and a CND leaflet on the effects of the bomb. In this cut-and-paste job, Milton's heroic line presses up against toneless descriptions of fallout and the bossy instructions of a cosmetics ad: 'Avenge O Lord thy slaughter'd saints, whose bones / Will cause up to 1 million deaths from leukaemia [...] / Now for the vitally important step. Cream your face and neck a second time.'[69] His 'Bomb Commercials', a set of parody adverts first performed at the apocalyptic event at the Cavern, imagine the advertising industry adapting, surreally and rather too smoothly, to a post-nuclear scenario. 'Everyday in cities all over England people are breathing in Fall-out. / Get the taste of the Bomb out of your mouth with OVAL FRUITS.' 'When he takes you in his arms for that final, four-minute kiss, you need an extra-special lipstick.'[70]

To us now, at a distance of sixty years, the idea of viewing bomb culture through the lens of consumer culture seems ridiculous, and comic because of it. Ads for face creams and lipsticks are inane, hyper-ordinary; the bomb threat is terrifying and extraordinary; the juxtaposition between the two is incongruous, and therefore funny. When the skit was first performed, it would also have prompted laughter, but of a less straightforward kind. The heightened, urgent scenarios into which ad-language is parachuted in Henri's lines remind us that, in the mid-1960s, its forms and techniques were new and strange, rapidly evolving: they were apt to be surprising rather than predictable, not yet ignorable background noise.[71] They were also, like 'the taste of the Bomb', everywhere – all-pervasive, in the atmosphere, part of the texture, physical and psychological, of the changing post-war environment. If it was the poet's business, as Henri argued, to capture the real language of the corner of the world he or she inhabited – the language, in his own case, of 'motor-bike specialists, consultant gynaecologists, Beatle fans, the people who write "Coronation Street", peeping toms, admen' – then slogans and jingles were part of that, a noisy element in the total landscape.[72]

Poetry could capture this landscape like an urban snapshot, reproducing fragments of found language from street hoardings and shopfronts. In McGough's 'Limestreetscene '64', a portrait of one of Liverpool's best-known streets, the slogan of the lit-up Guinness sign flickers into view, a 'neonic presence' against the dark civic architecture:

> St. George's Hall
> black pantheonic
> like a coalman's wedding cake
> glows in the neonic
> presence of Schweppervescence
> and 'Guinness is Good for You'

The same sign serves as a leitmotif in Henri's 'The Entry of Christ into Liverpool', where 'GUINNESS IS GOOD FOR YOU', in insistent caps, threads itself through the text of the poem, its letters appearing in sequential flashes as parts of the sign come to life: 'GUIN / GUINN / GUINNESS IS...'[73] Guinness crops up again in Henri's *Autobiography* (1971), this time flanked by rival ales, 'Newcastle Brown, Export and Exhibition'. In the memory, the recollected brand-names occupy the same kind of space as items on the young poet's library reading lists ('Kafka Auden MacNeice'), neither considered as more formative than the other.[74]

What poems could do with bits of text, books could do with a combination of text and image. In his introduction to *The Liverpool Scene*, Lucie-Smith explained that by accompanying his selection of poems with photographs of the poets and their city, he hoped to reconstruct something of the world they moved in – 'a kind of texture, both social and verbal.' Ad-language, in these photographs, is everywhere, supplying social and verbal 'texture' together. In one image, McGough and Henri are shown leaning nonchalantly outside a shop, next to an advert for pies aimed at young comic-book fans: 'ABC TV's Batman cometh with...

steak and kidney pies.' In another, Henri stares meaningfully at the camera from the interior of a grocer's, his head framed by stacks of Warhol-style Campbell's soup cans. On the back cover, a famous recent remark of Ginsberg's about Liverpool, made to a journalist during his stay with Patten and Henri on Canning Street in 1965, is given the glittering ad-man touch, laid out in giant red letters: 'Liverpool / is at / the / present / moment / the centre / of the / consciousness / of the / human / universe.'[75]

The problem with this dalliance with consumer culture, as several critics pointed out, was that it was sometimes hard to tell who was using whom. The danger, it was argued, when engaging with something as sophisticated and chameleon-like as advertising, was that even as you parodied it or imitated it, it would stay one step ahead: your attempts to make something real out of it, to assimilate it and transform it into art, would just end up corrupting whatever you produced. In ad-language, Lindop observed, poets were taking on 'an adversary without a conscience'. However thoughtful or self-conscious they were about their work, they were bound to come off worse, risking becoming the butt of the joke they were trying to make. Henri's 'slick evocation of the detritus of a consumer society,' Roy Fuller wrote, 'strikes us with […] uneasiness': it was like fraternizing with the enemy, 'junketing with the very forces designed to limit the imagination.'[76]

Henri's poem 'Me', according to Lindop, was the worst culprit. A regular hit on the Liverpool poets' performance set, 'Me' is a blur of names, a long, unpunctuated list of Henri's favourite composers, pop musicians, artists and writers:

Belà Bartók Henri Rousseau
Rauschenberg and Jasper Johns
Lukas Cranach Shostakovich
Kropotkin Ringo George and John[77]

By flattering the sensibilities, Lindop argued, of the select few who considered themselves acquainted with all these figures (plus, for good measure, Mick Jagger, Kurt Schwitters, Kafka and the Marquis de Sade), Henri appeared to be excluding, implicitly, those who weren't; he was forming a kind of club, membership of which depended on whether you possessed a particular 'blend of fashionable attitudes to life and art'. This appeal to a select audience, Lindop claimed, was closely related to the 'crudely explicit snobbery' of luxury adverts, which hooked in their prey by similar techniques of inclusion and exclusion. Both operated by sketching out the parameters of aspirational taste, gesturing to a lifestyle which, by definition, not everyone could share. 'The advertisement that asks us whether we are the kind of person who is capable of appreciating Someone's expensive brand of cigarettes,' he wrote, was just a step away from the 'implied question of Henri's poem: "Are you the kind of person who knows about Jarry, Coltrane, Debussy?"'[78]

The way in which Henri, McGough and Patten's work was marketed in the mid- and later 1960s indicates that a lot of people saw in it an endorsement of a particular lifestyle. Beatlemania saturated Liverpool with media attention, as executives competed with one another to scout for more local talent. 'Television crews would be filmed filming television crews filming television reporters reporting on the next big thing to come out of Merseyside,' McGough recalled.[79] In 1965, at the age of nineteen, Patten was offered his first book deal by a London publisher who happened to tune into Jack de Manio's *Today* programme on BBC radio, where he heard the young poet reading 'Little Johnny's Confession'. (A few months later, Patten told a journalist that because he had now had a 'brief television appearance', he hoped his mother would finally 'stop mentioning twice a week that there are good jobs going at

Ford's.'[80]) McGough, as part of his sketch group, The Scaffold, was scouted in 1966 by an ABC TV producer for a slot on a Saturday night chat show, *Gazette* (catchphrase: 'Famous in the North').[81] For its bumper piece on the Liverpool art scene in 1967, the *Weekend Telegraph* opened with a line that reminded everyone why the city was really in the public eye: 'From a decrepit, decaying part of the Beatle City, a whole new Mersey Scene is ready to burst out...'[82]

Within this context, when it came to publishing and promoting the Liverpool poets, there was only one way to go. 'I have looked at the book from every possible angle and am absolutely sure that the Liverpool label – however sick of it you may personally be – is the best sales pitch we have got,' Tony Richardson, Penguin's poetry editor, wrote to Patten in 1966. *The Mersey Sound* was the tenth volume in Penguin's long-running Modern Poets series (in total, there would be twenty-seven instalments between 1962–79, each introducing readers to a trio of contemporary writers), but the first to have its own title, set out in shocking orange comic-book lettering on the cover. In the context of pop music and Beatlemania, Richardson acknowledged, the idea of a 'Mersey sound' was already 'old hat', even 'corny'; but since it was a phrase that meant 'a great deal to a nation-wide audience', transposing it 'from pop music to poetry' would be guaranteed to pique interest.[83] Those who had never attended a reading at Streate's, never been to the Cavern, needed to be sold a way of life on the basis of what they did know about: the Beatles and Merseybeat. The book was to be a passport, a hot ticket to being young, 'in', and part of the scene, part of the pop life that Liverpool seemed to represent. 'The buyer must be made to feel that what's he getting will have less to do with poetry than with Liverpool,' Ian Hamilton wrote disapprovingly in the *TLS* in 1967.[84]

To sell this vision, the look of the books was key. '[We want] something very different from present PMP style,' Penguin's design team noted in their cover brief, 'something alive and rowdy and pop.'[85] On the first edition cover, the title phrase stood out against an edgy black background, framed by a dockland cityscape and pop art-style photographs of a hysterical female fan. Henri, McGough and Patten were unimpressed, disliking what McGough called 'the photographs of a teenage girl screaming orgasmically and *Yellow Submarine*-type typography that we considered too close to the pop music scene.'[86] But the cover succeeded in conveying what it was supposed to: that the 'young, fun, irreverent' voices collected in its pages were 'in some ways the equivalent in poetry of the Beatles.'[87] Liverpool poetry, it suggested, like the lyrics of a pop song, was about sound rather than words on a page: it was ephemeral, something that lived and died in the moment of performance and had been captured in print with difficulty. Penguin drew the line at Patten's suggestion that they 'put out a record' to accompany the book (a series of readings by the poets, perhaps 'backed by one of the beatgroups'), but only because they were unsure of how to go about marketing an LP simultaneously.[88] (Patten perhaps got the idea from the Beats: a special issue of *The Evergreen Review* dedicated to 'The San Francisco Scene' (1957), featuring Ginsberg's controversial poem 'Howl', was accompanied, a year later, by an LP of the poets reading their work.[89])

Tonight at Noon, Henri's solo collection, took a similar visual approach. On the cover, the large, surreally coloured portrait of the artist – sporting a Lennon-style cap, and framed by psychedelic title lettering – seemed designed to present him as a popstar as much as a poet.[90] *Love, Love, Love*, featuring the Liverpool poets alongside a selection of other avant-garde writers, was even more self-consciously zeitgeisty: on its 'writhingly psychedelic dust-jacket', the Beatles-inspired title, its letters formed by the draped bodies of semi-clothed female figures, sat beneath a large pink heart symbol and violently coloured acid clouds. The book was an object lesson, the *TLS* observed, in 'how marketing maketh myths'.[91]

Nothing quite compared, though, to *The Liverpool Scene*, which was launched, as McGough put it, 'on a French kiss of publicity'. Its publisher, the enthusiastic American Donald Carroll, knew exactly what he was doing by producing a glossy, square hardback which from a distance looked rather like a record sleeve, whose subtitle was 'Recorded live along the Mersey Beat'; he knew what he was doing, too, by dedicating the book 'To the Beatles, without whom…', as if the Fab Four were the guiding spirit of the enterprise; and by presenting the reader with a photo of Ringo in his pants on the first page.[92] A launch party (an event normally associated with pop record releases) was held at the Cavern, featuring live music from a local band, specially designed posters, stickers and badges, and a vast quantity of champagne.* Journalists 'shipped up from London' mingled with TV crews, poets, artists, local dignitaries from Liverpool City Council and the year's intake of female Liverpool Art College students. Some of the journalists' marriages did not survive.[93] Lucie-Smith had wanted the anthology to be a representation of the social 'texture' of a place, a 'record of a lifestyle'; what better way to convey that, and to sell it, than a blowout party everyone wished they'd been at?[94] 'This is what it's all about,' declared the music producer Hal Shaper on the cover of *The Incredible New Liverpool Scene* LP (1967), a recording of Henri and

---

* *The Mersey Sound* had its own impromptu version of a boozy launch in June 1967, when Patten won a Pernod Poetry Award and the ceremony turned into a 'massive party'.

McGough reading live brought out to accompany the book. 'Life along the Mersey Beat. Now.'[95]

Those who disliked the way *The Liverpool Scene* and *The Mersey Sound* were marketed – declaring them 'irritatingly modish', 'journalistically fashionable', flashy consumer products – probably disliked most of all the fact that the books weren't marketed for them.[96] Poetry books had always, of course, since the dawn of print, been presented as being for some kinds of people and not for others. What was different here was the fact that these books were so obviously and unapologetically not meant for the literary establishment. The difference between buying a copy of *The Mersey Sound* and not buying it wasn't, as in the past, a question of having the right educational background: it was a question of coolness.

In one sense, the publication of Henri, McGough and Patten's work did involve a rapprochement with the literary elite, because it located them squarely on the printed page. It brought their poetry out of the smoky bar and into the bookshop and university library, transforming a live act into material for the catalogues of publishing houses. 'The pop poets have been seduced into traditional publication, gathered into anthologies, flattered into betraying their aims,' Melly wrote.[97] For some performance poets (not the Liverpool poets), 'gathered' between two covers was, ultimately, the desirable place to be: the end-goal of their attempts to raise poetry's profile through live readings was to be able to stop doing the live readings. Robson, for instance, of the poetry and jazz movement, explained in the introduction to his anthology, *Poems from Poetry & Jazz in Concert* (1969), that he was delighted to have 'the opportunity to assemble these poems under one, more permanent, roof.'[98] But when it came to poets who championed live performance for its own sake, and whose identity was bound up with the 'scene' they'd emerged from, things got considerably more tricky. 'We are moving ever nearer,' the critic Jonathan Raban observed in 1971, 'to a charade in which editors, publishers, and critics reverently follow on the heels of infants who only want the freedom to be naughty and themselves.'[99]

In the case of the Liverpool poets, metropolitan publishers, sensing the way the wind was blowing, were only too eager to offer book deals and publicity, capitalising on Henri, McGough and Patten's proximity to pop in order to corner the burgeoning paperback market.[100] The poets themselves, though Patten in particular disliked the sudden upsurge of media attention, were happy to be in print, appreciating that publication meant not only stability but literary success of a lasting and important kind. But in their anthologies, all the same, it's hard not to see glimpses of what Lucie-Smith, writing after having seen Henri perform in Nottingham in 1966, called their 'essentially oral poetry' – glimpses of the difficulties involved in trying to pin down pop poetry's immediacy, its 'alive and rowdy' moment, onto the page, or of conveying something more like an environment, a three-dimensional scene, in flat lines of verse.[101]

In *The Mersey Sound*, what stands out is the provisional feeling that some of the poems, Henri's in particular, seem to possess – the way they let slip somehow that out in the world they would be different, more real and alive. 'Love Poem', with its collection of talismanic objects (the 'red bra', the 'chocolate Easter Egg'), is subtitled 'Sections from a work still in progress', as if its little details, like the affair they memorialize, are impermanent, liable to get lost or be replaced. 'I Want to Paint', having been rewritten from memory after Henri mislaid his original text, shape-shifted regularly in performance as he improvised extra lines and dropped others; on the page, it encapsulates, but only temporarily, the creative universe inside his head.[102]

In the case of *The Liverpool Scene*, much of the style of the book can be explained as a kind of resistance to the permanence of print. The candid, posed-unposed photographs portray snapshot moments that we can imagine looking different a second earlier or later; the snatches of conversation transcribed from interviews capture 'reactions of the moment' from the poets, rather than their 'considered formal statements'; the semi-haphazard, collage-style layout imparts a general air of 'fluidity and spontaneity', a suggestion that what's on the page is a set of possibilities, rather than a finished product. The most telling inclusion is Henri's 'Summer Poems Without Words', the 'action-piece' he'd created for live audiences, instructing them to clean their teeth consciously and look carefully at bus posters.[103] The piece is a draft for life in the same way a set of stage directions is a draft for performance: on the page, it's mere potential, coming into being only in the moment of action.*

The Mersey Sound sold forty thousand copies, twice Penguin's print run, in its first year of publication. Four revised editions and one restored edition later, it now ranks, according to its publisher, as the bestselling poetry anthology of all time, never once going out of print.[104] The appetite for verse in paperback among young people, which Penguin had identified and banked on when it launched its Modern Poets series in 1962, proved to be voracious. Large numbers of students and teenagers

---

* Michael Horovitz's anthology, *Children of Albion: Poetry of the Underground in Britain* (Penguin, 1969), was another collection of avant-garde performance poetry which seemed to push back against being a book. Horovitz refused to provide an introduction to his selection, instead writing a lengthy 'Afterwords' essay in an ungrammatical, slangy, countercultural style, which several critics suspected was designed specifically to annoy them.

devoured the book and sent in fan-mail; one, in a typical letter, wrote to Penguin to query whether they had printed a poem of Henri's she had heard live twice. The University of Bradford's Student Union wrote to request the presence of Henri, McGough and Patten at its arts festival. Editors at *Jackie*, the bestselling magazine for teenage girls, contacted Penguin in 1967 to ask permission to serialize extracts from *The Mersey Sound* for their readers.[105] (The publisher of *The Liverpool Scene*, having marketed it to the hilt, made a mistake in not 'going paperback' after a successful hardback run – it would have been, as Henri noted, a golden opportunity to 'cash in'.[106])

In a sense, both books, because they were printed objects that anyone could buy, saved Liverpool poetry from itself. To survive, last longer than the charmed atmosphere of the live reading or the visionary spectacle at the Albert Hall, poetry had to come out into the open, embrace the idea of its own permanence. 'I felt at the time I wanted poetry to become "overground",' Henri said after the Poetry Incarnation.[107] Going 'overground', to some, was akin to selling out, or making the Liverpool scene 'public property', as Melly put it: flattening and commercializing what was special about an art, a lifestyle, that previously only a select crowd had been in on. 'The city prospered and grew rich, happy at the feet of the Titans of Showbiz and the Titans of the Great God Art,' a satirical contributor to *Sphinx*, Liverpool University's student magazine, commented in 1970.[108] But it was also the only way to make that lifestyle spread and last, to give tens of thousands of teenagers who had never been to O'Connor's or the Cavern, and maybe never would, a taste of the pop moment. 'Remember that we are trying to extend [your] public greatly,' Richardson wrote to Patten in 1966. 'The public is by no means of the same kind that you already command.'[109] *The Mersey Sound*, one former fan recalled, 'made me feel somehow connected,' in touch from a distance with 'whatever it was that I thought was going on out there in that wider, long-haired world that I intuitively knew I wanted to be part of.'[110] Liverpool's bohemian district, not long after its glory days, was 'murdered by planners', as Henri put it, 'bulldozed' and 'uprooted'. Its poetry, though, pinned down, half-against its will, on the page, stayed alive.[111]

8

THERAPY

The Anthology and Self-Help (2000–)

*T*he Poetry Cure: A Pocket Medicine Chest of Verse, one
of the earliest psychotherapeutic collections of poetry in
English, appeared in 1925. Its creator, a poet and editor named
Robert Haven Schauffler, described it in his introduction as
'a cheap and convenient pocket anthology of remedies',
a little book that would give those suffering from common
psychological complaints – 'sorrow', 'fear', a 'swollen ego' –
the option of curing themselves through reading, rather than
employing the services of a therapist. His poems, he hoped,
would supply a rapid, easy means of treatment 'the instant the
first premonitory symptoms of a trouble are noticed.'[1] On the
cover leaf, Schauffler quoted from a recent essay by Robert
Graves. 'A well-chosen anthology,' Graves had written, 'is a
complete dispensary of medicine for the more common mental
disorders, and may be used as much for prevention as cure.'[2]
Neither Graves nor Schauffler was using the language of
medicine figuratively. Both men were convinced of poetry's
real abilities in the context of the developing science of
psychotherapy, understanding it as a powerful vehicle for
imaginative identification and healing. The idea wasn't a new
one – as Graves pointed out, the arguments for it were centuries

old, rooted in the ancient Greek idea of catharsis, the sense of emotional release and purgation experienced by spectators of dramatic performances.* But modern psychological theorists, following Freud and Jung, had also posited connections between the unconscious mind and the poetic imagination, between the writing and reading of poetry and the elucidation of healthy and unhealthy mental patterns for action.[3]

Schauffler, who had read widely in this literature, approached his subject from the perspective of a practitioner in the field. Rather than picking out poems which he imagined might have therapeutic uses for his readers, or which he'd found therapeutically useful himself, he conducted empirical research, seeking to generate a sufficient evidence base to be confident about what his book could achieve. 'For a long period, I studied, collected and tried the effects of various sorts of verse on patients in my poetic clinic,' he explained. 'Finally, a year ago, it grew evident that enough poems might be counted on to affect enough people with enough power and uniformity, to make possible a science of poetry therapeutics, and justify the present book.'[4]

In his anthology, Schauffler doesn't say exactly what took place in his 'poetic clinic' when patients came in with their complaints, but we can piece together the rudiments of his method. First, he was highly selective in his choice of poetic 'cure'. 'A large, ordinary anthology of verse is like a drug store,' he wrote in his introduction. 'It contains just the thing for your complaint – that is, if you know where to look for it. But an indiscriminate sampling of the stock may have serious consequences.' For some patients, 'bitter or cruel' poems would

---

* Graves 'explain[s] his theory of the medical value of poetry in a passage that reads like a page of Aristotle seen through the spectacles of Dr. Freud,' wrote the Irish essayist Robert Lynd in 1922.

be toxic rather than medicinal, exacerbating already-existing dark thoughts. For others, cheerful or frivolous poems were apt to have dangerous effects, making them feel misunderstood or alone. 'What is salvation for the average Jones may be poison for the exceptional Smith,' Schauffler said. Accordingly, when he came to compile his anthology, he subdivided it into sections corresponding to particular complaints ('Pills to Purge Melancholy', 'Spiritual Pick-Me-Ups'), and, within these, split up his poem recommendations into categories targeted at different 'psychological type[s]'. For the sort of person whose response to adversity was to want to escape from it, he offered poems calculated to provide a temporary diversion. For those who sought companionship in their emotional mood, he suggested poems likely to mirror or acknowledge the 'painful feelings' they were experiencing.[5]

Throughout, Schauffler wasn't interested in offering the finest or most famous poems in the English language. 'Why add one more to the myriad existing anthologies of the world's best poetry?' In his contents pages, notable Modernist poets were conspicuous by their absence; several major figures, including Philip Sidney, George Herbert and Robert Frost, had only one poem each (to two of Schauffler's own); others, such as Emily Dickinson, were represented by a selection that avoided their most interesting and complex material. A host of nineteenth-century British and American spiritual writers, on the other hand, fared considerably better. They had been chosen for their therapeutic efficacy: they were the 'highest grade' poetical 'drugs', as Schauffler put it, that he'd been able to obtain, and whose effects he'd managed to observe in his clinic. 'On the day when India paper editions of this work begin to dispute front window space in our drug stores with beauty clays, heating pads and gland preparations,' he declared, 'the market value of the poet will rise. He will shoot forward in popular esteem from the dubiously ornamental to the solidly useful class.'[6]

Although, in the United Kingdom, books had been available for more than twenty years in branches of Boots, the chemist chain, as part of a lending library scheme, the idea that they would one day displace medicines and cosmetics from the front windows of pharmacies seemed unlikely. Nonetheless, to sell the concept of his anthology, Schauffler needed to make the point that poetry could be 'solidly useful', a valuable tool in the pockets of readers, rather than merely 'ornamental', beautiful but useless. Many of those who disliked it, he believed, might be persuaded to change their minds if they were brought to see practical uses in it. The problem with trying to appeal to this group was the risk of alienating another: those who were fiercely protective of poetry's 'ornamental' qualities, and prized it because it offered them something intangible, ineffable – because it was useless, in other words. The 'deep reservoir of mistrust', in the literary critic Rita Felski's phrase, that such readers exhibited towards the idea of use tended to be informed by the kinds of poets and critics they read. Influenced by Romantic and post-Romantic attitudes, they held deep-rooted convictions about the special nature of art, poetry in particular, as a category of human endeavour, and about the impossibility of measuring its worth in terms of utility.[7]

The difference between these kinds of readers – between those seeking the closest thing to a 'pure' experience of artistic communion, and those wanting 'something to go on, something that will help them live their lives' – is apt to be overstated.[8] Often, poetry's ability to help comes from just those aesthetic qualities which seem to turn their backs on use value. In the last twenty years, however, a version of the old debate has resurfaced in the context of the growth of the market for self-help literature, and its spill-over into poetry publishing.

In the *London Review of Books* in 2004, the novelist and critic Andrew O'Hagan pointed to a difference between what he referred to as 'traditional' poetry anthologies – scholarly collections of the 'best' poems in the language, compiled by heavyweight publishing houses – and the collections now emerging onto the market. The 'old "Treasuries"', as he called them, had been 'collections of poems presented for their own qualities', the work of editors who foregrounded aesthetic or intellectual considerations. Now, he argued, many popular anthologies seemed to be focused not on poems but on readers: they presented poetry as a species of self-help, a tool of personal growth like any other, valuable as a plumbable well of advice, reassurance and emotional uplift.[9]

When did it become poetry's 'duty to give people a leg-up from one part of the day to another?' O'Hagan asked. New self-help-style collections, he and other critics argued, were bent on rebranding poetry as a 'lifestyle accessory' for the worried middle classes, placing it in the same 'sky-blue', 'touchy-feely' category as 'CD compilations for every mood', 'lavender bath oil' and 'state-of-the-art therapy'.[10] 'It is to sell poetry dreadfully short to treat it as a therapeutic tool rather than a serious art form,' Sam Leith remarked in the *Evening Standard* in 2016.[11] Rather than evaluating anthologists' selections – which, by and large, they didn't take issue with – critics attacked the basic idea that poetry was there to help. 'If you ignore the huggy, self-help element,' Daniel Soar commented in the *LRB* of Neil Astley's *Staying Alive: Real Poems for Unreal Times* (2002), 'it's a very good anthology indeed.'[12]

O'Hagan's example was *Poems to Last a Lifetime* (2004), edited by the writer and broadcaster Daisy Goodwin (also the editor of *101 Poems That Could Save Your Life* (1999), *101 Poems to Get You Through the Day (and Night)* (2000) and *101 Poems to Keep You Sane* (2001). Other self-help poetry collections published during the last two decades include Julia Darling and Cynthia Fuller's *The Poetry Cure* (2005); Deborah Alma's *The Emergency Poet: An Anti-Stress Poetry Anthology* (2015); Jonathan Bate, Paula Byrne, Sophie Ratcliffe and Andrew Schuman's *Stressed Unstressed: Classic Poems to Ease the Mind* (2016); and the publisher and broadcaster William Sieghart's two anthologies, *The Poetry Pharmacy: Tried-and-True Prescriptions for the Heart, Mind and Soul* (2017) and *The Poetry Pharmacy Returns: More Prescriptions for Courage, Healing and Hope* (2019).[13]

The kind of 'emotional utility', in O'Hagan's phrase, that such books offer varies. Sieghart and Goodwin's anthologies present themselves as self-help guides, selections of poems designed to support readers through emotional difficulties. Others, such as *The Poetry Cure* and *Stressed Unstressed*, have links to NHS institutions and may be recommended to patients by GPs or placed in clinic waiting rooms.[14] A third, looser, category involves anthologies without explicit therapeutic aims, but that open themselves up to readers who choose to use them in this way. The bestselling *Staying Alive* books – *Staying Alive* (2002), *Being Alive* (2004), *Being Human* (2011) and *Staying Human* (2020), all edited by Astley for Bloodaxe Books – are perhaps the most prominent examples of this group.[15] 'The best contemporary poetry is life-affirming and directly relevant to all our lives,' the introduction to *Staying Alive* argues. 'Poetry doesn't give answers as such, but it engages readers intellectually and emotionally.'[16]

What all therapeutic anthologies have in common is an openness to the idea behind Schauffler's 'poetry cure' experiment: that people come to poetry to feel better. Literary criticism of the modern era, in particular the kind of close reading dominant in American and British universities since the mid-twentieth century, has tended to 'rule out of bounds,' as

Louis Menand has argued, 'many things people naturally think about when they read literature' – among them 'the way it makes us feel'. Therapeutic poetry collections make it their mission to turn back the clock, explicitly reinviting an older, humanist mode of response.[17] They return empathy and connection to the list of things we can ask of a book, and uphold subjective responses – how this particular book makes me, a particular person, feel – as valid and useful readerly mechanisms.

Sieghart, who continues to run pop-up 'poetry pharmacies' at literary festivals, libraries and schools around Britain, listening to people's problems and prescribing them poems to help, argues that a key 'access point to poetry' for many readers is 'suffering'. The experience of going through a difficult time, he suggests, is what 'opens [...] ears, hearts and minds', prompting a yearning for solace and connection.[18] 'It is not a new idea that in times of loss, distress and pain we turn to poetry,' Darling and Fuller observe in their anthology. '[Poetry] allows us to acknowledge the intensity of what we are feeling – doesn't let us pretend we are "all right".'[19] Astley, likewise, though careful to emphasize that poetry rarely offers 'simple solace or [...] medication', has argued that contemporary verse should be prized for engaging 'with people and what people do and think and feel and fear in their lives.' 'If someone is drawn to reading poetry because of personal anxieties, or depression, or alienation, or bereavement, what's wrong with that?' he asked in a lecture of 2005. 'Once poems are written and published, they belong to the readers.'[20]

The idea that you might turn to literature for advice and comfort isn't a new one, as O'Hagan points out in his essay. Reading for self-help harks back to an early modern idea, derived from classical literary theory, of poetry as a source of utility as well as pleasure. Imaginative literature, for readers during the sixteenth and seventeenth centuries in particular, served as 'equipment for living': it was a storehouse of wisdom that could be practically applied, capable of helping individuals make sense of the problems they encountered in their lives.[21] Epic poems or history plays could supply models of conduct, or warnings about what not to do; elegies could be treasure-troves of comforting sentiments for the bereaved.

This way of reading meant consuming books in a particular manner. Many early modern readers kept commonplace books, or what we might call scrapbooks: personal notebooks into which they copied out passages from texts they found illuminating, grouping the various fragments together under thematic headings so that they could be easily consulted later. (Wavell's *Other Men's Flowers*, an anthology based on a notebook into which he'd copied down poems he knew by heart, grouping them by theme, is a twentieth-century version of the form, as is T.E. Lawrence's collection of his favourite 'minor poems', *Minorities*.[22]) What early modern readers chose to read, and how they read it, therefore, was both systematic and serendipitous. On one hand, they approached books as tools for making sense of the world, mining them for information, advice or anecdotes which might have some bearing on a personal situation. But they also read in a manner that we might think of as illogical or random. Rather than absorbing themselves in the forward movement of a poem or prose text, they read non-sequentially, 'in fits and starts', plucking out passages as they went, and hopping around and between books as their patterns of interest or emotional needs dictated.[23]

Modern self-help culture is the direct descendant of this instrumental, personal way of reading and using literature. Makers of self-help books don't expect readers to proceed through them in a linear fashion from cover to cover: instead, they encourage a practical approach, a method of locating and plucking out only those particular pieces of advice or model scenarios that are useful to the individual case. This way of reading is steered, partly, by the form the books take. Self-help texts, like early modern commonplace books, tend not to be cohesive wholes but collections of fragments, bodies made up of bits and pieces assembled from elsewhere. The book that brought an early version of self-help culture into the mainstream, more than a hundred and fifty years ago – Samuel Smiles's bestselling *Self-Help: With Illustrations of Character, Conduct, and Perseverance* (1859) – was a 'tapestry of literary anecdote and quotation', as the critic Beth Blum has argued, a storehouse of advice drawn from the characters and situations of literature.[24] It instructed its readers how to make and save money by quoting *Hamlet*; it taught self-reliance through Wordsworth and self-respect through Milton.[25] For many of the working-class autodidacts who drew on its wisdom, it represented a first encounter with classic literature – literature, that is, shredded and reformulated as a series of inspiring examples.[26]

Around the international success of *Self-Help*, a small Victorian publishing industry sprang up. Canny imitators adapted Smiles's model for the more lucrative middle-class market. A cousin of Oscar Wilde's, the Reverend E.J. Hardy, produced a semi-humorous book entitled *How to Be Happy Though Married* (1885), referring to himself as 'a graduate in the university of matrimony' on the cover.[27] In the decades that followed, the emergent self-help genre became a 'commercial juggernaut' in Britain and the United States, growing increasingly specialized in its methods and expanding into new territories: anxiety management, productivity, fear of ageing, weight control.[28] During the mid-twentieth century, the growth of popular interest in psychology and therapy encouraged greater numbers of middle-class readers to focus inwards, consulting self-help manuals for strategies of psychological improvement that would radiate outwards into other areas of their lives.[29] In recent decades, self-help has become more popular than ever, encouraging, under the banner of self-actualization, attention to the minutiae of individual physical and mental well-being. Reality genres with a self-improvement element – the weight-loss challenge, the interior design transformation, the fashion makeover – are stalwarts of television programming; self-help books, marketed as philosophy, psychology, romance, nutrition or health, dominate bestseller lists.[30]

In a saturated market, you need to be different to stand out. As Blum has pointed out, in an effort not to repeat the same old affirmative wisdom, self-help over the last two decades has returned to its beginnings, and to literature. Following the success of Alain de Botton's *How Proust Can Change Your Life* (1997), a number of recent books have adopted novelists, essayists and poets as their gurus – among them Marty Beckerman's *The Heming Way* (2011); Alexander McCall Smith's *What W.H. Auden Can Do for You* (2013); and *What Would Virginia Woolf Do?* (2018), by Nina Lorez Collins. Each of these reflects a belief that writers, sometimes despite themselves, make particularly trustworthy mentors. Life is complicated, uncertain and doesn't always give you what you want: advice capable of standing up to it has to be correspondingly nuanced, wary of easy answers. The more difficult works of literature are – the more 'faithfully' they represent human experience as 'complex, random, chaotic and multifaceted', as Blum has put it – the more they can be trusted, paradoxically, as guides to living.[31] Proust and Woolf, in their sheer recalcitrance (their 'vehemently anti-utilitarian agendas'), are far more use in the face of life's complexities than cheery proverbs or affirmations.

All novels, theoretically, regardless of their difficulty, 'have the power to transport you into another existence, and see the world from a different point of view,' as Ella Berthoud and Susan Elderkin argue in *The Novel Cure: An A–Z of Literary Remedies* (2013).[32] For every real quandary life presents, there's a fictional solution, a plot or character capable of modelling our problems for us and showing us what they look like from the outside, or from someone else's point of view. *Madame Bovary*, Berthoud and Elderkin suggest, could give you pause for thought if you were considering having an affair; the 'matter-of-fact' attitude to mortality in *One Hundred Years of Solitude* might go some way to curing you of a fear of death.[33] Fiction, it's claimed, sets up situations in which characters who resemble aspects of ourselves come up against predicaments that remind us of our own: it builds trial universes, spaces in which we're able to imagine and evaluate, without being compelled to take responsibility for, possible ways of being.[34] It encourages us to project and empathize.

Bibliotherapy – the practice of connecting literature and healthcare by encouraging people to read books to improve their well-being – is more popular than it's ever been. As a concept, reading therapy is over a century old, its principles first developed by librarians employed in hospitals after the First World War, as they sought innovative ways to treat traumatized soldiers. (Schauffler, a few years after the 1918 Armistice, dedicated his book to 'The noble army of CREATIVE LIBRARIANS, PRACTITIONERS ALL [...] OF THE POETRY CURE.'[35]) Since the millennium, it has been a site of rapid development, increasingly legitimized by public institutions. In the UK, bibliotherapy has been an element of NHS care for twenty years: the national Reading Agency charity, supported by Arts Council England, oversees a self-help scheme, Books on Prescription (which allows GPs to prescribe patients books on mental health conditions, in collaboration with public libraries), and runs the Reading Well Mood-boosting Books programme, which recommends lists of 'uplifting titles' in fiction, poetry and non-fiction for adults and children.[36] On the local level, there are bibliotherapeutic organizations and schemes, some supported by Arts Council funding. The Shared Reading initiative, launched in Birkenhead in 2002 by a charity, The Reader, oversees the establishment of community groups for reading and discussing classic novels.[37] In the academic world, the rapidly growing field of medical humanities investigates the workings of the mind and body using methodologies drawn from the spheres of literature, history and art.

In the for-profit domain, bibliotherapy has grown up as part of the self-help industry, emerging as an increasingly mainstream alternative to traditional therapy. Berthoud and Elderkin run their own private bibliotherapeutic practice at de Botton's School of Life in London, offering personalized consultations in which they assess clients' 'unique readerly identity' and prescribe curative doses of fiction or philosophy.[38] In rural Shropshire, Deborah Alma, editor of The Emergency Poet, has opened a bricks-and-mortar Poetry Pharmacy, an apothecary-style shop selling 'poetry, philosophy and well-being books', as well as miniature anthologies in the form of 'pill bottles' – collections of printed texts rolled up to look like lozenges, and sold thematically ('Broken Heart Pills'; 'Existential Angst Pills'; 'Blue Remembered Pills'). Like Berthoud and Elderkin, Alma also holds therapeutic 'consultation' sessions, from which clients emerge with a poem selected to assuage their anxieties.[39]

Do poems offer the same therapeutic resources as novels? Advocates argue that although most poems aren't able to supply the large-scale imaginative worlds that fiction builds, they offer other things that fiction can't, or which it doesn't foreground as effectively. The way a poem looks on the page, its shapeliness and repeating structures, can instil in readers 'a sense of order and harmony', as Darling and Fuller argue; images and metaphors can offer striking new ways of understanding the world; the musicality of rhythm can gesture towards balance and calm. Even a poem in a foreign language – whose force is largely experienced as a series of sounds – can have an 'extraordinary resonance', as Andrew Schuman, one of the editors of *Stressed Unstressed* and an NHS doctor, suggests. Schuman's GP surgery participates in Poems in the Waiting Room, a scheme devised in 1998, whereby local practices and other healthcare settings are issued with printed poem cards to display.* His patients, he tells me, respond enthusiastically to having lines from Emily Dickinson, Maya Angelou or Nâzim Hikmet to look at in the minutes before their appointments, and he notes that what they read often forms part of the consultation discussion. 'Patients bring me poems as well. It's a two-way thing, and it becomes something we talk about.'[40]

The therapeutic qualities Schuman sees in poetry – highlighting its unexpected, tangential approaches to problem-solving; its musicality – are cited by many practitioners who work between poetry and medicine. Poetry therapy as a field of clinical work emerged in New York City in the 1960s, as innovative psychiatrists (some of whom had personal experience of drawing on memorized poems under traumatic wartime conditions) sought to prove that poetry had a unique place in the 'total treatment of the emotionally ill'.[41] The US

---

* 'While Poems in the Waiting Room makes no formal therapeutic claim for its poetry cards,' its founder, Michael Lee, writes, 'the poetry cards exist and act in an explicit therapeutic context. The readers are waiting patients, who inevitably experience the process of reading the poems as an integral part of their visit to the doctor.'

National Association for Poetry Therapy, established in 1981, certifies practising therapists, holds annual conferences across the country and sponsors an academic journal.[42] In the UK, therapeutic poetry workshops, often led by poets, have taken place in hospitals, hospices, day and primary care centres and self-help groups since the late 1980s. During these sessions, patients are encouraged to read aloud, discuss and write creatively together. 'Poetry now crops up in many of the contexts we turn to when we're vulnerable, ill or at a loss,' Fiona Sampson, the former editor of *Poetry Review*, observed at the turn of the millennium.[43]

What links all forms of poetry therapy, across various settings, is their patient-focused approach to reading, the emphasis they place 'upon the person'.[44] A therapist who encourages a patient to read a poem isn't asking her to understand or evaluate it as a work of art, but instead to consider its relevance to her life situation: what matters, from the purely therapeutic point of view, is the perspective she comes away with – what the poem does to her or for her, not what kind of poem it is *qua* poem. Meaning arises, if it does, from the live interaction between the text and the psychological subject who happens to be reading it:

> The words on the page awaken a response: they bring to life a group of images, feelings and thoughts. The nature of these is determined (1) by our own past experiences with the words, and (2) by our present mental and emotional set. This response within us – the experience caused by the words – *is* the poem.[45]

The question poetry therapy asks, in other words, isn't 'What do you think it means?' but 'What does it mean for you?' The 'real' poem – the one that counts for the purposes of therapeutic activity – is internal, the 'group of images, feelings and thoughts' that the words on the page generate in a reader's mind, as she 'filters' them for insights that might inform her 'future attitudes and actions'.[46] The reader, in this framework, is powerful: she makes poems in her own image, rather than acting as a vessel for them to inhabit.[47] She might, in some contexts, be invited to transform what she reads in a more literal sense, to modify a poem's phrasing or 'provide a different ending' in order to make it reflect 'more accurately' her thoughts or feelings.[48]

Since all readers are individuals, and come to therapeutic reading with particular problems and anxieties, a single poem can generate many different internal texts, or 'poems within'. A poem that describes an emotional state, for instance, might be understood by one reader as reflecting the concerns of a past version of herself, but by another as reflecting those of a present or future self.[49] A poem that one patient might read as a liberating invitation to cast off old ties and securities might awaken in another profound anxieties about life's uncertainties. This individuality of response places the onus on therapists, who 'need to be aware of the effect a poem, a suggestion or an interpretation might provoke,' and to select the right piece accordingly.[50]

Much, here, depends on the nature of the psychological relationship between reader and poem. As Leah Price has argued, it's possible to conceptualize how bibliotherapy works in (at least) three ways: 'Do books work like a mirror, a painkiller, or a piece of exercise equipment?'[51] Does an effective therapeutic poem, in other words, show the reader a version of her own emotional state reflected back to her? Does it function like a sedative, calming heightened feelings? Or does it put the mind on the stretch by presenting a challenging new perspective? A reader might respond to the same poem differently on different days. John Stuart Mill, the philosopher and politician, recounted in his *Autobiography* (1873) that during a period of severe depression he had found solace in two opposite kinds of poetry. In the depths of his crisis, he had read and reread Coleridge's sonnet 'Work Without Hope', the dejected lines of which seemed to chime with and legitimize his low feelings. Then, as he sought a way out, he turned to 'joyful' poems by Wordsworth, whose sentiments, representing 'the very culture of the feelings, which I was in quest of,' as he put it, served as a kind of 'medicine' for his 'state of mind'.[52]

Patients suffering from depression, the American psychiatrist Jack Leedy observed in the 1960s, tended to be 'helped by poems sad and gloomy in tone, yet having lines or stanzas that reflect hope and optimism.' 'By reading, studying, memorizing, reciting or creating this kind of poem,' Leedy wrote, 'depressed patients come to feel that they are not alone in their depressions, that others are also depressed, that others have been depressed and recovered from their depressions.'[53] For such readers, cheery poems are likely to read as alienating, discounting the 'reality' and intensity of their experience, while unremittingly melancholic ones are liable to pose a risk too.[54] Michael Lee, the creator of Poems in the Waiting Room, notes that he was careful to avoid selecting poems of suicidal ideation (Keats's 'Now more than ever seems it rich to die / To cease upon the midnight with no pain...', for instance), on the grounds that they seemed likely to do damage rather than good.[55]

Those in the field of poetry therapy emphasize that curative reading is a collaborative process.[56] Poetry, Lee writes, 'is not, in itself, therapeutic': shaping it into a tool of therapy means drawing on the skills of a professional, someone able to mediate between poem and reader.[57] Therapists explain that what they do isn't just a question of 'handing out a poem at the end of a session' and informing the client that reading it will help her.

Instead, they direct the reading process, ask the right questions, draw out significant ideas, words or sounds. Poetry and the therapeutic conversation work together, practitioners argue, because in key respects poetry is '*like* therapy' (that is, traditional psychotherapy). Both are forms of expression whose medium is language; both employ symbols, images and metaphors to represent and try to organize complex forms of experience; both may appeal to the unconscious or pre-conscious mind as well as the conscious one.[58] The intimate kind of communication that takes place in the reading of a poem – the sense we have of 'an authentic voice speaking to us across time and space', often in a heightened emotional moment – resembles in key respects the therapeutic encounter, as an exchange between individuals reckoning with emotional difficulty.[59]

'You don't go to poetry for answers or absolutes, just as you shouldn't expect a psychotherapist to give you solutions to your problems, to make decisions for you,' Astley argues in *Staying Alive*. What both forms offer, instead, is dialogue, encouraging insights to emerge by and through the process of communication.[60] As poetry relies on readers to elicit its meanings, therapy guides its clients to come at self-knowledge. 'The emotional impact of a patient's sudden and dramatic insight during an analytic hour,' one clinician wrote in 1968, 'resembles the effect that a reader experiences when he seizes upon what is for him a particularly revealing intuitive communication from the poet.'[61]

✿

Therapy isn't easily available to everyone. One reason, as Price argues, that literature has become 'medicalized' in recent years – through, in the UK, programmes such as Books on Prescription – is that self-help is cheaper than help. Recommending someone a library book to read costs considerably less than subsidizing a series of individual sessions, and is potentially less risky than prescribing a course of medication.[62] Private therapy is expensive and NHS waiting lists are long, but a therapeutic method that involves visiting a GP for a prescription and exchanging it for a book opens up the resources of psychotherapy to anyone who might want them. 'From a medical vantage,' Price writes, 'books' selling points are largely negative: the money they don't cost, the side effects they don't produce, the addictions that they don't engender.'[63]

Several poetry anthologies feature on the current list of titles recommended by the Reading Agency's Mood-boosting Books website, among them Astley's *Being Alive* and *Being Human*, Alma's *The Emergency Poet*, and a collection edited by the poet Wendy Cope, *101 Happy Poems* (2001).[64] What makes such books potentially effective therapeutic recommendations is the variety and choice they contain. Most anthologies, like conventional self-help texts, don't make the assumption that everyone who reads them wants or needs the same kind of thing. Instead, they provide different routes and answers, though working within confined boundaries.[65] Astley's selections, in the *Staying Alive* series, mix consolatory poems – pieces such as Mary Oliver's 'Wild Geese', which, he says, possess 'great personal force for readers faced with similar tribulations in their own lives' – with poems that 'disturb, question and challenge', refusing to 'confirm what we already know'. The shifts of mood and tone push readers to make their way through the books idiosyncratically, discovering for themselves what interests or helps them.[66]

Those looking for more direct solutions are served by anthologies that strive to recreate, as best they can, the targeted, personalized work of talking therapy. Along similar lines to Schauffler's *Poetry Cure*, with its prescriptive formula for matching readers and texts, anthologies can steer the uncertain or unruly towards remedies for the specific problems that plague them. Berthoud and Elderkin's *The Novel Cure* covers every imaginable complaint (from 'abandonment' and 'addiction to sex' all the way down to 'yearning, general' and 'zestlessness'), for each of which the editors provide an appropriate fictional salve. Sieghart, who has said that poetry's therapeutic abilities 'only exist if you can find the right poem for the right state of mind,' adopts a similar method in his two *Poetry Pharmacy* anthologies, pairing problems ('Emotional Baggage'; 'Hopelessness'; 'Neediness'; 'Love Growing Stale') with poetic solutions.[67] Other books corral readers in the right direction by recommending poems for each of life's small daily trials and irritations. 'To help you find the right poem at the right time, the book is arranged like a medieval book of hours,' Goodwin writes of her arrangement in *101 Poems to Get You Through the Day (and Night)*. A 'survival kit for modern life', her anthology encourages readers to throw out the 'painkillers' and 'cigarettes' and use poems as crutches instead. For those who struggle to get out of bed, there's the alarm clock of Wordsworth's 'My Heart Leaps Up'; for the work-overwhelmed, desperate to leave the desk, Goodwin suggests the glimmer of freedom represented by Marvell's 'The Garden'.[68]

Using poetry for self-help, anthologists suggest, is as much about what you don't read as what you do. 'To use this book for self-help purposes,' Goodwin instructs in *101 Poems that Could Save Your Life*, 'first turn to the emotional index to find the condition from which you are currently suffering.' Devouring the book from cover to cover in one sitting, she emphasizes, should be avoided not only because it might distract you from finding from what you need, but also because, theoretically, picking out the wrong poem could make an emotional problem more acute. 'Chronic procrastinators should *not* put off turning to the "Just Do It" entry,' she says – where they can expect to be pummelled into productivity by Ezra Pound and Louis MacNeice – but the 'Stressed Out' should avoid it like the plague, sticking instead to their own, more zen section.[69] Poetry, this suggests, is like a drug both in its curative abilities and its potential for misuse. 'Better to take these poems little and often.'[70]

Medicinal verse requires dosage instructions. The prescriptive introductions and notes that self-help anthologies tend to contain – setting out not only what to read, but when, and how – reflect the higher stakes involved in picking up a book for bibliotherapeutic purposes. Schauffler's *Poetry Cure* features a lengthy preliminary section entitled: 'DIRECTIONS. (Read Well Before Using!)' The editors of *Stressed Unstressed* go back to basics in their introduction, providing a complete step-by-step guide to reading for self-help:

> Make yourself comfortable. Try to clear your head of all your worries. Breathe slowly and regularly. Listen to your own breathing as you breathe in and out: already you will feel slightly calmer. Now read slowly through your chosen poem, maybe in your head, ideally aloud, perhaps both. Then immerse yourself in its words. [...] By entering into the harmonized world of the poem, you have momentarily escaped your own world of stress and worry.[71]

Reading therapeutically, this passage suggests, is something you can master, given time and a willingness to be patient. Like meditation, discussed in the book as a related self-help practice, it comprises a set of techniques that work best when they become part of the fabric of daily life – when they become a lifestyle, a newly attentive way of being in the world. ('You can't pay full attention to a poem and worry about where you put your dry-cleaning stubs,' Goodwin remarks. [72]) Poetry's traditional rhythmic elements – 'the chime of rhyme, the reassurance of repetition, the sense of balance in the pattern of a stanza' – connect it with kinds of wellness activities that also involve ritualistic absorption in the moment: yoga, breathwork, mindfulness. Reading a poem, in this framing, eclipses reading a conventional self-help book, because what you get from it isn't just a download of advice. Poetry reading isn't a way of learning how to feel better, it *is* feeling better: it becomes, like a yoga class, 'nutrition for the soul', a repetitive practice that also counts as progress and change.[73]

In their second anthologies, Astley and Sieghart both reported being delighted and astonished by the degree of enthusiasm *Staying Alive* and *The Poetry Pharmacy* had elicited, from readers new to poetry or estranged from it in particular, who had discovered in their books a set of tools they found relevant and helpful. 'I knew full well the power of poetry to create that crucial sense of connection and security, of *not being the only one*,' Sieghart wrote. 'But even then I could not have predicted the scale of the reaction that slim volume would provoke.' Readers sent in poetic suggestions of their own; some asked him to find poems suitable for 'new maladies' the first book hadn't addressed.[74] For those who found poetry 'very helpful as an antidote for all kinds of difficulties', but weren't sure 'where to look', he tells me, *The Poetry Pharmacy* and other books provided a valuable mediating service – both connecting them with 'the right poem for the right moment', and prefacing poems with commentary to make them more approachable.[75]

Mediation of this kind, though, may not be for everyone. Almost a hundred years ago, during the first wave of interest in bibliotherapy, Graves and Riding had a warning for any editors and publishers contemplating entering the therapeutic poetry market. 'The possible medicinal value of an anthology for sick and disordered minds lies solely in the work which the sick and disordered mind does for itself if it compiles this anthology,' they insisted. Therapy happened, in other words, *through* anthologizing, through private acts of reading and collecting; it wasn't something you could absorb secondhand by reading other people's collections. Anthologists, in fact, were like 'bar[s] between the readers of the anthology and the poem,' imposing their sensibilities, their diagnoses, their views about what helped.[76]

Collecting, as the commonplace tradition indicates, whether for therapeutic ends or not, has always been something people have done privately, for themselves, guided by their interests and needs. Even the most culturally authoritative kinds of collections are personal, as the example of Yeats's eccentric *Oxford Book of Modern Verse* tells us; anthologies are loose affairs, assemblages of bits and pieces held together by curatorial ties that may come undone under pressure. Reading them well, especially in the therapeutic context, involves taking them apart, breaking them down in order to hunt through the pieces for what works best.

Being able to curate for oneself, of course, depends on access. Formerly, being able to put together a collection of poems meant possessing a large number of books and a cultural platform; now, online technologies have radically changed the way collecting happens. The growth of poetry sharing on social media has supplied readers with access to limitless texts and recommendations, establishing networks within which they're able to discover and gather new favourites. Algorithms accelerate the process, personalizing feeds so that what people see is also what they're most likely to consider appealing. Some readers scroll in order to collect material for private anthologies, which can either remain electronic or be printed and bound: Schuman, for instance, says that he 'scribbles down' poems posted by Twitter accounts he follows, then makes physical 'personal anthologies' out of his favourites.[77] Social media is its own kind of half-public, half-private anthology. Twitter and Instagram pages serve as miniature, constantly updateable, collections; on feeds, well-known poems are shared, commented on and parodied. Faber has responded to the movement towards self-curation by launching Pagesmith, a new personalization initiative, which allows readers to design 'bespoke poetry collections' of their own online.[78]

Anthologies are utopian. Since at least the early modern period, they have been tools for projecting and imagining, laying down the outlines of an ideal culture. For the creators of 'beauties' volumes during the eighteenth century, they represented a means of policing public morality, getting a handle on the explosion of print and the alarming social changes it threatened. For patriots during the First World War, they served as mechanisms to obscure and distract, retelling Britain's favourite stories about itself at a moment of national crisis. To the creators of *The Mersey Sound* and *The Liverpool Scene*, in the 1960s, they were portals to an alternative world, a ticket to a new way of being. What they may come to be in the future will depend on the cultural and social visions of those who make them: whom they curate for; what they take pleasure in; what they believe to be worth preserving; how they hope to continue the conversation. Not all designs are ambitious. 'I confess to a hope that my anthology may be read by a few other eyes than mine,' Samuel Courtauld wrote in 1939, introducing a deeply private collection of favourite poems he had compiled. 'Most of us, I suppose, feel a need at times to communicate our very personal feelings, even if only to one or two fellow creatures.'[79]

ENDNOTES

Introduction

1. [William Oldys], Preface to Thomas Hayward, ed., *The British Muse, or A Collection of Thoughts Moral, Natural, and Sublime, of our English Poets: Who flourished in the Sixteenth and Seventeenth Centuries*, 3 vols. (F. Cogan, 1738), vol. 1, pp. xviii–xix.
2. See Barbara M. Benedict, *Making the Modern Reader: Cultural Mediation in Early Modern Literary Anthologies* (Princeton University Press, 1996), pp. 167–8.
3. Laura Riding and Robert Graves, *A Pamphlet Against Anthologies* (Jonathan Cape, 1928), p. 51.
4. Ibid., p. 51.
5. A.P. Wavell, ed., *Other Men's Flowers* (Jonathan Cape, 1944), p. 15.
6. W.B. Yeats, ed., *The Oxford Book of Modern Verse, 1892–1935* (Clarendon Press, 1936), pp. xiii, xxi, xxxiv. On Yeats's selection, see Anne Ferry, *Tradition and the Individual Poem: An Inquiry into Anthologies* (Stanford, 2001), pp. 227–8; David Hopkins, 'On Anthologies', *Cambridge Quarterly*, 38 (2008), 285–304 (pp. 292–3).
7. Philip Larkin, ed., *The Oxford Book of Twentieth-Century English Verse* (Clarendon Press, 1973), p. v.
8. Rachel Hadas, 'On Poetry Anthologies', *New England Review* (1990–), 19 (1998), 126–39 (p. 127). On Larkin's *Oxford Book*, see Ferry, *Tradition*, pp. 236–43.
9. Florence Hardy quoted in Dennis Taylor, 'Hardy's Copy of "The Golden Treasury"', *Victorian Poetry*, 37 (1999), 165–91 (p. 165); Thomas Hardy, 'Apology', *Late Lyrics and Earlier, With Many Other Verses* (Macmillan and Co., 1922), p. xii.
10. Riding and Graves, *A Pamphlet*, p. 86.
11. Robert Irwin, 'Ecstasy in the desert', *Times Literary Supplement*, no. 5270 (2 April 2004), p. 4.
12. See Paul Fussell, *The Great War and Modern Memory* (Clarendon Press, 1975; repr. Oxford University Press, 2013), especially pp. 172–5.
13. Lawrence, *Minorities*, ed. J.M. Wilson, with a preface by C. Day Lewis (Jonathan Cape, 1971), pp. 17–18, 20, 53–64.
14. Simon Goldhill, *Preposterous Poetics: The Politics and Aesthetics of Form in Late Antiquity* (Cambridge University Press, 2020), pp. 74–5, 86; Goldhill and Emma Greensmith, 'Gregory of Nazianus in the

Palatine Anthology: The Poetics of Christian Death', *The Cambridge Classical Journal*, 66 (2020), 29–69 (p. 32).

15. Ferry, *Tradition*, pp. 14–15.
16. See William St Clair, *The Reading Nation in the Romantic Period* (Cambridge University Press, 2004), pp. 118, 135; and Chapter 3.
17. Benedict, *Making the Modern Reader*, pp. 182–3.
18. Richard D. Altick, *The English Common Reader: A Social History of the Mass Reading Public, 1800–1900* (Chicago University Press, 1957), p. 43.
19. See Ronald Schuchard, 'T.S. Eliot As An Extension Lecturer, 1916–1919', *Review of English Studies*, 25 (1974), 292–304 (p. 300); and Chapter 4.
20. Anne Stevenson, 'Why Palgrave Lives', *Victorian Poetry*, 37 (1999), 211–14 (p. 211); see also Ferry, *Tradition*, pp. 18, 127.
21. Ezra Pound, 'How to Read', in *Literary Essays of Ezra Pound*, ed. T.S. Eliot (New Directions, 1935; repr. 1968), p. 17.
22. Louis Menand, *The Free World: Art and Thought in the Cold War* (Farrar, Straus & Giroux, 2021), pp. 475–95.
23. Francis Turner Palgrave, *The Golden Treasury of the Best Songs and Lyrical Poems in the English Language*, ed. Christopher Ricks (Penguin, 1991), pp. 3, 5.
24. T.S. Eliot, 'What is Minor Poetry?', *The Sewanee Review*, 54 (1946), 1–18 (pp. 2–4).
25. Riding and Graves, *A Pamphlet*, pp. 160, 176, 67–8.
26. Anon., ed., *Poems on Affairs of State: From The time of Oliver Cromwell, to the Abdication of K. James the Second...* (n.p., 1697), p. v.

1 Revelation

1. Preface to George deF. Lord, ed., *Poems on Affairs of State: Augustan Satirical Verse, 1660–1714, Volume 1: 1660–1678* (Yale University Press, 1963), p. vii.
2. Anon., *An Impartial Account of the Arraignment, Tryal and Condemnation of Stephen Colledge for High-Treason...* (Richard Baldwin, 1682), p. 9.
3. Roger L'Estrange, *Notes Upon Stephen College. Grounded Principally upon his own Declarations and Confessions, And freely submitted to Publique Censure* (Joanna Brome, 1681), p. 47.
4. Stephen College, 'Truth brought to Light: Or, Murder will out', in *Poems on Affairs of State, From 1640 to this present Year 1704...,* [vol. 3] (no publisher, 1704), p. 180.
5. Stephen College, 'A Raree Show', in Lord, ed., *An Anthology of Poems on Affairs of State: Augustan Satirical Verse 1660–1714* (Yale University Press, 1975), p. 286.
6. L'Estrange, *Notes*, pp. 45–6.
7. Gary S. De Krey, 'Stephen College', *Oxford Dictionary of National Biography* (Oxford University Press, 2004), n.p.; preface to Lord, ed., *Poems on Affairs of State*, p. xxxiii.

8. John Ayloffe, 'Britannia and Raleigh', in Lord, ed., *An Anthology*, p. 123.
9. Preface to Lord, ed., *Poems on Affairs of State*, p. xxvi.
10. Harold Love, *English Clandestine Satire* (Oxford University Press, 2004), p. 13.
11. Anon., 'The Downfal of the French Bitch...', in *Poems on Affairs of State*, vol. 3, p. 211; The Earl of Rochester, 'Signior Dildo [Version B]', in Harold Love, ed., *The Works of John Wilmot, Earl of Rochester* (Oxford University Press, 1999), p. 254; [Charles Mordaunt], 'The Ladies March', in Harold Wilson, *Court Satires of the Restoration* (Ohio State University Press, 1976), p. 57; Andrew Marvell, 'Last Instructions to a Painter', in Lord, ed., *An Anthology*, p. 70.
12. [The Duke of Buckingham], 'Upon the Installment of Sir Of---n', in *The Second Volume of Miscellaneous Works, Written by George, Late Duke of Buckingham* (Samuel Briscoe, 1705), p. 88.
13. Anon., 'Satire on Old Rowley', in Lord, ed., *An Anthology*, p. 227.
14. See Harold Love, *Scribal Publication in Seventeenth-Century England* (Clarendon Press, 1993), particularly chs. 2 and 5; Ashley Marshall, *The Practice of Satire in England, 1658–1770* (Johns Hopkins University Press, 2013), p. 74.
15. Samuel Pepys, entry for 26 December 1666, in Robert Latham and William Matthews, eds., *The Diary of Samuel Pepys: Volume 7, 1666* (Harper Collins, 1971), p. 421.
16. See Love, *English Clandestine Satire*, pp. 45–51, on the spread from the mid-1670s of courtiers' lampoons to readers outside the court.
17. Ibid., p. 7.
18. Michael McKeon, 'What Were Poems on Affairs of State?', *1650–1850: Ideas, Aesthetics, and Inquiries in the Early Modern Era*, 4 (1998), 363–82 (pp. 371–3).
19. Preface to Lord, ed., *Poems on Affairs of State*, vol. 1, p. xxxix; see also Love, *English Clandestine Satire*, p. 2.
20. Dustin Griffin, 'Dryden and Restoration Satire', in Ruben Quintero, ed., *A Companion to Satire* (Blackwell, 2007), p. 178.
21. Preface to Anon., ed., *Poems on Affairs of State: From the Time of Oliver Cromwell, to the Abdication of K. James the Second...*, [vol. 1] (no publisher, 1697), sig. A5r.
22. Preface to Anon, ed., *State-Poems; continued from the time of O. Cromwel to the year 1697...* (no publisher, 1703), sig. A2v.
23. Preface to *Poems on Affairs of State*, vol. 1, sig. A5r.
24. Ibid., vol. 1, sigs. A3r, A4r.
25. Preface to Lord, ed., *Poems on Affairs of State*, p. xxxiii.
26. Paul Hammond, *The Making of Restoration Poetry* (Boydell and Brewer, 2006), p. 39.
27. See Joseph Hone, 'John Darby and the Whig Canon', *The Historical Journal*, 64 (2021), 1,257–80 (pp. 1,269–71).
28. Beth Lynch, 'John Darby', *Oxford Dictionary of National Biography* (Oxford University Press, 2004), n.p.

29. Hone, 'John Darby', p. 1,264.

30. Preface to *Poems on Affairs of State*, vol. 1, sig. A5r; see Hone, 'John Darby', p. 1,271.

31. Anon., 'The Mourners: Found in the Streets, 1702', in *Poems on Affairs of State*, vol. 3, p. 320.

32. Preface to Anon., ed., *Poems on Affairs of State, from The Reign of K. James the First, To this Present Year 1703* [vol. 2] (no publisher, 1703), p. iv.

33. [Arthur Maynwaring], 'Tarquin and Tullia', in *Poems on Affairs of State*, vol. 3, p. 319.

34. Ibid., p. 322.

35. Thomas Keymer, *Poetics of the Pillory: English Literature and Seditious Libel, 1660–1820* (Oxford University Press, 2019), p. 82.

36. See Hone, 'John Darby', p. 1268.

37. Lynch, 'John Darby'.

38. Marshall, *The Practice of Satire*, p. 74; McKeon, 'What Were Poems on Affairs of State?', pp. 364–6.

39. John McTague, 'Censorship, Reissues, and the Popularity of Political Miscellanies', *Eighteenth-Century Life*, 41 (2017), 96–115 (pp. 97–8).

40. See *Poems on Affairs of State, From 1620 to this present Year 1707...* [vol. 4] ([James Woodward], 1707), p. iv.

41. [William Shippen], 'Faction Display'd', in ibid., p. 95.

42. [Shippen], 'Moderation Display'd, A Poem, 1705. By the Author of *Faction Display'd*', in ibid., p. 102.

43. Shippen, *Moderation Display'd. A poem. By the same author. Now first correctly published, with large amendments...* (no publisher, 1705), pp. 18, 20.

44. Shippen, Preface to *Moderation Display'd*, n.p.

45. I'm indebted for my discussion of these censored satires to John McTague, 'Censorship, Reissues, and the Popularity of Political Miscellanies', *Eighteenth-Century Life*, 41 (2017), 96–115 (pp. 97–102).

46. Anon., ed. *Poems on Affairs of State, From the Year 1620 to the Year 1707...* (Thomas Tebb and Theophilus Sanders, 1716), pp. 114–15.

47. McTague, 'Censorship', pp. 99–100.

48. Ibid., p. 98.

49. Preface to *Poems on Affairs of State*, vol. 4, p. iv.

50. On these moral redefinitions of satire, see P.K. Elkin, *The Augustan Defence of Satire* (Clarendon Press, 1973).

51. Richard Steele, *The Tatler*, no. 92 (10 November 1709), p. 1.

52. See *A New Collection of Poems relating to State Affairs, from Oliver Cromwel to this present time... MS. notes* [by Alexander Pope], BL, shelf-mark C.28.e.15.

53. Pope's most famous smear is probably the attack on 'Sporus', a.k.a. Lord Hervey, in the *Epistle to Dr. Arbuthnot* (1735). Montagu probably collaborated with Hervey on her poem attacking Pope: see 'Verses Addressed to the Imitator of the First Satire of the Second Book of

Horace', in *The Letters and Works of Lady Mary Wortley Montagu*, 2 vols., ed. Lord Wharncliffe and William Moy Thomas (Cambridge University Press, 2011), vol. 2, pp. 464–7.

54. Anon. [George Canning], 'Poetry: Introduction to the Poetry of *The Anti-Jacobin*', in *The Anti-Jacobin; or, Weekly Examiner*, no. 1 (20 November 1797), p. 7.

55. Anon., 'Imitation. Sapphics. The Friend of Humanity and the Knife Grinder', in *The Anti-Jacobin*, no. 2 (27 November 1797), p. 15.

56. Anon., ed., *The Foundling Hospital for Wit. Intended for the Reception and Preservation of such Brats of WIT and HUMOUR, whose Parents chuse to Drop them* (G. Lion, 1743), p. i.

57. Ibid., pp. ii–iv.

58. Horace Walpole, Earl of Orford, *Memoires of the Last Ten Years of the Reign of George the Second*, 2 vols. (John Murray, 1822), vol. 1, p. 178.

59. Anon., 'Notes on Mr. Churchill's Fragment of a Dedication to the B----of G-----', in *The New Foundling Hospital for Wit. Being a Collection of Several Curious Pieces in Verse and Prose* (no publisher, 1769), pp. 71–5, 94. See Donald W. Nichol, '*The New Foundling Hospital for Wit: From Hanbury Williams to John Wilkes*', Studies in the Literary Imagination, 34 (2001), 101–17 (pp. 115–16).

60. Anon., 'An explanatory Note of a Passage in Mr. Churchill's Candidate…', in *The New Foundling Hospital for Wit… Part the Third* (J. Almon, 1769), pp. 72–4.

61. *The Political Register*, vol. 3, no. 16 (July 1768), p. 43.

2 Superstition

1. E.J. Clery, *The Rise of Supernatural Fiction, 1762–1800* (Cambridge University Press, 1995), pp. 13–14.

2. Ibid., p. 14.

3. Patricia Meyer Spacks, *The Insistence of Horror: Aspects of the Supernatural in Eighteenth-Century Poetry* (Harvard University Press, 1962; repr. 2013), pp. 26–7.

4. David Hume, 'Of Miracles', in *An Enquiry Concerning Human Understanding*, ed. Peter Millican (Oxford University Press, 2008), p. 119.

5. Samuel Johnson, 'Life of Tickell', in *Lives of the English Poets*, ed. G.B. Hill, 3 vols. (Clarendon Press, 1905) vol. 2, p. 311

6. Owen Davies, *Witchcraft, Magic and Culture, 1736–1951* (Manchester University Press, 1999), p. 1.

7. Joseph Addison, *The Spectator*, no. 419 (1 July 1712), p. 1.

8. Charles Lamb, 'Witches, and Other Night-Fears', in *Elia and The Last Essays of Elia*, ed. Jonathan Bate (Clarendon Press, 1987), p. 75.

9. Addison, *The Spectator*, no. 419, p. 1.

10. Addison, *The Spectator*, no. 110 (6 July 1711), p. 1.

11. See Davies, *Witchcraft*, p. 7.

12. George Birkbeck Hill and L.F. Powell, eds., *Boswell's Life of Johnson*, 6 vols. (Oxford University Press, 1934) vol. 2, pp. 178-9; vol. 3, pp. 297-8

13. Davies, *Witchcraft*, p. 50.

14. See Keith Thomas, *Religion and the Decline of Magic: Studies in Popular Beliefs in Sixteenth- and Seventeenth-Century England* (Penguin, 1971; repr. 1991), pp. 712–17, 638–67.

15. Quoted in ibid., p. 639.

16. Davies, *Witchcraft*, p. 26.

17. Thomas, *Religion*, p. 728.

18. Davies, *Witchcraft*, p. 16.

19. Ibid., pp. 136–7.

20. Anon., 'The Marriage of Sir Gawaine', in Thomas Percy, *Reliques of Ancient English Poetry*, ed. Henry B. Wheatley, 3 vols. (Bickers and Son, 1877), vol. 3, pp. 15, 17, 20, 24. This edition is hereafter referred to as *Reliques*.

21. *Reliques*, vol. 3, pp. 126–7.

22. Thomas Percy, *The Percy Letters: Vol. 7, The Correspondence of Thomas Percy and William Shenstone*, ed. Cleanth Brooks (Yale University Press, 1977), p. 94.

23. *Reliques*, vol. 3, p. 314.

24. *A Collection of Poems in Six Volumes. By Several Hands*, ed. Robert Dodsley, 6 vols. (R. and J. Dodsley, 1763), vol. 1, pp. 26–30; John Newbery, *The Art of Poetry on a New Plan: Illustrated with a great Variety of Examples from the best English Poets*, 2 vols. (J. Newbery, 1762), vol. 2, p. 47.

25. See Spacks, *Insistence of Horror*, p. 70 ff.

26. William Collins, 'Ode on the Popular Superstitions of the Highlands of Scotland', ll. 20, 60, 100–120, in *The Poems of Gray, Collins and Goldsmith*, ed. Roger Lonsdale (Longman, 1969; repr. 1976), pp. 503–12; Mark Akenside, *The Pleasures of the Imagination*, I. 456–71, in *The Poetical Works of Mark Akenside*, ed. Alexander Dyce (James Nichol, 1857; repr. AMS Press, 1969), p. 92. See Spacks, *Insistence of Horror*, pp. 75–6.

27. Horace Walpole's *The Castle of Otranto* (1765); James Macpherson's Ossian poems (1761–3); and Thomas Chatterton's Rowley poems (1768–70). Walpole revealed his own deceit by claiming authorship of the novel in a second edition. This met with a hostile reception: reviewers could accept the supernatural when they thought it had been dreamt up by an ignorant writer from the fifteenth century, but when it became clear the story was 'a modern performance', the rules of the game changed. 'That indulgence we offered to the foibles of a supposed antiquity, we can by no means extend to [...] a false tale in a cultivated period of learning.' See *Monthly Review* (May 1765), quoted in Emma Clery, 'Against Gothic', in *Gothick Origins and Innovations*, ed. Allan Lloyd Smith and Victor Sage (Rodopi, 1994), p. 34; Clery, *Supernatural Fiction*, pp. 54–5.

28. See Davies, *Witchcraft*, pp. 76–7.
29. Newbery, *Art of Poetry*, vol. 2, p. 154.
30. Percy, *The Percy Letters: The Correspondence of Thomas Percy and Richard Farmer*, ed. Cleanth Brooks (Louisiana State University Press, 1946), p. 7.
31. Arthur Johnston, *Enchanted Ground: The Study of Medieval Romance in the Eighteenth Century* (Athlone Press, 1964), p. 92.
32. R.B. [Nathaniel Crouch], *Wonderful Prodigies of Judgment and Mercy: Discovered in Above Three Hundred Memorable Histories...* (Nathaniel Crouch, 1682), title page. See Bertram H. Davis, *Thomas Percy: A Scholar-Cleric in the Age of Johnson* (University of Pennsylvania Press, 1989), p. 3.
33. Nick Groom, *The Making of Percy's Reliques* (Clarendon Press, 1999), pp. 39–40, 6.
34. Davis, *Thomas Percy*, p. 24.
35. Percy to Shenstone (24 November 1757), in *The Percy Letters: Vol. 7*, ed. Brooks, pp. 3–4.
36. Percy to Shenstone (9 January 1758), in ibid., pp. 9–10.
37. Hustvedt, *Ballad Criticism*, p. 160.
38. See Leah Dennis, 'Thomas Percy, Antiquarian vs. Man of Taste', *PMLA*, 57 (1942), 140–54.
39. Quoted in Davis, *Thomas Percy*, p. 92.
40. Approximately a quarter of the ballads in the *Reliques* originated from the manuscript Percy found. The remainder he discovered in other manuscripts or collections. See W.J. Bate, 'Percy's Use of His Folio Manuscript', *Journal of English and Germanic Philology*, 43 (1944), 337–48 (pp. 337–8).
41. Johnston, *Enchanted Ground*, pp. 95–6; Groom, *Making of Percy's Reliques*, pp. 92–9.
42. Johnston, *Enchanted Ground*, p. 9.
43. See ibid., p. 33.
44. George Crabbe, *The Library. A Poem* (J. Dodsley, 1781), p. 28.
45. Albert B. Friedman, *The Ballad Revival: Studies in the Influence of Popular on Sophisticated Poetry* (University of Chicago Press, 1961), pp. 130–2.
46. See Hustvedt, *Ballad Criticism*, p. 137.
47. Percy to Hailes (7 January 1763), in *The Percy Letters: Vol. 4, The Correspondence of Thomas Percy and David Dalrymple, Lord Hailes*, ed. A.F. Falconer (Louisiana State University Press, 1954), p. 19.
48. Shenstone to Percy (24 April 1761), in *The Percy Letters: Vol. 7*, p. 95.
49. [John Oldmixon], 'Of the Old English Poets and Poetry. An Essay', in *The Muses Mercury: Or, Monthly Miscellany*, vol. 1, no. 6 (June 1707), p. 132.
50. Addison, *The Spectator*, no. 70 (21 May 1711), p. 2. It's worth noting that Addison's trend-setting was inadvertent here: he wasn't interested in ballads *per se*, but in their use as a stress test for his idea that simplicity

in poetry was what tended to please readers most over the course of
time. See Friedman's discussion in *The Ballad Revival*, pp. 87–97.

51. Anon., 'Preface' to *A Pill to purge State-Melancholy: Or, a Collection of
    Excellent New Ballads* (no publisher, 1715), p. vi.

52. [Ambrose Phillips], ed., *A Collection of Old Ballads. Corrected from the
    best and most Ancient Copies Extant. With Introductions Historical,
    Critical, or Humorous*, 3 vols. (J. Roberts, 1723–5), vol. 1, pp. vi–vii.
    See Friedman, *The Ballad Revival*, pp. 151–2.

53. Phillips, ed., *A Collection of Old Ballads*, vol. 1, p. 261.

54. Addison, *The Spectator*, no. 12 (14 March 1711), p. 2.

55. *Reliques*, vol. 1, p. 8.

56. Davis, *Thomas Percy*, p. 127.

57. Paul Henri Mallet, *Northern Antiquities: Or, A Description of the
    Manners, Customs, Religion and Laws of the Ancient Danes*, tr. Thomas
    Percy, 2 vols. (T. Carnan, 1770), vol. 1, p. 55.

58. *Reliques*, vol. 3, pp. 196–7; italics mine.

59. Ibid., p. 200.

60. Ibid., pp. 210, 204.

61. Ibid., pp. 210–11.

62. Percy to Evans (6 December 1761); Percy to Evans (28 November
    1762); Percy to Evans (10 October 1762), in *The Percy Letters: Vol.
    5, The Correspondence of Thomas Percy and Evan Evans*, ed. Aneirin
    Lewis (Louisiana State University Press, 1957), pp. 33–45.

63. Evans to Percy (23 October 1762), in ibid., pp. 42, 44.

64. *Reliques*, vol. 3, p. 200.

65. For this argument, see Clery, *Supernatural Fiction*, p. 54.

66. Mallet, *Northern Antiquities*, tr. Percy, vol. 1, p. 56.

67. See Hustvedt, *Ballad Criticism*, p. 177.

68. Evans to Percy (17 April 1764), in *The Percy Letters: Vol. 5*, p. 82.

69. Henry Bourne, *Antiquitates Vulgares; or, the Antiquities of the Common
    People*, quoted in John Brand, *Observations on Popular Antiquities* (J.
    Johnson, 1777), pp. xvi–xvii, 58, 69–71.

70. Brand, *Observations*, pp. 71, iii–iv, ix.

71. Richard Hurd, *Letters on Chivalry and Romance* (A. Millar, 1762), p.
    98.

72. Johnston, *Enchanted Ground*, p. 27. On the political radical Thomas
    Spence's version of this idea, see Clery, *Supernatural Fiction*, pp. 68–9.

73. *Reliques*, vol. 3, pp. 281–2.

74. Groom, *Making of Percy's Reliques*, p. 225; Bate, 'Percy's Use of His
    Folio Manuscript', p. 340.

75. Percy to Hailes (23 October 1764); Percy to Hailes (16 December
    1764), in *The Percy Letters: Vol. 4*, pp. 88–9, 90.

76. Percy to Hailes (23 March 1765), in ibid., pp. 94–5.

77. Davis, *Thomas Percy*, pp. 132–3. See Walpole to Percy (5 February
    1765), in *Horace Walpole's Miscellaneous Correspondence: I*, ed. W.S.
    Lewis and John Riely (Yale University Press, 1980), p. 372.

78. Walpole to the Reverend William Cole (9 March 1765), in *Horace Walpole's Correspondence with the Rev. William Cole*, ed. W.S. Lewis and A. Dayle Wallace (Yale University Press, 1937; repr. 1961), p.89; Walpole to Horace Mann (26 March 1765), in *Horace Walpole's Correspondence with Sir Horace Mann: VI*, ed. W.S. Lewis, Warren Hunting Smith and George L. Lam (Yale University Press, 1960), p.289.

79. Groom, *Making of the Reliques*, p. 8.

80. Warton, *The History of English Poetry*, p. 36.

81. Brand, *Observations on Popular Antiquities*, pp. 118–119n.

82. Vicesimus Knox, 'On the Prevailing Taste for the Old English Poets', *Essays Moral and Literary... A New Edition*, 2 vols. (Charles Dilly, 1782), vol. 1, p. 218.

83. *The Monthly Review*, vol. 32 (April 1765), p. 241.

84. *The Critical Review*, vol. 19 (February 1765), pp. 119, 129–30.

85. *The Monthly Review*, vol. 32, p. 252.

86. Warton, *History of English Poetry*, vol. 2, pp. 462–3.

87. Edmund Burke, *A Philosophical Enquiry into the Sublime and Beautiful*, ed. Adam Phillips (Clarendon Press, 1998), p. 57. See Jonathan Brody Kramnick, *Making the English Canon: Print-Capitalism and the Cultural Past, 1700–1770* (Cambridge University Press, 1999), p. 77.

88. William Duff, *An Essay on Original Genius* (Edward and Charles Dilly, 1767), pp. 139–40, 143.

89. Elizabeth Montagu, *An Essay on the Writings and Genius of Shakespear* (J. Dodsley, 1769), p. 137.

90. Richard Hurd, *Letters on Chivalry and Romance* (A. Millar, W. Thurlbourn and J. Woodyer, 1762), p. 45.

91. Hugh Blair, *A Critical Dissertation on the Poems of Ossian, the Son of Fingal* (T. Becket and P.A. De Hondt, 1763), p. 33.

92. Quoted in Groom, *Making of Percy's Reliques*, p. 239.

93. Montagu, *Essay*, pp. 139–40, 160.

94. Mary Jacobus, *Tradition and Experiment in Wordsworth's Lyrical Ballads, 1798* (Clarendon Press, 1976), p. 209.

95. Robert Southey, 'Hayley's Memoirs', *Quarterly Review*, vol. 31 (1824–5), pp. 282–3.

96. Friedrich von Schlegel, *Lectures on the History of Literature, Ancient and Modern*, 2 vols. (William Blackwood, 1818), vol. 2, p. 218.

97. *Reliques*, vol. 3, p. 132.

98. [William Taylor, tr.], *Ellenore, A Ballad. Originally written in German by G. A. Bürger* (J. Johnson, 1796), pp. 7–8.

99. Ibid., pp. 13, 12.

100. See Jacobus, *Tradition and Experiment*, pp. 218–19.

101. *The Monthly Review* (July 1796), p. 322.

102. Jacobus, *Tradition and Experiment*, pp. 218–19; Lamb, 'Witches and Other Night-Fears', in Bate, ed., *Elia*, p. 77.

103. *The Collected Letters of Samuel Taylor Coleridge*, ed. Earl Leslie

Griggs, 6 vols. (Clarendon Press, 1956–71; repr. Oxford University Press, 2000), vol. 1, p. 438; *The Letters of William and Dorothy Wordsworth*, ed. Ernest de Selincourt, 2nd ed., 7 vols. (Clarendon Press, 1967–98), vol. 1, pp. 234, 246n; Southey, 'Donica', in *Poems* (Joseph Cottle, 1797), pp. 175–82.

104. On Shelley, see Matthew Gregory Lewis, *Tales of Wonder*, ed. Brett Rutherford, 2 vols. (Yogh & Thorn Books, 2017), vol. 1, p. ix.

105. Quoted in Lewis, *Tales of Wonder*, ed. Douglass H. Thomson (Broadview Editions, 2010), p. 17; on the composition of the volume, see pp. 13–14.

106. Ibid., pp. 15–20.

107. Lewis, *Tales of Wonder*, ed. Rutherford, vol. 2, pp. 268, 142, 163, 166; Lewis, *Tales of Wonder*, ed. Rutherford, vol. 1, pp. 162, 103–10, 173. The two new ballads in question are, respectively, Lewis's 'The Gay Gold Ring' and Southey's 'The Old Woman of Berkeley'.

108. Jacobus, *Tradition and Experiment*, pp. 215–16, 223–4.

109. Wordsworth, 'Essay, Supplementary to the Preface', in W.J.B. Owen and Jane Worthington Smyser, eds., *The Prose Works of William Wordsworth*, 3 vols. (Clarendon Press, 1974), vol. 3, p. 78.

110. Wordsworth, 'The Idiot Boy', in Ernest de Selincourt, ed., *The Poetical Works of William Wordsworth, Volume 2*, 2nd ed. (Clarendon Press, 1952), pp. 77–8; see Jacobus, *Tradition and Experiment*, p. 209, 220, 251, 254.

111. Lewis, *Tales of Wonder*, ed. Rutherford, vol. 1, pp. 75, 31, 110. On the tone of the notes, see Lewis, *Tales of Wonder*, ed. Thomson, p. 29.

112. Lewis, *Tales of Wonder*, vol. 1, ed. Rutherford, p. 110.

113. Lewis, 'Giles Jollup the Grave, and Brown Sally Green', in *Tales of Wonder*, ed. Rutherford, vol. 1, pp. 40–3.

114. Lewis, 'The Sailor's Tale', in ibid., vol. 1, p. 96. 'Quid' is a quantity of chewing tobacco.

115. Lewis, *Tales of Wonder*, ed. Thomson, p. 29.

3 Anxiety

1. The *Letters of John Keats*, ed. Hyder Edward Rollins, 2 vols. (Harvard University Press, 1958), vol. 1, p. 394.

2. Jack Stillinger, *Reading The Eve of St Agnes: The Multiples of Complex Literary Transaction* (Oxford University Press, 1999), pp. 116–17; Michael Gamer, *Romanticism, Self-Canonization, and the Business of Poetry* (Cambridge University Press, 2017), p. 33.

3. Gamer, *Romanticism*, pp. 30–2.

4. William St Clair, *The Reading Nation in the Romantic Period* (Cambridge University Press, 2004), pp. 109–115.

5. Quoted in Trevor Ross, 'Copyright and the Invention of Tradition', *Eighteenth-Century Studies*, 26 (1992), 1–27 (p. 3); St Clair, *Reading Nation*, pp. 114–15.

6. St Clair, *Reading Nation*, p. 124.
7. Thomas F. Bonnell, *The Most Disreputable Trade: Publishing the Classics of English Poetry, 1765–1810* (Oxford University Press, 2008), p. 231.
8. Gamer, 'Oeuvre-Making and Canon Formation', in *The Oxford Handbook of British Romanticism*, ed. David Duff (Oxford University Press, 2018), pp. 452–3.
9. Gamer, *Romanticism*, pp. 33–4.
10. St Clair, *Reading Nation*, p. 11.
11. Ibid., p. 135, and chapter 6.
12. Ibid., p. 118.
13. Ibid., pp. 118–19.
14. Louis-Sébastien Mercier, *L'An 2440*, quoted in Roger Chartier, *The Order of Books*, trans. Lydia Cochrane (Stanford University Press, 1994), pp. 68–9.
15. Vicesimus Knox, *Essays, Moral and Literary*, 2 vols. (Charles Dilly, 1778), vol. 2, p. 302.
16. Knox, *Winter Evenings, or Lucubrations on Life and Letters*, 2 vols. (Charles Dilly, 1788; repr. 1790), vol. 2, pp. 10–13.
17. Riding and Graves, *A Pamphlet*, p. 32.
18. Oliver Goldsmith, ed., *The Beauties of English Poesy*, 2 vols. (William Griffin, 1767), vol. 1, p. i; Knox, *Winter Evenings*, p. 10, quoted in Leah Price, *The Anthology and the Rise of the Novel: From Richardson to George Eliot* (Cambridge University Press, 2000), p. 4.
19. Barbara M. Benedict, *Making the Modern Reader: Cultural Mediation in Early Modern Literary Anthologies* (Princeton University Press, 1996), p. 198.
20. St Clair, *Reading Nation*, pp. 118, 135; Ferry, *Tradition*, p. 132.
21. On the ubiquity of 'beauties' anthologies in schools, see Altick, *The English Common Reader*, pp. 176–7.
22. A.T. Hazen, 'The *Beauties of Johnson*', *Modern Philology*, 35 (1938), 289–95 (p. 289); Daniel Cook, 'Authors Unformed: Reading 'Beauties' in the Eighteenth Century', *Philological Quarterly*, 89 (2010), 283–309 (pp. 283, 288–9, 291–2).
23. Altick, *The English Common Reader*, p. 43.
24. Cook, 'Authors Unformed', p. 292; see *The Lady's Magazine*, vol. 13 (1782), p. 123.
25. Barbara M. Benedict, 'The 'Beauties' of Literature, 1750–1820: Tasteful Prose and Fine Rhyme for Private Consumption', *1650–1850*, 1 (1994), 317–46 (p. 321).
26. Anon., *The Monthly Review*, vol. 66, p. 561.
27. Hannah More, *Strictures on the Modern System of Female Education*, 2 vols. (T. Cadell and W. Davies, 1799), vol. 1, p. 161.
28. [Samuel Johnson], *The Beauties of Johnson: Consisting of Maxims and Observations, Moral, Critical, and Miscellaneous* (G. Kearsley, 1781), p. v.

29. See Cook, 'Authors Unformed', p. 284.
30. Knox, *Elegant Extracts; or Useful and Entertaining Pieces of Poetry*, 2 vols. (James Moore, 1789), vol. 1, p. iv.
31. Henry Headley, ed., *Select Beauties of Ancient English Poetry*, 2 vols. (T. Cadell, 1787), vol. 1, p. vii.
32. Quoted in Ferry, *Tradition*, p. 132.
33. George Croly, ed., *The Beauties of the British Poets. With a few Introductory Observations* (R.B. Seeley and W. Burnside, 1828), p. xv.
34. Headley, ed., *Select Beauties*, p. vii; Knox, *Winter Evenings*, vol 1., p. 39.
35. Altick, *The English Common Reader*, pp. 85–7.
36. John Clarke, *An Essay Upon Study* (Arthur Bettesworth, 1731), pp. 223, 349–50.
37. Knox, *Winter Evenings*, vol. 1, p. 39; Knox, *Elegant Extracts... Poetry*, p. ii.
38. Knox, *Winter Evenings*, vol. 1, p. 39.
39. Altick, *English Common Reader*, p. 126.
40. Ibid., p. 126.
41. Thomas Bowdler, ed., *The Family Shakespeare, in one volume*, 4th edn. (Longman, Roberts, & Green, 1863), pp. vii–viii.
42. Friedrich Engels, *The Condition of the Working-Class in England in 1844*, ed. and trans. by Florence Kelley Wischnewetzky (Cambridge University Press, 1892; repr. 2010), p. 240.
43. Dodd, ed., *Beauties of Shakespear*, p. xvi; [William Shakespeare], *The Beauties of Shakespeare; Selected from his Plays and Poems* (G. Kearsley, 1783), p. ii.
44. Knox, *Elegant Extracts: or useful and entertaining Passages in Prose*, 2nd ed. (Charles Dilly, 1784), p. iii; Knox, *Elegant Extracts... Poetry*, pp. i–iii.
45. John Bullar, ed., *Selections from the British Poets, Commencing with Spenser, and Including the Latest Writers* (Thomas Baker, 1822), p. iv.
46. This approach was sanctioned by the conservative literary periodicals, in which 'not infrequently the reviewer frankly says that poor poetry is more than amply atoned for by sound morality'. See William S. Ward, 'Some Aspects of the Conservative Attitude toward Poetry in English Criticism, 1798–1820', *PMLA*, 60 (1945), 386–98 (pp. 392–3).
47. [Laurence Sterne], *The Beauties of Sterne: Including all his Pathetic Tales* (G. Kearsley, 1782), p. vii.
48. 'Advertisements', *The St James Chronicle*, issue 3347 (17–20 August 1782).
49. *European Magazine* (November 1782), quoted in Cook, 'Authors Unformed', p. 290; [Jonathan Swift], *The Beauties of Swift; or, the Favorite Offspring of Wit and Genius* (G. Kearsley, 1782), p. ii.
50. Lord Byron, *Don Juan*, II. 61, in Jerome J. McGann, ed., *The Complete Poetical Works*, 7 vols. (Clarendon Press, 1980–93), vol. 5, p. 108.
51. St Clair, *The Reading Nation*, pp. 280–2. On fears about the over-consumption of fiction, see Leah Price, *What We Talk About When We*

Talk About Books: The History and Future of Reading (Basic Books, 2019), pp. 128–32.

52. Ann Murry, *Mentoria: or, the Young Ladies Instructor*, 4th edn. (Charles Dilly, 1785), p. 274.
53. John Bennett, *Letters to a Young Lady, on a Variety of Useful and Interesting Subjects*, 2 vols. (W. Eyres, 1789), vol. 1, p. 208.
54. See E.J. Clery, *The Rise of Supernatural Fiction, 1762–1800* (Cambridge University Press, 1995), pp. 95–6; Alan Richardson, *Literature, Education, and Romanticism: Reading as Social Practice, 1780–1832* (Cambridge University Press, 1994), p. 169.
55. Knox, *Essays*, vol 2, p. 187.
56. J.A. James, *The Christian Father's Present to his Children*, 5th edn. (Frederick Westley & A.H. Davis, 1828), pp. 190–1; also Knox, *Essays*, pp. 185–7, 190; Chapone, *Letters*, vol. 2, pp. 144–5.
57. Hannah More, *Moral Sketches of Prevailing Opinions and Manners, Foreign and Domestic* (T. Cadell & W. Davies, 1819), p. 247.
58. James, *The Christian Father*, pp. 9, 72.
59. J. Aikin, M.D., *Letters to a Young Lady on a Course of English Poetry* (J. Johnson, 1804), pp. 2–3.
60. Ibid., pp. 2–3; 64–5.
61. Chapone, *Letters*, vol. 2, p. 132.
62. Jane Collier, *An Essay on the Art of Ingeniously Tormenting*, ed. Katherine A. Craik (Oxford University Press, 2009), p. 29.
63. Knox, *Essays*, vol. 2, pp. 358–9.
64. Byron, *Don Juan*, I. 22, in McGann, ed., *The Complete Poetical Works*, vol. 5, p. 15; Maria Edgeworth, *Letters for Literary Ladies* (J. Johnson, 1795), p. 35.
65. Collier, *Essay*, p. 29.
66. Edgeworth, *Letters*, pp. 36–7.
67. More, *Moral Sketches*, pp. 238–9, 245.
68. Clery, *Supernatural Fiction*, p. 95.
69. James, *The Christian Father*, p. 11.
70. More, *Strictures*, vol. 1, p. 163.
71. See, for instance, ibid., vol. 1, p. 164.
72. Knox, *Essays*, vol. 2, pp. 333–4, 310.
73. More, *Strictures*, vol. 1, pp. 163–5; vol. 2, p. 11.
74. 'On the Pleasure Derived from Objects of Terror', in J. and A.L. Aikin, *Miscellaneous Pieces, in Prose* (J. Johnson, 1773), pp. 46, 125. For a discussion of this, see Clery, *Supernatural Fiction*, pp. 81–3.
75. More, *Strictures*, vol. 1, pp. 164–6.
76. Ibid., vol. 1, pp. 160–2.
77. Sarah Fielding and Jane Collier, *The Cry: A New Dramatic Fable*, ed. Carolyn Woodward (University Press of Kentucky, 2017), p. 82.
78. Ibid., pp. 82–3.
79. More, *Strictures*, vol. 1, p. 161; vol. 2, p. 57.
80. Edgeworth, *Letters*, pp. 23–4.

81. Knox, *Essays*, vol. 2, pp. 358, 365.
82. Fielding and Collier, *The Cry*, pp. 161, 144–5.
83. Samuel Richardson, *Clarissa: or, The History of a Young Lady*, 4 vols., J.M. Dent & Sons, 1932, vol. 4, pp. 504–5. For this suggestion, see Price, *The Anthology and the Rise of the Novel*, p. 74.
84. Jane Austen, *Northanger Abbey*, ed. Marilyn Butler (Penguin, 1995; reissued 2003), p. 36.
85. Ibid., pp. 17–18.
86. Austen, *Pride and Prejudice*, ed. James Kinsley (Oxford University Press, 2019), p. 6; see Benedict, *Making the Modern Reader*, p. 217.
87. Austen, *Emma*, ed. Fiona Stafford (Penguin, 1996; reissued 2003), p. 67.
88. Ibid., p. 68. See *The New Foundling Hospital for Wit... Part the Fourth* (J. Almon, 1771), pp. 104–5.
89. Austen, *Emma*, pp. 424–5, 262.
90. More, *Strictures*, vol. 2, pp. 59, 56.
91. Naomi Schor, *Reading in Detail: Aesthetics and the Feminine* (Methuen, 1987), pp. 11–22.
92. J.J. Virey, *De l'Influence des femmes sur le gout dans la littérature et les beaux-arts, pendant le XVIIe et le XVIIIe siècle* (Deterville, 1810), pp. 13–15, quoted in Schor, pp. 150–1.
93. More, *Strictures*, vol. 2, p. 25-6; see Price, *The Anthology and the Rise of the Novel*, p. 75.
94. More, *Strictures*, vol. 2, p. 28; John Bennett, *Strictures on Female Education; Chiefly as it Relates to the Culture of the Heart* (E. Bushnell, 1787), p. 112.
95. Price, *The Anthology and the Rise of the Novel*, p. 75.
96. More, *Strictures*, vol. 2, pp. 3, 57–8.
97. J. Robertson, *An Essay on the Education of Young Ladies* (T. Cadell & W. Davies, 1798), p. 44.
98. Samuel Taylor Coleridge, *Biographia Literaria*, vol. 3, quoted in Price, *The Anthology and the Rise of the Novel*, p. 1.
99. St Clair, *Reading Nation*, p. 540.
100. Ross, 'Copyright', pp. 13–16.
101. Raymond Williams, *Culture and Society, Coleridge to Orwell* (Chatto & Windus, 1953; repr. Hogarth Press, 1987), p. 35.
102. Altick, *The English Common Reader*, pp. 54–5.
103. Williams, *Culture and Society*, pp. 33–5; Andrew Franta, *Romanticism and the Rise of the Mass Public* (Cambridge University Press, 2009), pp. 4–5.
104. Coleridge, *The Statesman's Manual*, in *Political Tracts of Wordsworth, Coleridge and Shelley*, ed. R.J. White (Cambridge University Press, 1953), p. 7.
105. Ibid., p. 8.
106. See St Clair, *Reading Nation*, p. 135.
107. Quoted in Christopher Ricks, 'The Making of *The Golden Treasury*',

in Francis Turner Palgrave, *The Golden Treasury* (Penguin Classics, 1991), p. 450.

108. Anon., Review of *The Beauties of Hume and Bolingbroke*, in *The Monthly Review*, vol. 67 (December 1782), p. 477.

109. Anon., Review of *The Flowers of Literature*, in *The London Magazine*, vol. 51 (November 1782), p. 532.

110. *The Public Advertiser*, issues 14240 (May 30 1780); 14777 (19 February 1782); 15008 (25 July 1782); 14579 (3 July 1781).

111. More, *Strictures*, vol. 1, p. 160; Clara Reeve, *The Progress of Romance*, 2 vols. (W. Keymer, 1785), vol. 2, p. 7. On the difference between the negative 'swarm' and Knox's positively-inflected 'hive', see Price, *The Anthology*, p. 75.

112. In a similar context, the growth of the readership for fiction, see Altick, *The English Common Reader*, p. 65.

113. Andrew Piper, *Dreaming in Books: The Making of the Bibliographic Imagination in the Romantic Age* (University of Chicago Press, 2009), p. 123; Altick, *The English Common Reader*, p. 66.

4 Education

1. Ezra Pound, 'How to Read', in *Literary Essays of Ezra Pound*, ed. T.S. Eliot (New Directions, 1935; repr. 1968), p. 18.

2. W. Macneile Dixon, 'Finality in Literary Judgment', *Westminster Review*, vol. 143 (January 1895), p. 401; Anon., 'An Authority in Poetical Criticism', *Saturday Review*, vol. 82 (19 September 1896), p. 312.

3. Pound to Ibbotson, 24 March 1936, in *Ezra Pound: Letters to Ibbotson, 1935–1952*, ed. Vittoria Mondolfo and Margaret Hurley (National Poetry Foundation, University of Maine, 1979), p. 24.

4. Martin Spevack, '*The Golden Treasury* 150 Years On', *Electronic British Library Journal* (2012), p. 3; Klaus Peter Müller, 'Victorian Values and Cultural Contexts in Francis Turner Palgrave's *The Golden Treasury*', in Barbara Korte, Ralf Schneider and Stefanie Lethbridge, eds., *Anthologies of British Poetry: Critical Perspectives from Literary and Cultural Studies* (Rodopi, 2000), pp. 128–9.

5. Quoted in Anne Ferry, *Tradition and the Individual Poem: An Inquiry into Anthologies* (Stanford University Press, 2001), p. 201.

6. Megan Jane Nelson, *Francis Turner Palgrave and The Golden Treasury*, unpublished Ph.D. thesis (University of British Columbia, 1985), p. 5.

7. Ibid., p. 9.

8. Gwenllian F. Palgrave, *Francis Turner Palgrave: His Journals and Memories of His Life* (Longmans, Green & Co., 1899), pp. 3, 14.

9. Ernest Hartley Coleridge, *Life and Correspondence of John Duke Lord Coleridge, Lord Chief Justice of England*, 2 vols. (William Heinemann, 1904), vol. 1, p. 76–7.

10. A.H. Clough to Tom Arnold, 16 July 1848, in *The Correspondence of*

Arthur Hugh Clough, ed. Frederick L. Mulhauser, 2 vols. (Clarendon Press, 1957), vol. 1, p. 181.

11. British Library Add. MS 45378 [Palgrave Papers, Vol. V], ff. 49r., 56v.–57r., 65v.; also in Bodleian Library, MS Eng. misc. e. 249 [Journal of Palgrave's visit to Paris, 1848], ff. 2, 6–7, 75–7.

12. F. Temple to Clough, 10 May 1853, in *The Correspondence of Arthur Hugh Clough*, vol. 2, p. 428.

13. Christopher Bischof, 'Masculinity, Social Mobility, and the Plan to End Pauperism in Mid-Victorian England: Kneller Hall Teacher's Training College', *Journal of Social History*, 46 (2013), 1039–59 (p. 1046).

14. Ibid., p. 1049.

15. J.F.C. Harrison, *Learning and Living 1790–1960: A Study in the History of the English Adult Education Movement* (Routledge & Kegan Paul, 1961; repr. 1963), pp. 77–8; see Altick, *The English Common Reader*, p. 85.

16. Harrison, *Learning and Living*, pp. 75–87; D.J. Palmer, *The Rise of English Studies: An Account of the Study of English Language and Literature from its Origins to the Making of the Oxford English School* (Clarendon Press, 1965), pp. 31–2; John R. Reed, 'Healthy Intercourse: The Beginnings of the London Working Men's College', *Browning Institute Studies*, 16 (1988), 77–90 (p. 78); William St Clair, *The Reading Nation in the Romantic Period* (Cambridge University Press, 2004), pp. 260–1.

17. Harrison, *Learning and Living*, p. 71; Altick, *The English Common Reader*, p. 202.

18. Palmer, *The Rise of English Studies*, p. 33.

19. Martyn Walker, *The Development of the Mechanics' Institute Movement in Britain and Beyond* (Routledge, 2017), p. 127; Philip Waller, *Writers, Readers, and Reputations: Literary Life in Britain, 1870–1918* (Oxford University Press, 2008), p. 605.

20. Altick, *The English Common Reader*, p. 203; Altick, 'From Aldine to Everyman: Cheap Reprint Series of the English Classics, 1830–1906', *Studies in Bibliography*, 11 (1958), p. 21n. On working-class readers' access to poetry, see Jonathan Rose, *The Intellectual Life of the British Working Classes* (Yale University Press, 2001), pp. 36–7, 118–121.

21. Altick, *The English Common Reader*, pp. 202–3.

22. Harrison, *Learning and Living*, pp. 66–8; Richard Buckley Litchfield, *The Beginnings of the Working Men's College* (Hudson & Co., 1902), pp. 6–7; Waller, *Writers, Readers*, p. 172.

23. Harrison, *Learning and Living*, pp. 86–7.

24. Robertson is quoted in Altick, *The English Common Reader*, p. 198; David Lester Richardson, ed., *Selections from the British Poets from the time of Chaucer to the Present Day, with Biographical and Critical Notes* (Baptist Mission Press, 1840), p. 16.

25. Harrison, *A History of the Working Men's College, 1854–1954* (Routledge & Kegan Paul, 1964), p. 12.

26. Martyn Lyons, 'New Readers in the Nineteenth Century', in Guglielmo Cavallo and Roger Chartier, eds., *A History of Reading in the West*, trans. Lydia G. Cochrane (Polity Press, 1999), p. 332.
27. Litchfield, *Beginnings*, pp. 5–8; Reed, 'Healthy Intercourse', pp. 79–81, 84–6.
28. Harrison, *History of the Working Men's College*, p. 61.
29. Lushington, 'Learning By Heart', p. 112.
30. Morley quoted in Palmer, *The Rise of English Studies*, p. 51.
31. See Palmer, *The Rise of English Studies*, pp. 37, 40.
32. A.J. Scott, *Suggestions on Female Education: Two Introductory Lectures on English Literature and Moral Philosophy* (Taylor, Walton, & Maberly, 1849), pp. 7, 21.
33. Matthew Arnold, 'The Study of Poetry', in P.J. Keating, ed., *Selected Prose* (Penguin, 1970; repr. 1987), pp. 340–1.
34. Stefan Collini, *Public Moralists: Political Thought and Intellectual Life in Britain, 1850–1930* (Clarendon Press, 1991), p. 354.
35. Palmer, *The Rise of English Studies*, p. 39; Anon., 'The Golden Treasury of English Song and Lyrics', *Spectator*, vol. 34 (27 July 1861), p. 814.
36. Michael Sadler, *Report of the Commission Appointed by the Government of India to Enquire into the Condition and Prospects of the University of Calcutta*, 13 vols. (H.M. Stationery Office, 1919–), vol. 2, pp. 305–7.
37. Ibid., vol. 2, pp. 310, 280.
38. Thomas Babington Macaulay *et al.*, *Civil Service of the East India Company: Report to the Rt. Hon. Chas. Wood, M.P.* (W. Thacker & Co., 1855), p. 9. See Waller, *Writers, Readers*, p. 172.
39. H.A. Dobson, *A Handbook of English Literature*, 2nd ed. (Crosby Lockwood and Co., 1880), pp. 82, 162.
40. See Matthew Reynolds, *The Realms of Verse 1830–1870: English Poetry in a Time of Nation-Building* (Oxford University Press, 2001), pp. 3–7.
41. 'The Visit of General Garibaldi', *The Morning Post* (5 April 1864), p. 5; 'Garibaldi in the Isle of Wight', *The Daily News* (7 April 1864), p. 5.
42. *The Westminster Review*, vol. 14 (1831), p. 224, quoted in Altick, *The English Common Reader*, p. 136.
43. Palgrave, 'The Growth of English Poetry' [Art. V. – *Bell's Annotated Series of British Poets*], *The Quarterly Review*, vol. 110 (October 1861), pp. 442–3, 451–2.
44. Nelson, *Francis Turner Palgrave*, p. 19.
45. Ibid., pp. 22–3, 37.
46. Palgrave, 'Method of Lectures on English Literature', *The Educational Expositor*, ed. T. Tate and J. Tilleard, vol. 1 (1853), p. 176; Lushington, 'Learning By Heart', pp. 109–10.
47. Palgrave, 'On Readers in 1760 and 1860', *Macmillan's Magazine*, no. 6 (April 1860), p. 488.
48. Palgrave, 'On the Scientific Study of Poetry', *The Fortnightly Review*, vol. 12 (August 1, 1869), p. 165.

49. Clough, 'Review of Some Poems by Alexander Smith and Matthew Arnold', in *The Poems and Prose Remains of Arthur Hugh Clough*, ed. Blanche Clough, 2 vols. (Macmillan & Co., 1869), vol. 2, pp. 361–2.

50. Palgrave, 'On the Scientific Study of Poetry', p. 173.

51. Palgrave, 'The Study of the English Language', *The Light Blue*, vol. 1 (April 1866), p. 83.

52. Palgrave, 'On the Scientific Study of Poetry', pp. 176, 166.

53. Ibid., pp. 173, 175.

54. Samuel Smiles, *Self-Help. With Illustrations of Character, Conduct, and Perseverance*, ed. Peter W. Sinnema (Oxford University Press, 2002), p. 266.

55. Palgrave, *The Golden Treasury of the Best Songs and Lyrical Poems in the English Language*, ed. Christopher Ricks (Penguin, 1991), p. 7.

56. [G.F.] Palgrave, *Francis Turner Palgrave*, p. 62; William Holman Hunt, *Pre-Raphaelitism and the Pre-Raphaelite Brotherhood*, 2 vols. (Macmillan & Co., 1905) vol. 2, p. 205.

57. Palgrave, 'Personal Recollections', in Hallam Tennyson, *Alfred Lord Tennyson: A Memoir By His Son*, 2 vols. (Macmillan & Co., 1897), vol. 2, p. 500; Holman Hunt, *Pre-Raphaelitism*, vol. 2, p. 205.

58. See Palgrave, *The Golden Treasury*, ed. Ricks, p. 441n.

59. B. Ifor Evans, 'Tennyson and the Origins of the *Golden Treasury*', *Times Literary Supplement* (8 December 1932), p. 941.

60. Palgrave, *The Golden Treasury*, ed. Ricks, p. 5.

61. See Lee Erickson, 'The Market', in Richard Cronin, Alison Chapman and Antony H. Harrison, eds., *A Companion to Victorian Poetry* (Oxford University Press, 2002), pp. 345–6.

62. Ferry, *Tradition*, p. 18.

63. Palgrave to Alexander Macmillan, 2 October 1874, BL Add. MS 54977, ff. 97r.–97v. See Nelson, *Francis Turner Palgrave*, p. iii.

64. Anon., ed., *Affection's Gift: Containing the Sacred Melodies of Thomas Moore; the Hebrew Melodies of Lord Byron; and the Sacred Poems of Mrs. Hemans* (Leavitt, Trow & Company, 1848); Charles Mackay, ed., *The Home Affections, Pourtrayed By the Poets* (George Routledge & Co., 1858), pp. v–vii. On *Affection's Gift* and other moralistic Victorian collections, see Linda H. Peterson, 'Anthologizing Women: Women Poets in Early Victorian Collections of Lyric', *Victorian Poetry*, 37 (1999), 193–209 (p. 195).

65. Arnold, 'The Study of Poetry', p. 347.

66. Lushington, 'Learning By Heart', p. 110.

67. Lyons, 'New Readers', p. 340.

68. A. Sonnenschein, 'Letters to the Editor', *Working Men's College Magazine*, no. 33 (1 September 1861), p. 135.

69. See Spevack, '*The Golden Treasury* 150 Years On', p. 9, on the absence of Donne and the other Metaphysical poets.

70. Palgrave, 'The Province and Study of Poetry', in *Oxford Lectures on Poetry*, ed. Mine Okachi (Tokyo, 1973), pp. 62–3.

71. William Wordsworth, Preface to *Lyrical Ballads* [1850], in *The Prose Works of William Wordsworth*, 2 vols., ed. W.J.B. Owen and Jane Worthington Smyser (Clarendon Press, 1974), vol. 1, pp. 138, 123; Palgrave, 'The Province and Study of Poetry', pp. 62–3, p. 44.

72. BL Add. MS 42126, e.g. ff. 190, 200, 203, 206.

73. See Palmer, *The Rise of English Studies*, p. 37.

74. On these readers, see Ferry, *Tradition*, p. 44.

75. Palgrave, *The Golden Treasury*, ed. Ricks, pp. 416, 417, 425.

76. BL Add. MS 42126, f. 83.

77. Rose, *Intellectual Life*, p. 37.

78. Palgrave, *The Golden Treasury*, ed. Ricks, p. 3.

79. Nelson, *Francis Turner Palgrave*, pp. 118, 152; Palgrave, *The Golden Treasury*, ed. Ricks, p. 444; Spevack, '*The Golden Treasury* 150 Years On', p. 3.

80. Spevack, '*The Golden Treasury* 150 Years On', p. 1.

81. Anon., 'Belles Lettres', *The Westminster Review*, vol. 20 (October 1861), p. 606.

82. Anon., 'Anthologies', *Spectator*, vol. 79 (30 October 1897), p. 591.

83. J.A. Froude, 'Some Poets of the Year', *Fraser's Magazine for Town and Country*, vol. 64 (October 1861), p. 466.

84. Matthew Arnold, 'The Literary Influence of Academies', *The Cornhill Magazine*, vol. 10 (August 1864), pp. 168–70.

85. A.J. Munby, 'A Noteworthy Book of Poems', *Working Men's College Magazine*, no. 35 (1 November 1861), pp. 171–2.

86. Altick, *The English Common Reader*, p. 244.

87. Lyons, 'New Readers', pp. 336–7.

88. Rose, *Intellectual Life*, p. 128.

89. Harold Brown, *Most Splendid of Men: Life in a Mining Community, 1917–25* (Littlehampton Book Services, 1981), p. 175.

90. Philip Inman, *No Going Back: An Autobiography* (Williams and Norgate, 1952), pp. 12–16, 43, 45, 47. I am indebted to Rose's *Intellectual Life* for this reference and the preceding one.

91. John Morley, 'On the Study of Literature', in *Literary Essays* (A.L. Humphreys, 1906), pp. 337, 345. On University Extension, and the place of English literature courses in the programming, see Waller, *Writers, Readers*, pp. 24–5. Of the 57 courses offered by Cambridge lecturers in the winter of 1886, ten were on literature. In the case of the London Extension programme, literary courses made up almost a quarter of the offering.

92. Ronald Schuchard, 'T.S. Eliot as an Extension Lecturer, 1916–1919', *Review of English Studies* 25 (1974), 292–304 (pp. 300–1).

93. Rose, *Intellectual Life*, p. 42.

94. V.W. Garratt, *A Man in the Street* (J.M. Dent & Sons, 1939), pp. 173–4.

95. Ibid., pp. 221, 253.

5 War

1. [Hall Caine], ed., *King Albert's Book: A Tribute to the Belgian King and People from Representative Men and Women Throughout the World* (*The Daily Telegraph*, 1914), pp. 6–7.
2. *The Glasgow Herald* (1 December 1914), p. 10.
3. *The New York Times* (16 December 1914), p. 3. See Nick Milne, 'Pen and Sword Pt. II: Advertising *King Albert's Book*' (http://ww1centenary. oucs.ox.ac.uk/?p=3241).
4. D.G. Wright, 'The Great War, Government Propaganda and English 'Men of Letters' 1914–16', *Literature and History*, 7 (1978), 70–100 (p. 75).
5. Paul Fussell, *The Great War and Modern Memory* (Clarendon Press, 1975; repr. Oxford University Press, 2013), p. 170.
6. John Gross, *The Rise and Fall of the Man of Letters: Aspects of English Literary Life Since 1800* (1969; repr. Penguin, 1973), p. 211.
7. Michael L. Sanders and Philip M. Taylor, *British Propaganda during the First World War, 1914–18* (Macmillan, 1982), p. 107.
8. Lucy Masterman, *C.F.G. Masterman: A Biography* (Nicholson & Watson, 1939), p. 276.
9. Florence Emily Hardy, *The Later Years of Thomas Hardy, 1892–1928* (Macmillan, 1930), p. 163.
10. Thomas Hardy, 'Sonnet on the Belgian Expatriation', in [Caine], ed., *King Albert's Book*, p. 21; Hardy, *The Later Years*, p. 164.
11. Hardy to John Galsworthy (15 August 1918); Hardy to Charles Watts (1 August 1915), both in *The Collected Letters of Thomas Hardy*, ed. Richard Little Purdy and Michael Millgate, 8 vols. (Clarendon Press, 1985), vol. 5, pp. 275, 117.
12. J.C. Bailey, 'War and Poetry', *Times Literary Supplement*, no. 664 (8 October 1914), p. 448.
13. Sir Arthur Quiller-Couch, 'Patriotism and Literature', quoted in Samuel Hynes, *A War Imagined: The First World War and English Culture* (Bodley Head, 1990), p. 73. See also Gross, *The Rise and Fall*, p. 206.
14. 'A Nation of Poets', *The Times* (12 March 1915), p. 10.
15. Gross, *The Rise and Fall*, p. 248.
16. Fussell, *The Great War*, pp. 172, 175–8; Robert Graves, *Goodbye to All That: An Autobiography* (Jonathan Cape, 1929), p. 224.
17. David Michael Jones, *In Parenthesis* (Faber and Faber, 1963), pp. 139, 95; William Dunbar, 'Lament for the Makers', in *The Oxford Book of English Verse, 1250–1900*, ed. Arthur Quiller-Couch (Clarendon Press, 1900; repr. 1912), pp. 30–3.
18. See Fussell, *The Great War*, ch. 5, especially pp. 172–3, 189; Simon Featherstone, *War Poetry: An Introductory Reader* (Routledge, 1995), p. 39.
19. Laurence Housman, ed., *War Letters of Fallen Englishmen* (Victor Gollancz, 1930), pp. 218, 186–7.

20. Quoted in Philip Waller, *Writers, Readers, and Reputations: Literary Life in Britain 1870–1918* (Oxford University Press, 2006), p. 186.

21. Ted Bogacz, '"A Tyranny of Words": Language, Poetry, and Antimodernism in England in the First World War', *The Journal of Modern History*, 58 (1986), 643–68 (p. 648).

22. 'Mr. Binyon's War Poems', *TLS*, no. 677 (7 January 1915), p. 4; 'The Poet-Prophet of Empire. Twenty Poems from Kipling', *The Times* (1 May 1918), p. 9.

23. Edmund Gosse, 'Some Soldier Poets', *The Edinburgh Review*, vol. 226 (1 October 1917), p. 315.

24. 'Mr. Binyon's War Poems', p. 4.

25. Bogacz, '"A Tyranny"', p. 647.

26. Reprinted in Charles F. Forshaw, ed., *One Hundred of the Best Poems of the European War. By Women Poets of the Empire* (Elliot Stock, 1916), p. 26.

27. A typical early example is Robert Bridges' 'Wake Up, England' (1914): 'Stand, England, for honour, / And God guard the Right!'

28. Featherstone, *War Poetry*, p. 39; Peter Parker, *The Old Lie: The Great War and the Public-School Ethos* (Constable, 1987), p. 215; Hugh Haughton, 'Anthologizing War', in Tim Kendall, ed., *The Oxford Handbook of British and Irish War Poetry* (Oxford University Press, 2009), p. 426.

29. Wright, 'The Great War', p. 75; *The Times* (6 August 1915), p. 7; 'The Poetry of War: National Inspiration in the Past Year', *The Times* (14 April 1915), p. 5; Hynes, *A War Imagined*, pp. 25–6.

30. Arthur Clutton-Brock, 'The Poetry of War', *TLS*, no. 718 (21 October 1915), p. 361.

31. Marion Scott, 'Contemporary British War-Poetry, Music, and Patriotism', *The Musical Times*, vol. 58 (1 March 1917), p. 120.

32. 'A Serious Outbreak of Poetry', *Daily Mail* (23 June 1915), p. 4; Hardy to Sydney Cockerell (28 August 1914), in *The Collected Letters*, vol. 5, p. 45.

33. Quoted in E.B. Osborn, ed., *The Muse in Arms: A Collection of War Poems, For the Most Part Written in the Field of Action, By Seamen, Soldiers, and Flying Men Who Are Serving, or Have Served, in the Great War* (John Murray, 1917), p. xiv.

34. Featherstone, *War Poetry*, p. 38.

35. Graves, *Goodbye*, p. 394. On book sales, see Hynes, *A War Imagined*, p. 104; Featherstone, *War Poetry*, p. 17.

36. Gosse, 'Some Soldier Poets', pp. 298–9.

37. Catherine W. Reilly, *English Poetry of the First World War: A Bibliography* (G. Prior, 1978), p. xix; Tim Kendall, 'Civilian War Poetry: Hardy and Kipling', in Santanu Das, ed., *The Cambridge Companion to the Poetry of the First World War* (Cambridge University Press, 2013), p. 200.

38. David A. Rennie, *American Writers and World War I* (Oxford University Press, 2020), p. 24.

39. Hynes, *A War Imagined*, p. 28. At least fifty anthologies were produced during the course of the war. See Haughton, 'Anthologizing War', p. 424.

40. 'Anthologies', *The Athenaeum*, no. 4550 (9 January 1915), p. 22.

41. See *The Times* (6 August 1915), p. 7, for a description of the anthology; the supplement appeared with the issue of 9 August.

42. Robert H. Ross, *The Georgian Revolt: Rise and Fall of a Poetic Ideal, 1910–1922* (Faber and Faber, 1967), p. 129; Parker, *The Old Lie*, p. 152.

43. Myron Simon, *The Georgian Poetic* (University of California Press, 1975), p. 12; Vincent Sherry, 'First World War Poetry: A Cultural Landscape', in Das, ed., *Cambridge Companion*, pp. 36–7.

44. Nicholas Murray, *The Red Sweet Wine of Youth: The Brave and Brief Lives of the War Poets* (Little, Brown, 2010; repr. Abacus, 2012), pp. 20, 23, 29; Ross, *The Georgian Revolt*, p. 127.

45. Francis Bickley, 'Notes on the Poets of To-Day', *The Westminster Gazette* (23 May 1914), p. 2; see also Gosse, 'Some Soldier Poets', p. 296.

46. Baldick, *The Modern Movement*, p. 109; Ferry, *Tradition*, p. 217.

47. Harold Monro, *Some Contemporary Poets* (L. Parsons, 1920), p. 25.

48. Charles Norman, *Ezra Pound* (Macmillan, 1960), p. 107; John G. Nichols, 'Ezra Pound's Poetic Anthologies and the Architecture of Reading', *PMLA*, 121 (2006), 170–85. See Ross, *The Georgian Revolt*, p. 129; Monro, *Some Contemporary Poets*, p. 25.

49. Quoted in Ross, *The Georgian Revolt*, p. 130.

50. Bailey, 'War and Poetry', p. 448.

51. William Watson, 'Duty', in *Poems of the Great War: Published on Behalf of the Prince of Wales's National Relief Fund* (Chatto & Windus, 1914), title page.

52. [John Lane], ed., *Songs and Sonnets for England in War Time: Being a Collection of Lyrics by Various Authors Inspired by the Great War* (John Lane, 1914), p. viii.

53. Charles F. Forshaw, ed., *One Hundred of the Best Poems on the European War. By Poets of the Empire* (Elliot Stock, 1915); Forshaw, ed., *One Hundred of the Best Poems... By Women Poets of the Empire*; Erskine Macdonald and Gertrude S. Ford, eds., *A Crown of Amaranth: Being a Collection of Poems to the Memory of the Brave and Gallant Gentlemen Who Have Given their Lives for Great and Greater Britain* (Erskine Macdonald, 1917).

54. See Parker, *The Old Lie*, p. 68, on the insistence that the English were not a militarist people.

55. Ian Colvin, 'The Answer'; Reginald R. Buckley, 'To the Aggressor', both in *Songs and Sonnets*, ed. Lane, pp. 16, 38.

56. Robert Bridges, ed., *The Spirit of Man: An Anthology in English & French from the Philosophers & Poets* (Longmans, Green & Co., 1916), p. iii.

57. Much like other contemporary forms of propaganda: see Sanders and Taylor, *British Propaganda*, pp. 130–1.

58. William Cryer, 'Have Faith in God', in Forshaw, ed., *One Hundred of the Best Poems... By Poets of Empire*, p. 55.

59. E.V. Lucas, ed., *Remember Louvain! A Little Book of Liberty and War* (Methuen & Co., 1914), pp. ii, v, 11, iv.

60. Bailey, 'War and Poetry', p. 448.

61. See Hynes, *A War Imagined*, p. 30.

62. Edgell Rickword, 'War and Poetry (1914–18)', *Life and Letters To-Day*, vol. 26 (July 1940), pp. 26–7.

63. See Parker, *The Old Lie*, pp. 99–105, on the prevalence of chivalric ideas in public school teaching in particular.

64. William Ernest Henley, ed., *Lyra Heroica: A Book of Verse for Boys* (Charles Scribner's Sons, 1891), p. vii.

65. Fussell, *The Great War*, pp. 22–3; see also Hynes, *A War Imagined*, pp. 109–10; Maurice Bowra, *Poetry and the First World War* [Taylorian Lecture, 1961] (Clarendon Press, 1961), p. 10.

66. R.E. Vernède, 'England to the Sea'; Alfred Noyes, 'The United Front'; James Bernard Fagan, 'The Hour', all in *Poems of the Great War*, pp. 20, 17, 21.

67. Henry de Vere Stacpoole, 'Britannia'; Sir Owen Seaman, 'Pro Patria'; Francis Coutts, 'To Britain (Before Her Declaration of War)'; Vernède, 'The Call', all in [Lane], ed., *Songs and Sonnets*, pp. 13, 26–7, 2, 66.

68. Forshaw, ed., *One Hundred of the Best Poems... By Women Poets of the Empire*, pp. 48, 118.

69. [The English Association], ed., *Poems of To-Day: An Anthology* (Sidgwick & Jackson, 1915; repr. 1918), pp. viii, 14.

70. See Samuel Hynes, *The Edwardian Turn of Mind* (Princeton University Press, 1968; repr. Pimlico, 1991), pp. 17–34; Featherstone, *War Poetry*, pp. 25, 27–8; Sherry, 'First World War Poetry', pp. 37–8; Bowra, *Poetry*, p. 8.

71. Quoted in Murray, *Red Sweet Wine*, p. 58.

72. Quoted in Hynes, *A War Imagined*, p. 111.

73. Binyon, 'England', in *Poems of To-Day*, pp. 20–2; Binyon, 'The Fourth of August', in *Poems of the Great War*, p. 13.

74. Bridges, ed., *The Spirit of Man*, p. iv.

75. Bowra, *Poetry*, p. 14.

76. Bailey, 'War and Poetry', p. 448.

77. Richard Aldington, 'Notes on the Present Situation', *The Egoist*, vol. 1, no. 17 (September 1914), p. 326.

78. John Gould Fletcher, 'On Subject-Matter and War Poetry', *The Egoist*, vol. 3, no. 12 (December 1916), p. 189.

79. Harold Monro, 'Varia', *Poetry and Drama*, vol. 2 (The Poetry Bookshop, 1914), pp. 251–2.

80. 'Solomon Eagle' [J.C. Squire], *The New Statesman*, vol. 3 (1914), p. 737.

81. [John Middleton Murry], 'French Poetry of the War', *TLS*, no. 695 (13 May 1915), p. 5.
82. [Arthur Clutton-Brock], 'The Poetry of War', *TLS*, no. 718 (21 October 1915), p. 361.
83. Jon Silkin, *Out of Battle: The Poetry of the Great War* (Palgrave Macmillan, 1998), pp. 67–9; Das, 'Reframing' First World War Poetry: An Introduction', in Das, ed., *Cambridge Companion*, p. 5; Featherstone, *War Poetry*, pp. 14–15; Murray, *Red Sweet Wine*, pp. 63–8.
84. Graves, 'The Poets of World War II', in *The Common Asphodel: Collected Essays on Poetry 1922–1949* (Hamish Hamilton, 1949), p. 307.
85. Jon Silkin, introduction to *The Penguin Book of First World War Poetry* (Allen Lane, 1979), pp. 26–7. The romanticism of the sonnets was 'atypical' of Brooke's poetry and sensibilities up to this point. See Elizabeth Vandiver, 'Early Poets of the First World War', in Das, ed., *Cambridge Companion*, p. 72.
86. Featherstone, *War Poetry*, p. 15; Waller, *Writers and Readers*, p. 232.
87. Quoted in Ross, *The Georgian Revolt*, p. 165. On 'Whom the Gods love die young', see Parker, *The Old Lie*, p. 96.
88. Galloway Kyle, ed., *Soldier Poets: Songs of the Fighting Men* (Erskine Macdonald, 1916), p. 107. On Kyle, see Elizabeth Vandiver, *Stand in the Trench, Achilles: Classical Receptions in British Poetry of the Great War* (Oxford University Press, 2010), pp. 144–5.
89. Kyle, ed., *Soldier Poets*, p. 10.
90. Ibid., pp. 8–9.
91. This argument has been described as an 'ideology' of 'combat gnosticism' by James Campbell – a privileging in both literature of the period and subsequent criticism of combat experience as the only basis for truth-telling about the war. See James Campbell, 'Combat Gnosticism: The Ideology of First World War Poetry Criticism', *New Literary History*, 30 (1999), 203–15; also Sarah Cole, 'Civilians Writing the War: Metaphor, Proximity, Action', in Das and Kate McLoughlin, eds., *First World War: Literature, Culture, Modernity* (British Academy and Oxford University Press, 2018), p. 100; Hynes, *A War Imagined*, p. 158.
92. Osborn, ed., *The Muse*, pp. xv–xxiii.
93. Haughton, 'Anthologizing War', pp. 426–7; Parker, *The Old Lie*, pp. 25–6; Murray, *Red Sweet Wine*, pp. 183–5.
94. Kyle, ed., *Soldier Poets*, pp. 7, 9.
95. Osborn, ed., *The Muse*, pp. vii–viii, xxii.
96. Galloway Kyle, ed., *More Songs by the Fighting Men: Soldier Poets, Second Series* (Erskine Macdonald, 1917), pp. 127, 18; Osborn, ed., *The Muse*, p. 151.
97. Osborn, ed., *The Muse*, pp. ix, xix. 'Those proud cliffs were calling clearly, / As Drake heard them in his day': Geoffrey H. Crump, 'Plymouth Mists', in Kyle, ed., *More Songs*, p. 54.

98. Joseph Courtney, 'As the Leaves Fall', in Kyle, ed., *Soldier Poets*, pp. 20–1; Herbert Asquith, 'The Volunteer', in Marsh, ed., *Georgian Poetry 1916–1917* (The Poetry Bookshop, 1918 [November 1917]), p. 181.

99. Parker, *The Old Lie*, pp. 86–7; Vandiver, 'Early Poets', p. 70.

100. On 'war as culture', see Cole, 'Civilians Writing the War', pp. 108–9; Brooke is quoted in Parker, *The Old Lie*, p. 218.

101. Vandiver, *Stand in the Trench*, pp. 335–6.

102. J.W. Mackail, ed., *Select Epigrams from the Greek Anthology, Edited with a Revised Text, Introduction, Translation and Notes* (Longmans, Green & Co., 1890), pp. 64–5, 240; on the cult of dying young, see Parker, *The Old Lie*, pp. 91–9.

103. Mackail, ed., *Select Epigrams*, p. 61.

104. Quoted in Murray, *Red Sweet Wine*, p. 63.

105. Robert Nichols, ed., *Anthology of War Poetry 1914–1918* (Nicholson & Watson, 1943), p. 51.

106. John Freeman, 'Happy is England Now', in Marsh, ed., *Georgian Poetry 1916–1917*, p. 138. On the contemporary trend of conflating 'England' with 'rural England', see Featherstone, *War Poetry*, pp. 29–30; on pastoral war literature more broadly, see Fussell, *The Great War*, ch. 7.

107. Dyneley Hussey, 'Youth'; Sydney Oswald, 'The Dead Soldier'; Oswald, 'Dulce et Decorum est pro Patria Mori'; H. Spurrier, 'The Guerdon'; J.W. Streets, 'Youth's Consecration', all in Kyle, ed., *Soldier Poets*, pp. 50–1, 68, 69, 94, 95.

108. Nichols, ed., *Anthology*, p. 61.

109. Paul Norgate, 'Wilfred Owen and the Soldier Poets', *Review of English Studies*, 40 (1989), 516–30 (p. 518); Parker, *The Old Lie*, p. 26.

110. Ross, *The Georgian Revolt*, p. 175; Hynes, *A War Imagined*, p. 299.

111. Vandiver, *Stand*, p. 129n.

112. Kyle, ed., *More Songs*, pp. 7–8.

113. Scott, 'Contemporary British War-Poetry', pp. 120–1.

114. Ibid., p. 121.

115. Rickword, 'War and Poetry', p. 29; Anon., 'Poetry and War', p. 4.

116. Gosse, 'Some Soldier Poets', pp. 299, 301, 311, 306, 309.

117. Fletcher, 'War Poetry', *The Egoist*, vol. 1, no. 21 (November 1914), p. 410.

118. Fletcher, 'More War Poetry', *The Egoist*, vol. 1, no. 22 (November 1914), pp. 426, 425.

119. Fletcher, 'War Poetry', p. 410; Fletcher, 'More War Poetry', p. 424.

120. Gosse, 'Some Soldier Poets', pp. 299, 316.

121. Middleton Murry, 'The Condition of English Poetry', *The Athenaeum*, issue 4675 (5 December 1919), pp. 1,283, 1,285.

122. Monro, *Some Contemporary Poets*, p. 28.

123. Laura Riding and Robert Graves, *A Survey of Modernist Poetry and A Pamphlet Against Anthologies* (Carcanet, 2002), pp. ?, 240.

124. Arthur Graeme West, 'God! How I Hate You, You Young Cheerful Men! On a University Undergraduate moved to verse by the war', in Tim Kendall, ed., *Poetry of the First World War* (Oxford University Press, 2014), p. 148.

125. Wilfred Owen, 'A Terre', in Kendall, ed., *Poetry*, p. 163.

126. Owen, 'Anthem for Doomed Youth', in Kendall, ed., *Poetry*, p. 153. Jon Stallworthy first noted the allusion to *Poems of To-Day*: see his *Wilfred Owen* (Clarendon Press, 1974; reissued 1998), p. 216. See also Norgate, 'Wilfred Owen', p. 522; Parker, *The Old Lie*, p. 249.

127. I am indebted for this suggestion to Norgate, 'Wilfred Owen', pp. 520–1.

128. Michael Cotsell, 'Wheels: An Introduction', *The Modernist Journals Project* (Brown and Tulsa Universities, ongoing; www.modjourn.org), n.p.

129. *TLS* and *The Lancet* quoted in *Wheels: An Anthology of Verse* (Basil Blackwell, 1916), pp. 89, 92.

130. Hynes, *A War Imagined*, p. 244. Quotations from the poetry are taken from, respectively, Osbert Sitwell, 'Therefore is the Name of it Called Babel'; Edith Sitwell, 'Thaïs in Heaven'; Edith Sitwell, 'The Mother'; Iris Tree, 'Zeppelins'; Osbert Sitwell, 'The End', all in *Wheels* (1916), pp. 24, 40, 50, 66, 16.

131. Sitwell, 'Babel'; Helen Rootham, 'The Great Adventure', both in *Wheels* (1916), pp. 24, 82.

132. Bertram Lloyd, ed., *Poems Written during the Great War, 1914–1918: An Anthology* (George Allen & Unwin, 1918), pp. 5–6; Lloyd, ed., *The Paths of Glory: A Collection of Poems Written During the War 1914–1919* (George Allen & Unwin, 1919), p. 7.

133. Wilfrid Wilson Gibson, 'The Bayonet'; Siegfried Sassoon, 'They', both in Lloyd, ed., *Poems*, pp. 42, 88.

134. Osbert Sitwell, 'Armchair'; Marcel Martinet, 'Civilians'; J.C. Squire, 'The Higher Life for Clergymen', all in Lloyd, ed., *Poems*, pp. 95, 65, 97.

135. Preface; Heinrich Hutter, 'Europe's All Souls' Day 1916', in Lloyd, ed., *Poems*, pp. 7–8, 62.

136. See Haughton, 'Anthologizing War', pp. 422–3; Das, 'Reframing', p. 6.

137. Lloyd, ed., *Paths*, p. 8.

138. Ibid., p. 5; Parker, *The Old Lie*, pp. 26–7.

139. Hynes, *A War Imagined*, pp. 300–1 (and on Owen's popularity versus Brooke's, see p. 302); Featherstone, *War Poetry*, pp. 15–16.

140. George Herbert Clarke, ed., *A Treasury of War Poetry: First Series* (Houghton Mifflin, 1917), p. xxv; Jacqueline T. Trotter, ed., *Valour and Vision: Poems of the War 1914–18* (Longmans, Green & Co., 1920), p. vii.

141. A.P. Wavell, ed., *Other Men's Flowers* (Jonathan Cape, 1944), pp. 5–6, 11.

142. Alexandra Harris, *Romantic Moderns: English Writers, Artists and the Imagination from Virginia Woolf to John Piper* (Thames & Hudson, 2010), pp. 144–7.

143. For this argument, see Jay Winter, *Sites of Memory, Sites of Mourning: The Great War in European Cultural History* (Cambridge University Press, 2014).
144. Rickword, 'War and Poetry', p. 27.
145. E.B. Osborn, *The New Elizabethans: A First Selection of the Lives of Young Men Who Have Fallen in the Great War* (John Lane, 1919), p. 4.

6 Politics

1. [Geoffrey Grigson] 'Why', *New Verse*, no. 1 (January 1933), pp. 1–2.
2. Martin Puchner, *Poetry of the Revolution: Marx, Manifestoes, and the Avant-Garde* (Princeton University Press, 2006), especially ch. 5.
3. F.T. Marinetti, 'Initial Manifesto of Futurism', in *Exhibition of Works by the Italian Futurist Painters* (Sackville Gallery, 1912), p. 3.
4. Ferry, *Tradition*, p. 223; Wyndham Lewis, ed., *Blast*, no. 1 (June 1914), p. 30.
5. John Middleton Murry, *The Problem of Style* (Oxford University Press, 1922), p. 77.
6. Puchner, *Poetry of the Revolution*, p. 11.
7. Lewis, ed., *Blast*, pp. 7–8; see Puchner, *Poetry*, pp. 116–17.
8. [Grigson], 'Politics: and a request', *New Verse*, no. 2 (March 1933), p. 1.
9. Samuel Hynes, *The Auden Generation: Literature and Politics in England in the 1930s* (Bodley Head, 1976; repr. Pimlico, 1992), p. 116; Porteus is quoted in Valentine Cunningham, *British Writers of the Thirties* (Oxford University Press, 1988; repr. 1993), p. 27.
10. John Lehmann, *New Writing in Europe* (Allen Lane, 1940), pp. 13, 19.
11. Cambridge Left, no. 1, quoted in Hynes, *The Auden Generation*, p. 100; Stephen Spender, 'Oxford to Communism', *New Verse*, no. 26–7 (November 1937), p. 10.
12. C. Day Lewis, ed., *The Mind in Chains: Socialism and the Cultural Revolution* (Frederick Muller, 1937), pp. 14–15.
13. 'Authors Take Sides on the Spanish War', *Left Review* (1937), n.p.
14. Stephen Spender and John Lehmann, eds., *Poems for Spain* (Hogarth Press, 1939), p. 7.
15. 'Authors Take Sides on the Spanish War', n.p.
16. Louis MacNeice, *Modern Poetry: A Personal Essay* (Oxford University Press, 1938), p. 5, Preface; Spender, *The Destructive Element: A Study of Modern Writers and Beliefs* (Jonathan Cape, 1935), pp. 190, 204.
17. Lehmann, *The Whispering Gallery: Autobiography I* (Harcourt, Brace and Company, 1955), p. 232.
18. Ibid., pp. 172–3.
19. Lehmann, *New Writing in Europe*, p. 26; Hynes, 'Michael Roberts' Tragic View', *Contemporary Literature*, 12 (1971), 437–50 (p. 437).
20. C. Day Lewis, 'Letter to W.H. Auden', in *From Feathers to Iron* (Hogarth Press, 1931); see Cunningham, *British Writers*, p. 167, for the suggestion.

21. Michael Roberts, ed., *The Faber Book of Modern Verse* (Faber and Faber, 1936), p. 9; Roberts, ed., *New Signatures: Poems by Several Hands* (Hogarth Press, 1932), p. 7.

22. Grigson, 'Faith or Feeling?', *New Verse*, no. 2 (March 1933), p. 16.

23. Lehmann quoted in John Haffenden, ed., *W.H. Auden: The Critical Heritage* (Routledge, 1983; repr. 1997), p. 5.

24. Hynes, *The Auden Generation*, pp. 27–9.

25. Roberts, ed., *Faber Book of Modern Verse*, p. 1. On the 'provocatively eccentric' nature of Roberts' pro-Modernist selections, see Baldick, *The Modern Movement*, p. 112.

26. Lehmann, *The Whispering Gallery*, pp. 177–8.

27. D.J. Enright, ed., *Poets of the 1950's: An Anthology of New English Verse* (Kenkyusha, 1955; repr. 1958), p. 3.

28. Roberts, ed., *New Signatures*, p. 10; Roberts, *Critique of Poetry* (Jonathan Cape, 1934), p. 42.

29. Roberts, ed., *New Signatures*, pp. 12–13.

30. Hugh l'Anson Fausset, 'The New Poetry', *TLS*, issue 1572 (March 17 1932), p. 197.

31. Foreword to Samuel Courtauld's unpublished anthology (1939), p. iii. I am very grateful to Inigo Thomas for allowing me to view and quote from this book.

32. Roberts, ed., *New Signatures*, pp. 18–19; see Hynes, *The Auden Generation*, p. 80.

33. Lehmann, *New Writing in Europe*, p. 28.

34. See, e.g. Alex Glendinning, Review of New Country, *TLS*, issue 1633 (18 May 1933), p. 345. In Robin Skelton, ed., *Poetry of the Thirties* (Penguin, 1964; repr. 1971), p. 15, it's described as 'violently propagandistic'.

35. Roberts, ed., *New Country: Prose and Poetry by the Authors of New Signatures* (Hogarth Press, 1933), pp. 13, 10, 14–15.

36. Ibid., pp. 15–18. See Cunningham, *British Writers*, pp. 211, 299, on the connection to the *Manifesto*.

37. Roberts, ed., *New Country*, p. 18; R.E. Warner, 'Hymn', in ibid., p. 254.

38. T.O. Beachcroft, 'A Week at the Union', in ibid., pp. 86–96.

39. John Lehmann, ed., *New Writing*, no. 1 (John Lane, 1936), n.p.

40. Quoted from the *Daily Worker*; see Hynes, *The Auden Generation*, p. 198.

41. E. Allen Osborne, ed., *In Letters of Red* (Michael Joseph, 1938), endpapers, epigraph, book jacket, p. 181.

42. See Puchner, *Poetry of the Revolution*, especially Introduction and ch. 1.

43. Glendinning, Review of New Country, p. 345.

44. Lehmann, *New Writing in Europe*, p. 28; on the hopeful use of 'more and more' among Left intellectuals, see Cunningham, *British Writers*, pp. 29–30.

45. Roberts, ed., *New Country*, pp. 18–19; Roberts, Critique, p. 154; Roberts, ed., *Faber Book of Modern Verse*, p. 6.

46. Day Lewis, *A Hope for Poetry* (Basil Blackwell, 1934; repr. 1936), pp. 29–30.
47. This is argued in depth by the Communist critic Alick West: see West, *Crisis and Criticism* (Lawrence and Wishart, 1937), pp. 112–34. 'Outworn forms and sentiments' is taken from John Lehmann's response to the 'Authors Take Sides' questionnaire.
48. Edward Upward, 'Sketch for a Marxist Interpretation of Literature', in Day Lewis, ed., *The Mind in Chains*, p. 54.
49. Spender, *The Destructive Element*, p. 204; Upward, 'Sketch', pp. 46–7.
50. Nancy Cunard, 'Does Anyone Know Any Negroes?', quoted in Cunard, ed., *Negro: An Anthology*, ed. and abridged by Hugh Ford (Frederick Ungar, 1970), p. xxvii.
51. Ibid., p. xxxi.
52. Ibid., pp. xxi, xvii.
53. Ibid., p. xxxii.
54. Ibid., pp. xxxi, 352.
55. Ibid., pp. 148, 151, xxxi–xxxii.
56. Ibid., pp. xii, xxiii–iv.
57. Ibid., p. xxiii.
58. Cunningham, *British Writers*, p. 297; on the makeup of Thirties reading audiences, see Julian Symons, *The Thirties: A Dream Revolved* (House of Stratus, 1975; repr. 2001), pp. 30–2.
59. Day Lewis, *A Hope*, p. 32; see also Spender, *The Destructive Element*, p. 230.
60. MacNeice, *Modern Poetry*, pp. 14–15.
61. Lehmann, *New Writing in Europe*, p. 13.
62. Charles Madge, 'Poetry and Politics', *New Verse*, no. 3 (May 1933), p. 2.
63. W.H. Auden and John Garrett, eds., *The Poet's Tongue* (G. Bell & Sons, 1935), p. vi; Auden, ed., *The Oxford Book of Light Verse* (Clarendon Press, 1938), p. vii.
64. Janet Adam Smith, ed., *Poems of Tomorrow: An Anthology of Contemporary Verse, Chosen from The Listener* (Chatto & Windus, 1935), p. v.
65. Roberts, ed., *New Signatures*, pp. 11–12. On Roberts and Empson, see Cunningham, *British Poets*, pp. 300–1.
66. Lehmann, *The Whispering Gallery*, pp. 233, 257.
67. Lehmann, *New Writing in Europe*, p. 79.
68. John Mulgan, ed., *Poems of Freedom* (Victor Gollancz/Left Book Club, 1938), pp. 11, 8.
69. Ibid., pp. 8–9.
70. Auden and Garrett, eds., *The Poet's Tongue*, pp. vi–vii, viii–ix.
71. On Auden's relationship to Oxford University Press, see Edward Mendelson, 'Light and Outrageous', *The New York Review of Books*, vol. 51 (12 August 2004).
72. Ibid., pp. xix–xx.

73. Quoted in D.S. Savage, 'Poetry Politics in London', *Poetry*, 53 (1939), 200–8 (p. 203).

74. Montagu Slater, 'The Turning Point', *Left Review*, no. 2 (October 1935), quoted in Hynes, *Auden Generation*, p. 166; Louise Bogan, 'Poetry's Genuine Fare', *Poetry*, vol. 48 (1936), pp. 45, 47.

75. Day Lewis, *A Hope*, pp. 36–7; see also Auden, 'Writing, or the Pattern Between People', in Naomi Mitchison, ed., *An Outline for Boys & Girls and Their Parents: Civilisation* (Victor Gollancz, 1932), p. 867; Arthur Calder-Marshall, 'Fiction', in *Fact*, no. 4 (July 1937), p. 44.

76. *Left Review* (February 1936); quoted in Cunningham, *British Writers*, p. 214.

77. Auden, 'Writing', pp. 867–8.

78. Auden, 'Writing', p. 864.

79. Auden, 'The Secret Agent', in *Collected Shorter Poems, 1927–1957* (Faber and Faber, 1966); p. 22; Madge, 'Letter to the Intelligentsia', in Roberts, ed., *New Country*, p. 233; Lehmann, 'A Little Distance Off', in Adam Smith, ed., *Poems of Tomorrow*, p. 55.

80. Day Lewis, *A Hope*, p. 38.

81. See Cunningham, *British Writers*, p. 219; for an example of this in practice, see Kohlmann, *Committed Styles*, pp. 180–1.

82. West, *Crisis and Criticism*, p. 80.

83. Spender, *The Destructive Element*, p. 229.

84. Jameson, 'Documents', pp. 17–18; Madge, 'Poetry and Politics', p. 3.

85. See Cunningham, *British Writers*, pp. 224–5.

86. See Skelton, *Poetry of the Thirties*, p. 17; Spender, 'The Left Wing Orthodoxy', *New Verse*, 31–2 (Autumn 1938), pp. 12–13.

87. Calder-Marshall, 'Fiction', p. 42; see also Jameson, 'Documents', p. 12.

88. Mitchison, 'We're Writing a Book', *New Masses*, vol. 20 (15 September 1936), pp. 15–17.

89. Jameson, 'Documents', pp. 14–15.

90. MacNeice, *Modern Poetry*, p. 196.

91. Madge, 'Oxford Collective Poem', *New Verse*, no. 25 (May 1937), pp. 16–18.

92. Roberts, ed., *New Signatures*, p. 7 and n.p.

93. Grigson, 'Faith or Feeling?', p. 15.

94. Roberts, ed., *New Country*, pp. 11–12, 13–14, 15.

95. Roberts, ed., *New Signatures*, pp. 18–19; Spender, 'The Funeral', in *New Signatures*, p. 95.

96. Roberts, ed., *New Country*, pp. 20–1.

97. See Hynes, *The Auden Generation*, p. 80.

98. Savage, 'Poetry Politics in London', p. 201.

99. Geoffrey West, 'A Cosmopolitan Miscellany: "New Writing" by Victims of Oppression', *TLS*, issue 1791 (May 30 1936), p. 11.

100. Lehmann, *The Whispering Gallery*, p. 248.

101. Lehmann, *The Whispering Gallery*, pp. 257–8; see Cunningham, *British Writers*, pp. 305–8.

102. Anthony Hartley, *A State of England* (Harcourt, Brace & World, 1963), p. 50.

103. Ibid., p. 38.

104. See Hynes, 'Michael Roberts', p. 438; Roberts, ed., *Faber Book of Modern Verse*, p. 3.

105. Auden, introduction to Mulgan, ed., *Poems of Freedom*, pp. 7–8.

106. Hartley, *A State*, p. 35.

107. J.D. Scott, 'In the Movement', the *Spectator*, vol. 193 (1 October 1954), p. 399; see also Cunningham, *British Writers*, p. 17.

108. Hartley, *A State*, p. 43.

109. Quoted in Blake Morrison, *The Movement: English Poetry and Fiction of the 1950s* (Oxford University Press, 1980; repr. Methuen, 1986), p. 55; on the class background of the new generation of poets, see Morrison's chapter 2, 'Class and Culture'.

110. Enright, ed., *Poets of the 1950's*, p. 5.

111. Morrison, The Movement, p. 3; Wain quoted in John Press, *Rule and Energy: Trends in British Poetry Since the Second World War* (Clarendon Press, 1963), p. 12.

112. Donald Davie, 'Remembering the Thirties', in Robert Conquest, ed., *New Lines: An Anthology* (Macmillan & Co., 1956), p. 70.

113. See Morrison, *The Movement*, p. 93.

114. Conquest, 'The Art of the Enemy', *Essays in Criticism*, 7 (1957), 42–55 (pp. 43–4).

115. See Eric Homberger, '*New Lines* in 1956', in Zachary Leader, ed., *The Movement Reconsidered: Essays on Larkin, Amis, Gunn, Davie and Their Contemporaries* (Oxford University Press, 2009), pp. 258–9.

116. According to Samuel Hynes, one 'central impulse of the thirties' was 'the search for a system'. See Hynes, 'Michael Roberts', p. 438. On the significance of *New Lines* for the careers of the Movement poets, see Morrison, *The Movement*, pp. 238–41.

117. Conquest, ed., *New Lines*, p. xv.

118. Davie, 'Too Late for Satire' and 'Rejoinder to a Critic', both in ibid., pp. 67–9. On Davie's 'Rejoinder' and similar poems, see Morrison, *The Movement*, pp. 87–9.

119. Enright, ed., *Poets of the 1950's*, p. 13.

120. Conquest, 'New Lines, Movements and Modernisms', in Leader, ed., *The Movement Reconsidered*, p. 307. Davie explained that there was a general desire among the group to pretend that 'we had never noticed how Larkin and Gunn and Amis had something in common, or that, if we had noticed, it didn't interest or excite us.' See Davie, 'Remembering the Movement', in *The Poet in the Imaginary Museum: Essays of Two Decades*, ed. Barry Alpert (Carcanet New Press, 1977), p. 72.

121. Conquest, ed., *New Lines*, p. xv; Enright, ed., *Poets of the 1950's*, pp. 15, 12.

122. Conquest, 'New Lines, Movements', p. 309. For an overview of the abuse, see Homberger, 'New Lines in 1956', pp. 264–8.
123. Charles Tomlinson, 'The Middlebrow Muse', Essays in Criticism, 7 (1957), 208–17 (pp. 215–16).
124. Press, Rule and Energy, pp. 19, 7–11.
125. A. Alvarez, Where Did It All Go Right? (Richard Cohen Books, 1999), p. 187.
126. Ibid., pp. 188–9.
127. Alvarez, ed., The New Poetry (Penguin, 1962), pp. 21–3; see also Alvarez's discussion of his argument in Where Did It All Go Right, p. 189.
128. Alvarez, ed., The New Poetry, pp. 23–5, 28; Alvarez, Where Did It All Go Right?, pp. 185–6.
129. Alvarez, ed., The New Poetry, pp. 23, 22.
130. Geoffrey Hill, 'Genesis', in ibid., p. 166.

7 Pop

1. [John Willett], 'Poems in Public', The Times Literary Supplement, issue 3098 (July 14 1961), p. 433; John O'Callaghan, 'Liverpool Letter', Guardian (14 February 1966), DM1107/D103, Bristol University Library Special Collections.
2. Quoted in Michael Horovitz, ed., Children of Albion: Poetry of the Underground in Britain (Penguin, 1969), p. 334.
3. For the whole argument, see Horovitz, ed., Children, pp. 316ff.
4. Jonathan Raban, The Society of the Poem (Harrap, 1971), p. 44.
5. Ibid., pp. 84–5; on the Beatles' avant-garde influences, see Jeff Nuttall, Bomb Culture (MacGibbon & Kee, 1968), p. 132; Ian MacDonald, Revolution in the Head: The Beatles' Records and the Sixties, 2nd ed. (Fourth Estate, 1997), pp. xiv–xix, 9–10, 20–1. See Grevel Lindop, 'Poetry, Rhetoric and the Mass Audience: The Case of the Liverpool Poets', in Michael Schmidt and Lindop, British Poetry Since 1960: A Critical Survey (Carcanet, 1972), pp. 92–3, for the counterargument.
6. Horovitz, ed., Children, p. 323; Edward Lucie-Smith, 'Poets in Conference', Encounter (June 1966), p. 41.
7. Pete Roche, ed., Love, Love, Love: The New Love Poetry (Corgi Books, 1967; repr. 1973), p. xiii.
8. C.B. Cox, 'Pop goes the poetry', Critical Quarterly, 10 (December 1968), pp. 309–11; George Melly, Revolt into Style: The Pop Arts in Britain (Allen Lane, 1970), pp. 208–9.
9. Roger McGough, Said and Done (Century, 2005), p. 109; Phil Bowen, A Gallery to Play To: The Story of the Mersey Poets (Liverpool University Press, 1999; 2nd ed. 2008), p. 12.
10. Bowen, A Gallery, pp. 30, 37–42.
11. McGough quoted in Edward Lucie-Smith, ed., The Liverpool Scene: Recorded Live Along the Mersey Beat (Donald Carroll, 1967), p. 79

12. Peter Brock, 'The newest sound', *Daily Express* (25 February 1966), DM1107/D103, Bristol University Library Special Collections.; Simon Neilson, 'Liverpool's Left Bank' [no. 1], *Liverpool Daily Post* (February 6 1967), p. 5.

13. Adrian Henri, 'The poet, the audience and non-communication', *Sphinx* (Autumn 1964), p. 27; John Cornelius, *Liverpool 8* (John Murray, 1982), p. 32; Bowen, *A Gallery*, p. 69.

14. Brock, 'The newest sound', DM1107/D103, Bristol University Library Special Collections.

15. Neilson, 'Liverpool's Left Bank' [no. 1], p. 5.

16. Sean Hignett, 'The Sound of Liverpool 8', *Weekend Telegraph* (31 March 1967), pp. 13–14; Darren Pih, 'Liverpool's Left Bank', in Christoph Grunenberg and Robert Knifton, eds., *Centre of the Creative Universe: Liverpool & the Avant-Garde* (Liverpool University Press, 2007), pp. 114–25.

17. O'Callaghan, 'Liverpool Letter', DM1107/D103, Bristol University Library Special Collections.

18. Neilson, 'Liverpool's Left Bank' [no. 3], *Liverpool Daily Post* (February 8 1967), p. 10.

19. Letter from Brian Patten to Anthony Richardson (undated), DM1107/D103, Bristol University Library Special Collections.

20. Brock, 'The newest sound', DM1107/D103, Bristol University Library Special Collections.

21. Neilson, 'Liverpool's Left Bank' [no. 3], p. 10.

22. Henri, 'Don't Worry/Everything's Going to be All Right'; 'Tonight at Noon'; 'Love Poem'; 'Love Is…'; 'Without You', all in Henri, Roger McGough and Brian Patten, *The Mersey Sound* (Penguin, 1967; restored ed. 2017), pp. 47, 3, 32, 12, 11.

23. Henri, 'Notes on Painting and Poetry' in *Tonight at Noon* (Rapp & Whiting, 1968; repr. D. McKay, 1969), p. 70; see Taylor, *Adrian Henri*, pp. 8, 175. On making art out of 'whatever was to hand', see Melly, *Revolt*, p. 10.

24. Melly, *Revolt*, p. 6; Horovitz, *Children*, p. 327.

25. See Ian MacDonald, *The People's Music* (Pimlico, 2003), pp. 192–3.

26. Publishers' advertising notice for Brian Patten, *Little Johnny's Confession* (George Allen & Unwin, 1967).

27. [Editorial], 'Making a Scene', *TLS*, issue 3432 (December 7 1967), p. 1,189.

28. Patten, *Little Johnny's Confession*, first edition dust jacket; Horovitz, *Children*, p. 369.

29. Nuttall, *Bomb Culture*, pp. 21–2.

30. Holmes quoted in Louis Menand, *The Free World: Art and Thought in the Cold War* (Farrar, Straus and Giroux, 2021), p. 478; Norman O. Brown, *Life Against Death: The Psychoanalytical Meaning of History* (Wesleyan University Press, 1959; repr. 1977), p. x; Nuttall, *Bomb Culture*, pp. 170, 184.

31. Quoted in Jonathan Dollimore, 'The challenge of sexuality', in Alan Sinfield, ed., *Society and Literature*, 1945–1970 (Methuen & Co., 1983), p. 51.
32. Adrian Mitchell, 'Peace is Milk', in Roche, ed., *Love, Love, Love*, p. 25.
33. McGough quoted in Lucie-Smith, *The Liverpool Scene*, p. 33; see also Brock, 'The newest sound', DM1107/D103, Bristol University Library Special Collections.
34. Patten, 'Before it happened', in Lucie-Smith, ed., *The Liverpool Scene*, p. 32.
35. McGough, 'At Lunchtime A Story of Love', in Henri, McGough and Patten, *The Mersey Sound*, pp. 64–5.
36. McGough, *Said and Done*, p. 180.
37. Henri, *Total Art: Environments, Happenings, and Performance* (Praeger Publishers, 1974), pp. 116–17; Nuttall, *Bomb Culture*, pp. 126–7.
38. Dominic Sandbrook, *White Heat: A History of Britain in the Swinging Sixties* (Little, Brown, 2006; repr. Abacus, 2010), pp. 524–5.
39. Taylor, *Adrian Henri*, pp. 208–9; Bowen, *A Gallery*, pp. 50–1.
40. Bill Harry, 'The Night the Bomb Dropped', *Mersey Beat* (December 19 1964), n.p., via http://www.triumphpc.com/mersey-beat/archives/bomb-dropped.shtml.
41. Ibid., n.p.; Taylor, *Adrian Henri*, pp. 210–11; Sandbrook, *White Heat*, pp. 533–4.
42. Harry, 'The Night the Bomb Dropped', n.p.
43. Henri, 'Notes on Painting', p. 68; and see Raban, *The Society of the Poem*, pp. 87–8.
44. Henri, 'Notes on Painting', p. 74. McGough has said in an interview (Deryn Rees-Jones, 'Finding a Rhyme for Alphabet Soup: An Interview with Roger McGough', in Rees-Jones and Michael Murphy, eds., *Writing Liverpool: Essays and Interviews* (Liverpool Press, 2007), pp. 141–2) that 'I never consciously write for performance. A poem has to be perfect on the page, and I write and rewrite… It's the poem first, then the poet, then the performer.'
45. Henri, 'I Want to Paint', in Henri, McGough and Patten, *The Mersey Sound*, p. 45; Taylor, *Adrian Henri*, p. 106.
46. Taylor, '"Reelin' an' a-rockin'": Adrian Henri and 1960s Pop', *East-West Cultural Passage*, 1 (2012), 109–25 (pp. 120–1).
47. Taylor, *Adrian Henri*, p. 204; Bowen, *A Gallery*, p. 49; McGough, *Said and Done*, p. 135.
48. Henri, 'Summer Poems Without Words', in Lucie-Smith, ed., *The Liverpool Scene*, p. 73; see Henri, 'Notes on Painting', p. 66; Peter Barry, 'The Hard Lyric: Re-registering Liverpool Poetry', in Wade, ed., *Gladsongs*, pp. 25–6.
49. Raoul Vaneigem, *The Revolution of Everyday Life*, trans. Donald Nicholson-Smith (Rebel Press, 1983; rev. ed., 2001), pp. 200, 202.
50. Douglas Dunn, 'To Still History', *Encounter* (November 1972), p. 62.
51. Horovitz, ed., *Children*, p. 338; Sandbrook, *White Heat*, p. 524; Bowen,

A Gallery, pp. 62–4; Lucie-Smith, 'A Wild Night', *Encounter* (August 1965), p. 65; Logue quoted in Jonathon Green, *Days in the Life: Voices from the English Underground, 1961–1971* (Heinemann, 1988; repr. Minerva, 1989), p. 73.

52. Horovitz, ed., *Children,* pp. 338–9; Gittings quoted in ibid., p. 340; Melly, *Revolt*, p. 205.

53. See Horovitz, ed., *Children*, pp. 321–2.

54. McGough, *Said and Done*, p. 86.

55. Wade, 'An Interview with Brian Patten', in Wade, ed., *Gladsongs*, p. 106; Patten, 'Prosepoem Towards a Definition of Itself', in Henri, McGough and Patten, *The Mersey Sound*, p. 101.

56. Letter from Anthony Richardson to Adrian Henri (20 September 1966); letter from Brian Patten to Anthony Richardson (undated), DM1107/ D103, Bristol University Library Special Collections.

57. Horovitz, ed., *Children*, pp. 360, 316.

58. Lucie-Smith, ed., *The Liverpool Scene*, pp. 7–8; Henri quotes this approvingly in 'Notes on Painting', p. 81. See Horovitz, *Children,* pp. 356–7, on the actor Peter O'Toole's reading of Mitchell's 'To Whom It May Concern' in Trafalgar Square during the CND's Easter March in 1965.

59. Henri quoted in Lucie-Smith, ed., *The Liverpool Scene*, p. 71; see also Henri, 'Notes on Painting', pp. 65–6, 69.

60. Nuttall, *Bomb Culture*, p. 92; Henri, 'The poet, the audience, and non-communication', p. 27.

61. See Bowen, *A Gallery*, p. 1; Dunn, 'To Still History', p. 61; Rees-Jones, 'Finding a Rhyme', p. 140.

62. Jeremy Robson, ed., *Poems from Poetry & Jazz in Concert: An Anthology* (Souvenir Press, 1969; repr. Panther Books, 1969), p. 13; Robson, ed., *The Young British Poets* (Chatto & Windus, 1971), p. 12; Horovitz, ed., *Children*, pp. 327–8.

63. Robson, ed., *Young British Poets*, p. 12; Lindop, 'Poetry, Rhetoric and the Mass Audience', pp. 92, 94, 102–3.

64. Lucie-Smith, 'A Wild Night', pp. 64–5; [Peter Porter], 'The Poet in the 'Sixties: Vices and Virtues – a recorded conversation with Peter Porter', in Schmidt and Lindop, eds., *British Poetry*, p. 203.

65. [Porter], 'The Poet in the 'Sixties', p. 203.

66. Lindop, 'Poetry, Rhetoric and the Mass Audience', pp. 95–101.

67. See, e.g. Henri, 'The poet, the audience and non-communication', p. 27.

68. Henri, 'Notes on Painting', p. 76; Henri, *Total Art*, p. 27.

69. Henri, 'On the Late Late Massachers Stillbirths and Deformed Children a Smoother Lovelier Skin Job', in Henri, McGough and Patten, *The Mersey Sound*, p. 15.

70. Henri, 'Commercials for 'Bomb' Event', in *Tonight at Noon*, p. 26; I am indebted to Taylor, *Adrian Henri*, p. 213, for the second quotation, part of an additional (unprinted) 'bomb commercial' performed in 1984.

71. See Taylor, *Adrian Henri*, p. 212.

72. Henri, 'Notes on Painting', p. 76.
73. McGough, 'Limestreetscene '64', in Lucie-Smith, ed., *The Liverpool Scene*, p. 15; Henri, 'The Entry of Christ into Liverpool', in Lucie-Smith, ed., *British Poetry since 1945* (Penguin Books, 1970, repr. 1978), p. 351.
74. Henri, *Autobiography* (Jonathan Cape, 1971), pp. 24–5, 37.
75. Lucie-Smith, ed., *The Liverpool Scene*, pp. 16, 24, back cover.
76. Lindop, 'Poetry, Rhetoric and the Mass Audience', pp. 100–1; Roy Fuller, 'Liverboom', *TLS*, issue 3411 (July 13 1967), p. 614; see also P.J. Kavanagh, 'A clutch of impresarios', *Guardian* (16 June 1967), p. 6 ('This is ad-man stuff').
77. Henri, 'Me', in Henri, McGough and Patten, *The Mersey Sound*, p. 20.
78. Lindop, 'Poetry, Rhetoric and the Mass Audience', p. 99; see also Raban, *The Society of the Poem*, pp. 119–22 ('either the reader becomes one of the faithful or else he is excluded, as a cynical onlooker, from the society of the poem').
79. McGough, *Said and Done*, p. 146.
80. O'Callaghan, 'Liverpool Letter', DM1107/D103, Bristol University Library Special Collections.
81. Bowen, *A Gallery*, pp. 58–9; Stephen Wade, 'The Arrival of McGough', in Wade, ed., *Gladsongs and Gatherings*, pp. 13–14.
82. Hignett, 'The Sound of Liverpool 8', p. 13.
83. Letter from Anthony Richardson to Brian Patten (13 October 1966); letter from Brian Patten to Anthony Richardson (undated), both DM1107/D103, Bristol University Library Special Collections.
84. [Ian Hamilton], 'Making a Scene', *TLS*, issue 3432 (December 7 1967), p. 1,189.
85. Penguin Modern Poets 10 Cover Brief, DM1107/D103, Bristol University Library Special Collections.
86. McGough, *Said and Done*, pp. 191–2.
87. Penguin Modern Poets 10 Cover Brief, DM1107/D103, Bristol University Library Special Collections.
88. Letter from Brian Patten to Anthony Richardson (undated); letter from Anthony Richardson to Brian Patten (13 October 1966), both DM1107/D103, Bristol University Library Special Collections.
89. Menand, *The Free World*, pp. 488–9.
90. See Bowen, *A Gallery*, p. 85.
91. [Hamilton], 'Making a Scene', p. 1,189.
92. McGough, *Said and Done*, p. 195. See Taylor, *Adrian Henri*, p. 95, on the dedication as a 'marketing tool'.
93. McGough, *Said and Done*, p. 195; Bowen, *A Gallery*, pp. 72–3.
94. Bowen, *A Gallery*, p. 72.
95. *The Incredible New Liverpool Scene LP*, prod. Hal Shaper (CBS, 1967), quoted in Taylor, 'Reelin' an' a-rockin'', p. 123.
96. See, among others, Kavanagh, 'A clutch of impresarios', p. 6; [Hamilton], 'Making a Scene', p. 1,189; Fuller, 'Oh Yeah?', *TLS*, issue 3398 (13 April 1967), p. 305.

97. Melly, *Revolt*, p. 210.
98. Robson, ed., *Poems from Poetry & Jazz in Concert*, p. 15.
99. Raban, *The Society of the Poem*, p. 180.
100. See William Wootten, 'To answer an appetite', *TLS*, issue 5691 (April 27 2012), p. 14, on Penguin's perception of the 'commercial wisdom of publishing verse in high-volume cheap paperbacks'.
101. Lucie-Smith, 'Poets in Conference', *Encounter* (June 1966), p. 41; Melly, *Revolt*, p. 210.
102. Henri, 'Love Poem'; 'I Want to Paint', both in Henri, McGough and Patten, *The Mersey Sound*, pp. 31–4, 44–6. See Taylor, *Adrian Henri*, p. 106, on the composition history of 'I Want to Paint'.
103. Lucie-Smith, ed., *The Liverpool Scene*, pp. 3, 73.
104. Taylor, *Adrian Henri*, p. 9; Henri, McGough and Patten, *The Mersey Sound*, back cover.
105. Letter from Clare Walker to Valerie Willey (2 August 1968); letter from Judith Wales to Lynne Wilson (28 October 1969); letter from E.A. Amsden to Jean Gardiner (11 April 1967), all DM1107/D103, Bristol University Library Special Collections.
106. Bowen, *A Gallery*, p. 75.
107. Quoted in ibid., p. 65.
108. Melly, *Revolt*, p. 214; Anon., 'The Myth of Liverpool (?)', *Sphinx* (Lent, 1970), p. 36.
109. Letter from Anthony Richardson to Brian Patten (13 October 1966), DM1107/D103, Bristol University Library Special Collections.
110. Sid Smith, 'Love Is…', at http://thebogbookblog.blogspot.com/2005/09/love-is.html.
111. Henri, *Autobiography*, p. 32.

8 Therapy

1. Robert Haven Schauffler, ed., *The Poetry Cure: A Pocket Medicine Chest of Verse, Compounded by Robert Haven Schauffler* (Dodd, Mead and Company, 1925), pp. xvii, xxxi, cover. See 'compound', v., sense 3, OED online (Oxford University Press, June 2021).
2. Robert Graves, 'The Use of Poetry', in *On English Poetry: Being an Irregular Approach to the Psychology of This Art, from Evidence Mainly Subjective* (Alfred A. Knopf, 1922), p. 85.
3. For instance, Frederick Clarke Prescott, *The Poetic Mind* (The Macmillan Company, 1922); David Seabury, *Unmasking Our Minds* (Boni & Liveright, 1924).
4. Schauffler, ed., *The Poetry Cure*, p. xviii.
5. Ibid., pp. xviii, xxvii–xxviii, xxix–xxx.
6. Ibid., pp. xxx–xxxii.
7. Rita Felski, *Uses of Literature* (Blackwell Publishing, 2008), p. 7.
8. Joseph North, *Literary Criticism: A Concise Political History* (Harvard University Press), p. 6, quoted in Beth Blum, *The Self-Help Compulsion:*

Searching for Advice in Modern Literature (Columbia University Press, 2020), p. 253.

9. Andrew O'Hagan, 'Flossing', *London Review of Books*, vol. 26, no. 21 (4 November 2004).

10. Robert Potts, 'Death by a thousand anthologies', *Guardian* (6 December 2003); O'Hagan, 'Flossing'; Neil Astley, 'Bile, Guile and Dangerous to Poetry': The StAnza Lecture 2005 (http://past.stanzapoetry.org/stanza06_archive/lecture.htm), quoting Steven Waling; Mark Ford, 'Categorically wrong', *Guardian* (7 September 2002).

11. Sam Leith, 'An unpoetic ode to therapy', *Evening Standard* (18 January 2016).

12. Daniel Soar, 'Short Cuts,' *London Review of Books,* vol. 24, no. 14 (25 July 2002).

13. Daisy Goodwin, ed., *101 Poems that Could Save Your Life: An Anthology of Emotional First Aid* (Harper Collins, 1999; repr. 2002); Goodwin, ed., *101 Poems to Get You Through the Day (and Night)* (Harper Collins, 2000; repr. 2003); Goodwin, ed., *101 Poems to Keep You Sane: Emergency Rations for the Seriously Stressed* (Harper Collins, 2001); Julia Darling and Cynthia Fuller, eds., *The Poetry Cure* (Bloodaxe and Newcastle University, 2005); Deborah Alma, ed., *The Emergency Poet: An Anti-Stress Poetry Anthology* (Michael O'Mara, 2015); Jonathan Bate, Paula Byrne, Sophie Ratcliffe and Andrew Schuman, eds., *Stressed Unstressed: Classic Poems to Ease the Mind* (William Collins/Harper Collins, 2016); William Sieghart, ed., *The Poetry Pharmacy: Tried-and-True Prescriptions for the Heart, Mind and Soul* (Particular Books, 2017); Sieghart, ed., *The Poetry Pharmacy Returns: More Prescriptions for Courage, Healing and Hope* (Particular Books, 2019).

14. Darling and Fuller, eds., *The Poetry Cure*, pp. 9, 11.

15. Neil Astley, ed., *Staying Alive: Real Poems for Unreal Times* (Bloodaxe, 2002); Astley, ed., *Being Alive: The Sequel to Staying Alive* (Bloodaxe, 2004); Astley, ed., *Being Human: The Companion Anthology to Staying Alive and Being Alive* (Bloodaxe, 2011); Astley, ed., *Staying Human: New Poems for Staying Alive* (Bloodaxe, 2020).

16. Introduction to Astley, ed., *Staying Alive*, pp. 19, 24.

17. Louis Menand, *The Free Play of the Mind: Art and Thought in the Cold War* (Farrar, Straus and Giroux, 2021), p. 457.

18. Sieghart, ed., *The Poetry Pharmacy*, pp. xviii, xv–xvi.

19. Darling and Fuller, eds., *The Poetry Cure*, p. 9.

20. Astley, 'Bile, Guile and Dangerous to Poetry'.

21. 'Equipment for living' is Kenneth Burke's term: see Burke, *The Philosophy of Literary Form: Studies in Symbolic Action* (Louisiana State University Press, 1941), p. 293 ff.

22. See Wavell, ed., *Other Men's Flowers*, p. 15.

23. Robert Darnton, *The Case for Books: Past, Present, and Future* (Public Affairs, 2009), pp. 149–50.

24. Blum, *Self-Help Compulsion*, p. 14.

25. Samuel Smiles, *Self-Help; With Illustrations of Character and Conduct* (John Murray, 1859), pp. 215, 240, 260.
26. Blum, *Self-Help Compulsion*, pp. 41–2.
27. Matthew Sturgis, *Oscar Wilde: A Life* (Alfred A. Knopf, 2021), p. 301; [E.J. Hardy], *How to be Happy Though Married: Being a Handbook to Marriage,* 3rd ed. (T. Fisher Unwin, 1886), front cover.
28. Blum, *Self-Help Compulsion*, pp. 16–18.
29. Timothy Aubry, *Reading as Therapy: What Contemporary Fiction Does for Middle-Class Americans* (University of Iowa Press, 2011), pp. 19–20.
30. Blum, *Self-Help Compulsion*, pp. 23–5.
31. Ibid., pp. 19–20, 26, 221.
32. Ella Berthoud and Susan Elderkin, *The Novel Cure: An A–Z of Literary Remedies* (Canongate, 2013), p. 2.
33. Ibid., pp. 13, 107.
34. Sarah McNicol, 'Theories of Bibliotherapy', in McNicol and Liz Brewster, eds., *Bibliotherapy* (Facet Publishing, 2018), pp. 27–8.
35. Liz Brewster, 'Bibliotherapy: a critical history', in McNicol and Brewster, eds., *Bibliotherapy*, p. 5; Schauffler, *The Poetry Cure*, dedication.
36. Leah Price, *What We Talk About When We Talk About Books: The History and Future of Reading* (Basic Books, 2019), pp. 119–22. See https://napc.co.uk/wp-content/uploads/2017/09/Reading-well.pdf.
37. Brewster, 'Bibliotherapy', p. 16; Blake Morrison, 'The reading cure', *Guardian* (5 January 2008).
38. https://www.theschooloflife.com/shop/eu/bibliotherapy/.
39. https://poetrypharmacy.co.uk/shoppe/; https://poetrypharmacy.co.uk/the-consulting-room/.
40. Interview with Andrew Schuman, 16 August 2021.
41. Jack J. Leedy, 'Principles of Poetry Therapy', in Leedy, ed., *Poetry Therapy: The Use of Poetry in the Treatment of Emotional Disorders* (J.B. Lippincott, 1969), p. 67; on poetry and the war, see Joost A.M. Meerloo, 'The Universal Language of Rhythm', in ibid.
42. Nicholas Mazza, *Poetry Therapy: Theory and Practice*, 2nd edn. (Routledge, 2017), pp. 3, 7; N.F. Mazza, 'Therapy and Poetry', in *The Princeton Encyclopaedia of Poetry and Poetics*, ed. Roland Greene, 4th edn. [online edition] (Princeton University Press, 2017), n.p.
43. Fiona Sampson, *The Healing Word: A Practical Guide to Poetry and Personal Development Activities* (The Poetry Society, 1999), pp. 7–10.
44. Arthur Lerner, 'Some Semantic Considerations in Poetry Therapy', *ETC: A Review of General Semantics*, 48 (1991), 213–19 (p. 213); see Mazza, *Poetry Therapy*, p. 4.
45. Quoted in Geri Giebel Chavis, *Poetry and Story Therapy: The Healing Power of Creative Expression* (Jessica Kingsley Publishers, 2011), p. 26.
46. McNicol, 'Theories of Bibliotherapy', p. 30.
47. See Blum, *Self-Help Compulsion*, p. 36.
48. Mazza, *Poetry Therapy*, pp. 19, 26–7.

49. Chavis, *Poetry and Story Therapy*, pp. 26–7.
50. Diana Hedges, *Poetry, Therapy and Emotional Life* (Radcliffe Publishing, 2005), p. 95.
51. Price, *What We Talk About*, p. 134.
52. See Peter Garratt, 'Victorian Literary Aesthetics and Mental Pathology', in *The Edinburgh Companion to the Critical Medical Humanities*, eds. Anne Whitehead and Angela Woods (Edinburgh University Press, 2016), pp. 431–3.
53. Leedy, 'Principles of Poetry Therapy', pp. 67–8.
54. Chavis, *Poetry and Story Therapy*, p. 42.
55. Michael Lee, 'Poems in the Waiting Room: Aspects of Poetry Therapy', *Journal of Poetry Therapy*, 19 (2006), 91–8 (p. 92).
56. Mazza, *Poetry Therapy*, p. 19.
57. Lee, 'Poetry in the Waiting Room', p. 94.
58. Mazza, *Poetry Therapy*, p. 10; Hedges, *Poetry, Therapy*, p. 6.
59. Chavis, *Poetry and Story Therapy*, p. 25.
60. Astley, ed., *Staying Alive*, pp. 23–4.
61. Lewis R. Wolberg, 'Preface: The Vacuum', in Leedy, ed., *Poetry Therapy*, p. 9.
62. Price, *What We Talk About*, pp. 121–3.
63. Ibid., p. 123.
64. https://reading-well.org.uk/books/mood-boosting-books.
65. My thanks to Sophie Ratcliffe for this suggestion.
66. Astley, ed., *Staying Alive*, pp. 20–1; Astley, ed., *Being Alive*, p. 18. 'I've heard many people say that they don't read the [*Staying Alive*] anthologies through from cover to cover,' Astley told me over email. 'They read them slowly, reading and re-reading [favourite] poems.'
67. Sieghart, ed., *The Poetry Pharmacy*, pp. xvi–xvii, 22, 18; Sieghart, ed., *The Poetry Pharmacy Returns*, pp. 8–9, 106–7.
68. Goodwin, ed., *101 Poems to Get You Through*, pp. xi–xiii, 3, 88.
69. Goodwin, ed., *101 Poems that Could Save Your Life*, pp. xii–xiii.
70. Goodwin, ed., *101 Poems to Get You Through*, p. xiii.
71. Schauffler, ed., *The Poetry Cure*, p. xvii; Bate *et al.*, *Stressed Unstressed*, p. 5.
72. Goodwin, ed., *101 Poems to Keep You Sane*, p. x.
73. Bate *et al.*, *Stressed Unstressed*, p. 4.
74. Astley, ed., *Being Alive*, pp. 18–20; Sieghart, ed., *The Poetry Pharmacy Returns*, pp. xiii–xiv.
75. Interview with William Sieghart, 12 July 2001.
76. Riding and Graves, *A Pamphlet*, pp. 34–5.
77. Interview with Schuman.
78. https://pagesmithbooks.com/. My thanks to Joe Dunthorne for pointing me towards this.
79. Foreword to Samuel Courtauld's unpublished anthology, p. i.

ACKNOWLEDGEMENTS

I am very grateful to Richard Milbank for commissioning this book, then for editing it with care, attentiveness and kindness. My thanks to everyone at Head of Zeus, but especially to Aphra Le Levier-Bennett, Matilda Singer and Kathryn Colwell: thank you for your hard work and patience. *The Treasuries* wouldn't be here without my agent, Cara Jones, who has always fought my corner and told me to stop worrying. Here's to many more tiny beers together.

Thank you to Neil Astley, Sophie Ratcliffe, Andrew Schuman and William Sieghart for agreeing to be interviewed, and for encouragement and advice. Thank you to Ailsa McNicol for beady-eyed fact-checking. I am very grateful to Inigo Thomas for showing me Samuel Courtauld's marvellous anthology, and to Richard Davenport-Hines for sending me down new reading trails. Santanu Das provided invaluable help with chapter 5. Joseph Hone kindly read chapter 1 and saved me from a multitude of errors (all those remaining are mine). Alice Spawls cast an artist's eye over the front cover. I'm especially grateful to Brian Patten for his comments on chapter 7, and to Hannah Lowery at the University of Bristol's Special Collections for archival assistance.

To All Souls College, Oxford, and the support and inspiration I found there, I owe the impetus for this book and the time and self-belief I needed to begin it.

Thank you to my dear friends for encouraging me and putting up with me. To my Dutch family: hartelijk bedankt voor de aanmoediging en de gezelligheid! Greatest thanks to my parents and brother, for everything. And this book is for Paul, with gratitude and love.

TEXT PERMISSIONS

Image Credits

1. Album / Alamy Stock Photo
2. British Library
3. Gift of Sarah Lazarus, 1891 / Wikimedia Commons
4. Yale Center for British Art / Wikimedia Commons
5. Internet Archive.org
6. The History Collection / Alamy Stock Photo
7. © Bristol Museums, Galleries & Archives / Purchased with the assistance of the subscribers, 1913. / Bridgeman Images
8. © National Portrait Gallery, London
9. Look and Learn / Peter Jackson Collection
10. Wikimedia Commons
11. Leonard McCombe / Intermittent / Getty Images
12. Old Visuals / Alamy Stock Photo
13. British Library
14. © Carcanet publisher
15. Bettmann / Contributor / Getty Images
16. Gordon Anthony / Stringer / Getty Images
17. © Edward Lucie-Smith / National Portrait Gallery, London
18. Pictorial Press Ltd / Alamy Stock Photo
19. © Edward Lucie-Smith / National Portrait Gallery, London
20. © The Estate of Tom Picton, Tate Images
21. sjbooks / Alamy Stock Photo
22. © Adrian Henri estate, courtesy of Catherine Marcangeli

Index

101 Happy Poems (Cope), 278
101 Poems series (Goodwin), 265, 279–80, 281

Achilles (mythological figure), 171
Adam Smith, Janet, *Poems of Tomorrow*, 203
Addison, Joseph, 42, 54, 55
adult education, 7, 114–29, 137–41, 144–5
advertising jingles and slogans, 247, 248–51
Aeneid (Virgil), 61, 113
Affection's Gift (19th-century pocket volume), 131
afterlife, 41
Aga Khan, 143
Agincourt, Battle of (1415), 157–8, 170
Aikin, Anna, 96
Aikin, John, 96; *Letters to a Young Lady on a Course of English Poetry*, 91–2
Akenside, Mark, *The Pleasures of the Imagination*, 47
Albert I, King of the Belgians, 142; see also *King Albert's Book*
Aldington, Richard, 162–3
Alexander the Great, 158
Allen, Donald M., *The New American Poetry*, 8, 223
Alma, Deborah, 272; *The Emergency Poet*, 266, 278
Almon, John, 36, 37
Altick, Richard, 83, 107
Alvarez, Al, 222–4; *The New Poetry*, 222–3, 224
Amis, Sir Kingsley, 220, 222
Anderson, Robert, *Complete Edition of the Poems of Great Britain*, 77, 79, 81, 91

Angelou, Maya, 273
Anne, Queen, 23–4, 27–9, 31–2
Anschluss (1938), 219
Anthologia (Meleager of Gadara), 6
anthologists, role of, 1–3, 87, 261–2, 281–3
Anthology of War Poems, An (Brereton), 182
'Anthology Wars' (United States; 1950s/60s), 8
anti-capitalism, 4, 188, 194, 200
anti-Catholicism, 12–13, 15, 23, 26n, 89
anti-Fascism, 188–9, 196–7, 216, 222
anti-German sentiment, 124, 144, 146–7, 156–60
Anti-Jacobin (newspaper), 34–5
Antiquitates Vulgares (Bourne), 61–2
Arber, Edward, *The Shakespeare Anthology*, 7
Aristophanes, 5
Aristotle, 262n
Armistice (1918), 11, 271
Arnold, Matthew, 113, 114, 115, 121, 131, 136
Arnold, Tom, 113
Arras, Battle of (1917), 169
Arthurian legend, 44–5, 51, 52, 53
Asquith, Herbert, 170, 183
Asquith, Herbert Henry (*later* 1st Earl of Oxford and Asquith), 145, 170
Astley, Neil, *Staying Alive* series, 265, 266, 267, 278, 281
astrology, 44
Athenaeum (magazine), 152
atomic and nuclear weapons, 219, 223, 233–6, 248, 249
Auden, W.H., 189n, 190–1, 202–3, 204–5, 216–18, 250; introduction to *Poems of Freedom*, 205,

216–17; 'Night Mail', 211; *The Orators*, 193*n*, 218; *The Oxford Book of Light Verse*, 205–9; *The Poet's Tongue*, 205–7; 'The Secret Agent', 209
Auschwitz concentration camp, 223
Austen, Jane, 105, 139*n*; *Emma*, 99–100; *Northanger Abbey*, 99; *Pride and Prejudice*, 99
'Authors Take Sides on the Spanish War' (questionnaire), 189, 213*n*
autobiography, 122, 208
Ayloffe, John, 15, 17, 22

Bagster, Samuel, *The Poets of Great Britain*, 77, 79
Bailey, John Cann, 146, 158
Ball, John (Jones: *In Parenthesis*), 148
ballad singers, 13–14, 44, 54
ballads, 12–14, 44–60, 62, 63, 65, 68–74, 133, 206
Balliol College, Oxford, 15, 113, 114, 135
Bate, Jonathan, *Stressed Unstressed*, 266, 280
Beachcroft, Thomas Owen, 'A Week at the Union', 195–6
Beat poets, 8, 233, 234, 241, 242–3, 254
Beatles (pop group), 227, 228, 233, 238, 252, 253, 255; 'All You Need is Love', 227; 'When I'm Sixty-Four', 231; 'Yellow Submarine', 254
'beauties' volumes, 76–109; aims, 85–6, 87–8, 92, 104–5; finances, 77–8, 83, 85, 86, 105, 106–9; readership, 7, 9, 79–80, 82, 83, 85–6, 90–2, 104–9; reception and criticism, 80–1, 88, 96–8, 103–9, 122*n*; sales, 79, 105, 106–7; selection and editing, 81–2, 83–4, 87–92; structure and arrangement, 83–4
Beauties of Byron (Lake), 88–9
Beauties of English Poesy (Goldsmith), 85
Beauties of Shakespeare (Dodds), 88
Beauties of the British Poets (Croly), 86–7

Beauties of the Poets of Great Britain (Roach), 7, 83, 85, 86, 106
Beauties series (Kearsley), 82–5, 88, 89–90, 92, 98, 104–5, 107
Beckerman, Marty, *The Heming Way*, 270
Belgian Fund (refugee organization), 143
Bell, John, *The Poets of Great Britain Complete from Chaucer to Churchill*, 76–7, 78–9, 81, 91
Bell, Julian, 190
Bennet, Mary (Austen: *Pride and Prejudice*), 99
Bennett, John, 103
Berlin, 192, 196
Berryman, John, 222, 223–4
Berthoud, Ella, *The Novel Cure*, 271, 272, 279
bias, 3–4; *see also* propaganda
bibliotherapy, 261–83
Binyon, Laurence, 161, 179, 183; 'For the Fallen', 156
Birkenhead, 272
Birmingham, 117
Black writers, 198–201
blackshirts (British Union of Fascists), 188
Blackstone, Sir William, 42–3
Blair, Hugh, 67
Blake, William, 147, 205
Blast (magazine), 186, 187
Blenheim, Battle of (1704), 29
Bloodaxe Books (publishing company), 266
Blum, Beth, 269, 270
Boer War (1899–1902), 159
Bogan, Louise, 207
Bomb Culture (Nuttall), 233–4, 245
Books on Prescription (NHS scheme), 271–2, 277
Boots (retailer), 264
Boswell, James, 43, 67
Bourne, Henry, *Antiquitates Vulgares*, 61–2
Bowdler, Thomas, 87; *Family Shakespeare*, 87–8, 104
bowdlerism, 87
'Boy and the Mantle, The' (ballad), 63

Bradford University, 259
Brand, John, *Observations on Popular Antiquities*, 60–1, 64
Brereton, Frederick, *An Anthology of War Poems*, 182
Bridges, Robert, 149, 162; *The Spirit of Man*, 156–7, 162; 'Thou Careless, Awake!', 162
Bridgnorth, Shropshire, 49, 50
Brighton Mechanics' Institute, 118
British Communist Party *see* Communist Party of Great Britain
British Empire, 156, 160, 161, 168; *see also* colonialism
British Muse, The (Oldys), 1–2, 3
British Museum, 8
Brontë, Patrick, 117
Brooke, Rupert, 2, 153, 161, 164–6, 169, 171, 172, 179, 183; *1914, and Other Poems*, 165–6; *Collected Poems*, 182–3; 'The Soldier', 165
Brown, Alec, 196
Brown, Ford Madox, 120
Brown, Harold, 138
Brown, Maggie, 231
Brown, Norman O., 234
Brown, Pete ('Pete the Beat'), 228
Brown, Tom, *A Satyr upon the French King*, 25
Browning, Robert, 147
Brownsword, Bertha, 150
Bullar, John, *Selections from the British Poets*, 88–9
Bürger, Gottfried: 'Der Wilde Jäger', 71; 'Lenore', 68–71, 72, 74
Burke, Edmund, 64, 66
Burne-Jones, Sir Edward, 120
Burns, Robert, 122, 123, 133
Burroughs, William, 241
Byrne, Johnny, 228
Byrne, Paula, *Stressed Unstressed*, 266, 280
Byron, George Gordon, 6th Baron, 77, 87, 89–90, 91, 159, 205; *Don Juan*, 89–90, 93; *Hebrew Melodies*, 131
Byzantine Empire, 6

Caine, Sir Hall, *King Albert's Book*, 142–4, 145–6, 152

Calder-Marshall, Arthur, 211
Calves' Head Club, 24
Cambridge University, 64, 139, 146; Library, 51
Campbell, Thomas, *Specimens of the British Poets*, 77
Canning, George, 34
Canning, William, 26
Carlyle, Thomas, *Sartor Resartus*, 140
Carnegie, Andrew, 143
carols, Christmas, 206, 239
Carroll, Donald, 255
Catholicism, 41, 43; anti-Catholicism, 12–13, 15, 23, 26n, 89
Catullus, 21
censorship, 7, 17, 18–19, 22–3, 28, 32, 196; *see also* bowdlerism
Chalmers, Alexander, *Works of the English Poets*, 77, 79
Chapone, Hester, 92
Charles I, King, 13, 24
Charles II, King, 13–17, 19, 21–2, 22–3, 24, 31
Charterhouse School, 112–13
Chartist(s), 113, 117, 137, 205
Chatterton, Thomas, 47
Chatto Book of Modern Poetry, The (Day Lewis/Lehmann), 218n
Chaucer, Geoffrey, 44, 77
chauvinism, 124, 145, 146–7
Chesterton, G.K., 150; 'France', 156
Chicago, 151
Children of Albion (Horovitz), 258n
children's education, 7, 53–4, 82n, 106, 144, 171
Choate, Joseph, 144
Christ Church, Oxford, 50
Christian Socialists, 119
Christianity, 61, 84, 87, 88, 90, 193, 214; and war, 150, 160, 165, 168, 183; *see also* Catholicism; Protestantism
Christmas carols, 206, 239
Christ's Hospital (school), 82n, 106
church attendance, 44
Churchill, Sir Winston, 143, 149n, 153; obituary of Rupert Brooke, 165, 172

City Poems (Smith), 127, 135

Clare, John, 105–6

Clarissa (Richardson), 99

Clarke, Charles Cowden, 117

Clarke, George Herbert, *A Treasury of War Poetry*, 183

Clarke, John, 86

Clayton Squares (beat group), 229, 238

Cleveland, Barbara Palmer, Duchess of, 16, 21

Clough, Arthur Hugh, 113, 114, 115, 127, 135; 'Say not the Struggle Naught availeth', 6

Club, the (London dining society), 64

Clutton-Brock, Arthur, 164

CND (Campaign for Nuclear Disarmament), 245, 248

Cock Lane Ghost (1762), 40–1, 47, 63

'Cock Lorrel's Treat' (ballad), 63

Cohen, Francis *see* Palgrave, Sir Francis

Cohen, Leonard, 227

Coleridge, Samuel Taylor, 34, 70, 105, 106; 'Work Without Hope', 276; 'Youth and Age', 6

Collection of Old Ballads, A (Phillips), 54–6

Collection of Poems in Six Volumes, A (Dodsley), 47

College, Stephen, 12–15, 17, 22, 37–8

Collier, Jane, 93; *The Cry*, 97, 98–9

Collini, Stefan, 122

Collins (publishing company), 2n

Collins, Nina Lorez, *What Would Virginia Woolf Do?* 270

Collins, William, 'Ode on the Popular Superstitions of the Highlands of Scotland', 47

colonialism, 122–3; *see also* British Empire

Colvin, Ian, 'The Answer', 156

commonplacing, 6, 50, 268, 269, 281–2

Communism, 4, 185–224

Communist Manifesto (Marx/ Engels), 186, 195

Communist Party of Great Britain, 188–9, 216, 219

Communist Party of the USA, 199, 200

Complete Edition of the Poems of Great Britain (Anderson), 77, 79, 81, 91

concentration camps, 219, 223

Connolly, Cyril, 171, 188

Conquest, Robert, 219–21, 222; *New Lines*, 220–1, 223

Conservative Party, 161

Cooke, Charles: *The Flowers of Literature*, 107; *Pocket Edition of Select British Poets* series, 79, 106

Coombes, Bert Lewis, 204

Cooper, Thomas, 137

Cope, Wendy, 101 *Happy Poems*, 278

copyright, 77–8, 79, 105, 155

Corgi Books (publishing company), 227

Corso, Gregory, 242

Counter-Attack (Sassoon), 182

Courtauld, Samuel, 193, 283

Courtney, Joseph, 170

Coutts, Francis (*later* 5th Baron Latymer), 159

Cowper, William, 91

Crabbe, George, 53

Craftsman, The (newspaper), 35

Crane, Hart, 191n

Credulity, Superstition, and Fanaticism (Hogarth), 39–40

Critical Quarterly (journal), 227–8

Critical Review (journal), 65

Croly, George, *Beauties of the British Poets*, 86–7

Cromwell, Oliver, 19–20, 124

Crouch, Nathaniel, 49–50

Cruttwell, Edith Mary, 'Gallipoli, May, 1915', 160

Cry, The (Collier/Fielding), 97, 98–9

Cunard, Nancy, 198–201, 213n; *Negro: An Anthology*, 198–200, 201

Daily Mail, 151

Daily Telegraph, 143, 175, 230, 253

Danby, Thomas Osborne, Earl of (*later* 1st Duke of Leeds), 16

Darby, John, 22–8, 32

Darby, John, Jr., 28

Darling, Julia, *The Poetry Cure*, 266, 267, 273

Davie, Donald, 219, 222; 'Rejoinder to a Critic', 220–1, 222; 'Remembering the Thirties', 218–19; 'Too Late for Satire', 220

Dawson, George, 117

Day Lewis, Cecil, 190–1, 203, 205, 212, 217; *Chatto Book of Modern Poetry*, 218n; *A Hope for Poetry*, 198, 202, 209; 'Letter to W.H. Auden', 190; *The Mind in Chains*, 188

de Botton, Alain, 272; *How Proust Can Change Your Life*, 270

de Manio, Jack, 252

Debussy, Claude, 143, 252

Decade Club (Oxford debating society), 113

Depression (1930s), 188

Dickens, Charles, 117, 119

Dickinson, Emily, 263, 273

Discourse Concerning the Original and Progress of Satire (Dryden), 19, 33

Dobson, Henry Austin, *Handbook for English Literature*, 123

doctors, 43, 266, 271–2, 273, 278

Dodd, William, *Beauties of Shakespeare*, 88

Dodsley, Robert, *A Collection of Poems in Six Volumes*, 47

Don Juan (Byron), 89–90, 93

Donaldson, Alexander, 78

'Donica' (Southey), 70–1

Donne, John, 10

'Dragon of Wantley, The' (ballad), 62, 63–4

dragons, 44, 46, 62, 63–4

Drake, Sir Francis, 158, 159, 160, 163, 164, 170, 184

Dryden, John: *Discourse Concerning the Original and Progress of Satire*, 19, 33; 'Heroic Stanzas on the Death of Oliver Cromwell', 19–20

Duff, William, 66

Dugdale, Florence, 4, 151

Dunbar, William, 'Lament for the Makers', 148

Dunn, Douglas, 242, 246

Dylan, Bob, 227

Early Italian Poets (Rossetti), 139

East India Company, 123

Edgeworth, Maria, *Letters for Literary Ladies*, 93, 94, 98

Edinburgh, 70

Edinburgh Festival: Fringe, 226, 240; Poetry Conference (1964), 245

Edinburgh Review, 87n, 175

education *see* adult education; children's education; female education

Education Office (government department), 114, 121, 125, 126, 130

Educational Expositor, The (journal), 126

Egoist, The (magazine), 163, 176

Elderkin, Susan, 272; *The Novel Cure*, 271, 279

Elegant Extracts (Knox series), 81, 88, 98, 104, 105, 122n

Eliot, T.S., 4, 7, 9, 139–40, 192, 202; *The Waste Land*, 192

Elizabethan age, 139, 153–4, 160–1, 170, 184

Elton, Mrs (Austen: *Emma*), 100, 104

embroidery, 101–2, 104

Emergency Poet, The (Alma), 266, 278

Emma (Austen), 99–100

Empson, Sir William, 190, 194, 203n; *Seven Types of Ambiguity*, 203n

Encounter (magazine), 242

Endymion (Keats), 76

Enfield, William, 71–2; *The Speaker*, 7

Engels, Friedrich, 88; *Communist Manifesto*, 186, 195

English Poets, The (Ward), 140n

Enlightenment, The, 60–2, 65–6

Enright, D.J., 218, 221, 222; *Poets of the 1950's*, 221

Erskine Macdonald (publishing company), 166

Essay on the Education of Young Ladies, An (Robertson), 104

Eton College, 171
Euripides, 134
Evans, Evan, 58–9, 64
Evans, Mike, 238
Evening Standard (newspaper), 265
Evergreen Review, The (magazine), 254
Everyman's Library (publishing series), 140
Excelles (pop group), 239

Faber Book of Modern Verse, The (Roberts), 3–4, 111, 191*n*, 192, 197–8, 216
Faction Display'd (Shippen), 28–9, 30
Fagan, J.B., 159
Fainlight, Harry, 243
'Fair Margaret and Sweet William' (supernatural ballad), 45–6, 48, 71
Fairies and Fusiliers (Graves), 152
'Fairies Farewell, The' (ballad), 58
fairy beliefs, 40, 41–4, 48, 57–60
'family editions', 87–8, 104
Family Shakespeare, The (Bowdler), 87–8, 104
Farmer, Richard, 51–2
Farringford House, Isle of Wight, 123, 130
fascism, 188–9, 196–7, 216, 219, 222
Featherstone, Simon, 148*n*
Felski, Rita, 264
female education, 7, 87, 90, 93–104; *see also* women readers
Ferlinghetti, Lawrence, 242
Ferry, Anne, 8
Fielding, Henry, 83; *Tom Jones*, 80
Fielding, Sarah, *The Cry*, 97, 98–9
Fingal (Macpherson), 48
First World War (1914–18), 3, 5, 139–41, 142–84, 187, 210, 213; *see also* Armistice (1918)
Flaubert, Gustave, *Madame Bovary*, 271
Fletcher, John Gould, 163, 176
florilegia, 6
Florio (More), 97*n*
flowers, anthologies as gatherings of, 1, 6, 88, 89, 107
Flowers of Literature, The (Cooke), 107

folksongs, 206
Ford, James W., 199, 200
Foreigners, The (Tutchin), 24
Forshaw, Charles, *Women Poets of the Empire*, 160
fortune-telling, 44
Foulis, Robert and Andrew, 78
Foundling Hospital for Wit, The (18th-century anthology series), 35
Fox, Ralph, 196
Franco, Francisco, 188
Fraser's Magazine, 135
Freeman, John, 172
Freke, John, 22
Freud, Siegmund, 234, 262
'Friend of Humanity and the Knife Grinder, The' (18th-century parody), 34–5
Frost, Robert, 112, 263
Froude, James Anthony, 135–6
Fuller, Cynthia, *The Poetry Cure*, 266, 267, 273
Fuller, Roy, 246, 251
Fussell, Paul, 144, 147, 148
Futurism, 186, 194

Galsworthy, John, 146
García Márquez, Gabriel, *One Hundred Years of Solitude*, 271
Garden Revisited, A (Lehmann), 190
Garibaldi, Giuseppe, 123
Garratt, V.W., 140–1
Garrett, George, 204
Garrett, John, *The Poet's Tongue*, 205–7
Garrick, David, 100
Gaudier Brzeska, Henri, 186
Gay, John, 78
Gazette (television chat show), 253
George, St, 44, 52, 158
Georgian Poetry (Marsh), 153–4, 163, 172, 177, 183
ghost beliefs, 39–43, 48, 57, 59–62, 65–7
ghost stories and ballads, 44–9, 51, 52, 55–60, 65–75
Gibson, Wilfrid Wilson, 'The Bayonet', 180–1
Ginsberg, Allen, 233, 242–3, 251; 'Howl', 254

Gittings, Robert, 243
Glasgow, 78
Glasgow Herald (newspaper), 143
Glorious Revolution (1688), 23, 25n
Goethe, Johann Wolfgang von, 124, 147
Golden Treasury, The (Palgrave), 110–41; aims, 126–9, 130–1; contents and selection, 9, 129–35; historical context, 112–29; publication, editions and reprints, 111, 135, 137–8; readership, 126–9, 131–2, 135–6, 137–41; reception, 135–7; reputation and importance, 4, 7, 9, 10, 107, 110–12, 137–41, 153; sales, 111, 135; structure and arrangement, 133–4; title, 130–1, 139
Goldman, Willy, 204
Goldsmith, Oliver, 83; *The Beauties of English Poesy*, 85
Goodwin, Daisy: *101 Poems* series, 265, 279–80, 281; *Poems to Last a Lifetime*, 265, 266
Gosse, Sir Edmund, 150, 152, 170n, 175, 176
Gothic, 47, 71–2, 73, 96
Göttingen University, 68
Graves, Robert, 165, 169, 182, 183, 207, 261–2; *Fairies and Fusiliers*, 152; *Pamphlet Against Anthologies*, 2–3, 5, 9–10, 81, 177, 281–2
Gray, Thomas, 'Elegy Written in a Country Churchyard', 100, 111
Great War *see* First World War
Great Yarmouth, Norfolk, 112
Greece, ancient, 6, 57, 61, 67, 121, 171–3, 178, 261–2
Greek Anthology, The (Mackail), 171–3, 175
Grenfell, Julian, 182n, 183
Grenville, Thomas, 163
Griffin, Dustin, 19
Grigson, Geoffrey, 185–6, 187, 191, 204, 213
Gross, John, 145
Guardian (newspaper), 206n, 225, 230, 231, 245–6

Guernica bombing (1937), 219
Gunn, Thom, 222

Hailes, David Dalrymple, Lord, 54, 63
Hall, Donald, *New Poets of England and America*, 8
Halward, Leslie, 204
Hamburg, 70
Hamilton, Ian, 253
Hammond, Paul, 22
Handbook of English Literature, A (Dobson), 123
happenings (performance events), 237–40
Hardy, E.J., *How to Be Happy Though Married*, 269
Hardy, Thomas, 4, 143, 145–6, 150; *Late Lyrics and Earlier*, 4–5; 'Men Who March Away', 146, 156; 'Sonnet on the Belgian Expatriation', 146
Harlem Renaissance, 199
Harris, Alexandra, 183
Harsent, David, 245–6
Hartley, Anthony, 216, 217
Hawkins, John Frederick 'Spike', 228
Hazlitt, William, 105–6
Headley, Henry, *Select Beauties of Ancient English Poetry*, 84, 85, 86, 104
Heaney, Seamus, 206; *The Rattle Bag*, 206n
heart, learning by, 82n, 113, 126, 132, 137, 268; *see also* quotation, public
Hebrew Melodies (Byron), 131
Hector (mythological figure), 171
Hemans, Felicia, 131
Heming Way, The (Beckerman), 270
Henley, William Ernest, 183
Henri, Adrian: appearance and character, 228; life and career, 227, 228–9, 230, 231, 243; marketing and sales, 252–9; performance events, 237–42, 249, 257, 258; reputation and criticism, 232n, 242, 245–8, 251–2, 256–7; style and subject matter, 232, 235, 237–8, 240–2,

247–52, 257–8; views, 229, 244, 245, 247–8, 249, 259, 260; *Autobiography*, 250; 'Bomb Commercials', 249; 'Bomb Event', 238–40; 'City', 238; 'The Entry of Christ into Liverpool', 241, 250; 'I Want to Paint', 240, 247, 257; 'On the Late Late Massachers Stillbirths and Deformed Children a Smoother Lovelier Skin Job', 248–9; 'Love Poem', 257; 'Me', 251–2; 'The New "Our Times"', 240; 'Nightblues', 238; 'Notes on Painting and Poetry', 248; 'Silent Poems', 241; 'Summer Poems Without Words', 258; *Tonight at Noon*, 238, 248, 254; see also *Mersey Sound, The*
Henry V, King, 157–8
Herbert, George, 263
Hikmet, Nâzim, 273
Hill, Sir Geoffrey, 222; 'Genesis', 224
Hiroshima bombing (1945), 220–1, 233
Hitler, Adolf, 188, 194, 216
Hodge, Herbert, 204
Hodgson, W.N., 167
Hogarth, William, *Credulity, Superstition, and Fanaticism*, 39–40
Hogarth Press (publishing company), 190
Holloway, John, 217–18
Holmes, John, 234
Home Affections, The (Mackay), 131
Homer, 54, 61, 67–8; *Iliad*, 61, 171
Hood, Robin (legendary figure), 44
Hood, Thomas, 'The Bridge of Sighs', 133
Hope for Poetry, A (Day Lewis), 198, 202, 203
Hopkins, Gerard Manley, 149, 197–8
Horace, 173
Horovitz, Michael, 226, 232–3, 242, 244, 246; *Children of Albion*, 258n
Housman, A.E., 2, 4, 147
How Proust Can Change Your Life (de Botton), 270
How to Be Happy Though Married (Hardy), 269

Howard, Geoffrey, 167
Hughes, Langston, 199
Hughes, Ted, 222; *The Rattle Bag*, 206n
Hull University, 244
Hume, David, 41, 83, 98
Hungarian revolution (1956), 222
Hunt, Leigh, 105–6
Hunt, William Holman, 129
Hurd, Richard, 61–2
Hussey, Dyneley, 'Youth', 172
Hutter, Heinrich, 181
Huxley, Thomas Henry, 126n
Hyde, Anne, 16
Hynes, Samuel, 193n

Iliad (Homer), 61, 171
Ilkley, Yorkshire, 139
Imagism, 154, 176, 186
Imagistes, Des (Pound), 154, 186
In Letters of Red (Osborne), 196–7, 204–5
In Parenthesis (Jones), 148
Incredible New Liverpool Scene LP, The (1967), 255–6
India, 118, 122–3
Inman, Philip (*later* 1st Baron Inman), 138–9
International Brigades (Spanish Civil War), 189
International Poetry Incarnation (1965), 227, 242–3, 246–7, 259
Introduction à l'Histoire de Dannemarc (Mallet), 56–7, 58, 60
Isherwood, Christopher, 189n, 196
Isle of Wight, 123, 130

'Jack and Gill' (nursery rhyme), 206
Jackie (magazine), 259
Jacobites, 28
Jacobus, Mary, 70
Jagger, Sir Mick, 228, 252
James, John Angell, 91, 95
James II, King, 15, 16, 19, 21, 22–3, 24, 25n, 26
Jameson, Storm, 210, 211
Jarvis, Harold John, 'Dulce et Decorum est pro Patria Mori', 179
jazz, 199, 225, 240; poetry-and-jazz

movement, 226, 228, 238, 246, 256
Johnson, Samuel, 85; and Percy's *Reliques*, 51, 64; and supernatural phenomena, 40, 43, 53; *The Beauties of Johnson*, 82, 83, 85; *Works of the English Poets*, 79
Jones, David, *In Parenthesis*, 148
Jonson, Ben, 140
Jowett, Benjamin, 113, 114, 123
Julius Caesar, 21
Jung, Carl, 262

Kafka, Franz, 250, 252
Kaprow, Allan, 237, 239
Kearsley, George, *Beauties* series, 82–5, 88, 89–90, 92, 98, 104–5, 107
Keats, George, 76, 77
Keats, Georgiana, 76, 77
Keats, John, 10, 76–7, 117, 147; *Endymion*, 76; 'Ode to a Nightingale', 276
Keighley, Yorkshire, 117
Kemble, Charles, 117
Kemble, Fanny, 117
Kenrick, William, 65
Kéroualle, Louise de, Duchess of Portsmouth, 15, 16
King Albert's Book (Caine), 142–4, 145–6, 152
King's College, London, 119, 120
Kingsley, Charles, 122
Kipling, Rudyard, 3, 150, 159, 183; 'Hymn Before Action', 156
Kneller Hall (training college), 114–16, 119, 125
Knox, Vicesimus, 64, 80–1, 82, 86, 91, 93, 95; *Elegant Extracts*, 81, 88, 98, 104, 105, 122*n*
Kyle, William Galloway, 166–75; *More Songs by the Fighting Men*, 169*n*, 174, 179; *Soldier Poets: Songs of the Fighting Men*, 166–8, 169, 172–5, 179

Labour Party, 188, 192
Lackington, James, 79–80
Lady's Magazine, 83
Lagger, Peter, 204–5

Lake, J.W., *Beauties of Byron*, 88–9
Lamb, Charles, 42, 70, 82*n*
lampoons, 16–17
Lane, John, *Songs and Sonnets for England in War Time*, 155–7, 159, 176
Langland, William, 205
Larkin, Philip, 220, 222; *The Oxford Book of Twentieth-Century English Verse*, 4
Lawrence, D.H., 153
Lawrence, T.E., 5–6; *Minorities*, 5–6, 268; *Seven Pillars of Wisdom*, 5*n*
Le Despencer, Francis Dashwood, 11th Baron, 36–7
Lear, Edward, 206
learning by heart, 82*n*, 113, 126, 132, 268; *see also* quotation, public
Lee, Michael, 273*n*, 276
Leedy, Jack, 276
Left Review (magazine), 189, 207, 213*n*, 214–15
Lehmann, John, 187, 190, 192, 194, 197, 202, 222, 224; *A Garden Revisited*, 190; 'A Little Distance Off', 209; *New Signatures*, 4, 190–4, 203, 212–14, 220, 223; *New Writing*, 196, 203–4, 214–16, 220; *Poems for Spain*, 188
Leith, Sam, 265
Lessing, Gotthold Ephraim, 147
L'Estrange, Sir Roger, 13
Letters for Literary Ladies (Edgeworth), 93, 94, 98
Letters to a Young Lady on a Course of English Poetry (Aikin), 91–2
Lewis, Matthew: *The Monk*, 71; 'The Sailor's Tale', 73–4; *Tales of Wonder*, 71–5
Lewis, Wyndham, 186–7
Lindop, Grevel, 246, 247, 251–2
Lingen, Ralph (*later* 1st Baron Lingen), 114
literacy, 144
live readings *see* performance events
Liverpool, 225, 227, 229–33, 251, 252–3, 260; Art College, 230, 231, 255; Canning Street, 230; Cavern Club, 229, 238, 249, 253;

Everyman Theatre, 229; Lime Street, 250; O'Connor's Tavern, 229, 241, 259; Sampson & Barlow's folk club, 229, 241, 245; Streate's Coffee Bar, 228, 253

Liverpool Daily Post, 230

Liverpool Scene, The (Lucie-Smith), 227, 235, 244–5, 250–1, 255–6, 258, 259, 283

Liverpool University, 230, 259

Lloyd, Bertram, 180; *The Paths of Glory*, 182; *Poems Written during the Great War*, 180–2

Logue, Christopher, 243

London: Albert Hall, 227, 242–3; Bartholomew Close, 22, 27; Blackfriars Road, 126*n*; British Museum, 8; Camden, 119, 126*n*, 129; Cock Lane, 40; Hyde Park, 228; National Gallery, 8; Newgate Prison, 26; Northumberland House, 63; Notting Hill, 231; Paternoster Row, 106; Southall, 139; Southwark, 126; St Paul's Cathedral, 165; Wellington House, 145; Working Men's Colleges, 119–22, 125, 126–7, 128, 129, 132, 139; *see also* Twickenham

London, University of, 7, 139; *see also* King's College, London; University College, London

London Magazine, 54, 107

London Review of Books (LRB), 265

Louis XIV, King of France, 15, 25

Love, Love, Love (1967), 227, 235, 254–5

Lowell, Robert, 222, 223–4

Lozère (France), 63–4

LRB see London Review of Books

Lucas, E.V., *Remember Louvain!* 155, 157

Lucie-Smith, Edward, 235, 246–7, 257; *The Liverpool Scene*, 227, 235, 244–5, 250–1, 255–6, 258, 259, 283

'Lucy and Colin' (supernatural ballad), 46–7

Lushington, Vernon, 120

Lynd, Robert, 262*n*

Lyra Heroica (1891), 159, 160

Lyrical Ballads (Wordsworth), 72, 133

Macaulay, Dame Rose, *Keeping Up Appearances*, 2*n*

Mackail, John William, *The Greek Anthology*, 171–3, 175

Mackay, Charles, *The Home Affections*, 131

Macmillan (publishing company), 110–11, 135

Macmillan, Alexander, 131, 134, 135

MacNeice, Louis, 189, 202, 211, 250, 280

Macpherson, James, *Fingal*, 48

Madame Bovary (Flaubert), 271

Madge, Charles, 194, 202, 208; 'Oxford Collective Poem', 211–12

magic, 42, 44, 45, 48, 50, 58, 61

Mallet, David, 'William and Margaret', 46, 47, 48

Mallet, Paul Henri, *Introduction à l'Histoire de Dannemarc*, 56–7, 58, 60

Malory, Sir Thomas, *Le Morte d'Arthur*, 5

Manchester Free Library, 119

Marconi, Guglielmo, 143

'Margaret's Ghost' (supernatural ballad), 65

Marinetti, Filippo Tommaso, *Manifesto of Futurism*, 186

Marlborough, John Churchill, 1st Duke of, 29, 30, 31

Marlborough, Sarah, Duchess of, 28, 29, 31

Marlowe, Christopher, 140, 153–4

marriage, 93–4, 118

'Marriage of Sir Gawaine, The' (Arthurian ballad), 44–5, 48, 71

Marsh, Sir Edward, 153, 165; *Georgian Poetry*, 153–4, 163, 172, 177, 183

Marvell, Andrew, 18; 'The Garden', 279

Marx, Karl, *Communist Manifesto*, 186, 195

Marxism, 187, 194, 207–8, 209–10; *see also* Communism

Mary II, Queen, 23, 26

Masefield, John, 153

Masterman, Charles, 145–6, 150, 159

Maurice, Frederick Denison, 119, 120, 125, 133, 138, 145

Maynwaring, Arthur, *Tarquin and Tullia*, 25–6, 28

McCall Smith, Alexander, *What W.H. Auden Can Do for You*, 270

McCartney, Sir Paul, 232, 242

McConnell, Robert Wallace, 148–9

McGough, Roger: appearance and character, 228; life and career, 227–9, 231, 238, 243, 252–3; marketing and sales, 252–9; reputation and criticism, 232*n*, 245–8, 256–7; style and subject matter, 235–7, 240, 247, 250–1; views, 229, 231, 244, 247–8; 'Limestreetscene '64', 250; 'At Lunchtime A Story of Love', 235–7; 'Why Patriots are a Bit Nuts in the Head', 246; see also *Mersey Sound, The*

McTague, John, 30, 31

mechanics' institutes, 116–19

Medmenham Abbey, Buckinghamshire, 36–7

Meleager of Gadara, *Anthologia*, 6

Melly, George, 232, 243, 256, 259

Men of Good Will (Romains), 211*n*

Menand, Louis, 8, 267

Mercier, Louis-Sébastien, *L'An 2440*, 80*n*

Mersey Beat (magazine), 238, 240

Mersey Sound, The (Henri/McGough/Patten), 7, 9, 11, 227, 244, 248, 253–60, 283

Methodism, 39–40, 41

Middleton, Jane, 16

Middleton Murry, John, 164, 176–7, 186

Miles, Barry, 243

Miles, Sue, 243*n*

Mill, John Stuart, *Autobiography*, 276

Miller, George, 130, 133

Milton, John, 7, 9, 79, 83, 91, 99, 105, 120, 123, 124, 149, 153, 157, 205, 269; *Paradise Lost*, 132, 137, 148; Sonnet XXXVIII, 248–9

Mingus, Charles, 238

Minorities (Lawrence), 5–6, 268

minstrels, 53

Mitchell, Adrian, 226, 246–7; 'Peace is Milk', 235

Mitchell, Sir Peter Chalmers, 196

Mitchison, Naomi, Baroness, 211

Moderation Display'd (Shippen), 29–30

Modernism, 154, 202, 263

Molotov-Ribbentrop Pact (1939), 216, 219

Monet, Claude, 143

Monk, The (Lewis), 71

Monmouth Rebellion (1685), 24

Monro, Harold, 151*n*, 154, 163, 165*n*, 177

Montagu, Elizabeth, 66

Montagu, Mary Wortley, Lady, 34

Monthly Review (journal), 65, 70, 107

Moore, Thomas, 105, 106, 131

Moral Sketches of Prevailing Opinions and Manners (More), 91, 94

More, Hannah: *Florio*, 97*n*; *Moral Sketches of Prevailing Opinions and Manners*, 91, 94; *Strictures on the Modern System of Female Education*, 85, 95–8, 100–4, 105, 108

More Songs by the Fighting Men (Kyle), 169*n*, 174, 179

Morier, Sir Robert, 114

Morland, Catherine (Austen: *Northanger Abbey*), 99

Morley, Henry, 120

Mosley, Sir Oswald, 188

Movement, The (1950s), 217–19, 222–3

Mulgan, John, *Poems of Freedom*, 205, 216–17

Munby, Arthur, 136–7

Murray, Gilbert, 161

Murry, Ann, 90

Murry, John Middleton, 164, 176–7, 186

Muse in Arms, The (Osborn),
168–70, 174, 178, 184
Mussolini, Benito, 188

Nagasaki bombing (1945), 233
National Association for Poetry
Therapy (United States), 274
National Gallery, London, 8
National Government (1930s), 218*n*
National Health Service *see* NHS
national identity *see* patriotism and
national identity
Nazism, 188, 194, 216
Nazi-Soviet Pact (1939), 216, 219
Negro: An Anthology (Cunard),
198–200, 201
Nelson, Horatio, 1st Viscount, 159,
160
New American Poetry, The (Allen),
8, 223
'New Ballad, A' (18th-century satire),
31–2
*New Collection of Poems Relating to
State Affairs, A* (1705), 33–4
New Country (Roberts), 4, 193–6,
197, 212–14, 220, 223
New Elizabethans, The (Osborn), 184
New Foundling Hospital for Wit, The
(18th-century anthology series),
36–7, 100
New Lines (Conquest), 220–1, 223
New Masses (magazine), 211
New Poetry, The (Alvarez), 222–3,
224
*New Poets of England and America,
The* (Hall/Pack/Simpson), 8
New Signatures (Lehmann/Roberts),
4, 190–4, 203, 212–14, 220, 223
New Statesman (magazine), 166
New Verse (magazine), 185–6, 187,
188, 191
New Writing (periodical), 196,
203–4, 214–16, 220
New York, 230, 237, 273
New York Herald Tribune, 111
New York Times, 143, 146
New York Times Magazine, 234
Newbery, John, 47, 48
Newbolt, Sir Henry, 151*n*, 176, 179,
183; 'The Vigil', 150–1, 156

newspapers: 17th-century, 18;
18th-century, 18, 34–5, 46; 19th-
century, 126; 20th-century, 143,
145, 146, 150–2
Newton, Sir Isaac, 64, 65
NHS (National Health Service), 266,
271–2, 273
Nichols, Robert, 161*n*, 172, 173
Nitsch, Hermann, 237–8
nonsense poems, 206
Northanger Abbey (Austen), 99
Northumberland, Elizabeth Percy,
Countess of, 62–3
Nottingham, 257
Novel Cure, The (Berthoud/Elderkin),
271, 279
Noyes, Alfred, 159; 'The Moon is
Up', 159, 160–1
nuclear weapons *see* atomic and
nuclear weapons
nursery rhymes, 206
'Nut Brown Maid, The' (ballad), 54
Nuttall, Jeff, *Bomb Culture*, 233–4,
245

Observations on Popular Antiquities
(Brand), 60–1, 64
Observer (newspaper), 221, 222, 224
O'Hagan, Andrew, 265–6, 267
Old Huntsman, The (Sassoon), 150
Oldmixon, John, 54
Oldys, William, *The British Muse*,
1–2, 3
Oliver, Mary, 'Wild Geese', 278
One Hundred Years of Solitude
(García Márquez), 271
Orators, The (Auden), 193*n*, 218
Orton, Joe, 234
Orwell, George, 189*n*; *The Road to
Wigan Pier*, 211
Osborn, Edward Bolland: *The Muse
in Arms*, 168–70, 174, 178, 184;
The New Elizabethans, 184
Osborne, Eric Allen, *In Letters of
Red*, 196–7, 204–5
Oswald, Sydney: 'The Dead Soldier',
172–3; 'Dulce et Decorum est pro
Patria Mori', 173, 179
Other Men's Flowers (Wavell), 3,
149*n*, 183, 268

Owen, Wilfred, 4, 169, 174, 178–9, 182; 'Anthem for Doomed Youth', 179; 'Dulce et Decorum Est', 173, 179; 'A Terre', 178
Oxford, 13, 38; Ashmolean Library, 58; Oxford Castle, 12
Oxford Book of English Verse, The (Quiller-Couch), 6, 7, 9, 111, 140, 147–8, 153
Oxford Book of Light Verse, The (Auden), 205–9
Oxford Book of Modern Verse, The (Yeats), 4, 282
Oxford Book of Twentieth-Century English Verse, The (Larkin), 4
'Oxford Collective Poem' (Madge), 211–12
Oxford University, 139, 211–12; see also Balliol College; Christ Church
Oxford World's Classics (book series), 79

pacifism, 179–80, 235, 246
Pack, Robert, The New Poets of England and America, 8
Palatine Anthology (10th century), 6
Palgrave, Elizabeth, 112–13
Palgrave, Sir Francis (né Cohen), 107, 112–13, 125
Palgrave, Francis Turner: background, 107, 112; character, 112, 124–5, 132n; childhood and education, 112–14, 124–5, 135; ideas and beliefs, 114, 116, 124–9, 133, 138; life and career, 111, 114–16, 125, 145; preparation and selection of anthology, 129–35; publication of The Golden Treasury, 135–7; reputation and importance, 111, 137–41; see also Golden Treasury, The
Palgrave, Gifford, 112–13
Pamphlet Against Anthologies (Riding/Graves), 2–3, 5, 9–10, 81, 177, 281–2
Pankhurst, Emmeline, 143
Paradise Lost (Milton), 132, 137, 148
Paris, 80n, 114, 125, 231
Parker, Peter, 171

Parsons, Elizabeth, 40
Parsons, Richard, 40
Paths of Glory, The (Lloyd), 182
patriotism and national identity, 3, 84, 122, 142–6, 150, 153–84; see also chauvinism
Patroclus (mythological figure), 171
Patten, Brian: life and career, 227, 228–9, 231, 233, 238, 243, 244, 252–3; marketing and sales, 252–9; reputation and criticism, 232n, 233, 245–8, 252–3, 255n, 256–7; style and subject matter, 235, 240, 247; views, 231, 244, 245, 247–8, 252–3; 'Before it happened', 235, 237; 'Little Johnny's Confession', 252; 'Prosepoem Towards a Definition of Itself', 244; Underdog, 244; see also Mersey Sound, The
Penguin (publishing company), 222, 244, 253–4, 258–9; Modern Poets, 253, 258; Penguin Classics, 79
Pepys, Samuel, 16n, 17
Percy, Arthur, 49
Percy, Thomas, Bishop of Dromore, 48–65; see also Reliques of Ancient English Poetry
performance events, 225–6, 228–9, 237–43, 245–8, 249, 256–7, 258, 259
Pernod Poetry Award, 255n
pharmacies, 264, 266, 267, 272
Phillips, Ambrose, A Collection of Old Ballads, 54–6
Pitt, Humphrey, 50
Plath, Sylvia, 222, 224
Pleasures of the Imagination, The (Akenside), 47
Pocket Edition of Select British Poets series (Cooke), 79, 106
Poems for Spain (Spender/Lehmann), 188
Poems from Poetry & Jazz in Concert (Robson), 256
Poems in the Waiting Room (therapeutic initiative), 273, 276
Poems of Freedom (Mulgan), 205, 216–17

Poems of the Great War (1914), 155–6, 159–60, 162, 176

Poems of To-Day (The English Association), 160–1, 178–9

Poems of Tomorrow (Adam Smith), 203

Poems on Affairs of State (17th/18th-century series), 12–38; aims, 11, 14, 20–1, 25, 27; contents and selection, 14–15, 19–23, 24–32; editors and publishers, 22–3, 28, 32–3; historical context, 12–19, 22–4, 37–8; publication and editions, 14, 19–20, 23–4, 27–8, 32; reception and readership, 9, 30–1, 32–3, 35, 37–8; reputation and importance, 9, 33–5, 37–8

Poems to Last a Lifetime (Goodwin), 265, 266

Poems Written during the Great War (Lloyd), 180–2

Poètes de la Guerre, Les (1915), 164

Poetry Cure, The (Darling/Fuller), 266, 267, 273

Poetry Cure, The (Schauffler), 262–4, 266, 271, 278–9, 280

Poetry Pharmacy series (Sieghart), 266, 279, 281

poetry therapy, 261–8, 272–83

poetry-and-jazz movement, 226, 228, 238, 246, 256

Poets of Great Britain Complete from Chaucer to Churchill (Bell), 76–7, 78–9, 81, 91

Poets of Great Britain, The (Bagster), 77, 79

Poets of the 1950's (Enright), 221

Poet's Tongue, The (Auden/Garrett), 205–7

Polack, Ernest, 148

Political Register, The (newspaper), 37

pop music, 7, 226–30, 245, 254, 255

Pope, Alexander, 33–4, 78, 83, 99, 220; *The Rape of the Lock*, 206

Popish Plot (17th century), 13–14

Porter, Peter, 247

Porteus, Hugh Gordon, 187

Potter, Thomas, 36

Pound, Ezra, 8, 110–11, 154, 186,

280; *Des Imagistes*, 154, 186; *The Egoist*, 163, 176

Pre-Raphaelites, 120, 129

Press, John, 218n, 222

Press Licensing Act (1662), 17, 18

Price, Leah, 103–4, 275, 277–8

Pride and Prejudice (Austen), 99

Prince of Darkness, The (17th-century satire), 26n

Prinsep, Valentine, 129

Prior, Matthew, 99

Private Eye (magazine), 27

propaganda: political and ideological, 4, 18, 194, 224; wartime, 3, 144–5, 154–8, 219

Protestantism, 19, 24, 41; *see also* Methodism

Proust, Marcel, 270

psychoanalysis, 223, 262

psychotherapy, 261–2, 269–70

public libraries, 108, 117, 119, 138, 201, 272

Public Records Office, 112

Puck (Shakespeare: *A Midsummer Night's Dream*), 57

Pulteney, William (*later* 1st Earl of Bath), 35

Punch (magazine), 155, 157

Quiller-Couch, Sir Arthur, 146; *The Oxford Book of English Verse*, 5, 6, 7, 9, 111, 140, 147–8, 153

quotation, public, 98–101, 132

Raban, Jonathan, 232n, 257

race and racism, 198–201

Raleigh, Sir Walter, 170, 184

Rape of the Lock, The (Pope), 206

Ratcliffe, Sophie, *Stressed Unstressed*, 266, 280

Rattle Bag, The (Heaney/Hughes), 206n

Reading Agency (charity), 271, 278

reading process: of anthologies, 4–6, 82, 96–7, 103–4, 268–9, 282–3; of novels, 271–2; of poetry, 274–7, 280–1

recitation *see* quotation, public

Reeve, Clara, 108–9

religion: and profanity, 87–9, 90; and

superstition, 39–40, 41, 42, 61, 66; and war, 150, 160, 165, 168, 183, 223; *see also* Catholicism; church attendance; Methodism; Protestantism

Reliques of Ancient English Poetry (Percy), 39–75; aims, 48–9, 52–3; contents and selection, 48, 50–2, 56, 57–8, 62, 63, 68–9; historical context, 39–48; preparation and publication, 48, 53–4, 56–63, 64; reception and readership, 48–9, 63–5; reputation and importance, 10, 49, 55, 64–75; structure and arrangement, 52, 62–3

Remember Louvain! (Lucas), 155, 157

Revolutions of 1848, 113–14, 125

Richardson, David Lester, 118

Richardson, Samuel, *Clarissa*, 99

Richardson, Tony, 253, 259

Rickword, Edgell, 158, 175, 184

Riding, Laura, *Pamphlet Against Anthologies*, 2–3, 5, 9–10, 81, 177, 281–2

Ritson, Joseph, 49

Roach, John, *Beauties of the Poets of Great Britain*, 9, 83, 85, 86, 106

Road to Wigan Pier, The (Orwell), 211

Roberts, Michael, 3–4, 190–6, 197–8, 224; *The Faber Book of Modern Verse*, 3–4, 111, 191*n*, 192, 197–8, 216; *New Country*, 4, 193–6, 197, 212–14, 220, 223; *New Signatures*, 4, 190–4, 203, 212–14, 220, 223

Robertson, F.W., 118

Robertson, Joseph, *An Essay on the Education of Young Ladies*, 104

'Robin Good-Fellow' (ballad), 58, 59

Robson, Jeremy, 246; *Poems from Poetry & Jazz in Concert*, 256

Rochester, John Wilmot, 2nd Earl of, 18, 21–2

Roderick Random (Smollett), 80

Rolling Stones (rock band), 228

Romains, Jules, *Men of Good Will*, 211*n*

Romanticism, 67–74, 105–6, 264

Rome, ancient, 21, 25–6, 28–9, 57, 121, 125, 171

Rootham, Helen, 180

Rose, Jonathan, 138

Rosenberg, Isaac, 169

Rossetti, Dante Gabriel, 120; *Early Italian Poets*, 139

Rossiter, William, 126*n*

Ruskin, John, 120, 126*n*

Rye House Plot (1683), 23

Sade, Marquis de, 252

Sadler Commission on Indian Education (1917–19), 123

'Sally in our Alley' (ballad), 133

Sampson, Fiona, 274

San Francisco, 231, 254

Sandwich, John Montagu, 4th Earl of, 36–7

Sartor Resartus (Carlyle), 140

Sassoon, Siegfried, 169, 182, 183; 'Absolution', 169; *Counter-Attack*, 182; *The Old Huntsman*, 150; 'They', 181

satires, 17th/18th-century, 9, 12–38, 93, 97*n*

Saturday Review (newspaper), 182*n*

Satyr upon the French King, A (Brown), 25

Savage, Derek Stanley, 212*n*

Scaffold, The (sketch group), 227, 253; 'Lily the Pink', 227–8

Scanlon, Bob, 199

Schauffler, Robert Haven, *The Poetry Cure*, 261–4, 266, 271, 278–9, 280

Schiller, Friedrich, 124, 147

Schlegel, Friedrich von, *Lectures on the History of Literature*, 68

schools and schooling *see* children's education

Schor, Naomi, 102

Schuman, Andrew, 273, 283; *Stressed Unstressed*, 266, 280

Schwitters, Kurt, 252; 'Sneezing Poem', 243

Scott, Sir Walter, 71, 122, 159; 'William and Helen', 70

Scott, Alexander John, 121

Scott, Marion, 151, 174–5

Scottsboro Boys, 199
scrapbooks *see* commonplacing
sea shanties, 206
Seaman, Sir Owen, 159
Second Dutch War (1665–7), 15
Second World War (1939–45), 3,
   149*n*, 183, 216, 219–21, 223
Seghers, Anna, 196
*Select Beauties of Ancient English
   Poetry* (Headley), 84, 85, 86, 104
Selections from the British Poets
   (Bullar), 88–9
Self-Help (Smiles), 128, 269
self-help guides, 128, 268–71
self-help poetry collections, 261–8,
   272–83
Seven Pillars of Wisdom (Lawrence),
   5*n*
Seven Types of Ambiguity (Empson),
   203*n*
Sexton, Anne, 222
sexuality, 234–6
Shakespeare, William, 3, 10, 27, 52,
   120, 122, 205, 206; 'beauties'
   volumes, 7, 77, 78, 79, 83, 84,
   87–8, 98, 104, 105; wartime
   anthologizing, 147, 148–9, 153,
   159; witches and ghosts, 57, 66,
   67; *Hamlet*, 67, 82*n*, 148, 269;
   Henry V, 157–8; *The Merchant
   of Venice*, 149; *A Midsummer
   Night's Dream*, 57; 'Under the
   Greenwood Tree', 111
Shakespeare Anthology, The (Arber), 7
Shakespearean Chartist Association,
   137
Shaper, Hal, 255–6
Shared Reading (charitable initiative),
   271–2
Shelley, Percy Bysshe, 9, 10, 71, 77,
   106, 228
Shenstone, William, 46, 51, 54
Shetland, 206
Shifnal, Shropshire, 50
Shippen, William, 28–30
Shirley, James, 'Death the Leveller', 6
Sidney, Sir Philip, 153–4, 170, 184,
   263
Sieghart, William, 267; *Poetry
   Pharmacy* series, 266, 279, 281

Simonides of Ceos, 171
Simpson, Louis, *The New Poets of
   England and America*, 8
Sitwell, Dame Edith, 179; *Wheels*,
   179–80
Sitwell, Sir Osbert, 179
Skyros (Greece), 164
Slater, Montagu, 207
Smiles, Samuel, *Self-Help*, 128, 269
Smith, Adam, 64
Smith, Alexander, *City Poems*, 127,
   135
Smith, Harriet (Austen: *Emma*),
   99–100
Smollett, Tobias, *Roderick Random*,
   80
Soar, Daniel, 265
social media, 282–3
*Soldier Poets: Songs of the Fighting
   Men* (Kyle), 166–8, 169, 172–5,
   179
Somme offensive (1916), 140, 148,
   161*n*, 166, 174, 179
Songes and Sonettes (Tottel), 6
*Songs and Sonnets for England in
   War Time* (Lane), 155–7, 159,
   176
Sorbonne, 114
Sorley, Charles Hamilton, 165*n*
Southey, Robert, 34, 68, 71; 'Donica',
   70–1; 'The Widow', 34
Spanish Civil War (1936–9), 188–9,
   204, 210, 216, 219
Speaker, The (Enfield), 7
Specimens of the British Poets
   (Campbell), 77
Spectator (magazine), 42, 54, 55,
   122, 135
Spender, Sir Stephen, 188, 189, 190,
   192, 198, 203, 205, 210, 213,
   217, 218, 222; *Poems for Spain*,
   188
Spenser, Edmund, 76–7, 124, 153–4
Sphinx (Liverpool University
   magazine), 259
Spirit of Man, The (Bridges), 156–7,
   162
'spouting' pieces (texts learned by
   heart), 82*n*, 99, 113, 132
Spurrier, H., 173

Squire, Sir John Collings, 163–4, 166
St Clair, William, 78, 79–80
St Helens Reporter (newspaper), 150
Stacpoole, Henry de Vere, 159
Stalin, Joseph, 216
Stalinism, 219
Stanley, Arthur, 114
Starr, Sir Ringo, 255
Stationers' Company, 27
Staying Alive series (Astley), 265, 266, 267, 278, 281
Steele, Sir Richard, 33
Stephens, James, 154
Sterne, Laurence, 83, 87, 89; *Tristram Shandy*, 89
Streets, John William, 'Youth's Consecration', 173
Stressed Unstressed (Bate/Byrne/Ratcliffe/Schuman), 266, 280
Strictures on the Modern System of Female Education (More), 85, 95–8, 100–4, 105, 108
Stuart, James Francis Edward, 28
Stuarts (dynasty), 18–32, 37; *see also* Anne, Queen; Charles I, King; Charles II, King; James II, King
supernatural ballads, 44–9, 51, 52, 55–60, 65, 68–74
superstition, 39–75
Surrey, Henry Howard, Earl of, 6
'Sweet William's Ghost' (Scottish ballad), 46, 68–9, 71
Swift, Jonathan, 7, 78, 83, 87, 89, 92

Taft, William Howard, 143
Tales of Wonder (Lewis), 71–5
Tarquin and Tullia (Maynwaring), 25–6, 28
Tatler, The (magazine), 33
Taylor, William, 70, 71
television, 225, 245, 246, 247, 252–3, 270
Temple, Frederick, Archbishop of Canterbury, 115, 116
Tennyson, Alfred, 1st Baron, 2, 3, 115, 123–4, 153; and Palgrave's *Golden Treasury*, 129–31, 132, 133, 134
Thomson, James, 118
Times, The (newspaper), 130n, 135n, 146, 149, 150–1, 152, 158, 165, 195
Times Literary Supplement (TLS), 146, 149, 150, 151, 155, 158, 162, 164, 180, 193, 215, 225, 233, 253, 255
Today (radio programme), 252
Toft, Mary, 40
Tom Jones (Fielding), 80
Tomlinson, Charles, 222
Tonight at Noon (Henri), 238, 248, 254
Torch (Hull University magazine), 244
Tories, 25, 34, 39
Tottel, Richard, *Songes and Sonettes*, 6
Trafalgar, Battle of (1805), 163, 164
Treasury of War Poetry, A (Clarke), 183
Tristram Shandy (Sterne), 89
Trotter, Jacqueline, *Valour and Vision*, 183
Turner, Elizabeth (*later* Palgrave), 112–13
Tutchin, John, 24–5
Twickenham, Middlesex, 115; Kneller Hall (training college), 114–16, 119, 125

Underdog (magazine), 244
University College, London, 121
University Extension movement, 7, 139–40
Upward, Edward, 194, 196, 198, 204

Valour and Vision (Trotter), 183
Vaneigem, Raoul, *The Revolution of Everyday Life*, 242
Vernède, R.E., 151n, 159; 'The Call', 159–60
Vietnam War (1955–75), 235, 247
Virey, Julien-Joseph, 102
Virgil, 54, 61, 68, 134; *Aeneid*, 61, 113
Vorticists, 186, 194

Wain, John, 218
Walpole, Horace (*later* 4th Earl of Orford), 35, 47, 63–4

Walpole, Sir Robert (*later* 1st Earl of Orford), 35
war *see* Boer War; First World War; Second Dutch War; Second World War; Spanish Civil War; Vietnam War
War Propaganda Bureau, 145–6
Ward, Thomas Humphry, *The English Poets*, 140n
Warner, Rex, 205; 'Hymn', 195
Warren, Sir Herbert, 147
Warton, Thomas, *The History of English Poetry*, 64, 65
Waste Land, The (Eliot), 192
Watson, Sir William, 150, 151n, 155, 159, 183
Watts, Charles, 146
Watts, Isaac, 85
Wavell, Archibald (*later* 1st Earl Wavell), *Other Men's Flowers*, 3, 149n, 183, 268
West, Alick, 210
West, Arthur Graeme, 177–8
Westminster Gazette, 153–4
Westminster Review, 135
Wharton, Edith, 143
What W.H. Auden Can Do for You (McCall Smith), 270
What Would Virginia Woolf Do? (Collins), 270
Wheels (Sitwell), 179–80
Whigs, 23, 25, 55
Wilde, Oscar, 117, 269
Wilkes, John, 36–7
Willett, John, 225–6, 227
William III, King, 19, 21, 22, 23–5, 26
Williams, Sir Charles Hanbury, 35
Wintringham, Tom, 196
Wishart & Company (publishing company), 201
Witchcraft Act (1736), 41–2

witches and witchcraft, 39, 40, 41–5, 48, 57, 59–60, 66–7
'Witches' Song, The' (ballad), 57
Women Poets of the Empire (Forshaw), 160
women readers, 55–6, 82, 86–7, 90–104
women's education *see* female education
Woodhouse, Emma (Austen: *Emma*), 99–100
Woodhouse, Mr (Austen: *Emma*), 99–100
Woodward, James, 28, 32–3
Woolf, Leonard, 190
Woolf, Virginia, 190, 270
Woolner, Thomas, 129–30, 133
Wordsworth, Dorothy, 70
Wordsworth, William, 9, 34, 70, 72, 106, 120, 132–3, 147, 162, 269, 276; 'The Idiot Boy', 72–3; *Lyrical Ballads*, 72–3, 133; 'My Heart Leaps Up', 279
Workers' Educational Association, 138
workhouses, 115
Working Men's College Magazine, 126, 132, 136
Working Men's Colleges, 119–22, 125, 126–7, 128, 129, 132, 139
Works of the English Poets (Chalmers), 77, 79
Works of the English Poets (Johnson), 79
Writers' Association for Intellectual Liberty, 210
Wyatt, Sir Thomas, 6

Yeats, W.B., *The Oxford Book of Modern Verse*, 4, 282
Young, Edward, 91
Ypres, Battle of (1915), 183